DIRECT
INSTRUCTION
A PRACTITIONER'S
HANDBOOK

KURT E. ENGELMANN

JOHN CATT
FROM HODDER EDUCATION

Every effort has been made to trace all copyright holders, but if any have been inadvertently overlooked, the Publishers will be pleased to make the necessary arrangements at the first opportunity.

Although every effort has been made to ensure that website addresses are correct at time of going to press, Hodder Education cannot be held responsible for the content of any website mentioned in this book. It is sometimes possible to find a relocated web page by typing in the address of the home page for a website in the URL window of your browser.

Hachette UK's policy is to use papers that are natural, renewable and recyclable products and made from wood grown in well-managed forests and other controlled sources. The logging and manufacturing processes are expected to conform to the environmental regulations of the country of origin.

Orders: please contact Hachette UK Distribution, Hely Hutchinson Centre, Milton Road, Didcot, Oxfordshire, OX11 7HH. Telephone: +44 (0)1235 827827. Email education@hachette.co.uk. Lines are open from 9 a.m. to 5 p.m., Monday to Friday.

ISBN: 9781036003289

© Kurt E. Engelmann 2024

First published in 2024 by
John Catt from Hodder Education,
An Hachette UK Company
15 Riduna Park, Station Road,
Melton, Woodbridge IP12 1QT
Telephone: +44 (0)1394 389850
www.johncatt.com

A catalogue record for this title is available from the British Library

Direct Instruction: A Practitioner's Handbook is a comprehensive guide for users of DI who want to improve their implementation and also for educators who are considering implementing these effective instructional programs. With sections covering the rationale and research behind DI, detailed guidance for successful implementation, and suggestions for avoiding pitfalls, reading this book is like being coached through a course on how to teach reading and why it should be done that way. The actionable information will help users of DI programs achieve the optimal instructional efficacy and efficiency that can lead to academic success for all students.

> *Stephanie Stollar, PhD, assistant professor at Mount St. Joseph*
> *University and founder of the Reading Science Academy*

To the uninitiated, Direct Instruction might seem complex, peculiar, or even intimidating. Thankfully, Dr. Engelmann is here to show us what's under the hood of the most effective teaching system ever devised. Whether you are a long-time practitioner of Direct Instruction, or a new adopter like me, the book you hold in your hands will tell you everything you need to know about implementing DI for the best results.

> *Zach Groshell, PhD, instructional coach, consultant, host of the*
> Progressively Incorrect *podcast.*

Kurt Engelmann's book is a must-read for educators. It is both comprehensive and accessible, and comes at an important time as the world of education has a renewed interest in scientifically based reading instruction. Engelmann demonstrates that the Direct Instruction reading, mathematics, and spelling programs set the standard for tools designed to ensure academic success with every student. The scope of the book is impressive, encompassing the aspects of design that make *Reading Mastery* and the other DI programs the most carefully engineered and effective set of curricula in existence; what it takes to implement the programs effectively; and how to sustain success. The book is filled with the invaluable wisdom of decades of implementation efforts from around the world. This book is an outstanding resource for educators interested in accelerating the achievement of all students.

> *Laura Doherty, president and CEO, Baltimore Curriculum Project,*
> *implementor of Direct Instruction since 1996*

This is an accessible book for anyone who is interested in finding out about the theory, implementation, and day-to-day monitoring of DI programs. Myths about DI are addressed throughout the book, and specific discrete issues are explored in various standalone 'topic brief' sections. I recommend this book to those who like and know a little about DI as well as to those who have never heard of or initially struggle with DI.

Dr Nazam Hussain, specialist senior educational psychologist

The evidence on Direct Instruction offers the strongest hope for narrowing our nation's glaring educational disparities, but DI must be implemented correctly to be fully effective. Dr. Engelmann gives us clear and complete directions for uplifting our students' and our nation's academic achievement.

Bill Sower, president, The Sower Center for Successful Schools

Kurt Engelmann's *Direct Instruction* provides a fundamental advance for education. Any educators who are responsible for curriculum decisions or implementing DI programs – regardless of whether they say they love or hate DI – should not just read this book, but keep it available as a resource. It covers everything from the rationale and history of DI to the details of conducting daily lessons. Readers will find clear explanations of both the underlying philosophy and design of DI as well as guidance about how to implement DI effectively. *Direct Instruction: A Practitioner's Handbook* explains why and how to teach DI in one accessible source.

John Wills Lloyd, PhD, professor emeritus, University of Virginia, founder and editor of SpecialEducationToday.com

Direct Instruction: A Practitioner's Handbook is an ambitious effort to create a comprehensive unpacking of one of the important pieces of scaffolding for deeper learning.

Drew Perkins, director of ThoughtStretchers Education

This practitioner's guide to implementing Direct Instruction is the most up-to-date, thorough, and comprehensive guide to the implementation of DI available. Dr. Engelmann draws upon and cites many of his father's writings to elucidate details of implementation that may be less well understood among practitioners. He shares insights gained from implementing DI in multiple complex settings around the world. School personnel who implement Direct Instruction while attending to the details presented in this guide will be assured remarkable success in the classroom!

Bonnie Grossen, PhD, DI author and implementer, executive director, Center for Applied Research in Education

Dr. Engelmann delivers the ABCs of DI in *Direct Instruction: A Practitioner's Handbook*, a how-to manual that should be part of the curriculum toolbox of both beginning and experienced educators. This book provides a comprehensive review of both the philosophy and research behind this proven educational approach, in addition to strategies and recommendations for successful implementation. In my over 30 years as a Direct Instruction consultant, I have never found a publication that addresses DI in its totality – until this one.

Donna Dressman, president/senior consultant, Conquest Consulting, LLC

TABLE OF CONTENTS

ACKNOWLEDGEMENTS

I want to thank all of those who have made this book possible. In the first instance, I am grateful to the readers of the chapter drafts – Dr. Bonnie Grossen, Rochelle Davisson, Elise C. Engelmann, Ashly Cupit, and Tamara Bressi – who provided me with terrific feedback on content as well as wording. It is difficult to imagine what this book would have looked like had I not received their careful and insightful input. I am also thankful for the feedback and support provided by John Catt: Mark Combes, Natasha Gladwell, and Rebecca Taylor. They helped transform the component chapters and other bits of writing into a coherent, polished book.

I am grateful to the many mentors and thought partners I have had in the Direct Instruction (DI) community over the years. My most influential mentors include Dr. Mary Gleason, Gary Davis, Jerry Silbert, Dr. Vicky Vachon, Siegfried "Zig" Engelmann, Dr. Geoff Colvin, and Dr. Douglas Carnine. Other critical thought partners have included Owen Engelmann, Dr. Sheri Wilkins, Dr. Kathy Madigan, Randi Saulter, Shep Barbash, Dr. Jean Stockard, Dr. Nancy Woolfson, Christine Wlaschin, Bryan Wickman, and my wife, Dianna Carrizales-Engelmann.

Observing instruction in classrooms has provided a strong basis for my understanding of the application of DI to actual school settings. I am grateful to Dr. Vicky Vachon, whom I accompanied on visits to several dozen schools over the years, as well as to other Direct Instruction coaches. These include, but are not limited to, the following implementation managers and project directors from the National Institute for Direct Instruction (NIFDI): Kris Althoff, Kathy Anderer,

Susan Borden, Maria Collins, Michele Davidson, Tara Davis, Laura Doherty, Dr. Donna Dwiggins, Betsy Frisch, Linda Frost, Rosella Givens, Dr. Phyllis Haddox, Ray Hall, Ginger Herrman, Lyn House, Dr. Kathy Jungjohann, Alisa Kerr, Sue Martin, Tami McGrattan, Billie Overholser, Sue Owens, Toni Rice, Rose Rios, Cheryl Shelton, Tenisha Smith, Deborah Steely, Judy Towns, Beverly Trent, Maria Vanoni, and Brenda Williams. I have also been able to draw on the work done by Dr. Mary Gleason and others at NIFDI in developing many of the implementation support procedures described in this book.

Without the input and insights gained from these mentors, thought partners, and DI expert coaches, I would not have possessed the background knowledge required to write a handbook on DI for practitioners. The handbook has also benefited from the input of DI program authors Susie Andrist, Bonnie Grossen, Steve Osborn, and Bernie Solano, who generously shared their knowledge of the design and content of specific DI programs described in chapter 4.

Lastly, I am grateful to my father, Siegfried "Zig" Engelmann, who, along with early colleagues and co-authors, established the theory, fundamental research, curricula, and training conventions that have allowed me and the aforementioned professionals to help teachers, coaches, and school and district leaders learn the skills and procedures they need to ensure that all of their students succeed.

Kurt E. Engelmann   June 4, 2023

LIST OF TABLES

LIST OF FIGURES

INTRODUCTION

Those of you who are reading this book may have different experiences with Direct Instruction (DI). You may be the principal or headmaster of a school who is considering implementing DI for the first time, and you want to understand the DI approach and its implications to your school's structure and culture before you purchase DI programs. You may be a teacher who has implemented DI for a year with positive results as you've observed your students acquire skills at a faster rate than cohorts of students in previous years. Or you may be a curriculum director in a school district where DI has been implemented successfully in one school, and you are considering whether to recommend that other schools also adopt the DI approach. Whatever your experience level or your position, this book will provide essential information to support your journey with DI.

This book is intended to serve as a guide for teachers, school or district leaders, and other educational practitioners who are interested in implementing DI successfully. As such, the content of the book focuses on the *practical issues that practitioners face when implementing DI* and does not devote much space to other aspects of DI. This book includes a *summary* of the theoretical aspects of DI and research on the efficacy of the DI approach, and it provides references in the bibliography to other sources on DI's theory and research base. More space is devoted to the design of the DI programs, the understanding of which is critically important for practitioners as it provides the rationale for the procedures that teachers, coaches and school leaders should follow to implement DI successfully. The overall focus of the book is to inform practitioners in the field who are considering implementing DI or want to improve the effectiveness of their current implementations of DI.

The essence of this book is to provide a roadmap for teachers and school leaders to ensure that students taught with DI are highly successful. This roadmap is divided into three sections, and each section is divided into several chapters. The first section addresses what DI is and why it has the features it does. The second section addresses how to implement DI successfully. Understanding the elements of DI and their rationale is a prerequisite to ensuring that users implement these elements with fidelity. The third section is devoted to cautions to consider when implementing DI. It describes potential pitfalls and the consequences of ignoring the programs' provisions as it addresses the real-life dilemmas that many teachers and school leaders face when attempting to implement DI along with other priorities and mandates. As a supplement to the chapters, the book includes nine "topic briefs" – short summaries of important topics that provide additional background information on the research base and other aspects of DI.

The sections are meant to be read consecutively by most readers, especially those who are new to DI. However, the second section on how to implement DI can be used as a reference guide by all readers as they implement the DI approach, and they can revisit the section at different stages of the implementation process. The last section may resonate more deeply with experienced DI users than those new to DI as the content of the section is designed to relate to the personal experiences of seasoned DI users. However, the last section provides rationale for specific implementation requirements that many new DI practitioners may find useful.

The first step in this journey is to explain *what Direct Instruction is*, a task that is surprisingly complex, as described in the first section of this book.

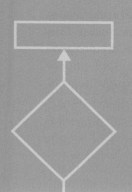
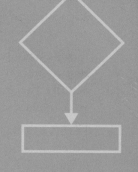

SECTION 1:
WHAT IS DIRECT INSTRUCTION?

INTRODUCTION TO THE SECTION

This section of the book is devoted to explaining what Direct Instruction (DI) is. At first glance, this would seem to be a simple task that could be addressed succinctly. After all, the name "Direct Instruction" implies a type of explicit teaching that is performed directly by a teacher to their students. What more can be involved in DI than simply teaching students directly in contrast to having students acquire skills and concepts through projects, cooperative learning or some other indirect learning activity?

Directly and explicitly teaching students a given subject matter is indeed a correct characterization of DI. Yet, *DI is much more complex than simply direct teaching.* It involves a set of practices and procedures that, taken together, form a comprehensive model of teaching and learning. A sophisticated communication theory lies at the center of the DI model. The published DI programs have been constructed in conformity with this theory as the DI authors have woven together a complex design of instructional elements to create programs that lead to successful outcomes for every student who meets the programs' entry requirements. The complexity is hidden, just as the complexity of a high-performance automobile is hidden from the driver, who operates the auto through simple and accessible user controls (e.g. the steering wheel). With DI, teachers provide instruction by following the provisions of the scripted programs and the teacher's guides that accompany the programs. As long as school and district leaders ensure that the structural and training requirements of the programs have been met, students successfully acquire the program's content when the teacher delivers the program with fidelity.

In this section, I will "open the hood" on the DI approach and explain the different components that go into making DI successful. Many of these components, such as signals and choral responses, are readily observable and may already be known to the reader. Others are less readily observable. For each component, I will explain the rationale behind its inclusion – why it is part of the DI approach.

Understanding the rationale is critical to a successful implementation of DI. The DI approach involves many components, each of which often requires a great deal of effort on the part of teachers and school leaders to implement successfully. For teachers and leaders who don't fully understand the rationale, there may be a tendency by some to cut corners. Perhaps the teacher does not provide a full correction for every student performance error. Or perhaps they continue with an exercise when one student responds later than the rest of the students during group instruction. Or perhaps the school leader reduces the time devoted to the DI programs by 20 minutes a day to allocate additional time to test preparation. Or perhaps the school leader places all students in grade-level material rather than providing instruction of students at their performance level. Each one of these types of adjustments to the implementation parameters has a predictable, negative effect on student progress through the DI programs and reduces the rate at which students acquire the skills and concepts addressed in the programs. Understanding the rationale increases the likelihood that teachers and school leaders will implement the DI programs with fidelity, to the benefit of students' learning.

CHAPTER ONE
THE GOAL OF DIRECT INSTRUCTION: ACCELERATION OF STUDENT PERFORMANCE

To understand DI, it is important to start with the goal that the creator of DI, Siegfried "Zig" Engelmann (father of the author of this book), set before himself when he developed this unique instructional approach. The overriding goal of DI is to accelerate the performance of students. S. Engelmann defined acceleration as "simply teaching more in less time" (Engelmann, S., 2014, 106). If students learn more in less time year after year from an early grade level, the positive results can be compounded so that they will be performing considerably higher than expected after several years.

EXAMPLES OF ACCELERATION

An example of this acceleration can be seen in a grainy, black-and-white 1966 film of a young Siegfried Engelmann demonstrating the mathematics skills and concepts possessed by kindergarten students who had attended the Bereiter-Engelmann preschool at the Institute for Research on Exceptional Children at the University of Illinois the previous year as 4-year-olds or 5-year-olds. Each of the African American students in the preschool was highly at risk of academic failure and received academic instruction in the preschool for only 20 minutes per day. They were recruited for this experimental early-learning program because an older sibling had been identified as having special needs.

The film does not show an instructional session. Instead, the film captures a joyfully spirited back-and-forth interaction between Engelmann and the children as he defies them to solve a variety of mathematical problems. Unphased and up to the challenge, students eagerly work math problems that students usually don't learn until third grade or later – problems involving the fundamental operations (addition, subtraction, multiplication, and division), basic algebra, fractions, and area. For over 50 years, this remarkable film has served as a prime example of the power of his approach to accelerate the performance of highly at-risk students starting at an early age. (See: *Preschool Students Demonstrate Exceptional Math Skills*, available at www.nifdi.org/videos/siegfried-zig-engelmann. html#Pre.)

Fast forward three decades, and Siegfried Engelmann and colleagues have translated the methodology he developed, Direct Instruction, into a comprehensive set of instructional programs covering the major academic subject areas (reading, language/writing, and mathematics) along with a comprehensive reform model involving training, coaching, and school leader capacity building. This model was applied at the elementary school level and, selectively, remedially at the middle and high school levels.

CITY SPRINGS ELEMENTARY, BALTIMORE 1997–2003

A schoolwide example of accelerated performance through the implementation of this comprehensive reform model at the elementary school level is City Springs School in Baltimore, Maryland. In the 1990s, City Springs was one of Baltimore's lowest performing schools with nearly all of the students eligible for free and reduced lunch. As Muriel Berkeley, founder of the Baltimore Curriculum Project, a non-profit organization that operates several charter schools in the city of Baltimore, wrote:

> In the spring of 1996, City Springs Elementary was a place of failure for both students and teachers. Many children could not read, and test scores were abysmal. No remnant of a one-time implementation of "Success for All" remained. Children listened to teachers only when they felt like it, roamed the halls, and left the building. The faculty, spinning like tops, reacted to one crisis after another. When DI was implemented the following fall, the

primary focus was behavior management, as the faculty had to establish order before they could teach children to read and write. (Berkeley, 2002, 222)

The 2000 PBS documentary, *The Battle of City Springs*, captured the difficulty of transforming the school during the second year of DI implementation, 1997–1998. The opening scenes of the documentary focus on a tattered American flag flapping in the wind, which was symbolic of the extraordinarily low levels of academic success at the school. (See www.nifdi.org/videos/nifdi-schools.html.)

After years of conscientious attention to implementing DI with fidelity and tremendous effort on the part of the school's leadership and staff, City Springs became a place of academic success. Several reporters from local news outlets wrote about the implementation of DI in Baltimore and its positive results in the early 2000s. Mike Bowler of the *Baltimore Sun* noted in 2001 that the 17 schools implementing DI at the time were "pulling ahead of citywide averages" on standardized test results (Bowler, 2001). He wrote that the five schools that had started DI first were performing at an even higher level.

In reading, all five of the original DI schools outpaced citywide averages on the Comprehensive Test of Basic Skills, taken in March, and in four of five grades their kids scored above the national median. (The fourth grade, for reasons no one can explain, is a problem everywhere.) City Springs Elementary, smack in the middle of one of the city's poorest neighborhoods, is a case in point. If Baltimore schools in general have done well on the CTBS, City Springs has performed even better, improving reading scores by 54 percentage points in the first grade and 53 points in the fifth since Direct Instruction arrived. (Bowler, 2001)

Although other schools in the city implemented DI with considerable success, none matched the performance gains of City Springs. The short video, *The Battle of City Springs Epilogue*, reveals the stunning improvement of student performance that took place at the school since the original film on the school was taken.

Grade	1998	2001
1st	28	82
2nd	26	63
3rd	28	50
4th	20	32
5th	14	67

Table 1.1 City Springs Elementary median percentile scores on the Comprehensive Test of Basic Skills (CTBS), 1998–2001. Source: *The Battle of City Springs Epilogue*, https://youtu.be/EjwribR0qbQ.

In City Springs, students weren't just mastering decoding and other basic skills. They were acquiring critical content and higher-order concepts, too. On a visit to the school in 2001, Bowler reported that the students' reading comprehension of the texts they read was high:

> Upstairs, a U.S. history class is eagerly discussing a recent field trip to Monticello, President Thomas Jefferson's home in Virginia. One of the raps against DI is that while it might do a good job at teaching the mechanics of reading with its highly scripted instruction, it falls down when it comes to comprehension. I saw no evidence of that among the fifth- and fourth-graders in the stuffy U.S. history classroom. They had done their reading with understanding; they knew about the Lewis and Clark expedition, about slavery and even about Jefferson's gardens. I've heard first-graders at City Springs reading with evident understanding, but that hasn't silenced the critics who charge that DI is simply "rote learning". (Bowler, 2001)

The academic success of DI at City Springs and other schools improved over the years. Two years later, Bowler wrote:

> It's getting to be a broken record, but City Springs Elementary, one of Baltimore's poorest, led the city again in this year's TerraNova testing ... Four of the top five city schools in first-grade scoring use Direct Instruction. Yet the curriculum is seldom credited by the school system's leaders. One wonders why. (Bowler, 2003)

Muriel Berkeley credited the exceptional results at City Springs to the dedication of Bernice Whelchel, the school's principal, to implementing the comprehensive DI model and Core Knowledge with fidelity. DI was the academic focus of the school instead of prepping the children for taking the state test, the Maryland School Performance Assessment Program (MSPAP). Berkeley wrote in 2002:

> The focus at City Springs Elementary School from Day 1 of implementation has been on using DI and Core as they are intended to be implemented, as defined by the BCP and the National Institute for Direct Instruction. During the first and second years of the implementation, years when the priorities were to be DI reading, writing, spelling and mathematics programs, the principal devoted her time and energy to learning about the design and techniques of DI, and she held her teachers accountable for the same. The principal's message to teachers about the importance of handling behavior consistently and effectively and of implementing DI as it was designed to be used was unambiguous. The principal noticed when teachers let their praises fall below their corrections, when their lesson progress fell below what was possible, and when students' written work showed lack of mastery or was not checked. In addition, when the principal noticed a lapse in the implementation she informed the teacher in question. Several teachers left the school because of the relentless pressure to perform. The principal did not distract herself or her teachers from the implementation of DI with initiatives recommended by MSPAP experts. She knew that the faculty had chosen DI as the tool to best teach students critical academic skills, and that the students would be unable to perform on MSPAP until they have mastered reading, writing, and mathematics skills. (Berkeley, 2002, 234–35)

The school accomplished these goals despite severe challenges of mobility and inconsistent support at home. According to Karin Chenoweth, reporter at *The Washington Post*, City Springs suffered from:

> a highly mobile student body (almost 50 percent of her students move in or out during the year); a highly mobile teaching force

(47.6 percent of her teachers are conditionally certified, which means that they don't have full teaching certification); and parents who don't always know how to help their children succeed in school. (Chenoweth, 2003)

OTHER EXAMPLES OF ACCELERATION WITH DI

Acceleration of academic performance through the use of DI programs can occur with more advantaged students as well as with highly at-risk students. Students with greater background knowledge and skills are simply placed higher in the program and taught at a faster rate. In the late 1970s, 30 children from middle-class families in Springfield, Oregon were taught the *Reading Mastery* program as first and second graders at an accelerated rate by University of Oregon practica students with very positive results, as reported by S. Engelmann in *Teaching Needy Kids in our Backward System*:

> At the end of their second grade, children read at the middle fourth-grade level according to the Stanford Achievement Test. They performed on the fifth-grade level of an oral reading test. The top ten children received a fourth-grade test that measured speed and accuracy. (We could find no test for the second or third grade.) Students performed on the seventh-grade level. The children were not taught science as a subject, but level 3 of our reading program has stories that are heavy in science content. The class performed at the fourth-grade level in science. (Engelmann, S., 2007, 172–73)

Another example of using DI to accelerate achievement of high-performing students is Thales Academy, a private school network with eight campuses, mostly in North Carolina. Students at Thales score consistently in the 97th–99th percentiles on the Iowa Test of Basic Skills in reading, language, and math (Thales Academy, 2016, 19:05). More examples of accelerating student performance at the elementary school level are provided in a video produced in 2009 by the award-winning Palfreman Film Group. *Helping Kids Soar: Children Reaching Their Full Potential with Direct Instruction* portrays the experience of two schools in different parts of the country as they accelerated the performance of all of their students with DI: Emerson Elementary in Alliance, Nebraska and Fickett Elementary in Atlanta, Georgia. Students are shown in both schools reading at a much higher proficiency level than has historically been the case for children of their ages at their schools. Fourth and fifth graders at Fickett Elementary read *Understanding U.S. History*, a middle-school social studies textbook, and discuss the role of Harriet Tubman during the Civil War among other topics. The video contains testimonials about the profound change that DI has made on students' reading, including the following from first-grade teacher Becky Lawrence at Emerson Elementary:

> I've been teaching school for 34 years. Never had kids read like this before in first grade. Even my low ones are reading... like crazy! (NIFDI, *Helping Kids Soar: Children Reaching Their Full Potential with Direct Instruction*)

And from second-grade teacher Linda McMeekin:

> It was my privilege this year to teach a higher-level reading group, and because they were all at the same level, they could just soar. And they did. I've had first graders this year who are reading at a fourth/fifth grade level, and they're doing very, very well with it. (Ibid.)

Acceleration can apply to any learner of any age in any subject area. For remedial students, it often takes the form of "closing the gap" between their performance and grade-level expectations. But it can also imply increasing their performance beyond grade-level expectations. To accommodate remedial students' advanced learning, several of the DI remedial programs contain strategies or information that their grade-level peers do not know. For instance, in the first lesson of the lowest level of the *Corrective Reading Comprehension* program, the first vocabulary word that students learn is *masticate*. (See Level A, L. 1, Exercise 6, task A.) That's not a word that students in fourth grade typically know. When students in remedial programs master this type of advanced content, they gain the self-confidence that they can learn complex and difficult material.

EFFECTIVENESS AND EFFICIENCY

Two of the foundational principles of acceleration are *effectiveness* and *efficiency*. *Effectiveness* implies student mastery of the material. The importance of this principle is reflected in the titles of two of the most prominent DI programs – *Reading Mastery* and *Spelling Mastery* – but the concept of mastery is at the core of all of the DI programs. In DI, all skills and concepts are taught to mastery in each lesson. Passing rates in the DI approach are much higher than in traditional approaches to provide frequent verification that students have mastered the content:

- 85% correct on independent work
- 90% correct on in-program mastery tests.

If students experience difficulty with parts of the lesson, these parts are repeated the following day until students demonstrate mastery. This high level of mastery provides a solid foundation for students to learn new skills and concepts. Because each skill covered in earlier lessons in the DI programs lays the foundation for later lessons, mastering earlier lessons facilitates students' acquiring new content. These high passing criteria also emphasize the need for proper placement. If students are not properly placed in the programs, they will not be able to meet these passing criteria. This will result in the student either repeating the lessons many times or proceeding through the program without mastering the content and being unprepared for more advanced lessons. If a student has difficulty with earlier material and is "dragged" through the program without meeting the passing criteria, the student will experience even greater difficulty mastering the content as time goes on.

Teaching to mastery involves correcting all errors that students commit. Some of the specific error correction procedures are indicated in the scripts, and there are more generalized error correction procedures that can be applied to different classes of exercises. Most error corrections involve giving students the answer immediately and repeating the missed item, which leads to positive practice of the items by the students. (An exception is when there is a rule or strategy to be applied, in which case the teacher prompts the students to apply the appropriate rule.) Correct answers should greatly exceed the number of errors that students commit so the instructional sessions are positive for the students and teachers. This requires students to be placed at the spot in the program that matches their skill level so they can be successful and commit few errors.

Mastery of the programs' content ensures a solid foundation for future learning in the programs and outside material. It also has a very positive effect on students' self-image and their motivation to learn. Students in DI had the highest affective (self-image) scores in Project Follow Through, the largest educational experiment in the history of the US. The evaluation results of Follow Through demonstrated that "competence enhances self-esteem and not *vice versa*" (Engelmann, S. et al., 1988, 311). Especially for students who have not had a history of academic success, mastering the DI content every day provides a strong motivation to come to school and work hard because each student knows that they will be successful every day.

Efficiency is the second foundational principle of acceleration. It involves using time as prudently as possible to maximize student learning in any given time frame. If a student can master a given skill or concept in less time, there is more time for students to learn other content. If the entire curriculum teaches all skills and concepts more efficiently than traditional teaching approaches, significant overall student performance gains can be achieved. If a student receives instruction in the major subject areas using an accelerated approach for a number of years, these gains will be translated into major changes in the student's performance. If, for example, students in an accelerated curriculum achieve a 20% performance gain per year in comparison to students in a traditional curriculum, students in the accelerated approach will have gained a full year's performance over the comparison students after five years.

Maximizing efficiency has been scrupulously applied to the Direct Instruction curriculum, the delivery of lessons, and classroom organization. The quest for efficiency has driven the formation of many of the most well-known components of the DI approach, including the following:

- **Scripts** provide consistent wording and examples that have been selected according to a sophisticated communication theory that ensures all students will learn the content. The scripts have been field-tested and revised to verify that they are effective with a wide range of students who meet the programs' entrance qualifications. Scripts also greatly facilitate teachers' professional development as trainers and coaches can refer to specific formats when modeling effective teaching practices or observing and providing feedback to teachers as they use the DI programs.

- **Skill-based placement** is a prerequisite for teachers to provide instruction that will accelerate student achievement. All DI programs come with placement tests that teachers use to determine which levels of the DI programs match each student's instructional level. Schools purchase programs according to where students place, not according to their grade level. For example, second-grade students may place into the kindergarten level of the reading program. Thus, the "kindergarten" level of the program is merely a nominal designation indicating that it is the most basic level of the program, followed successively by the first-grade level of the program, the second-grade level of the program, etc. If students are in fourth grade or higher, they may place into the DI remedial programs, which do not have any nominal grade-level designations.

- **Homogeneous grouping** allows for more efficient teaching. If the skills and background knowledge of students in an instructional group are highly similar, the type of material one student in the group is ready for is probably the same as the type of material the other students in the group are ready for. And the mistakes one student makes are probably similar to the mistakes other students in the group will tend to make. In contrast, if students are not at the same skill level, the teacher is presented with the dilemma of whom to target with her teaching. If she focuses on the high-performing students in the group, her presentation will be at a level that is too advanced for the other members of the group. In contrast, if she focuses on the lower-performing students in the group, she will not be meeting the needs of the high-performing students, who will probably get bored and may start acting out. If she directs her teaching in between the skill levels of the higher- and lower-performing students, the group will experience a combination of these two sets of problems.

- **Unison responses** allow for much more efficient instruction than relying solely on individual turns for several reasons. First, each and every student is required to think and respond to all questions. Thus, the amount of practice each student has increases dramatically over individual turns. Second, when students are required to respond to each question, they are on task all the time; classroom behavior can improve dramatically as a result. Third, the teacher gets a lot of information from a group response to each question. When a teacher presents students successively the same question through individual turns, the teacher will only know whether the first student understood the task because the other students who follow might simply be copying the response of the first student (or the correction by the teacher if the first student answered the question incorrectly). For instance, if the teacher asks a student, "What is 8 + 6?" and the student answers it correctly, "14", the teacher has no way of knowing whether other students who subsequently answer correctly already knew that fact or whether they were simply copying the first student's response.

- **Signals** indicate to students when to respond in unison during group instruction. If the teacher provides a consistent and predictable signal, the students will know when to respond. Without a consistent signal, some of the students may respond before others, undermining the purpose of the group response, which is to provide information to the teacher about the performance of each student on the instructional tasks. The effective use of signals allows the teacher to evaluate the performance of all students on group tasks at the same time.

- **Strategic seating** allows the teacher to monitor student responses and interact with students during group instruction and independent work more easily, especially highly at-risk students, which bolsters the mastery of student work and the rate at which students progress through the lessons.

(How to implement each of these components is addressed in section 2 of this book.)

At the curricular level, efficiency implies first teaching the skills and content that will provide the strongest foundation for future learning. In the case of the *Reading Mastery Signature Edition*, the *sounds* letters make are taught to students in the kindergarten level of the program so that students learn to blend them together to read words. Later, in the first-grade level of the program, students learn *letter names*. Letter names are taught later because students don't need to know them to read words. For students who do not already know their letter names, postponing teaching letter names until the first-grade level of the *Reading Mastery* program allows students to start learning to read much earlier than if time were taken to teach students the names of the letters.

In contrast, three other DI reading programs – *Reading Mastery Transformations Edition, Horizons,* and its semi-automated version, *Funnix* – have been designed for students who already know many letter names (Engelmann, S., 2000). These programs make acquisition of reading skills as efficient as possible by taking advantage of students' knowledge of letters. In these programs, the sounds letters make are not presented in isolation. Instead, students derive the sounds from the names of the letters. (The design of these reading programs is discussed more thoroughly later in the book.)

The concept of efficiency has also been applied to classroom organization in the DI approach. Efficient classroom organization is stressed during training sessions offered by the National Institute for Direct Instruction (NIFDI) on routines, expectations and instructional "games". In these sessions, teachers learn to identify the critical behavior expectations and routines that are needed for their classrooms to run efficiently. They then translate these routines and expectations into "games" that students practice as they try to improve upon their previous fastest time for lining up for recess, getting out red pens for correcting their independent work, putting away their instructional materials, etc. These efficient practices are not limited to Direct Instruction classrooms, of course, as they have been widely adopted in "no excuses" schools that may use other instructional approaches.

THE RELATIONSHIP BETWEEN EFFECTIVENESS AND EFFICIENCY

The relationship between effectiveness and efficiency is mostly predominated by the former. *Instruction first needs to be effective before it can be efficient.* In other words, teachers must ensure that students are given material that matches their skill level and master it before focusing on how students can master material at a faster rate. If students go through the lessons too quickly without mastering the content, then, ironically, this will lead to much slower progress through the program. The teacher will need to go back and review the content that the students didn't master because *success with lessons that appear later in the programs is predicated on students mastering all of the previous content.*

The "mastery-first" approach should be applied to all DI subject areas. In reading, it is best known by the adage "accuracy before fluency." If students make errors when they read a text, the focus of instruction first and foremost should be on remediating those decoding errors so students are able to read the text accurately. If the teacher prompts students to reread the text without first correcting the errors, the number of errors the students make will stay the same or even *increase* during a second read of the same passage as error patterns become fixed in the students' responses. Repeating errors can reinforce guessing and other habits that lead to inaccurate reading, which are more difficult to undo the more they become the pattern for students. For mathematics, the mastery-first approach involves ensuring that students understand facts and operations at a high level of accuracy before prompting them to solve mathematics problems at a faster rate. Again, if students are prompted to meet timed performance expectations in math fact worksheets without having mastered the facts sufficiently, error rates will stay the same or even increase over time.

An important time for teachers to slow down to ensure mastery is when they are providing "think time" to students to process a direction or question before signaling them to respond as a group. The amount of processing time needed varies by task and by student. Tasks that are new to students or are complex usually require more "think time" in comparison to tasks that are less complex or more familiar to students. The amount of time that teachers provide should be based on each student's performance. Some students may need more time than others to formulate their response on any given task. Often, literally only a second or two more is needed for some students to process the tasks. If a teacher provides think time for the group that *matches the needs of the student who requires the most time*, the group will answer together in unison. If the students' responses are correct, the group can proceed through the lesson. If the teacher provides insufficient think time for all of the students, they will not all answer correctly in unison. As a result, the teacher will need to repeat the item, slowing down the group's progress. In these cases, the difference between providing sufficient think time and rushing the students can lead to tremendous differences in progress through the program when compounded over the course of a school year. Groups given appropriate think time will progress much faster than those whose responses are rushed.

Student mastery of material can lead to faster learning when students are presented with similar content. This relationship was discovered by Siegfried Engelmann in the 1960s as he and colleagues developed the *classification* track of the first DI language program:

> Early work in the Direct Instruction Preschool provided many examples of the acceleration achieved in specific areas of knowledge by teaching to mastery. One of the cleanest demonstrations came from the teaching of classification concepts – vehicles, clothing, food, animals, etc. – to four-year-olds. For this demonstration, the order of introduction for the classes differed from one group of children to another. ... Children learned one class to mastery, then learned the next in their sequence. ...

> The number of trials required for the children to learn different classes followed a predictable trend regardless of which class they learned first and which they learned fourth or fifth. The class that required the largest number of trials was the first class or second class in their sequence. The fourth or fifth class in the sequence required less than half the number of trials required for the children to learn the first class.

> One of the reasons for this accelerated learning is that the children did not have to learn as much to master the fifth class as they had to learn to master the first. In learning the first class, they had to learn the names of a higher-order class (vehicles, for instance) and some members of this class (boat, train, bus, etc.). Children also had to learn the relationship between the higher-order class and the members of the class. They had to learn basically that all trucks are vehicles, but that all vehicles are not necessarily trucks. This relationship is tricky and requires practice.

All the classes have the same structure. Children who learn the structure for the first class do not have to relearn it for each of the other classes. They still have to learn the name for the new higher-order class and the names for the various members. But the children do not have to relearn the structure or relationship of a higher-order class to members. Therefore, the children do not have to learn as much to master later examples. Consequently, children are able to master these classes faster, in fewer trials. (Engelmann, S., 2014, 54–56)

In this manner, students' mastery of content can accelerate their learning in any given subject area. Once students have mastered a certain format or a problem type – whether it is a classification task, a math story problem, map reading skills, constructing analogies, or reading words with silent Es – students will be able to learn similar content in less time than it took them to learn the first format or problem type.

Although the relationship between effectiveness and efficiency usually favors the former, there are times when being more efficient can lead to greater mastery. When teachers present the program at a brisk pace overall (while still providing sufficient think time), this can not only help students progress through the program at a faster rate, but it also captures their attention, which is a prerequisite for them to master the program's content. The opposite is also true. Students' attention will often drift if a teacher is overly methodical and presents the program at a consistently slow rate. Varying the rate of presentation as well as varying tone and body position can be important for holding students' attention.

MAXIMIZING STUDENT PERFORMANCE THROUGH ALL AVAILABLE FACTORS

The other foundational principle of acceleration is *maximization*, which is related to both effectiveness and efficiency. Maximization has to do with the scope of the effort to improve student performance and the effect that each factor has on performance. When applying this principle, schools are analyzed through the lens of identifying all resources that can be used to their maximum extent to help students succeed. This principle is best expressed by the axiom that *in order to maximize students' learning, you must maximize the influence of all factors that positively affect students' learning.* For example, since time on task is a factor that positively affects students' learning, it is important to use the time scheduled for key subject areas as judiciously as possible so that a maximum amount of time within the allotted schedule is actually devoted to instruction. Since contingent reinforcement is another factor that can positively affect students' learning, it is important to maximize the effect of reinforcement that students receive for their efforts and their accomplishments.

Of course, *the goal is to maximize the effect of all the factors taken together,* which often requires a trade-off in resource allocation. In balancing the two factors mentioned above, instead of long celebrations recognizing student success every day, mini-celebrations can take place throughout the day. Teachers and students can simulate riding a roller coaster, peeling a banana, setting off fireworks or dozens of other in-your-seat play-acting celebrations that require a minute or less and are still very reinforcing to students.

THE SCHOOL'S RESPONSIBILITY FOR ACADEMIC LEARNING

A critical question is whether factors in the home environment can be maximized to help students learn. Indeed, there is considerable research that the home is a place where significant learning can take place, including before formal schooling begins. (See, for example, Hart and Risley (1995).) Since the home environment can greatly influence students' acquisition of critical skills and knowledge, does the DI approach include a program for parents and other caregivers? As discussed later in this section, there are some DI programs that were created with the express purpose of home use. But the use of these programs is not a mandatory expectation of the comprehensive DI model. Although in theory the home environment could be analyzed in the same way as the classroom environment to identify and maximize the effect of factors that affect student learning, home environments vary so extensively even across the population of one elementary school that requiring parents and other caregivers to maximize their home environment to support DI would be unrealistic. For this reason, DI does not count on parents to contribute directly to the academic learning of their children. The support of parents and guardians, such as reinforcing students for their performance on independent work when it is taken home, is "icing on the cake" of the instructional program at school.

Instead of counting on the home environment to be a consistent contributor to students' learning, DI assumes that all academic learning takes place at school because the home environment cannot be relied upon to contribute appreciably to students' acquisition of critical skills and knowledge, especially for highly at-risk students and students with unstable home environments. In the DI approach, school leaders and staff assume responsibility for providing instruction that meets the needs of the students. This principle involves pledging that regardless of how unfavorable the lives of students may be outside of school – at home, in the park, on the streets – school leaders and staff commit to ensuring that students master the lessons that match their skill level each and every day. If this is not achieved, teachers and school leaders devise ways to help children who struggled so they succeed the next day.

The urgency tied to this relentless approach lies in contrast to the logical consequences of teaching methods that assume students should develop at their own pace without targeted instruction from teachers. Rather than assume unseen "development" is taking place inside a child, DI practitioners use each student's demonstrated performance to determine what a child does and does not know. In this way, the DI approach is "behavioral", although not in a strict behaviorist sense that reinforcement and punishment are the sole determinants of learning. DI is "behavioral" because the observed student performance on specific tasks in reaction to the teacher's presentation is used at the heart of all decisions in a DI implementation. Certainly, successful DI instructors use positive behavioral management techniques to engage students and reinforce them for their efforts and their accomplishments. But *the role of behavior management is to facilitate and support the academic instruction that takes place rather than to act as the main causal agent of students' learning*. It is the step-by-step design and sophisticated communication system undergirding the DI programs, discussed later in this book, that are the main drivers of students' success with DI.

HIGHER-ORDER THINKING SKILLS

In contrast to a common myth that DI is a "basic skills" approach, the ultimate focus of DI is to foster higher-order, critical thinking. In order for students to become critical thinkers though, they must master more basic elements of complex operations. So the DI programs involve rote learning, especially at the beginning of program levels. When students can reliably identify fundamental elements such as the sounds letters make, symbols for basic operations (+, –, ×, ÷), and the names of different objects, they provide a basis for more advanced learning in reading, mathematics and language, respectively. For example, when students can reliably identify the names of a truck, a car, a bicycle, and an airplane, they can learn the class of vehicles and the rule that *if it can take you places, it's a vehicle.* If they do not know the names of vehicles, they cannot learn the concept of a class of vehicles. Nor can they learn the rule above that students can apply to different objects to determine whether it belongs to the class of vehicles – a higher-order operation that students learn to do reliably in the Grade K level of the language track of *Reading Mastery.*

In this way, *rote elements do not appear randomly in the DI programs but appear in close relationship with higher-order skills.* Learning the sounds letters make lays the foundation for the strategy of blending the sounds together to form words rather than memorizing words or guessing at their identity based on the shape of the words. Counting backwards lays the foundation for subtraction. And identifying the sequence of events in a story lays the foundation for students to summarize stories.

In several DI programs, students refer to an explicit model that can be used to organize facts and processes. An example is *Understanding U.S. History,* which uses a problem-solution-effect structure for analyzing historical events. Students learn that historical actors have options to choose from in response to problems – **a**ccommodating, **d**ominating, **m**oving, **i**nventing, or **t**olerating the problem. Students learn to apply this ADMIT model to past events, identify which option historical actors chose, and determine the consequences these choices had for future events and the choices taken by other actors. With this model, the rote elements of specific historical events (names of people, dates, actions, and results) are easier for students to retain as they are incorporated into a broader narrative. As DI program author Doug Carnine explains in the introduction to *Higher Order Thinking: Designing Curriculum for Mainstreamed Students*:

> ... hierarchically organized information is easier to remember than randomly organized information ... the number of terms and isolated facts required of students can be reduced because they are learning higher order organizations that subsume many of these bits and pieces. (Carnine and Kame'enui, 1992, 17)

Despite the emphasis on conceptual acquisition in the DI programs, much of the field of education is either unaware of or has ignored DI's emphasis on higher-order thinking. Many in the field have conflated DI's structure with a lack of higher-order thinking or creativity. For example, during Project Follow Through 1968–77, DI was officially classified by the US federal government as a "behavioral approach" with the assumption that students in the DI model would score well on basic skills but not so well on cognitive measures or self-esteem. Ironically and unexpectedly for others in the field, the results showed that students in the DI model performed best of *all* of the nine major models on *all* skills, *with the biggest discrepancy in cognitive skills*. Students in the models involving more open-ended discovery approaches performed the lowest out of the group of models, with almost all of the models showing negative effects on cognitive measures in comparison to matched Title 1 schools (Engelmann, S. et al., 1988, 312). (See Topic Brief 8 on Project Follow Through.)

Still today, DI is classified as a "teach to the test" approach that eschews students' higher-order thinking. An example is the following from a webpage on the "teacher-centered approach to learning":

> Taken to its most extreme interpretation, teachers are the main authority figure in a teacher-centered instruction model. Students are viewed as "empty vessels" who passively receive knowledge from their teachers through lectures and direct instruction, with an end goal of positive results from testing and assessment. In this style, teaching and assessment are viewed as two separate entities; student learning is measured through objectively scored tests and assessments. (Teach.com, 2020)

The webpage quoted did not mention upper-case DI explicitly (the difference between upper-case DI and lower-case di is explained later in this section), but it is a common myth that DI has "an end goal of positive results from testing and assessment." However, that is not the goal of DI. It is to accelerate student learning in both basic and higher cognitive skills as a means for preparing students for more advanced learning. The objective metric of the students' acquisition of these skills is the in-program assessments (mastery tests and reading checkouts discussed later), not external, high-stakes tests. The mastery tests are composed entirely of the material covered in previous lessons. Teachers repeat selected exercises in response to students' errors on the mastery tests. In this way, teaching and assessment are an integral part of the same process of students' acquisition of critical skills and knowledge as a basis for more advanced learning without reference to high-stakes tests. (One of the cautions discussed in the third section of this book is how students can fail to reach their full potential with DI when teachers teach only to the in-program mastery tests.)

Ironically, some of the most critical higher-order thinking skills covered in the DI programs never appear directly on high-stakes tests. The *Reading Mastery Signature Edition Language, Grade 5* program places a great deal of emphasis on students learning to analyze deductions, arguments, and statements of claims, evaluate them for missing information or inadequate evidence, test hypotheses, and identify contradictions. After they demonstrate that they've mastered these skills of analysis, they construct alternative arguments from evidence that's presented and write conclusions that are specific to the evidence available. The students work cooperatively in groups to complete projects that require them to apply these higher-order thinking skills:

Project 1   Create an argument that has inadequate evidence.

Project 2   Create an argument that has false cause.

Project 3   Simplify and critique a passage that uses complex vocabulary.

Project 4   Create an outline diagram for critiquing a new problem type.

Project 5   Write an improbable inference and a description of the illustration.

Project 6   Rewrite a passage, using difficult vocabulary, and critique the content of the passage.

Project 7   Use reference tools to identify a mystery location and write how the place was identified.

Project 8   Write an improbable inference and a description of the illustration.

Project 9   Prepare a debate about homework.

Project 10   Write a persuasive proposal for improving school. (Engelmann S., Grossen and Osborn, 2008, 80)

The mastery of these skills is not reflected directly in high-stakes tests, such as reading comprehension tests that measure vocabulary to a great extent. Yet, these thinking skills are critical for each student to master in order to become a contributing citizen in our society. Our democratic processes work well only if citizens can analyze arguments, identify deficiencies in arguments, and apply logical processes to come up with counter-arguments that inform their decisions. If students do not master these critical thinking skills, they can be swayed by false advertisements, misleading claims, and demagogic rhetoric, to the detriment of their well-being and the well-being of society as a whole.

SUMMARY

In sum, the overriding goal of DI is to accelerate the performance of students. This requires that instruction should be effective (students are taught to mastery) first and foremost and efficient (using as little time as possible). Mastery itself leads to faster learning as students have a solid basis for acquiring new skills and knowledge.

To maximize student learning, all the factors that have been proven to have a positive effect on student learning should be made as efficient and effective as possible. This means behavior management and classroom routines as well as all aspects of instruction should be streamlined in such a way as to ensure that time is utilized with maximum effect on student performance every day. Utilizing all parts of the school day with maximum effect is critical for instruction that is as equitable as possible for students without the advantage of language-rich and information-rich homes as they rely almost exclusively on school as the sole place for acquiring the skills, knowledge, and confidence they need for more advanced learning. DI provides a coherent set of skills and knowledge integrated with higher-order thinking skills that will serve all students who master the content well in the future with the goal not of helping them pass high-stakes tests but of laying the basis for their success and well-being as productive citizens later in life.

CHAPTER TWO
DESIGN OF THE DIRECT
INSTRUCTION CURRICULA

If the long-term goal of Direct Instruction is to accelerate the performance of all students, the daily objective of each DI lesson is to ensure that every child masters critical skills and concepts in a way that lays the basis for more advanced learning while building students' confidence that they are competent and successful learners. This daily objective is accomplished by *targeting instruction at each student's skill level* using a very precise metric that can be objectively measured (first-time correct performance, discussed in section 2). Teachers adjust the amount of practice needed according to each student's performance on every task. If a student's performance indicates a consistent pattern of not meeting predetermined criteria for success, the student receives targeted support to stay in the existing group or is placed in a group that is receiving instruction at the student's skill level. Student performance is maximized when instruction is customized for each student in this manner. A school's ability to provide instructional groupings, which is limited by such factors as classroom space, trained instructor availability, and the amount of time in the day, impacts the level of customization for each student.

The Direct Instruction curricula support the successful achievement of this daily objective through their unique design, which allows students to master every lesson every day if they are placed in lessons that match their skill level. DI is often referred to as a "scripted" approach, which is true but insufficient to describe the powerful design that ensures students' mastery of the material if they are properly placed in the programs and taught by teachers who follow the programs' directions precisely. This chapter describes the components of the DI programs that allow for students' daily mastery of the content: faultless communication, an incremental step design, the track structure of the programs, consistent exercise formats, frequent in-program assessments that are closely tied to the lessons' content, and the integration of all components into coherent programs that enable students to perform higher-level, cognitively complex tasks.

FAULTLESS COMMUNICATION

The design of the DI programs involves the application of a sophisticated communication theory that ensures students comprehend the targeted skill or concept introduced by the teacher in new material. Called "faultless communication" or the "single interpretation principle," students who possess the necessary preskills learn the new skill or concept without fail as a result of the type of examples presented and their arrangement as well as the specific, consistent wording used by the teacher. The approach reduces possible misunderstandings to a minimum to the extent that students can't help but learn the intended content. (For a detailed explanation of faultless communication, see Engelmann and Carnine (1991), *Theory of Instruction* or Engelmann, S. (1969b), *Conceptual Learning*. It has also been referred to as "clear teaching," the title of the booklet on DI by Shepard Barbash (2012), which offers a more accessible summary of Direct Instruction theory. See also Scott (2017) and Boxer (2019).)

The great care involved in the arrangement of examples and their strategic introduction to limit misunderstanding in the DI approach can be illustrated by the introduction of sounds in the kindergarten level of *Reading Mastery Signature Edition*. (The program refers to symbols that students learn initially as sounds and not letter names because students do not need to know the name of a letter to know the sound that the letter makes when it is read.) As discussed in chapter 3, other very effective DI designs for teaching beginning reading exist. The design used in *Reading Mastery Signature Edition* has proved to be successful with children with below-average foundational skills, who often have difficulty discriminating between different letters that are highly similar in appearance. The most common example is the discrimination between the letters *b* and *d*, which many students confuse when learning to read or write.

The reason for the confusion is easy to understand if viewed from the context of young children's lack of familiarity with symbols. Until they are introduced to symbols, children spend their entire lives observing and manipulating physical objects. In the physical world, an object retains its identity regardless of its position or orientation. For example, a pencil is still a pencil if the tip is pointed up, or if the eraser is pointed up, or if the pencil is lying flat on a table or in any other position. However, this is not the case for almost all symbols. If you make a physical object that represents the letter *b*, when you rotate the object so the ball is on the other side of the stick, you have created the lower-case letter *d*. If you flip that object 180 degrees so the stick is now pointing down rather than up, you have created the lower-case letter *q*. If you rotate the object one more time as you did for the first rotation so the ball is on the other side of the stick, you have created the lower-case letter *p*. In sum, the same object rotated in different ways produces the symbols *b*, *d*, *q* and *p*. It is no coincidence that students often confuse these pairs of symbols, *b* and *d*, and *p* and *q*, because they are identical to the same physical object oriented in different ways.

Students' confusion of these symbols is exacerbated by the order that they are usually introduced in the classroom. In most classrooms, letters are introduced in the same order they appear in the alphabet. Consequently, the letters *b* and *d* are introduced very early to students as these letters are second and fourth in order in the alphabet. The letters *p* and *q* are introduced back-to-back as they appear sequentially in the alphabet.

In contrast to the traditional, alphabetical order of introducing symbols, great care is taken in the *Reading Mastery* program to prevent confusing students by 1) altering the appearance of symbols so they do not resemble each other, and 2) spacing out the introduction of these symbols over many lessons. Research has proved that extended practice with one of a pair of highly similar letters before introducing the second minimizes students' confusion of the letters (Carnine, 1980). The *Pronunciation*

Guide (Table 2.1) displays the 40 symbols used in the kindergarten level of the program. These symbols represent the most common sounds in the English language. With very few exceptions, they convert the English alphabet into an orthography with one-to-one correspondence between each symbol and the sound it makes when read. The table provides information on the pronunciation of the sounds the symbols represent as well as the lessons where the symbols first appear.

Symbol	Pronounced	As in	Voiced or Unvoiced *	Introduced in Lesson
a	aaa	and	v	1, 12
m	mmm	ram	v	4, 11
s	sss	bus	uv	9, 16
ē	ēēē	eat	v	19
r	rrr	bar	v	23
d	d	mad	v	27
f	fff	stuff	uv	31
i	iii	if	v	34
th	thththth	this and bathe (not thing)	v	38
t	t	cat	uv	41
n	nnn	pan	v	44
c	c	tack	uv	48
o	ooo	ox	v	51
ā	āāā	ate	v	58
h	h	hat	uv	61
u	uuu	under	v	64
g	g	tag	v	68
l	lll	pal	v	72
w	www	wow	v	76
sh	shshsh	wish	uv	80

Symbol	Pronounced	As in	Voiced or Unvoiced *	Introduced in Lesson
I	(the word I)		v	88
k	k	tack	uv	92
ō	ōōō	over	v	98
v	vvv	love	v	102
p	p	sap	uv	108
ch	ch	touch	uv	113
e	eee	end	v	118
b	b	grab	v	121
ing	iiing	sing	v	124
ī	īīī	ice	v	127
y	yyy	yard	v	131
er	urr	brother	v	135
x	ksss	ox	uv	139
oo	oooo	moon (not look)	v	142
j	j	judge	v	145
ȳ	īīī	my	v	149
wh	www or wh	why	v or uv	152
qu	kwww (or koo)	quick	v	154
z	zzz	buzz	v	156
ū	ūūū	use	v	158

* Voiced sounds are sounds you make by vibrating your vocal chords. You do not use your vocal chords for unvoiced sounds—you use air only. To feel the difference between voiced and unvoiced sounds, hold your throat lightly and say the sound **vvv**. You will feel your vocal chords vibrating. Then, without pausing, change the sound to **fff**. The vibrations will stop. The only difference between the sounds is that the **vvv** is voiced and the **fff** is not.

Sound Combinations, Digraphs, and Diphthon

al (also)	er	sh
ar (arm)	ing	th
ch	oo	wh
ea (meat)	ou (out)	
ee (need)	qu	

Table 2.1 Pronunciation guide for *Reading Mastery Signature Edition Grades K & 1*. Source: Engelmann, S. and Bruner, E. C. (2008b). *Reading Mastery Signature Edition Teacher's Guide Grade K*, p. 87, © McGraw Hill.

As the table shows, students practice the *d* sound for 94 lessons before they are introduced to the *b* sound. The *d* sound is the sixth symbol introduced (on Lesson 27), whereas the *b* sound is the 29th symbol introduced (on Lesson 121). Moreover, the authors of *Reading Mastery* adjusted the shapes of these symbols so they resemble each other less. The ball for the *d* sound is oval and slanted, whereas the ball for the *b* sound is a circle. Similar steps were taken to reduce potential confusion between the *p* and *q* sounds. Their introduction is separated by over 40 lessons, and the *q* has been incorporated into a *qu* consonant cluster symbol. (See chapter 10 of Engelmann and Carnine (1991) for a more detailed discussion of the effects on student learning of different sequences for introducing minimally different members of a set of phenomena.)

The shapes of other pairs of symbols that students often confuse are altered to help students discriminate between them. The crossbar of the *t* has been raised, and the top of the *f* has been exaggerated in length. The hump of the *h* is much smaller than the hump of the *n*. And the *j* appears without a ball in contrast to the *i*, which has a ball. All of these adjustments help ensure that students can differentiate between the symbols and learn to identify the sounds they make reliably.

Once students have mastered all of these symbols, the modifications are gradually removed. The bars over long vowels disappear; conjoined letters are separated; and the letters take on their traditional sizes and shapes. The transition to the traditional alphabet is completed by Lesson 92 of the first-grade level of the program. These changes occur incrementally so students readily master each change as it happens. As a result, students' transition to reading text composed of "regular letters" occurs seamlessly. (See the video, *Why is Reading So Hard?* at www.nifdi.org/videos.html for an excellent animated depiction of the transition from the *Reading Mastery* alphabet to the traditional alphabet in the first-grade level of the program.)

Students' success in the *Reading Mastery* sequence calls into question the notion that the difficulties many students experience when learning to read are neurobiological in origin. The very high rate at which students in the *Reading Mastery* program learn to differentiate between letters and avoid the difficulties that many students experience during traditional reading instruction indicates that the origin of many of the problems students experience in learning to read may be instructional, not neurobiological.

INCREMENTAL STEP DESIGN

In his book, *Teaching for Mastery*, Mark McCourt characterizes the subject of mathematics as being like a giant Jenga tower with bricks located higher in the structure dependent on support from bricks located lower in the tower:

> Turning to my own subject, mathematics, for a moment: I often describe the subject as being like one massive Jenga tower. Each brick in the tower represents an idea, concept, skill or leap in knowledge. It is glaringly evident that the main reason that pupils fail to acquire all of the knowledge expected of them by the end of schooling is not that the bricks at the top of the tower are somehow beyond them, but that the bricks lower down are loose, wobbly or missing entirely. Attempting to learn a new mathematical idea without the necessary foundations in place is pointless. (McCourt, 2019, 31)

Direct Instruction programs promote mastery of critical skills and concepts systematically through a unique incremental step design that puts each "brick" in the learning "tower" firmly in place as content increases in complexity and sophistication. Only 10–15% of the content of any lesson is new. The remaining 85–90% of any lesson contains material that was introduced in previous lessons. If students are placed properly in the program and have mastered the content of the previous day's lesson, they will have a relatively small amount of material to master in today's lesson (10–15%), which should be possible for the overwhelming majority of students who receive proper instruction. They will spend most of their time in the lesson applying skills and concepts learned in previous lessons and increasing their automaticity with this content (85–90%). This structure provides a firm foundation for mastering new content in later lessons as everything that is introduced in the DI programs is incorporated into later lessons.

The incremental design of DI programs can be viewed from two different perspectives:

1. Everything learners need to know to perform a targeted skill is pre-taught.
2. Everything introduced in the programs is used and integrated into increasingly more complex tasks.

These statements are different sides of the same coin. They both describe the same structure. The first statement is taken from the perspective of how the more advanced skills in the DI programs are supported completely by skills introduced earlier in the programs, and the second statement is taken from the perspective of how all skills and concepts introduced lead to more advanced skills and applications.

The structure of the DI programs can be visualized as a staircase with stairs representing lessons that incorporate new material at a steady rate. In this metaphorical representation, the small rise of each step represents new content introduced in the lesson, and the part of the staircase underneath the step represents content introduced in previous lessons. *Just as it is easier for a student to proceed up a physical staircase to the next step if the student is standing just one step below, it is easier for students to proceed to the next highest lesson if they have mastered all of the content presented in the preceding lessons and are being taught the lesson that corresponds to their current skill level.* For example, in Figure 2.1, each number represents a lesson in a DI program. Students are presented with Lesson 6 and have mastered all the content in the previous lessons. Only the relatively small, bracketed amount of content is newly introduced in the lesson. The rest represents the amount of content that students are reviewing from previous lessons and applying to new contexts.

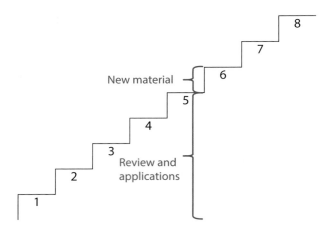

Figure 2.1 Mastery teaching staircase with proper placement.

However, if students are placed in lessons that are too advanced for them, their current skill level is actually much lower than their placement in the program. Because they are misplaced, they must master much more than the 10–15% of the lesson that is new. This percentage can increase dramatically in proportion to the extent of the misplacement. If the actual skill level of a student is one lesson behind the current lesson, she must master 20–30% of the lesson that is functionally new to her. If she is two lessons behind the current lesson, she must master 30–45% of the lesson that is functionally new to her, and so forth.

In Figure 2.2, a group of students is presented with Lesson 6 but for whatever reason, they have only mastered all the content through Lesson 4. Consequently, these students need to learn roughly twice as much new material as the students in the previous example who had mastered the content through Lesson 5. Learning this greater amount would be a challenge for any student, but it is an even greater challenge to at-risk students and students who may lack confidence in their ability to learn the material.

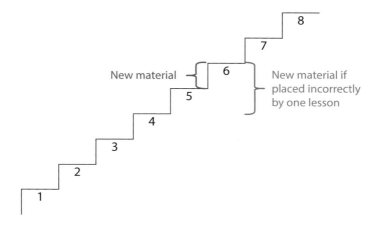

Figure 2.2 Mastery teaching staircase with improper placement.

Thus, the incremental structure of the DI programs is a double-edged sword. If students are placed precisely at the current skill level and taught to mastery every day, they will proceed through the lessons with minimal backtracking as they acquire all of the skills and concepts presented by the programs. If, however, the students are presented with lessons that are significantly above their skill level, they will have difficulty mastering the lessons. This lack of mastery will most likely grow as the program introduces new content at a steady pace. (Ensuring that students are placed appropriately initially and brought to mastery on all content daily will be a major focus in the chapters ahead.)

If there is a gap between what the students know and what they are presented with, the incremental design is lost, and the prospect of bringing students to mastery on the current lesson is essentially nil. S. Engelmann cautioned that "the benefits of the design of the program are obliterated if a student falls below the level of the stair" (Engelmann, S., 2014, 14). Indeed, even if the teacher is following the script and correction procedures, using the proper signals, providing positive feedback to students, and implementing all of the other components of the DI programs with fidelity, they will not be providing the type of instruction that is inherent in the approach because of the high number of student performance errors, which makes it impossible to bring the students to mastery on the content. In these cases of significant misplacement, students need to be re-placed and presented with material that matches their skill level, which may involve regrouping the students if some have the skills to continue through the program at the current lesson and others need to be pushed back in the program. Placing students in material that matches their skill levels must be done before the teacher can "do DI" as envisaged by the programs' authors.

Note that experienced teachers who have been trained in DI delivery techniques may be able to close small learning gaps in an instructional group through separate one-on-one intervention sessions if the instructional level of the lower-performing students is off by only a few lessons. Less experienced and untrained teachers usually have much more difficulty closing small learning gaps, which would allow instructional groups to remain intact.

EXAMPLES OF INCREMENTAL STEP DESIGN

The staircase is simply a conceptual model for visualizing how the sophistication of the content increases steadily and incrementally in the DI programs. But what do these learning "steps" actually look like, and how do they make learning relatively easy at first for students and then gradually more challenging? A pair of examples serve to illustrate the incremental design of two different DI programs.

The first example involves the way in which carrying is taught in the addition module of *Corrective Mathematics*. *Corrective Mathematics* is a seven-level program designed to address specific sets of deficits that students in Grade 4 and higher often have. The first four levels, called modules, address the basic mathematical operations of addition, subtraction, multiplication, and division. The final three modules cover: basic fractions; fractions, decimals, and percentages; and ratios and equations. In all of the modules, the program addresses the most common mistakes that remedial students make when working math problems. In the addition module, carrying is taught in a way that is designed to eliminate or greatly reduce the confusion that many students experience when they are learning to work column addition problems that result in a two-digit sum. This requires that students add the numerals with the same place value together correctly and then write the two numerals in two different places – in the answer space of the lower place value column (the ones column, for example) and at the top of the column of the next higher place value column (the tens column in this case). Here is an example of a problem with two-digit numbers that involves carrying from the ones to the tens column:

$$
\begin{array}{r}
28 \\
13 \\
+\ 42 \\
\hline
\end{array}
$$

Here is an example of a problem with two-digit numbers that doesn't involve carrying from the ones to the tens column:

$$
\begin{array}{r}
21 \\
13 \\
+\ 42 \\
\hline
\end{array}
$$

When working problems that involve carrying, remedial students often write the incorrect number in the incorrect spot. So the addition module provides scaffolding ("learning steps") in the following ways so students work the problems correctly:

> First, the students add columns of single-digit numbers. Then, they are taught to add columns of numbers that have more than one digit but that do not require renaming (carrying). When carrying is introduced, the sum for the ones column is given, and the students write only the number being carried in a box at the top of the tens column. Later, the sum is no longer written, and then, the carrying box is dropped. The operation is expanded so that carrying occurs not only from the ones column but also from the tens and hundreds columns. (Adapted from: Engelmann, S., Carnine and Steely, 2005, 8.)

This careful, step-by-step scaffolding of how to teach carrying is spread out over many lessons. Table 2.2 describes each of the tracks (sets of exercises with a common focus) that support students learning this critical operation.

Step one	Determine the sum of two 2- or 3-digit numbers. No regrouping. Vertical format.
Step two	Determine the sum of two 2- or 3-digit numbers. No regrouping. Horizontal format.
Step three	Determine the sum of three or four single-digit numbers. With and without regrouping.
Step four	Determine the sum of three or four 2-digit numbers. No regrouping.
Step five	Determine the sum of three or four 1- or 2-digit numbers. The sum of the ones column is greater than 9.
Step six	Determine the sum of three or four 1-, 2-, or 3-digit numbers. The sum of the ones column as well as the sum of the tens column is greater than 9. Regrouping required.
Step seven	Determine the sum of three or four 1-, 2-, 3-, or 4-digit numbers. The sums of the ones, tens, and/or hundreds columns are between 10 and 20. Regrouping required.
Step eight	Determine the sum of three or four 2-, 3-, or 4-digit numbers. The sums of the ones, tens, and/or hundreds columns are between 10 and 35. Regrouping required.

Table 2.2 Sequence of carrying operations in the addition module of *Corrective Mathematics*. Adapted from: Engelmann, S., Carnine, D. and Steely, D. (2005). *Corrective Mathematics Series Guide*, p. 13.

The simplest operation is introduced first – summarizing two 2- or 3-digit numbers without regrouping. The students' repertoire is slowly expanded to include more advanced versions of the operation while previous skills are maintained. The different subsets of problem types extend until the end of the module – through Lesson 65. With this very gradual ramp up in the sophistication of the exercises, students who could not add two one-digit numerals together reliably when they started the program reliably solve such problems as the following after only 12 weeks of instruction:

$$
\begin{array}{r}
1818 \\
1943 \\
2775 \\
+\ 559 \\
\hline
\end{array}
$$

The second example of DI's incremental step design is from the kindergarten level of *Reading Mastery Signature Edition*. As previously discussed, students learn the sounds that letters make in this level of the program. After they can identify a symbol reliably, they learn to blend the sounds together to form words, which they read in isolation. After the students can read the words reliably, the words appear in stories. Thus, the stories are completely decodable; they consist solely of words that students have read successfully, and the words are composed of sounds that students can identify reliably. Because of this structure, students are able to decode the stories at a high level of accuracy, which *allows students to focus more on reading with prosody and text comprehension than if students are struggling to decode words in a passage.*

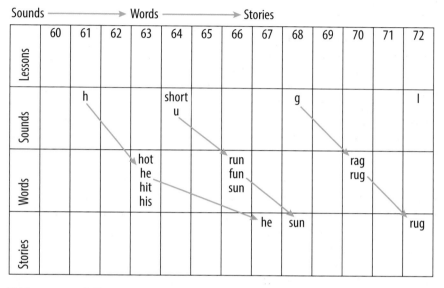

Sounds ⟶ Words ⟶ Stories

Lessons	60	61	62	63	64	65	66	67	68	69	70	71	72
Sounds		h			short u				g				l
Words				hot he hit his			run fun sun				rag rug		
Stories								he	sun				rug

Table 2.3 How skills are taught in *Reading Mastery Signature Edition Grade K.*

This progression of skills is played out over many lessons for any particular sound. As Table 2.3 demonstrates, the introduction of the sounds *h*, *u*, and *g* are spaced out over several lessons. The sound *h* is introduced in Lesson 61. Students practice identifying the sound and differentiating it from other sounds that they've already learned for a couple of lessons. Then, in Lesson 63, the students start to read words that contain the *h* sound – *he*, *hit*, *his*. They practice reading words that contain the *h* sound in isolation for several lessons before they appear in stories in Lesson 67. Thus, *students have the opportunity to practice the* h *sound for nearly seven full lessons before it appears in a story.* The likelihood of their reading the story successfully is increased dramatically through this carefully engineered ramp up of the use of the *h* sound in the program in comparison to traditional approaches to reading that involve presenting the letter *h* and words that start with the letter *h* in the same lesson.

This same careful progression from sounds to words to stories occurs for all of the other sounds in the program. As the table shows, students have the opportunity to practice the short *u* and the *g* sounds for nearly five full lessons before they appear in stories. By that time, the *l* sound is introduced, continuing the sophisticated pattern of sound introduction in the program, which enables all students with the prerequisite skills to master the program's content and read by the end of kindergarten.

TRACKS

Both of the examples of skill progressions provided previously – the carrying operation in the addition module of *Corrective Mathematics* and the identification and blending of sounds in the kindergarten level of *Reading Mastery Signature Edition* – illustrate the "tracks" organizational structure of the DI programs. Lessons in the DI programs are not devoted to a single topic. Instead, DI lessons are composed of several exercises that represent different tracks (sequences of exercises that introduce and expand on a specific skill type over many lessons). Each lesson contains exercises that span a variety of topics, with the exercises belonging to several different tracks. In this way, what would be a topical unit in traditional instructional programs is distributed over several lessons, which facilitates students' engagement during instruction and acquisition of the content.

Each exercise in a lesson usually lasts only a couple of minutes with a great deal of variability with regard to programs and levels. For example, Lesson 125 of the *Language for Thinking* program contains five exercises plus the workbook introduction representing the following tracks:

Exercise 1: Questioning skills

Exercise 2: Homonyms

Exercise 3: Inferences

Exercise 4: Reporting on pictures

Exercise 5: Description

Workbook Lesson: True/false, classification, months

The lesson is intended to last about half an hour for an average of around five minutes per exercise (including the Workbook Lesson) with some of the exercises lasting longer than others. During the Workbook Lesson part of group work, the teacher introduces the tasks that students will complete during independent work time. An additional five to 10 minutes should be scheduled for students to complete the workbook activities.

In contrast, Lesson 11 of the *Reading Mastery Signature Edition* Grade 1 reading program, which is intended to last about the same duration, contains 23 exercises representing four tracks (the SOUNDS, READING VOCABULARY, STORIES and INDEPENDENT WORKSHEET tracks):

Exercise 1: Sounds firm-up (SOUNDS track)

Exercise 2: Sound out first (READING VOCABULARY track)

Exercise 3: Sound out first (READING VOCABULARY track)

Exercise 4: "ar" (READING VOCABULARY track)

Exercise 5: "ar" words (READING VOCABULARY track)

Exercise 6: Read "ar" word the fast way (READING VOCABULARY track)

Exercise 7: Sound out first (READING VOCABULARY track)

Exercise 8: Last part, first part (READING VOCABULARY track)

Exercise 9: Read the fast way first (READING VOCABULARY track)

Exercise 10: Read the fast way (READING VOCABULARY track)

Exercise 11: Read the fast way first (READING VOCABULARY track)

Exercise 12: Read the fast way first (READING VOCABULARY track)

Exercise 13: Read the fast way (READING VOCABULARY track)

Exercise 14: First reading – title and three sentences (STORIES track)

Exercise 15: Remaining sentences (STORIES track)

Exercise 16: Second reading – sentences and questions
(STORIES track)

Exercise 17: Picture comprehension (STORIES track)

Exercise 18: Read the story items (INDEPENDENT
WORKSHEET track)

Exercise 19: Read sentence to copy (INDEPENDENT
WORKSHEET track)

Exercise 20: Identify sounds to be written (INDEPENDENT
WORKSHEET track)

Exercise 21: Read story, answer items (INDEPENDENT
WORKSHEET track)

Exercise 22: Write words for picture (INDEPENDENT
WORKSHEET track)

Exercise 23: Introduction to independent activity
(INDEPENDENT WORKSHEET track)

As with Lesson 125 of the *Language for Thinking* program, Lesson 11 of the *Reading Mastery Signature Edition* Grade 1 reading program is intended to last about half an hour for an average of just over a minute per exercise during group instruction with additional time allocated for independent work. Some of these exercises involve reading a single word, so these exercises can take just a few seconds *if the students are at mastery.* Exercises 18–23 should also be quick as they involve the teacher introducing students to the independent work and do not involve students actually completing all of the independent work tasks. Story reading is expected to take up much more time than exercises involving a single word or exercises introducing students to the independent work. Completing the lesson in a reasonable amount of time is possible only if the students are appropriately placed in the program. If they are not, and the exercises involve many error corrections, the students won't be able to complete the group work in half an hour.

The progression of the exercises within this lesson follows the same pattern as the lessons in the kindergarten level of the program after students are able to read connected text: students identify sounds, read words of different types, read the story that is composed of words students have mastered, and engage in independent work that reinforces skills they learned in today's lesson and previous lessons. The tracks listed earlier are composed of sub-tracks that merge together to form more sophisticated tracks. Content that has been mastered is integrated with new material to develop more advanced exercises.

The teacher's guide for each level of the DI programs contains a *Scope and Sequence Chart* that shows the range of lessons covered by the different tracks and their sub-tracks. The transition to the use of the traditional alphabet is illustrated in Figure 2.3 through the Scope and Sequence Chart of the *Reading Mastery Signature Edition* Grade 1 reading program. The following bullet points summarize the tracks that contribute to the transition to the traditional alphabet. Student mastery of the tracks described in bullet points 1–4 lays the basis for students to participate successfully in the spelling track, which appears in Lessons 86–160:

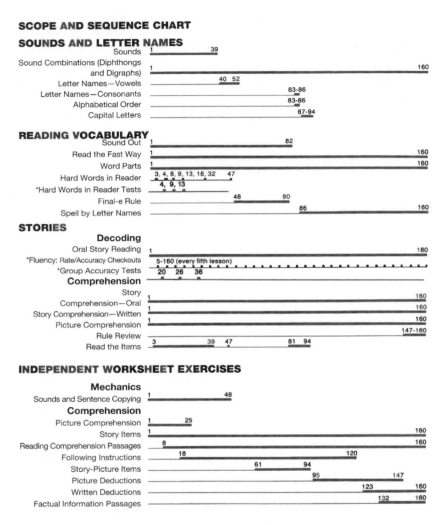

Figure 2.3 Scope and Sequence Chart. Source: Engelmann, S. and Bruner, E. C. (2008a). *Reading Mastery Signature Edition Teacher's Guide Grade 1*, p. 112, © McGraw Hill.

- From Lessons 1–39, all letters are identified as "sounds" using the same modified orthography taught in the Grade K level of the program (the first track in the chart).

- From Lessons 40–52, students learn the names for vowels, and the long vowels are presented as they appear in the normal alphabet with no lines (macrons) over them (the third track in the chart).

- From Lessons 48–80, students learn to apply the long-vowel rule when words end in the letter *e* rather than follow the rule learned in the kindergarten level of the program of ignoring silent *es*, which appeared much smaller in size than other symbols (the 12th track in the chart).

- From Lessons 83–86, students learn the letter names of consonants (the fourth track in the chart).

- From Lesson 86 through to the end of the program, students spell words using letter names (the 13th track in the chart).

FORMATS

The content of the DI programs is not merely "scripted." Within each of the instructional tracks, exercises are constructed in a clear, consistent way and written in a specified form, which facilitates the teacher's presentation of the lesson and the students' mastery of the content. Each format has the same basic structure for all exercises with similar content. The format remains the same with minor modifications across several lessons. Each new exercise of the same type retains the wording and the structure of the previous lesson but includes different examples of the targeted skill or concept. The *Corrective Reading* program authors explain the advantage of the "format" system to teachers and students:

> The format exercises have these advantages:
>
> 1. They are easy to present because your behavior in the basic steps remains the same for all examples of a given format.
> 2. They are easy for students to comprehend because the directions and wording are the same for all examples of a particular format. (Engelmann, S. et al., 2008a)

Students and teachers alike benefit from the reliability and predictability of the formats. They can concentrate on the content rather than expend mental energy trying to figure out what type of presentation is required of the teacher, and what type of responses are expected of the students.

The "format" system can be illustrated by comparing the exercises in Figure 2.4 that are both part of the Sound Combinations track of *Corrective Reading Decoding*, Level B2, a remedial Direct Instruction reading program. Before doing so, here are some critical script conventions:

Teacher talk – what the teacher says – is in blue.

(Directions to the teacher – what the teacher does – are in parentheses.)

Student responses – what the students say or do – are in italics.

<table>
<tr>
<td valign="top">

■ EXERCISE 2 ■

(NEW) SOUND COMBINATION: tch

Task A

1. Open your Student Book to Lesson 14. ✓
   • Touch the letters T–C–H in part 1. ✓

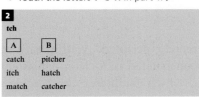

   • The letters T–C–H go together and make the sound **ch**. What sound? (Signal.) *ch.*
2. You're going to read words that have the letters T–C–H.
3. Touch the first word in column A. ✓
   • What word? (Signal.) *Catch.*
   • Spell catch. (Signal for each letter.) *C–A–T–C–H.*
4. Next word. ✓
   • What word? (Signal.) *Itch.*
   • Spell itch. (Signal for each letter.) *I–T–C–H.*
5. (Repeat step 4 for **match.**)
6. (Repeat steps 3–5 until firm.)

Task B

1. Touch the first word in column B. ✓
   • What word? (Signal.) *Pitcher.*
2. Next word. ✓
   • What word? (Signal.) *Hatch.*
3. (Repeat step 2 for **catcher.**)
4. (Repeat steps 1–3 until firm.)

</td>
<td valign="top">

■ EXERCISE 1 ■

(NEW) SOUND COMBINATION: oi

Task A

1. Open your Student Book to Lesson 30. ✓

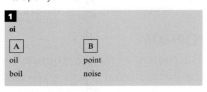

   • Touch the letters O–I in part 1. ✓
   • The letters O–I go together and make the sound **oy**. What sound? (Signal.) *oy.*
2. You're going to read words that have the letters O–I.
3. Touch the first word in column A. ✓
   • What word? (Signal.) *Oil.*
   • Spell oil. (Signal for each letter.) *O–I–L.*
4. Next word. ✓
   • What word? (Signal.) *Boil.*
   • Spell boil. (Signal for each letter.) *B–O–I–L.*
5. (Repeat steps 3 and 4 until firm.)

Task B

1. Touch the first word in column B. ✓
   • What word? (Signal.) *Point.*
2. Next word. ✓
   • What word? (Signal.) *Noise.*
3. (Repeat steps 1 and 2 until firm.)

</td>
</tr>
</table>

Figure 2.4 Two exercises from the Sound Combination track of *Corrective Reading Decoding*, Level B2, from Lessons 14 and 30 respectively. Source: Engelmann, S. et al. (2008a). *Corrective Reading Decoding, Level B2 Teacher's Guide*, pp. 96 and 182, © McGraw Hill.

The two exercises are identical in script structure with the relevant places in the script modified to accommodate the new examples. In Exercise 2 of Lesson 14, the sound combination is *tch*; the example words contain *tch*; the teacher wording in steps 1 and 2 refers to *tch*; and the students' spelling responses all contain *tch*. In Exercise 1 of Lesson 30, the sound combination is *oi*; the example words contain *oi*; the teacher wording in steps 1 and 2 refers to *oi*; and the students' spelling responses all contain *oi*. This same format is used in the track throughout the program, which introduces the sound combinations listed in Table 2.4.

Lesson	Sound Combinations
14	tch
15	ir, ur, er
20	wa
30	oi
37	ce, ci
47	tion
49	ea
52	ge, gi
54	kn

Table 2.4 Sound combinations introduced in *Corrective Reading Decoding*, Level B2. Source: Engelmann, S. et al. (2008a). *Corrective Reading Decoding, Level B2 Teacher's Guide*, p. 15.

In general, there is a progression of the content and an evolution of formats in all DI programs as exercises proceed from more structured and teacher-led activities to more independent activities as part of the generalization process. The formats often become simpler because students require less support to complete the exercise successfully. The format above is used to introduce sound combinations. In any exercise modeled on this format type, all of the words contain the same sound combination. This "mass practice" of the isolated skill facilitates students' acquisition of the new content. After students master the format in which only the new sound combination appears, they will proceed to a more challenging format that presents a mixture of words with different types of sound combinations.

Figure 2.5 is a more advanced, "mixed set" format from Lesson 16.

=== EXERCISE 2 ===

WORD READING

1. Touch the first word in part 2. ✓

2			
proudly	batch	our	salt
stormed	pitcher	foolish	

- What sound? (Signal.) *ow.*
- What word? (Signal.) *Proudly.*
2. Next word. ✓
- What sound? (Signal.) *ch.*
- What word? (Signal.) *Batch.*
3. (Repeat step 2 for each remaining word.)

Figure 2.5 A mixed set of sound combinations from Lesson 16. Source: Engelmann, S. et al. (2008a). *Corrective Reading Decoding, Level B2 Teacher's Guide*, p. 108, © McGraw Hill.

This exercise includes words containing *tch*, which was introduced just two lessons earlier, with other sound combinations that students mastered in the previous level of the program. The format requires much less teacher talk because at this point 1) the teacher does not need to explain the sounds the letter combinations make, and 2) students do not need to practice spelling the letter combinations because they've already done that for several lessons. Throughout the program, as students master the sound combinations, the combinations are moved over to this less-structured format – just as the sounds were moved into the word reading formats and then story reading in *Reading Mastery*, as discussed previously in this section.

FREQUENT, FUNCTIONAL ASSESSMENTS

The incremental design of the Direct Instruction programs is effective only if students are placed at their current skill level and taught to mastery every day. In order to ensure ongoing proper placement and mastery, the DI programs incorporate several types of assessments that occur at different frequencies. All of the assessments are *functional* in that *the results inform teachers and school leaders on specific next actions*: whether students should repeat exercises or whether they are ready to proceed in the program. They occur frequently, which enables teachers and school leaders to adjust instruction in a timely manner and keep students as close as possible to the lesson that matches each student's learning "step."

There are three types of assessments embedded in the DI programs: mastery tests, cumulative tests, and checkouts. *Mastery tests* verify students' acquisition of material that was introduced over a specific range of lessons as well as skills and concepts from earlier lessons. Mastery tests usually occur every 10 lessons in most DI programs, but their frequency varies considerably by program and level. For instance, mastery tests in *Essentials for Writing*, a high-school-level DI composition program, occur every five lessons through Lesson 20, then every 10 lessons through Lesson 80 with the last mastery test occurring in Lesson 95, the last lesson of the program (Engelmann, S. and Grossen, 2010, 91). The first level of the *Direct Instruction Spoken English* program has just three mastery tests – at Lessons 15, 30, and 60 – and an end-of-level test at Lesson 100 (Engelmann, S. et al., 2011, 211).

There are three different sets of criteria for passing the mastery tests. The first is the *overall percentage correct*. The passing criterion for the mastery tests as a whole is 90% or as close as mathematically possible to 90%. For instance, if a student scores 88% correct on a mastery test, the student will pass the test if the next possible score would be 92% correct. However, if it is mathematically possible for a student to score 90%, then 88% would not be a passing score. If a student fails to pass the mastery test, the teacher reteaches content in the form of specified "remedies" (exercises covering the skills and content addressed in the missed items). The teacher delivers the remedies that match the errors students made and re-tests the students on the missed items until each student passes the test.

The second set of passing criteria is for the *individual parts of each test*. In several of the DI programs, such as *Connecting Math Concepts: Comprehensive Edition* (CMC CE) and the language track of *Reading Mastery Signature Edition*, mastery tests are divided into different parts with specific passing criteria for each part. For example, Mastery Test 7 of CMC CE Level B contains six parts with passing scores ranging from 9 points to 18 points (see Table 2.5). If a student earns less than the passing score for any part, the student must be given the instructional remedies specific to that item-type and retested for that part.

Part	Description	Score	Possible Score	Passing Score
1	New Number Families	2 for each problem	20	18
2	Count-on (Rulers)	4 for each problem	20	16
3	Bills	3 for each problem	15	12
4	3 Addends (Columns)	3 for each problem	15	12
5	Coins (Quarters)	3 for each problem	15	12
6	Column Subtraction	3 for each problem	15	9
		Total	100	

Table 2.5 Passing criteria for Mastery Test 7, CMC CE Level B. Adapted from: Engelmann, S., Engelmann, O. and Carnine, D. (2012). *Connecting Math Concepts Comprehensive Edition Level B Teacher's Guide*, p. 25.

The third criterion for passing the mastery tests is the *group passing percentage*. If more than a quarter of the students in an instructional group fail any part of the mastery test, then all students in the group must be given the instructional remedies and retested for that part. This ensures that the group as a whole is firm on each component of the material covered, which increases the likelihood that the group can remain intact as students progress through the lessons.

Several of the DI programs assess students' acquisition of skills through *cumulative tests*. In contrast to the content of mastery tests, which concentrate on the most recently introduced material, cumulative tests are designed to test all of the major skills and concepts introduced up to that point in the program. Remedies for the cumulative tests are specified in the program in the same manner that remedies for the mastery tests are specified.

As with mastery tests, the frequency of cumulative tests varies by program. For example, each level of the CMC CE program contains a mid-level cumulative test, which assesses students' knowledge of the first half of that level, and an end-of-level cumulative test, which assesses students' knowledge of the whole level, with a strong emphasis on material covered in the second half of the level. In contrast, Levels A and B of the *Spelling Master* program contain weekly optional 10-word tests beginning with Lesson 10. In the other levels of *Spelling Mastery* (Levels C, D, E and F), cumulative tests occur every five lessons. (Dixon and Engelmann, S., 1999, 48).

The reading programs contain informal assessments called *checkouts*, which test students' proficiency in reading familiar material. Individual students read a selected passage from a story that they already read as a group as part of their daily lesson. In *Reading Mastery*, the teacher records the time of the reading and the errors made and matches them against a preset time and error limit. If students do not meet the rate and accuracy criteria, they reread the passage until they can. In *Corrective Reading Decoding*, students have a set time to read rather than a set passage length to read. The teacher records the number of words students are able to read in the time limit for the *Decoding* checkouts.

Checkouts occur once students can read connected text. In *Reading Mastery Signature Edition*, this occurs in Lesson 108 of the kindergarten level of the program. The students are given checkouts on Lessons 109 and 110, then every five lessons through the Grade 3 level of the program. Checkouts appear every 10 lessons in the upper two levels of the program (Grade 4 and Grade 5). In contrast, the *Corrective Reading Decoding* program contains daily checkouts in all levels of the program to provide a close check on remedial readers' accuracy and fluency.

COHERENT RELATIONSHIP BETWEEN A PROGRAM'S COMPONENTS

In order for a Direct Instruction program to function as an effective and efficient learning "stairway" for all students who meet the program's entrance requirements, the program's components must be coordinated so they reinforce the positive effect of the other components at each level of the program's structure. These components must all fit together in a seamless and mutually supportive way as outlined in *Rubric for Identifying Authentic Direct Instruction Programs*, by S. Engelmann and Geoff Colvin (2006). In the rubric, Engelmann and Colvin identify seven different levels across which seamless coordination must take place:

1. Presentation of information
2. Tasks
3. Task chains
4. Exercises
5. Sequences of exercises (tracks)
6. Lessons
7. Organization of content. (Engelmann, S. and Colvin, 2006, 15)

At each level, Engelmann and Colvin articulate a set of axioms that authentic DI programs must incorporate fully. Here are the axioms for the sixth category – lessons – that indicate the type of coordination that is required at that level of a DI program:

- Everything taught in a lesson must be consistent with what had been taught earlier.
- Each lesson provides additional practice on everything introduced in the preceding one or two lessons.
- Part of each lesson has some form of cumulative review or applications that address skills and information presented in earlier lessons.
- Any lesson may be used as a test to determine whether students are placed appropriately and whether they are performing at a high level of mastery. (Engelmann and Colvin, 2006, 15)

Because the components are so well coordinated, DI programs may actually give the impression of being overly simple to the casual observer. As Engelmann and Colvin noted:

> Possibly the most difficult concept for observers of DI programs to understand is that although the programs seem simple, they meet multiple design criteria that make them simple. The superficial impression of a program done right is that the authors may not understand some of the complexities of the content. The complexities, however, have been addressed and have been reduced to non-complexities that do not sacrifice the integrity of what is taught earlier or what is to be taught later. (Engelmann and Colvin, 2006, 14)

Thus, the by-product of a well-designed program is that it "will seem easy, possibly even too easy" (Engelmann and Colvin, 2006, 22). Just as the advanced engineering of a high-performance automobile makes it easy to drive, the advanced design of the DI programs makes it seem easy to the casual observer.

FIELD-TESTING AND REVISING THE PROGRAMS

In order to ensure that the DI programs meet these high standards of quality and effectiveness, they are field-tested with students in real classroom settings and revised based on the field test results before they are published. The DI authors design the first draft of programs through a careful and thorough logical analysis of the content. However, the structure and content of the programs often change considerably in subsequent drafts in response to the performance of students in the field tryouts. Potential areas of improvement of the programs are revealed through the tryout process, which lead to revisions of the draft programs.

Field tryouts involve different sites that test lessons at different stages of revision. If a draft version of Lesson 50 of a program, for instance, is tested with an initial group of students, the DI authors will make the changes indicated by the field test and have the revised version ready for the next instructional group when they reach Lesson 50. In the meantime, the first instructional group will have continued through the program. They might be on Lesson 75, for example, when the second group reaches Lesson 50. If the tryout of the revised version of Lesson 50 with the second group indicates the need for more revisions, the authors will revise the lesson yet again in time for a third group to test the lesson. This process continues until the lesson meets the high standards for DI programs.

Managing this process of multiple revisions can be very demanding. S. Engelmann describes the process of developing the *Corrective Reading* program:

> When we develop a program, the tracks are in separate folders. We chart all the information about the program to show which exercises and examples appear on every lesson. Lessons are then assembled and field-tested. ... The specific types of mistakes the students make during the first field test imply both what has to

change and how it has to change. To obtain this information, we need copies of actual student work and annotated scripts that teachers used, with their comments about specific problems (including problems of a lesson or part taking too much time).

To verify that we have adequately addressed the problems, we have to do a field test of the revised material. When all work is finished, we have enough charts to paper a 12-foot wall from ceiling to floor, enough copies of student material to fill four standard filing cabinets, and probably more than 2,000 pages of manuscript for each iteration of the program. (Engelmann, S., 2007, 209)

This thorough tryout-revision process is done with painstaking care to ensure that the implementation of the programs will result in effective and efficient instruction consistently for all students who meet the programs' entrance requirements. The incredible effort and expertise needed to design and produce such products are barriers to teachers to create their own versions of DI programs, as discussed in later chapters.

CHAPTER THREE
CONTENT AND TASK ANALYSIS
OF KEY STRATEGIES

The most critical instructional design elements were described in the previous chapter of this book, which addressed the question of how the DI programs are structured to accelerate student performance. Several examples of the way content is handled in the programs were used to illustrate those critical DI design elements. This chapter provides more in-depth examples of how the specific content is structured with a focus on *key strategies* that make the DI programs uniquely effective. These examples are:

- blending three spelling strategies across six levels
- teaching sounds through letter names
- building background knowledge for reading comprehension
- writing clear descriptions of events
- teaching fractions and their relationship to integers.

BLENDING THREE SPELLING STRATEGIES ACROSS SIX LEVELS

Teaching students to spell words accurately is a major challenge due to the inconsistent relationship between sounds (phonemes) and symbols (graphemes) in the English language. In languages with a high phonetic correspondence between symbols and sounds, such as Spanish, spelling can be taught solely through a phonetic analysis. If each letter produces one and only one sound, students can spell all words phonetically and don't need to master other spelling strategies and learn when to apply them. Speakers of regularly phonetic languages only need to follow a simple, three-step process:

1. Learn the sounds that each letter produces.
2. Practice saying words a sound at a time.
3. Write the letters that represent these sounds.

Of course, these three steps may require years of practice to master, but the process is much simpler than the process needed to learn to spell words in the English language or other languages that do not have a consistent sound-to-symbol relationship.

In languages that are mostly phonetic but have regular exceptions, students need to take the additional steps of memorizing and applying the exceptions before they can spell words accurately. For instance, in Russian, several vowels make different sounds depending on their placement relative to the main stress in a word. If the vowels appear precisely one syllable before the main stress, they make the short /a/ sound. If the vowels appear after or more than one syllable before the main stress, they make the short /u/ sound. As an example, the word *khorosho*, which can be translated into English as "fine," contains the letter *o* as the only vowel. Yet it is pronounced *khurasho* because the stress falls on the last syllable. Russian speakers must take this rule into account when spelling words containing multiple vowels.

Due to the historical influence of various Germanic and Romance languages, English is far from phonetically regular. A popular device to illustrate the degree of mismatch between sounds and symbols in English is the phonetic spelling of the word "fish" as *ghoti*, in which:

- *gh* is pronounced /f/ as in tough,
- *o* is pronounced /i/ as in women, and
- *ti* is pronounced /sh/ as in nation.

The *ghoti* device, which originated in 1855, underscores how the phonetic strategy is limited in its applicability to the English language. The lack of consistently phonetic relationships in English have prompted some to describe it as "a bizarre mishmash" (Zimmer, 2010). The spelling of vowel sounds is particularly variable. For instance, the long /e/ sound can be made by the following letters and letter combinations:

- *e* as the first vowel in *refer*
- *y* as in *crazy*
- *ie* as in *shriek*
- *ee* as in *meek*
- *ea* as in *speak*.

The Direct Instruction approach to address the complexities of the English language is to teach students the simplest spelling patterns first and then introduce more complex patterns incrementally over time. *Spelling Mastery*, a six-level developmental DI spelling program, utilizes three different strategies to move from simple to complex spelling tasks:

1. phonemic (phonetic)
2. whole-word
3. morphemic.

The phonemic strategy involves teaching the most common sound–symbol correspondences in the English language. As discussed below, the phonemic strategy is the most straightforward of the three strategies, and it is emphasized in the lower levels of *Spelling Mastery*. In this strategy, each letter represents one and only one sound. Words taught through the phonemic approach include:

- split
- run
- dog
- mat
- end
- bats.

The whole-word approach involves teaching words that do not adhere to the common sound–symbol correspondences. Examples of this type of word include:

- many

- through
- thought
- what
- speak
- year.

The whole-word approach is more complex than the phonemic approach. Even though it is more complex, it is introduced early because of the number of high-frequency words that are spelled irregularly in the English language.

The *Spelling Mastery* program employs two types of scaffolding to assist students in learning the whole-word approach. The first type of scaffolding is to provide students with practice in *applying the phonemic approach to the parts of irregularly spelled words that still follow general phonetic patterns.* Students are presented with written words and sentences with the irregularly spelled parts provided and the regularly spelled parts missing. For instance, students are presented a workbook exercise with "_any" and told to write the word "many." Students need to only write an *m* in the blank to spell the word correctly, which they can easily do because it follows the phonemic strategy they've already mastered.

Here is an exercise from the teacher presentation book and student workbook of *Spelling Mastery*, Level A, Lesson 18. In this exercise, students write words that are completely phonemic (rest, mash, hand, win, and fast) as well as those that are irregular (many and what) with letters provided for most of the irregular sounds.

EXERCISE 3

FILL-IN

1. Find Part A on your worksheet. ✔
2. First you'll say what each word should be.
   Then you'll fill in every blank.
3. Word 1 should be **rest**.
   What word? (Signal.) *Rest*.
   Fill in every blank.
4. Word 2 should be **mash**.
   What word? (Signal.) *Mash*.
   Fill in every blank.
5. (Repeat Step 4 for **what, win, hand, many, fast**.)

A

1. __ e __ __
2. __ __ __ __
3. w h __ __
4. w i __
5. __ __ __ __
6. __ a n y
7. f __ __ __

Figure 3.1 Exercise applying the phonemic approach to parts of irregularly spelled words. Source: Dixon, R. and Engelmann, S. (2007a). *Spelling Mastery Series Guide*, pp. 44–45, © McGraw Hill.

Over time, this scaffolding is removed. By the time students are asked to spell the word "many" with no scaffolding (four blanks appear in the workbook), they have had sufficient practice seeing and spelling the word orally that they can write the word correctly without any assistance.

The second type of scaffolding is to teach groups of irregular word "families" that share a common spelling. The program has a *Vowel Patterns* track in which students systematically learn the major word families that share a common vowel spelling. For instance, in Level B of the program, students learn that the long sound /a/ is usually spelled "a-y" when it appears at the end of words. Here is the exercise from Lesson 106 of *Spelling Mastery*, Level B in which students spell words with the "a-y" ending:

EXERCISE 2

VOWEL PATTERNS

1. Some words end in the sound /ā/.
   Tell me how that sound is usually
   spelled at the end of a word.
   Get ready. (Signal.) *a-y.*
2. Listen: **day.** What word? (Signal.) *Day.*
3. Say the end sound in **day.** Get ready.
   (Signal.) /ā/.
4. Spell /ā/. Get ready. (Signal.) *a-y.*
5. Spell **day.** Get ready. (Signal.) *D-a-y.*
6. Listen: **spray.** What word? (Signal.)
   Spray.
7. Say the end sound in **spray.**
   Get ready. (Signal.) /ā/.
8. Spell /ā/. Get ready. (Signal.) *a-y.*
9. Spell **spray.** Get ready. (Signal.)
   S-p-r-a-y.
10. (Repeat Steps 6–9 for **play, stray.**)
11. (Call on individual students to spell
    spray, day, stray, play.)

Figure 3.2 Exercise teaching the spelling of the "a-y" family of words. Source: Dixon, R. and Engelmann, S. (2007a). *Spelling Mastery Series Guide*, pp. 44–45, © McGraw Hill.

Another family in the *Vowel Patterns* track consists of words that contain the long /e/ spelled "ea", including:

- repeat
- leader
- speak
- leave
- year.

Presenting the words in families helps students learn these vowel spelling patterns initially. After students master the spelling of the word families, the words are integrated into more challenging "mixed set" formats that contain irregular words from several families as well as phonetically spelled words. This approach is much more conducive to the development of students as reliable, confident spellers than just rote memorization; the scaffolding in *Spelling Mastery* allows students to recognize spelling patterns of irregularly spelled words that they are able to apply when they encounter words in isolation.

The morphemic (morphographic) approach to spelling involves teaching students *morphemes* (affixes and bases) and *spelling rules* to apply to words containing morphemes. Students learn that each morphograph has meaning, which helps students remember the meaning of words containing morphographs. Once students learn several morphographs, they can combine them to create numerous words. Table 3.1 illustrates how learners can combine a handful of affixes and bases to create over two dozen words.

Prefixes	Bases	Suffixes	Words
re- dis- un-	cover pute	-ed -able	coverable, covered, discover, discoverable, discovered, disputable, dispute, disputed, disreputable, disrepute, recover, recoverable, recovered, reputable, repute, reputed, uncover, uncoverable, uncovered, undiscoverable, undiscovered, undisputable, undisputed, unrecoverable, unrecovered

Table 3.1 Example of morphemic word construction. Source: Dixon, R. and Engelmann, S. (2007a). *Spelling Mastery Series Guide*, p. vii, © McGraw Hill.

Students learn that combining some morphographs does not require a change in spelling. An example from the list of words in Table 3.1 is "recoverable," which is spelled exactly as its constituent morphographs are spelled – "re" + "cover" + "able." They also learn that combining certain morphographs *does* require a change in spelling. The word "disputed" is not spelled "disputeed." In *Spelling Mastery*, students first learn to combine morphographs that do not require a change in spelling because this is the easiest type to master. Then they are systematically taught rules on combining morphographs that result in a change in spelling. Two of the most important rules are:

1. If a morphograph ends in *e* and you are adding a morphograph that starts with a vowel, drop the final *e* of the first morphograph when spelling the word.
2. If a short word ends in consonant-vowel-consonant (cvc), double the final consonant when adding a morphograph that begins with a vowel.

Initially, students learn these rules separately. Later, students are presented with discrimination (mixed-set) exercises to ensure they can apply the rules appropriately. Here is an example of a discrimination exercise from *Spelling Mastery*, Level D, Lesson 54:

EXERCISE 2

RULE DISCRIMINATION

1. I'll say words.
   Let's figure out whether the doubling rule, the final-**e** rule, or no rule applies.
2. The first word begins with **world**.
   Spell **world**. Get ready. (Signal.)
   Could a rule apply? (Signal.) *No*.
   Why not? (Call on a student.)
   World does not end with an e or cvc.
3. The word is **worldly**.
   Say it. (Signal.) *Worldly*.
   Spell **worldly**. Get ready. (Signal.)
4. The next word begins with **bar**.
   Spell **bar**. Get ready. (Signal.)
   Could a rule apply? (Signal.) *Yes*.
   Which rule? (Call on another student.)
   The rule about doubling a letter.
   Everybody, how do you know the doubling rule could apply? (Signal.)
   Bar is a short cvc word.
5. The word is **barred**. Say it. (Signal.)
   Barred.
   Does the doubling rule apply?
   (Signal.) *Yes*.
   How do you know? (Call on another student.)
   Bar is a short cvc word, and e-d begins with v.
   Spell **barred**. Get ready. (Signal.)
6. The next word begins with **like**.
   Spell **like**. Get ready. (Signal.)
   Could a rule apply? (Signal.) *Yes*.
   Which rule? (Call on another student.)
   The rule about dropping the final e.
   Everybody, how do you know the final-**e** rule could apply? (Signal.) *Like ends with an e.*
7. The word is **likeness**.
   Say it. (Signal.) *Likeness*.
   Does the final-**e** rule apply?
   (Signal.) *No*.
   How do you know? (Call on another student.)
   Ness does not begin with v.
   Spell **likeness**. Get ready. (Signal.)
8. The next word begins with **mother**.
   Spell **mother**. Get ready. (Signal.)
   Could a rule apply? (Signal.) *No*.
   Why not? (Call on another student.)
   Mother is not a short cvc word, and it does not end with an e.
9. The word is **mothering**.
   Say it. (Signal.) *Mothering*.
   Spell **mothering**. Get ready. (Signal.)
10. The next word begins with **safe**.
    Spell **safe**. Get ready. (Signal.)
    Could a rule apply? (Signal.) *Yes*.
    Which rule? (Call on another student.)
    *The rule about dropping the final-**e**.*
    Everybody, how do you know the final-**e** rule could apply? (Signal.) *Safe ends with an e.*
11. The word is **safest**.
    Say it. (Signal.) *Safest*.
    Does the final-**e** rule apply?
    (Signal.) *Yes*.
    How do you know? (Call on another student.)
    Est begins with v.
    Spell **safest**. Get ready. (Signal.)

Figure 3.3 Morphographic spelling rule discrimination exercise. Source: Dixon, R. and Engelmann, S. (2007a). *Spelling Mastery Series Guide*, p. 57, © McGraw Hill.

After students can discriminate whether a spelling change rule applies, and if so, which one, the scaffolding is systematically removed. Eventually, students spell multisyllabic words without any prompting from the teacher regarding spelling change rules. Because students have learned to apply the rules reliably, they spell the words with great accuracy.

As mentioned above, the *Spelling Mastery* program blends these three strategies – phonemic, whole-word and morphemic (morphographic) – by teaching the simplest strategies in the lower levels of the program and the more advanced strategies in the upper levels of the program. As Table 3.2 indicates, the types of strategies students learn as they progress through the levels of the program shift from the phonemic and whole-word approaches to the morphemic (morphographic) approach in a carefully controlled manner.

Level	Content	Spelling Strategy
A	• teaches a sound-symbol strategy for spelling simple, regularly spelled words • teaches the spelling of a set of high-frequency, irregularly spelled words	phonemic ■■■■ whole-word ■■■
B	• expands the sound-symbol strategy to more difficult, regularly spelled words • increases the number of irregularly spelled words that students spell	phonemic ■■■■ whole-word ■■■
C	• makes the transition from the phonemic approach to the morphographic approach • teaches a small number of key structural spelling rules	phonemic ■■ morphographic ■■■■■■ whole-word ■■
D	• expands students' morphographic strategies by introducing nonword bases • teaches an additional set of spelling rules that address multisyllabic words	phonemic ■■ morphographic ■■■■■■ whole-word ■■
E	• emphasizes useful nonword bases • expands on morphographic principles taught in Levels C and D	phonemic ■■ morphographic ■■■■■■ whole-word ■■
F	• presents information about international spellings and the history of unusual spellings • acquaints students with the interrelationships of spelling, vocabulary, etymology, usage, and syntax	phonemic ■■ morphographic ■■■■■■ whole-word ■■

Table 3.2 Strategies used in different levels of *Spelling Mastery*. Source: Dixon, R. and Engelmann, S. (2007a). *Spelling Mastery Series Guide*, p. viii, © McGraw Hill.

The first two levels of the program contain phonemic and whole-word approaches only as students rely principally on sound–symbol relationships to spell words. The third level of the program (Level C) acts as a bridge to the higher levels. Level C introduces the morphographic approach, which then becomes the dominant approach in Levels D–F. In Level F, students address such advanced spelling topics as word etymology and international spellings. Because the program blends these approaches from simplest to most challenging seamlessly, students are able to spell more than 4,000 words reliably by the end of the program (Dixon and Engelmann, S., 1999, v).

TEACHING SOUNDS THROUGH LETTER NAMES

As described in the previous chapter, the first two levels of the *Reading Mastery Signature Edition* use a modified orthography with 40 symbols that correspond to sounds made in the English language. Students learn these symbols, referred to as "sounds" in the program, and how to blend the sounds together, which provides the basis for decoding regularly spelled words. Students do not need to possess prior knowledge of letter names to learn the 40 symbols. Instead, students learn the normal English alphabet in the Grade 1 level of the program – after they have had a great deal of practice reading connected text with the modified orthography.

There is another beginning DI reading sequence that uses a different approach to teaching the sounds that students blend together to form words. Instead of teaching the symbols as "sounds," *Horizons, Funnix* and *Reading Mastery Transformations* (the newest DI language arts program series) teach students sounds through letter names. These programs are designed to take advantage of students' knowledge of letter names to help them learn the sounds that letters make. As such, the programs are intended for students who either know their letter names or can learn them easily (Engelmann, S., 2000, 19).

The authors of *Horizons/Funnix/Transformations* analyzed the relationship between the names of letters and the sounds letters usually make when they appear in words. The result of their analysis is a typology of letter groupings that provides the basis for how students learn the sounds letters make. Tables 3.3 and 3.4 show two of the most critical letter types used in the programs:

- sounds made from the last part of letter names
- sounds made from the first part of letter names.

Letter	Sound as in	Introduced in Lesson
m	came	6
s	kiss	6
n	pan	7
l	bell	8
f	fir	9
r	ear	10
y	my	25
x	box	101

Table 3.3 Sounds derived from the last part of letter names. Adapted from: Engelmann, S. and Engelmann, O. (2012b). *Funnix Reading Programs Teacher's Guide*, p. 23.

Letter	Sound as in	Introduced in Lesson
t	rat	19
p	map	32
d	mad	38
v	live	48
j	jail	50
k	hike	50
b	grab	73

Table 3.4 Sounds derived from the first part of letter names. Adapted from: Engelmann, S. and Engelmann, O. (2012b). *Funnix Reading Programs Teacher's Guide*, p. 24.

As Tables 3.3 and 3.4 show, letters from the first group appear earlier in the programs than letters from the second group because *it's easier for students to learn the sound that is the last part of the letter name*. The last part is easier because it's the last sound students produce when saying letter names a part at a time. In contrast, the first part is further temporally distanced and the more recent sound potentially inhibits recall, which can be difficult for some young learners.

Early in the programs, students learn to say the names of selected letters from the first group a part at a time. In Exercise 6 of Lesson 18 in the Grade K level of *Reading Mastery Transformations*, the teacher leads the students as they say the names of the letters *l*, *s*, *f*, and *m* a part at a time:

Exercise 6: Saying Letters a Part at a Time

a. (Display **l s f m**)

• Everybody, look at the board. ✓

  My turn to touch and say the letters.

• (Point to **l**.) L.

• (Point to **s**.) S.

• (Point to **f**.) F.

• (Point **m**.) M.

b. Everybody, go back to your workbook and find the row of black letters below the mouse trail. ✓

  Your turn to touch the letters and tell me their names.

c. Touch under the first letter. ✓

• What letter? (Signal.) *L*.

d. Next letter. ✓

• What letter? (Signal.) *S*.

e. Next letter. ✓

• What letter? (Signal.) *F*.

f. Last letter. ✓

• What letter? (Signal.) *M*.

(Repeat steps c through f until firm.)

g. I'll say the name of each letter a part at a time. Then you'll say it with me.

h. Listen: **eee . . . fff**.

- Say it with me. *eee . . . fff.*
- Touch **eee . . . fff**. (Signal.) ✓
- What letter are you touching? (Signal.) *F.*

i. Listen: **eee . . . sss**.

- Say it with me. *eee . . . sss.*
- Touch **eee . . . sss**. (Signal.) ✓
- What letter are you touching? (Signal.) *S.*

j. Listen: **eee . . . mmm**.

- Say it with me. *eee . . . mmm.*
- Touch **eee . . . mmm**. (Signal.) ✓
- What letter are you touching? (Signal.) *M.*

k. Listen: **eee . . . lll**.

- Say it with me. *eee . . . lll.*
- Touch **eee . . . lll**. (Signal.) ✓
- What letter are you touching? (Signal.) *L.*

In the next lesson, students learn that the sound for the letters *m* and *s* is the last part of each letter's name. From Lesson 19 of the Grade K level of *Reading Mastery Transformations*:

Exercise 4: Sounds from Letter Names

a. (Display **m s**)

- Everybody, look at the board. ✓

b. (Point to **m**.) Everybody, what letter? (Signal.) *M.*

- (Point to **s**.) Everybody, what letter? (Signal.) *S.*

(Repeat step b until firm.)

c. (Point to **m**.) Again, what letter? (Signal.) *M.*

I'll say **M** a part at a time. Listen: **eee . . . mmm**.

• Your turn. Say **M** a part at a time. Get ready. (Signal.) *eee* (Signal.) *mmm*.

d. Listen: When you read words, you don't say the names of the letters. You say the **sounds**.

The sound that **M** makes is the last part of the letter name. It's **mmm**.

• Everybody, say the sound that **M** makes. (Signal.) *mmm*.

e. (Point to **s**.) Everybody, what letter? (Signal.) *S*.

I'll say **S** a part at a time. Listen: **eee . . . sss**.

• Your turn. Say **S** a part at a time. Get ready. (Signal.) *eee* (Signal.) *sss*.

The sound that **S** makes is the last part of the letter name. It's **sss**.

• Everybody, say the sound that **S** makes. (Signal.) *sss*.

f. This time I'll say each letter name a part at a time. You'll say the sound.

g. My turn. The letter is **eee . . . mmm**, so the **sound** is **mmm**. What's the sound? (Signal.) *mmm*.

• Listen: The letter is **eee . . . sss**, so the **sound** is **sss**. What's the sound? (Signal.) *sss*.

h. Your turn.

• (Point to **m**.) This letter is **eee . . . mmm**. What's the sound? (Signal.) *mmm*.

• (Point to **s**.) This letter is **eee . . . sss**. What's the sound? (Signal.) *sss*.

(Repeat steps g and h until firm.)

Later, students discriminate between letter names and the sounds they make. Note the use of bold in the script to indicate that the teacher should emphasize the critical discrimination between **names** and **sounds**. From Lesson 22 of the Grade K level of *Reading Mastery Transformations*:

Exercise 3: Sounds vs. Letter Names

a. I'll say things. Then you'll say them.

b. Listen: **S, M, F**. Say those letter **names**. Get ready. (Signal.) *S* (Signal.) *M* (Signal.) *F*.

c. I'll say **sounds** for those letters.

d. Listen: **sss . . . mmm . . . fff**. Say those letter **sounds**. Get ready. (Signal.) *sss* (Signal.) *mmm* (Signal.) *fff*.

(Repeat step d until firm.)

e. Your turn to tell me if I say a letter name or a sound.

f. Listen **mmm**. Is **mmm** a letter name or a sound? (Signal.) *Sound.*

• Listen: **sss**. Is **sss** a letter name or a sound? (Signal.) *Sound.*

• Listen: **fff**. Is **fff** a letter name or a sound? (Signal.) *Sound.*

• Listen: **S**. Is **S** a letter name or a sound? (Signal.) *Letter name.*

• Listen: **M**. Is **M** a letter name or a sound? (Signal.) *Letter name.*

• Listen: **F**. Is **F** a letter name or a sound? (Signal.) *Letter name.*

(Repeat step f until firm.)

g. Listen: **M**. Is **M** a letter name or a sound? (Signal.) *Letter name.*

• Listen: **fff**. Is **fff** a letter name or a sound? (Signal.) *Sound.*

• Listen: **S**. Is **S** a letter name or a sound? (Signal.) *Letter name.*

• Listen: **mmm**. Is **mmm** a letter name or a sound? (Signal.) *Sound.*

• Listen: **sss**. Is **sss** a letter name or a sound? (Signal.) *Sound.*

• Listen: **F**. Is **F** a letter name or a sound? (Signal.) *Letter name.*

(Repeat step g until firm.)

Eventually, students simply say the sound each letter makes, which they can do reliably because the previous exercises systematically built their recognition of letter sounds based on letter names. Once students have successfully mastered the sounds of six letters from the first group, they move on to the more challenging task of learning the sounds from the second group of letters, which involves recalling the first sound of the letter name.

Consonants not part of these two groups are considered to be irregular letters. Students learn the specific, idiosyncratic sounds for these letters starting at Lesson 51 in the *Funnix* program after students have had a great deal of practice with the first two groups of sounds. See Table 3.5.

Letter	Sound as in	Introduced in Lesson
c	cat	51
w	wow	57
g	gum	59
h	hat	65

Table 3.5 Sounds for irregular consonants. Adapted from: Engelmann, S. and Engelmann, O. (2012b). *Funnix Reading Programs Teacher's Guide*, p. 24.

Note that the letters *c* and *g* can indicate sounds in the English language other than those listed in the table. In some words, these letters make the *first* part of their names. The sounds for the letter name *c* are /sss/ /eee/ so the first part of the letter name is /sss/ as in the word "nice." The sounds for the letter name *g* are /j/ /eee/ so the first part of the letter name is /j/ as in the word "genius." However, the /sss/ and /j/ sounds do not appear in the beginning level of the *Horizons/Funnix/Transformations* programs for two reasons: 1) there are many more words for *c* and *g* that make the "irregular" sound in Table 3.5, and 2) the authors did not want the students to have to deal with the ambiguity of more than one sound for *c* and *g* initially. Students learn that these letters can also make the first part of their names in higher levels of the program after they have become familiar with *c* and *g* making the hard /k/ and /g/ sounds respectively.

The programs deftly address the ambiguity regarding the sounds that vowel letters make. As mentioned previously, the sounds that vowel letters make in the English language are highly variable. The *Horizons/Funnix/ Transformations* programs utilize "blue letter" prompts to signal to students that a letter in the word represents a long sound. Students learn the convention that *if a word contains a blue letter (which is silent), another letter in the word says its name*. For instance, the letter *i* is silent in the word, rain, as the *a* says its name in the word (i.e. it produces a long /a/ sound).

As shown in Table 3.6, vowels are introduced relatively early in the programs. With the exception of the short /a/ sound, which is introduced in Lesson 15 of *Funnix*, long vowels predominate in the early part of the *Horizons/Funnix/Transformations* programs. *If students already know their letter names, long vowel sounds are easier than short vowel sounds for students to learn because long vowels are simply the names of the letters.* If students already know their letter names, they can learn to read the long vowels quickly. For this reason, *three long vowel sounds are introduced in the same lesson* (Lesson 10) in contrast to the customary practice of spacing out the introduction of new sounds in DI reading programs to allow students time to master each sound.

Letter	Long sound as in	Introduced in Lesson	Short sound as in	Introduced in Lesson
a	rain	10	ran	15
e	meet	10	met	110
o	hope	10	hop	92
i	like	15	lick	42
u	use	56	us	68

Table 3.6 Introduction of sounds for vowels. Adapted from: Engelmann, S. and Engelmann, O. (2012b). *Funnix Reading Programs Teacher's Guide*, p. 24.

The predominance of long vowel sounds has a profound effect on the selection of words and the composition of stories in the *Horizons/Funnix/Transformations* programs. Because sounds are introduced in a different order in these programs in comparison to the *Reading Mastery Signature Edition* (RMSE), which introduces short vowels earlier, the composition of the words differs markedly between the Signature edition and the *Horizons/Funnix/Transformations* programs. As mentioned previously, the words that appear in the DI reading programs only contain letters with sounds that students have mastered so they are completely decodable. Stories in turn contain only words that students have already read successfully so they are completely decodable, too.

Based on the careful analysis of the relationship between letter names and the sounds they make, the *Horizons/Funnix/Transformations* programs take advantage of students' knowledge of letter names to advance their literary skills more rapidly than in RMSE. By the end of the kindergarten level of *Reading Mastery Transformations*, students are able to read over 900 words – at least 500 more words than students who finish the kindergarten level of RMSE. Students know proportionally an even greater number of words in comparison to RMSE by the Grade 1 level of the programs (communication with Engelmann, O., program author, October 2020). Again, this rapid progress is possible only if students already know their letter names. Transformations has a pre-program that teaches students their letter names as well as other critical background information to prepare students who do not know their letter names for the program.

Once students reach the third level of the reading programs (*Horizons* C, RMSE Grade 2 or *Reading Mastery Transformations* Grade 2), the content is highly similar across the programs. Students have learned how to decode and answer fundamental literal and inferential questions of the material they read. When they reach the third level, they possess the decoding skills *to learn content systematically through reading* – an approach to enhancing students' reading comprehension that is the next focus of this chapter.

BUILDING BACKGROUND KNOWLEDGE FOR READING COMPREHENSION

Several recent publications in the field of education have emphasized the superiority of building students' content knowledge to promote reading comprehension in comparison to teaching them comprehension strategies (finding the main idea, determining cause and effect, distinguishing between fact and opinion, etc.). In an article in *Edutopia*, Holly Korbey asks the question, "Is it time to drop 'finding the main idea' and teach reading in a new way?" (Korbey, 2020). She advocates building students' background knowledge as a means of improving reading comprehension, a thesis more fully developed in a book she refers to: *The Knowledge Gap: The Hidden Cause of America's Broken Education System–and How to Fix It* by Natalie Wexler (New York: Avery, 2019).

The idea advocated in these publications is not new. They echo the arguments that E. D. Hirsch at the Core Knowledge Foundation (which he founded in 1986) has made for years: that background knowledge – vocabulary and the "reality" that the vocabulary represents in any particular passage – is key to students' ability to comprehend the passage. If students do not possess the requisite background knowledge, they will fail to comprehend the meaning of content-rich texts despite having mastered the skills needed to decode the passage. Hirsch explained the importance of building background knowledge in the Spring 2006 issue of *American Educator*:

> The importance of systematically and effectively teaching decoding cannot be overstated ... But becoming a skilled decoder does not ensure that one will become a skilled reader. There are students who, after mastering decoding, and reading widely can, under the right circumstances, gain greater knowledge and thence better reading comprehension. But such gains will occur only if the student already knows enough to comprehend the meaning of what he or she is decoding. Many specialists estimate that a child (or an adult) needs to understand a minimum of 90 percent of the words in a passage in order to understand the passage and thus begin to learn the other 10 percent of the words. Moreover, it's not just the words that the student has to grasp the meaning of—it's also the kind of reality that the words are referring to. ... When a child doesn't understand those word meanings and those referred-to realities, being good at sounding out words is a dead end. Reading becomes a kind of Catch-22: In order to become better at reading with understanding, you already have to be able to read with understanding. (Hirsch, 2006)

The upper levels of *Reading Mastery* (Grades 2–5) are designed to provide students with the knowledge they need to comprehend grade-level texts. Students learn critical vocabulary and background information as well as critical thinking skills in these levels of the program, which enable them to understand a wide range of grade-level reading selections. The lower levels of the program (kindergarten and Grade 1) emphasize *learning to read*, with a focus on decoding (although literal and interpretive comprehension activities are included). The upper levels (Grades 2 and above) emphasize *reading to learn* with a heavy emphasis on building students' background knowledge in various domains – *a focus that has been part of the* Reading Mastery *programs since they were first published in the 1970s.*

Starting in the Grade 2 level of the program, students read separate informational/comprehension passages that provide the background knowledge needed for them to comprehend stories and other literary selections in the program. The informational content is also integrated into other elements of the program – the independent work, fact games, mastery tests and special projects. Just as other DI programs are designed around continuous incremental introduction of new skills, the upper levels of the *Reading Mastery* program are designed around *the incremental introduction of new content*, which is integrated into the stories and in-program mastery tests as well as special projects that further the students' acquisition of critical background information. The teacher's guide for Grade 2 of *Reading Mastery* describes how the content is integrated into the different components of the program:

1. Information is introduced in a comprehension passage.
2. Within two lessons of the introduction, the information is used in the main story.
3. A variation of the information also appears in the independent-work items.
4. The items are reviewed in subsequent lessons.
5. Information that is particularly important or difficult appears in the fact games or in fact reviews. The game format provides the students with massed practice on a lot of information.
6. The ten lesson tests assess students' understanding of the information.
7. The final step is the integration of recent information with information taught earlier. This integration provides for increasingly complex applications and review. For major story sequences the integration culminates with a special project, in which students research additional facets of the story theme. (Engelmann, S. and Hanner, 2008, 19)

The stories in the Grade 2 and 3 levels of *Reading Mastery* were written specifically for the program to help build students' scientific knowledge while providing narratives that interest young readers. Here is a partial list of the stories that appear in the Grade 2 level of the program:

- A Tricky Toad Named Goad—Goad has amusing adventures in which she tricks people.
- Nancy Learns About Being Small—A girl becomes very small and learns important facts about common objects.
- Herman Travels the World—A fly goes around the world on a jet. Students use maps to follow the jet's progress.
- Linda and Kathy Alone on an Island—Two shipwrecked girls struggle to survive on an island.
- Bertha and Her Nose—A girl with a great sense of smell helps an investigator capture a group of polluters.
- Andrew Dexter's Dreams—A bank teller gets superhuman powers and is hired by a football team.
- The Time Machine—Two boys find a Time Machine and go back and forth in time. (Engelmann, S. et al., 2008b, 24)

Students are pre-taught the specific science facts that are incorporated into the stories. For the Goad stories, students learn important features of amphibians in general and toads in particular. For the stories about Herman the Fly, who travels around the world, students learn key geographic places that he visits. They also learn rules about how jet airplanes work – that air emitted in one direction propels the vehicle in the opposite direction. In this way, the stories reinforce students' knowledge of important science facts and rules.

Figure 3.4 is an excerpt from the *RMSE Teacher Presentation Book* for Exercise 3 of Lesson 61. It provides background information on the relationship between the general time of day and the position of the sun in the sky, which is integrated into the story *Linda and Kathy Alone on an Island*. The content of the student textbook is represented in the colored boxes of text along with the graphic of the sun in the sky. The students read the passage until they reach designated spots in the text, at which point the teacher asks them the questions shown in the exercise.

Figuring Out the Time of Day

Linda and Kathy do not have any clocks, so they cannot tell exactly what time it is. But they can figure out if it is morning, noon, afternoon, evening, or night. To figure out the time, they use facts about the sun.

- Everybody, what do they use to figure out the time of day? (Signal.) *Facts about the sun.* (ND)

Here are those facts:
The sun always comes up in the east. That's called sunrise.

- Listen to that fact again: The sun always comes up in the east. Everybody, say that fact. (Signal.) *The sun always comes up in the east.* (RF/R)

The sun always goes down in the west. That's called sunset.

- Listen to that fact again: The sun always goes down in the west. Everybody, say that fact. (Signal.) *The sun always goes down in the west.* (RF/R)
- What is it called when the sun comes up? (Signal.) *Sunrise.* (RF/R)
- What is it called when the sun goes down? (Signal.) *Sunset.* (RF/R)

When the sun is coming up in the east, it is morning.

- Everybody, in the morning is the sun in the **east** or **west**? (Signal.) *East.* (RF/R)

When the sun is right overhead, it is noon.

- Everybody, what time is it when the sun is right overhead? (Signal.) *Noon.* (RF/R)

When the sun sets in the west, it is evening.

- Everybody, in the evening is the sun in the **east** or **west**? (Signal.) *West.* (RF/R)

The picture below shows the sun at different times of day. The arrows show which way the sun is moving.

- The picture shows many suns, but there really is only one sun.

Touch sun A.

- Everybody, do it. ✔

That is the first sun Linda and Kathy see in the morning. It is in the east.

- Everybody, where is the first sun they see in the morning? (Signal.) *In the east.* (ND)

Touch sun B.

- Everybody, do it. ✔

That sun is higher in the east. They see that sun later in the morning. Touch sun C.

- Everybody, do it. ✔

That sun is right overhead. When they see this sun, they know it's around noon.

- Everybody, what time of day is it? (Signal.) *Noon.* (ND)

Touch sun D.

- Everybody, do it. ✔

That sun is moving down in the west. It is an afternoon sun.

- How do you know it's an afternoon sun?
  (Call on a student. Idea: *Because it's
  going down in the west.*) (RF/R)

  > Sun E is the last sun they see. That
  > sun is in the west.

- Everybody, touch the first sun that you
  see in the morning. ✔
- In which direction is that sun? (Signal.)
  East. (VA)
- Touch the last sun that you see at the
  end of the day. ✔
- In which direction is that sun? (Signal.)
  West. (VA)
- Touch the sun that you would see at
  noon. ✔
- What's the letter of that sun? (Signal.)
  C. (VA)

  > If you know where the sun is, you
  > can figure out directions. If you face
  > the sun that you see early in the
  > morning, in which direction are you
  > facing?

- Everybody, what's the answer? (Signal.)
  East. (VA)

  > If you face the sun that you see at
  > the end of the day, in which direction
  > are you facing?

- Everybody, what's the answer? (Signal.)
  West. (RF/R)
- Was the author's purpose to persuade,
  inform, or entertain? (Signal.) *Inform.* (AP)

Figure 3.4 Excerpt from the Informational Reading Track, Grade 2. Source: Engelmann, S. and Hanner, S. (2008). *Reading Mastery Signature Edition Teacher Presentation Book B Grade 2*, L. 61, pp. 59–60, © McGraw Hill. (The abbreviations circled in pink are explained in Figure 3.6.)

When students reach the Grade 4 level of the program, the reading selections shift from stories written specifically for the program to reinforce scientific knowledge to various types of literature. Here is a list of the literature genres in the Grade 4 level of the program:

Genre	Reading selection
Biography	Jackie Robinson
	Jane Addams
	Samuel Clemens and Mark Twain
Factual Article	Amazing Animal Journeys
	Animals in Danger
	The Domestication of Animals
	England in the 1500s
	Journey to Dawson
Folktale	Beauty and the Beast
Myth	The Golden Touch
	The Miraculous Pitcher
Novel	The Prince and the Pauper
	The Wonderful Wizard of Oz
Poem	In the Time of Silver Rain
	Open Range
	The Spider and the Fly
	Trees
Short Story	Adventure on the Rocky Ridge
	Buck
	The Cat that Walked by Himself
	A Horse to Remember
	Ron's Summer Vacation
	The Ugly Duckling

Table 3.7 Genres addressed in *Reading Mastery Signature Edition Grade 4*. Source: NIFDI. (2013). *Literature in Reading Mastery Signature Edition*, p. 2.

Although the program emphasizes literature, students learn critical background information in conjunction with each story. Here's what they learn about domestic animals in Grade 4 (lesson and exercise types appear in parentheses):

I. Domestic animals

A. Definition

1. Domestic animals live with people in people's houses or farms (lesson 41, factual article)
2. Dogs, horses, cows, chickens, and goats are domestic animals (lesson 41, factual article)

B. Domesticating animals

1. Dogs were the probably the first animal to be domesticated (lesson 41, factual article)
   a. Dogs were domesticated by cave people (lesson 41, factual article)
   b. Dogs helped cave people hunt (lesson 41, factual article)
   c. Dogs can track other animals (lesson 41, factual article)
   d. Dogs warned cave people of danger by growling (lesson 41, factual article)
2. Domesticating goats and sheep made it possible to farm (lesson 41, factual article)
3. Animals were domesticated to hunt (lesson 42, factual article)
   a. Cats were domesticated over 3,000 years ago in Egypt to kill mice and rats (lesson 42, factual article)
   b. Mongoose[s] were domesticated to kill cobras (lesson 42, factual article)
   c. Ferrets were domesticated to catch mice and rats (lesson 42, factual article)
4. Animals were domesticated to give milk, eggs, meat, wool, and leather (lesson 42, factual article)
5. Animals were domesticated to carry things (lesson 42, factual article)
   a. Camels can carry large loads for long distances (lesson 42, factual article)

      b. Llamas can climb high mountains without roads (lesson 42, factual article)

      c. Elephants carry tremendous loads and lift trees (lesson 42, factual article)

      d. Donkeys and horses carry large loads (lesson 42, factual article)

  6. Tame animals, like dogs, live with people (lesson 42, factual article)

  7. Animal breeding made animals more useful (lesson 42, factual article)

C. Dogs

  1. A litter is a group of puppies born at the same time (lesson 54, story reading)

  2. A runt is the smallest puppy in the litter (lesson 54, story reading)

  3. Hound dogs have a powerful sense of smell (lesson 54, story reading)

  4. Hound dogs are used to track other animals (lesson 54, story reading)

  5. A kennel is a place where dogs are kept (lesson 54, story reading)

D. Facts about horses

  1. A thoroughbred is a breed of horse used for racing (lesson 34, vocabulary)

  2. A nag is an old broken-down horse (lesson 34, vocabulary)

  3. A swaybacked horse has a back with a big dip in it (lesson 34, vocabulary)

  4. [When horses gallop, they run almost as fast as they can] (lesson 36, vocabulary)

E. Horse racing

  1. A steeplechase is a type of horse race (lesson 35, story reading)

a. The horse jumps barriers and obstacles [in a steeplechase] (lesson 35, story reading)

b. The jumps include fences, hedges, shelf, and water barriers (lesson 35, story reading)

2. When the horse jumps up, the rider leans forward (lesson 36, story reading)

3. When the horse lands, the rider leans back (lesson 36, story reading)

4. The Grand National Steeplechase Championship in England is a famous steeplechase (lesson 39, story reading)

   a. Horses come from all over the world to race (lesson 39, story)

   b. The course is four and a half miles long with 30 jumps (lesson 39, story reading)

   c. The course is triangular (lesson 39, story reading). (Woolfson, 2014, 57–59. Item D4 is in brackets as it has been changed by the program author.)

Students learn information about these additional subjects in similar detail in the Grade 4 level of the program:

- wild animals
- endangered animals
- physical geography – landforms, glaciers, tides, tornadoes
- political geography – selected countries, states, cities
- history – early cave dwellers, Ancient Greece and Rome, England in the 1500s, The Yukon Gold Rush
- biographies – Jackie Robinson, Jane Addams, Samuel Clemens, and Mark Twain.

In conjunction with the Jackie Robinson biography, students learn fundamental information about the game of baseball. They learn some baseball vocabulary, including: *major leagues, rookie, dugout,* and *umpire.* Here's the first of the information passages on baseball from Lesson 61, which appears in the students' textbook along with a graphic representation of a baseball diamond with players from two teams:

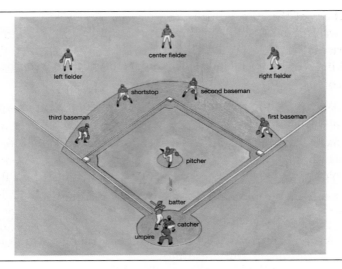

Facts about Baseball

The picture on the opposite page shows a game between two baseball teams, the Reds and the Blues. There are nine players on each team. All nine Blues are in the field. One player from the Reds is standing at home plate. That player is called the batter. The other Reds players are in the dugout, waiting for their turn at bat.

The pitcher on the blue team throws the ball toward the catcher, who plays behind home plate. There are players at first base, second base, and third base. Between second and third base is another player called the shortstop. In the outfield, there are three more players: the left fielder, the center fielder, and the right fielder.

When the pitcher throws the ball, the batter tries to hit the ball to a spot where nobody on the blue team can catch it. Then the batter runs as far as possible around the bases, starting with first base. If the batter can run all the way around the bases and come back to home plate, the batter scores a run.

The picture also shows an umpire right behind the catcher. The umpire calls out "Strike!" for good pitches and "Ball!" for bad pitches.

In this lesson, you will begin reading a biography of a famous baseball player, Jackie Robinson. Jackie's story is told by a fictional person. The narrator is fictional, but he tells facts about Jackie Robinson.

Figure 3.5 Information about baseball. Source: Engelmann, S. et al. (2008c). *Reading Mastery Signature Edition Grade 4 Textbook B*, © McGraw Hill.

As a point of interest, background information on baseball is the focus of one of the most well-known studies on background knowledge and its relationship to reading comprehension. (See Recht and Leslie, 1988.)

The authors of the study concluded that prior knowledge, not reading ability, was the main factor in students' ability to comprehend a story about baseball. E. D. Hirsch has also used baseball to illustrate the need for building background knowledge as a prerequisite for students to be able to comprehend subject-specific texts (Hirsch, 2006).

The range of information that students learn through the *Reading Mastery* program by the end of the Grade 5 level is substantial. The best source for seeing the range of background information taught in the program is *Science and Social Studies in Reading Mastery Signature Edition* by Dr. Nancy Woolfson (the source of the Grade 4 facts listed earlier). The book presents an outline of the information taught in the Grade 2–5 levels of the program along with the lessons where the information appears and the exercise type in parentheses. The book is nearly 100 pages long, which underscores the amount of content that students master in the program.

The information students learn in the program not only provides a strong foundation for comprehending the content of the literature in the program, but also provides a foundation for them to read and understand outside material, *especially the textbooks they encounter in other subject areas.* For instance, the knowledge students acquire in the Grade 4 level of the program about the United States immediately before and during the Civil War provides a strong basis for them to learn about the US during Reconstruction. Similarly, what students learn about the solar system and galaxies provides a basis for learning about other topics in astronomy. In each of these cases, it would be important for the teacher to review the relevant information the students already learned in the *Reading Mastery* program to set the stage for the outside units so the students can see how the new information is related to what they already know.

While the reading-to-learn levels of *Reading Mastery* have a strong emphasis on vocabulary and background knowledge, they also include critical comprehension strategies and skills, which occur in the context of the stories and other selections students read. In the Grade 2 level of the program, each of the story series addresses skills for determining cause-and-effect strategies and finding supporting evidence. In addition, each story series teaches at least one additional comprehension skill. For instance, the *Herman the Fly* series provides students with practice in narrative sequencing as they trace the route that Herman takes. Temporal sequencing is a focus of *The Time Machine* series as students use a timeline to track the two boys' journey to different points in time. Character development is a focus of both of these story series as well as several others in the Grade 2 level of the program as students interpret the characters' feelings, infer motives, and predict what choices the characters will make.

The Grade 2–5 levels of the program use a system of abbreviations to help teachers track the different types of comprehension activities in the program. These abbreviations appear in pink letters throughout the teacher presentation book. In the informational segment about *Linda and Kathy Alone on an Island*, which appears in Figure 3.4 (Exercise 3, Lesson 61 of RMSE Grade 2), the abbreviations stand for:

- author's purpose (AP)
- noting details (ND)
- recall facts or rules (RF/R)
- refer to visual aids (VA).

Here is a complete list of the abbreviations for the different types of comprehension questions presented to students in the program:

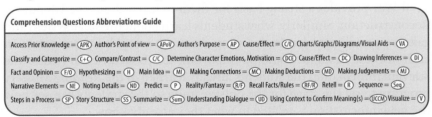

Comprehension Questions Abbreviations Guide

Access Prior Knowledge = (APK) Author's Point of view = (APoV) Author's Purpose = (AP) Cause/Effect = (C/E) Charts/Graphs/Diagrams/Visual Aids = (VA)

Classify and Categorize = (C+C) Compare/Contrast = (C/C) Determine Character Emotions, Motivation = (DCE) Cause/Effect = (DC) Drawing Inferences = (DI)

Fact and Opinion = (F/O) Hypothesizing = (H) Main Idea = (MI) Making Connections = (MC) Making Deductions = (MD) Making Judgements = (MJ)

Narrative Elements = (NE) Noting Details = (ND) Predict = (P) Reality/Fantasy = (R/F) Recall Facts/Rules = (RF/R) Retell = (R) Sequence = (Seq)

Steps in a Process = (SP) Story Structure = (SS) Summarize = (Sum) Understanding Dialogue = (UD) Using Context to Confirm Meaning(s) = (UCCM) Visualize = (V)

Figure 3.6 Key to comprehension question abbreviations in *Reading Mastery*. Source: Engelmann, S. et al. (2008b). *Reading Mastery Signature Edition Series Guide for the Reading Strand*, p. 76, © McGraw Hill.

In this way, *Reading Mastery* combines "the best of both worlds." It systematically builds students' background information as a means of developing a strong basis for students to understand the content of the stories that appear in the program and related outside material. At the same time, the program provides students with the skills to be able to perform such critical tasks as summarizing story plots, analyzing the motivations of the characters, differentiating fact from opinion, and making predictions about story developments.

WRITING CLEAR DESCRIPTIONS OF EVENTS

One of the biggest challenges for young writers is to convey a sequence of events clearly so that it is comprehensible to readers. When many students write multiple-paragraph narrative accounts of events, it is sometimes difficult for readers to discern what the setting is for the events, which events took place first, what caused the events, and what the outcome was of the actions depicted. The goal of one of the key standards for third grade writing as articulated in the Common Core State Standards is for students to describe event sequences clearly:

> Write narratives to develop real or imagined experiences or events using effective technique, descriptive details, and clear event sequences.

> (Source: Common Core State Standards Initiative, English Language Arts Standards » Writing » Grade 3, accessible at https://corestandards.org/wp-content/uploads/2023/09/ELA_Standards1.pdf)

The Grade 3 level of the language track of *Reading Mastery Signature Edition* and *Expressive Writing*, a two-level remedial writing program, are designed to teach students to describe event sequences clearly as an integral part of narrative composition writing. In *Reading Mastery*, the explicit teaching of writing starts in the second half of the Grade 2 language program and continues into the Grade 3 program. At the end of the Grade 2 program, students possess the following skills:

- They can write simple, regular order sentences to describe the main action a person took, as depicted in a picture.
- They can write simple paragraphs that are prompted by a series of pictures. The students basically report on what the pictures show.
- They also have begun the process of editing paragraphs.
- They have worked on pronoun usage and clarity, capitalization, ending marks, verb tense, subject/predicate, and apostrophes.

These skills are expanded greatly in the Grade 3 program. By the end of the Grade 3 program, students write multi-paragraph passages with quotations based on a single picture prompt. They edit paragraphs for pronoun clarity, inclusion of important details, and sequence and mechanical problems such as punctuation, capitalization, ending marks, and parts of speech.

The approach to teaching writing in the Grade 3 program involves a focus on teaching students explicitly how to describe a sequence of events. In contrast to other approaches that provide an open-ended topic to students and allow them to structure their own writing, the DI approach limits students' writing by topic and structure, which makes it much easier for the teacher to teach the critical elements of good writing systematically. Using open-ended prompts with little structure in other approaches to writing may encourage students' self-expression and creativity, but it often doesn't lead to students' acquisition of critical writing skills because the teacher has more difficulty giving them feedback on specific, critical elements of good writing. The DI approach is to teach critical writing skills first as students apply the skills in carefully structured writing assignments. The program initially controls the prompts and directions to students so that they produce written responses with very specific foci. The prompts and directions are gradually eased as students master critical elements of clear writing. Over time, the writing tasks become more open-ended.

In the DI approach, limiting the variability of the students' writing initially makes it much easier for the teacher to direct students' attention to critical elements of *sequence, clarity and fundamental writing conventions* as each student's written product possesses many features identical to the products of their classmates. The structure for writing assignments in the *Reading Mastery Grade 3* language program includes:

- prompts with a very specific focus depicted in pictures that portray concrete actions
- key vocabulary words that correspond to the actions indicated in the pictures
- use of the past tense exclusively initially until students learn to quote characters depicted in the pictures.

An early emphasis of the program is for students to *report* exactly what occurred in the pictures. The students do not describe the character's motivation or thought process at this stage of their writing. The authors of the program explain the advantage of limiting students' writing to reporting initially:

> Students of varying abilities will tend to write the same set of sentences if they are required to report. However, if students are permitted to write whatever their imagination dictates, great variation will occur. Although some of the students will write clever passages, these passages don't serve as good models to the other students because they are the product of many skills that have not been taught to the other students. Also, the lines between acceptable and unacceptable passages will not be clear to many students because the passage they write may be quite different from those other students created. In this context, students find it difficult to figure out what's acceptable and what isn't. In summary, when the assignment is restricted to "reporting," the criteria for an acceptable passage are clear, the variability from student to student is reduced, and all students are able to succeed because the assignment does not involve skills that have not been taught in the program. The goal is not to teach a few students well, but to teach all of them well. (Engelmann, S., Silbert and Hanner, 2008a, 11)

Reporting lays the basis for students to make inferences as they describe what must have occurred between or before the events shown in pictures. The authors explain that:

> ... reporting sets the stage for "inferring," which is taught later. If students understand what it is to report, they can appreciate the difference between reporting and inferring, which involves interpretations based on a picture sequence but not shown by the sequence. (Engelmann, S., Silbert and Hanner, 2008a, 11)

In the early part of the Grade 3 level of the language program, students are provided with the subject for each sentence of the paragraph they write and the order of the sentences in the paragraph. A picture with four panels shows the initial word students are to use for each sentence, and the numbers indicate the order of the sentences. An example is Lesson 13. The students' textbook depicts an interaction between a man named Hector and a monkey over a freshly baked pie. (See Figure 3.7.)

D Write a paragraph that reports on what happened.
Write a sentence for each name shown in the pictures.

1. Hector
2. He
3. A monkey
4. The monkey
5. Hector

	grabbed	window sill	started	yelled
ate	piece	pie	answered	phone	scolded

Check 1
Does each sentence tell the main thing? (M)

Check 2
Does each sentence begin with a capital and end with a period? (CP)

Check 3
Does each sentence tell what somebody or something **did?** (DID)

Figure 3.7 Hector and the monkey from Lesson 13. Source: Engelmann, S., Silbert, J. and Hanner, S. (2008b). *Reading Mastery Signature Edition Language Arts Presentation Book A Grade 3*, pp. 66–67, © McGraw Hill.

Before students write, the teacher leads them in constructing the story of Hector and the monkey orally. For each sentence, the teacher calls on several students to say what the character did. The teacher is provided with example sentences in the teacher presentation book. Here are the five example sentences for Lesson 13:

1. Hector put a hot pie on the window sill.
2. He went inside the room to answer the telephone.
3. A monkey grabbed the pie.
4. The monkey ate the pie.
5. Hector scolded the monkey. (Engelmann, S., Silbert and Hanner, 2008b).

The teacher praises students who come up with different sentences that describe the actions depicted at each step, and the class orally repeats the students' sentences if they accurately portray the actions. The teacher reads the example sentences as a story to the students. Then and only then do the students write a paragraph. When they are finished with a draft of their paragraph, they review the three "checks" located below the vocabulary box silently to themselves as a guide for their work, which they revise as needed. The students already demonstrated mastery on each of the elements of composition described in the checks earlier in the program, so they can revise their paragraph based on these checks completely independently.

As in all DI programs, the exercises become more complex and sophisticated as students master the content of lessons and are ready for more advanced work. The next step in the students' acquisition of sequencing skills is for them to go beyond merely reporting what is shown in pictures and infer what events or actions must have taken place in between pictures. The vehicle used in the DI programs to teach students to infer actions that are not depicted in the prompt is *the missing picture*. In Lesson 23 of the Grade 3 level of *Reading Mastery*, the students' textbook contains the following:

> **Write a paragraph that tells about the middle picture.**

| climbed | growled | against | bush | missed |

Check 1
Did you write sentences that give a clear picture of what must have happened in the middle picture? (WH)

Check 2
Are all your sentences written correctly? (CP, RO, DID)

Figure 3.8 Missing picture exercise from Lesson 23. Source: Engelmann, S., Silbert, J. and Hanner, S. (2008b). *Reading Mastery Signature Edition Language Arts Presentation Book A Grade 3*, p. 114, © McGraw Hill.

The teacher reads the following paragraph, which tells what happened before the first picture took place and describes the first picture:

> Mr. Wingate collected rare and beautiful butterflies. One day he was out in the woods when he saw a huge blue butterfly. He chased the butterfly for a while. Finally, it landed on the top of some bushes. Mr. Wingate did not know that a mother bear was sitting on the other side of the bushes watching her cub. He ran toward the butterfly. He held his butterfly net over his head. (Engelmann, S., Silbert and Hanner, 2008b, 114)

The teacher then leads the students in a step-by-step comparison of Picture 1 with Picture 3 to figure out what must have happened in Picture 2. For Picture 1, the teacher asks:

- Where is the mother bear?
- Where is the butterfly?
- What is Mr. Wingate doing?

For picture 3, they ask:

- Where is the net?
- Where is Mr. Wingate?
- Where is the mother bear?
- Where is the butterfly?

The teacher calls on individual students to help construct a paragraph orally that describes what must have happened in the missing picture. Here is the excerpt for this step of the exercise:

---

6. You're going to make up sentences that tell what must have happened in the missing picture.

- Raise your hand when you can say a sentence that tells what Mr. Wingate did with the net. (**Call on a student. Idea:** *Mr. Wingate swung the net at the butterfly.*)
- Everybody, did the net miss the butterfly? (**Signal.**) *Yes.*
- The net missed the butterfly. Say that sentence. (**Signal.**) *The net missed the butterfly.*
- Raise your hand when you can say a sentence that tells where the net went. (**Call on a student. Idea:** *The net went over the mother bear's head.*)
- Raise your hand when you can say a sentence that tells what Mr. Wingate did when he saw the mother bear. (**Idea:** *He ran away. He climbed a tree.*)
- Raise your hand when you can say a sentence that tells what the mother bear did when the net went over her head. (**Idea:** *The mother bear growled. She ran after Mr. Wingate.*) (Engelmann, S., Silbert and Hanner, 2008b, 114–15.)

Students answer the questions, which the teacher accepts if they address what the question asks. Then students repeat an example paragraph orally as a group, sentence by sentence. After that, the students write a paragraph on their own. This high level of scaffolding ensures that the students successfully write a clearly sequenced paragraph.

By Lesson 41 students are writing two paragraphs – a paragraph about what happened in the first picture, and a paragraph about what must have happened in the middle picture. Starting at Lesson 73, students learn to set the scene for the action that occurs in pictures. The first of the two paragraphs they write includes a description of what was taking place before the first picture as well as what happened in the first picture. For setting the scene, students learn the rule that you can use the past continuous tense to describe what was happening. The students' textbook contains this rule, which the teacher reviews orally with the class. From Lesson 73:

D Here's a rule about using verbs when you write a story: When you start a story, you can write sentences that tell where somebody **was**, or what somebody **was doing**. After you tell where somebody was or what somebody was doing, you tell what the person **did, not** what the person was doing.

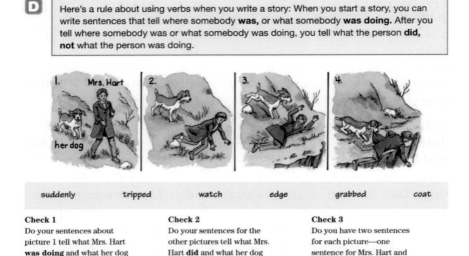

Check 1	Check 2	Check 3
Do your sentences about picture 1 tell what Mrs. Hart **was doing** and what her dog **was doing?** (WH)	Do your sentences for the other pictures tell what Mrs. Hart **did** and what her dog **did?** (WH, DID)	Do you have two sentences for each picture—one sentence for Mrs. Hart and one sentence for her dog? (WH)

Figure 3.9 Mrs. Hart and her dog from Lesson 73. Source: Engelmann, S., Silbert, J. and Hanner, S. (2008c). *Reading Mastery Signature Edition Language Arts Presentation Book B Grade 3*, p. 11, © McGraw Hill.

As shown above, the first check that the students do of their work is whether they properly set the scene. An example of the first two sentences of this exercise that set the scene are:

> Mrs. Hart was walking down the hill with her dog. Her dog was walking behind her.

(Engelmann, S., Silbert and Hanner, 2008c, 11.)

Notice that the authors waited until more than halfway through the program before teaching students how the verb tense used in setting the scene for the main action differs from the tense used in the rest of the narrative. The students practice writing narrative accounts in the simple past tense for over 70 lessons, which ensures that they are at mastery on the use of the past tense for narrative writing before the program introduces the exception involved in setting the scene.

In Lesson 85, students begin writing narratives with three paragraphs: a paragraph setting the scene and two paragraphs about what happened in the other pictures. In Lesson 91, they learn that 1) they need to start a new paragraph whenever someone new talks and 2) quotes can be in the present tense. They also learn to identify problems that characters face as part of setting the scene. For instance, in Lesson 91, the main characters couldn't see a parade because a crowd was in front of them and blocked their view.

In Lesson 97, students start writing narratives in which they construct their own sequence of events. They finish stories their teacher reads that establish the setting, describe the characters, and indicate a problem. The endings that students write to these stories are at least three paragraphs long. The problem in Lesson 97 is that Barbara found a wallet with money, and her sister needs to have an operation. Figure 3.10 is from the student textbook for the paragraph writing exercise for that lesson.

> Write an interesting ending to the story your teacher read. Your ending should have at least three paragraphs.

money   operation   hundred   enough   decide

sidewalk   because   wallet   thousand

	Barbara took the wallet and
	went to ▮▮▮▮.

Check 1

Does each paragraph have no more than one person talking?

Check 2

Did you write at least two sentences that begin with a part that tells when?

Figure 3.10 Barbara found a wallet from Lesson 97. Source: Engelmann, S., Silbert, J. and Hanner, S. (2008c). *Reading Mastery Signature Edition Language Arts Presentation Book B Grade 3*, p. 106, © McGraw Hill.

Note how the writing review checks in Figure 3.10 have changed to match the students' expanded skills and understanding of narrative writing.

Beginning in Lesson 101, students write whole stories. They are given a picture with some vocabulary and a list of guiding steps for writing an interesting story, and are told to "write an interesting story." Here are the guiding steps:

1. **Tell about the characters at the beginning of the story.** Tell where they were. Describe them and name them.
2. **Tell about their problem.** Tell what they wanted to do and why they couldn't do it.
3. **Tell the things they did to solve their problem.**
4. **Tell how the story ends.** Tell whether they solved their problem. (Engelmann, S., Silbert and Hanner, 2008c, 106)

Figure 3.11 shows the prompt for story writing for Lesson 105.

Write an interesting story.

spaceship　　　creature　　　frightened　　　suddenly

Figure 3.11 Story-writing prompt from Lesson 105. Source: Engelmann, S., Silbert, J. and Hanner, S. (2008c). *Reading Mastery Signature Edition Language Arts Presentation Book B Grade 3*, p. 106, © McGraw Hill.

After students finish their first draft of the story, they follow a series of checks to determine what, if anything, should be rewritten. Then they work in groups to refine their stories even more. Each student reads their story and critiques their own writing in front of the group, after which each of the other members of the group provides feedback in turn. After the cooperative work session, students return to their writing to incorporate the feedback that resonates with them into a final draft of their composition.

Students are able to work cooperatively and edit their work effectively and independently because of the systematic instruction and practice they received for over 100 lessons on setting the context of their stories, describing the action clearly and sequentially, and other essential elements of good writing. Students who go through this sequence write with the same imagination and creativity as students who go through other writing approaches. The difference is that students who go through this sequence all have the skills to convey their ideas sequentially and clearly so readers can understand their imaginative and creative thoughts.

FRACTIONS AND THEIR RELATIONSHIP TO INTEGERS

Many elementary and middle school students have difficulty working problems with fractions. They do not have a firm grasp on the relationship between different types of fractions or the relationship between fractions and integers. These students have misapprehensions about the nature and characteristics of fractions, such as the false understanding that fractions are always less in value than one. Many students make errors when performing different operations involving fractions (adding, subtracting, multiplying, and dividing them), and they have great difficulty converting fractions into mixed numbers, decimals, or percentages. Some students have not mastered the basic nomenclature of fractions as they confuse the terms "numerator" and "denominator." The difficulty that many students experience with fractions and their lack of a clear understanding of the nature of fractions lead many of them to become anxious whenever they encounter fractions – an anxiousness that follows them throughout their lives.

The DI math programs teach fractions in a way that ensures students develop a firm understanding of fractions and their relationship to integers, mixed numbers, decimals, and percentages. Graduates of the programs can manipulate fractions easily, perform operations involving fractions reliably, and use fractions to solve word problems or in other applications. The DI math programs accomplish this by:

- introducing the different features of fractions incrementally so students can master each key concept as it is introduced before encountering other features
- using graphic representations of fractions initially, which help students understand the features of fractions, and fading the use of graphic representations as students master key concepts
- providing examples that show the full range of fraction types so students do not develop misapprehensions about the nature of fractions
- delaying the introduction of specialized nomenclature, such as "numerator" and "denominator," the use of which is not necessary for understanding and manipulating fractions.

Although some teaching of fractions occurs in earlier levels, the systematic teaching of fundamental concepts of fractions for elementary students occurs in Lessons 29–130 of Level D of *Connecting Math Concepts Comprehensive Edition*. From the very beginning (Lesson 29), the program shows that *fractions can be greater than one as well as less than one*. Here is the first set of fractions that students see in the program:

$$\frac{2}{3} \quad \frac{10}{2} \quad \frac{1}{5} \quad \frac{8}{7}$$

Two of the four fractions in this initial set are greater than one (ten halves and eight sevenths). Other examples of fractions greater than one appear throughout the fractions track to ensure that students don't draw the incorrect conclusion that fractions are always less than one in value.

The initial teaching of fractions takes place *without the use of unnecessary nomenclature*. The terms that are used in the program are limited to those that make critical concepts easier for students to grasp. Students are introduced to the terms "units" and "parts." In the program, graphic units – rectangles and circles – are divided into uniform parts. Students learn that "the bottom number" of a fraction (the denominator) is simply the number of parts that a unit has been divided into. Students eventually learn the specialized terms for fractions in the program, which are defined as follows in the students' glossary that is part of the program:

Denominator: The bottom number in a fraction.

The denominator tells the number of parts in a whole.

Numerator: The top number in a fraction.

The numerator tells how many parts we have. (Engelmann, S. et al., 2014, 2–4)

As a first step in understanding fractions, students practice simply counting the number of parts in units to determine the denominator for different fractions. Here is the display the teacher shows in Lesson 29 as students count the parts in each unit, which is then shown as the denominator in the fraction to the right:

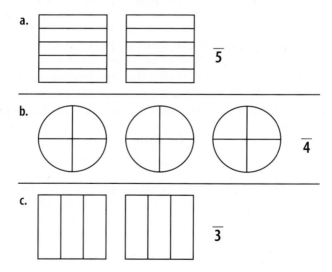

After students demonstrate that they understand that "the bottom number" is determined by counting the number of parts per unit, they are presented with a version of the display with parts shaded, which represents "the top number" (the numerator):

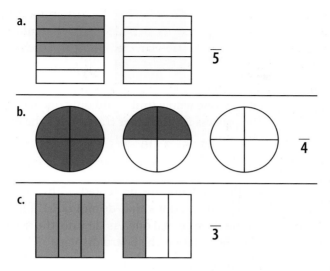

Students simply count the number of units that have been shaded to determine "the top number" for these fractions. Note that the shaded parts exceed one unit in the second and third items, *b* and *c*, so the fractions are each greater than one – six fourths and four thirds.

After several lessons in which students practice identifying the top and bottom numbers from graphic representations of fractions by counting parts per unit and parts that have been shaded, students learn to identify fractions that equal one. They learn the rule that "if the top number and the bottom number of the fraction are the same, the fraction equals one unit." (Engelmann, S. et al., 2014, 123.) In Lesson 34, students are presented with the following fraction and asked to describe what the graphic representation of this fraction would look like:

$$\frac{4}{4}$$

The teacher asks the students to predict how many parts a unit in the graphic representation of this fraction will have and how many parts will be shaded. Then she shows the following display to the students so they can verify their answers:

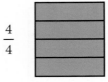

$$\frac{4}{4}$$

The teacher points out that one whole unit – and only one whole unit – is shaded. She repeats the process for the other fractions in the exercise:

$$\frac{7}{7} \quad \frac{5}{5} \quad \frac{3}{3} \quad \frac{10}{10} \quad \frac{2}{2}$$

In the same exercise, the students are presented with a mixed set of fractions that equal one and fractions that do not equal one. They are asked to identify which fractions equal one. As they do, the teacher writes "= 1" to indicate the equality. Here is the board display:

$$\frac{8}{9} \quad \frac{3}{3} = 1 \quad \frac{7}{7} = 1 \quad \frac{2}{5} \quad \frac{5}{5} = 1$$

Starting in Lesson 38, students write inequality signs (greater than ">" and less than "<") as well as the equal sign to indicate the relative value of the fractions.

At Lesson 42, the program introduces a very powerful tool to help teach students several critical aspects of fractions – the number line. Fractions are represented graphically on number lines with each unit representing an integer that is divided into smaller parts. Students are able to understand dividing units on a number line to represent fractions because of the earlier examples of dividing rectangles. The number line closely resembles rectangles with no spaces between them.

Students count the parts in each unit on the number line, which are separated by larger lines. As before, students determine the denominator first. They are presented with several number lines with units divided into different numbers of parts and are asked to "find the bottom number". Here is the display for Exercise 2 of Lesson 42 with the denominators filled in:

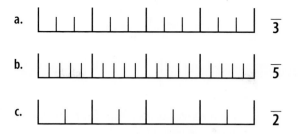

Students then determine the numerator by counting the number of parts shaded:

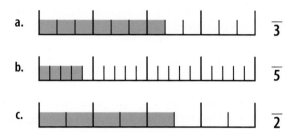

The program builds on this use of number lines to teach important relationships between fractions and integers, such as the relative value of a given fraction and a given integer. For instance, in Lesson 47, the teacher prompts students to construct two inequality statements based on a number line with parts shaded to represent a fraction:

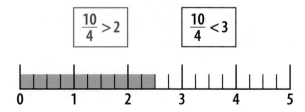

In their workbook for the lesson, students write fractions independently based on a number line representation of a fraction. Then they construct an inequality statement:

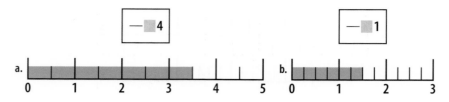

They determine that seven halves is less than four in problem A, and that six fourths is greater than one in problem B.

Number lines are also used to demonstrate conditions of equality between integers and fractions. Starting on Lesson 88, students calculate the numerator of fractions that equal a given whole number. Students complete the following equation:

$$3 = \frac{}{4} = \frac{}{5} = \frac{}{1} = \frac{}{9}$$

To determine the numerators of the fractions, students multiply the denominator of each fraction by the whole number that the fraction equals with the products equaling the numerators for the different fractions:

$$3 = \frac{12}{4} = \frac{15}{5} = \frac{3}{1} = \frac{27}{9}$$

Students apply this knowledge about the relationship between whole numbers and fractions to number lines. In Lesson 99, they determine the equivalent fractions to whole numbers for each of the units on different number lines. They apply the rule of multiplying the bottom number by the number of units to determine the top number. In Exercise 3 of Lesson 99, students apply this rule to a number line with two parts per unit:

They also apply it to a number line with four parts per unit:

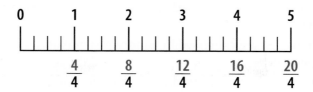

Number lines are then used to teach students about mixed numbers. As before, integers are used to represent the number of units on a number line, but now fractions represent the parts of each unit. From Lesson 108:

This work provides students with a solid understanding of mixed numbers. Note that the steps above are much easier for students who have achieved automaticity with multiplication facts. After the initial teaching of these concepts, number lines are faded from the program. In later lessons, students work problems with fractions involving addition, subtraction, inequality, and mixed numbers without reference to number lines.

The systematic teaching of fundamental concepts of fractions in Level D lays the foundation for more advanced work with fractions in Level E. Following a review of these concepts in the first 30 lessons of Level E, students learn to convert fractions into decimals and vice versa. For instance, in Lesson 60 of Level E, students complete the following table:

	Fraction	Decimal
a.		23.04
b.	7/100	
c.		.3
d.	219/10	
e.		.08

In this exercise in Lesson 60, students learn to convert each of the following:

- fractions that are expressed in tenths into decimals expressed as tenths
- fractions that are expressed in hundredths into decimals expressed as hundredths
- decimals that are expressed in tenths into fractions expressed as tenths
- decimals that are expressed in hundredths into fractions expressed as hundredths.

Note that the numbers used in the exercise represent a range of values greater and less than one so students will not develop the misunderstanding that decimals apply only to values less than one.

In subsequent lessons in Level E, students complete similar tables involving decimals and percentages. By the end of the level, students are able to convert numbers between fractions, decimals and percentages reliably and confidently. This is made possible by building upon the systematic teaching of fundamental fraction concepts that took place in Level D of the program.

SUMMARY

The examples provided in this chapter are just that – examples of the content analysis performed by the authors of the published DI programs. There are many other examples that could have been described in this chapter. Every critical skill or concept that is addressed in the DI programs has been analyzed by the authors to determine the student performance goals, the possible sources of students' confusion in learning the content, and ways in which the content can be structured to reduce or eliminate any confusion on the part of the students. The simplest preskills (prerequisite skills) have been identified for *all* of the content addressed in the DI programs, and students master these preskills before learning more advanced concepts and skills. As the examples in this chapter indicate, students who are placed appropriately in the programs will learn the content to mastery and be able to perform much more sophisticated applications at the end of the instructional sequences than they were able to at the start of the programs. The correct implementation of any of the sequences described in this chapter can be expected to have a profoundly positive impact on the performance of students who possess the necessary preskills. The positive impact on student performance is increased manifold when it is combined with the rest of the instructional sequences in the DI programs, which provide a strong basis for future learning.

The range of these examples indicates that there is no "cookie cutter" formula for structuring content in the DI approach. The relationship between critical concepts in a given subject area – rather than a predetermined formula – influences the structure of the programs. For instance, the authors of *Spelling Mastery* didn't a priori decide to focus on the phonetic approach to spelling in the lower levels of the program and then transition to the morphemic approach in the higher levels. They let the specific subject matter guide them in identifying the most fundamental and easiest-to-master spelling skills that would lay the foundation for students to learn more advanced spelling skills. The example of the two different beginning DI reading sequences illustrates how the same content can be structured in different ways in the DI approach with the difference between the two reading sequences centered around the children's knowledge of letter names. Indeed, there are many ways that the content of any of the programs could be structured so that critical preskills are taught systematically to mastery and then integrated into more advanced applications. The authors approach instruction in each subject area scientifically and without hesitation adapt or completely change all material as the evidence informs them.

The present chapter and chapter 2 were designed to describe the critical features possessed by all authentic Direct Instruction programs. As the examples in both of these chapters show, the DI methodology has been applied to several critical subject areas to address a wide range of student performance levels. The next chapter provides a systematic overview of the scope of the DI curricula and the performance levels addressed by each of the published DI programs.

CHAPTER FOUR
SCOPE OF THE DIRECT INSTRUCTION CURRICULA

The two previous chapters of this book described the design of Direct Instruction and provided examples of the analysis of critical content in selected DI programs. This chapter addresses the scope of the DI curricula, which can be divided into *programs for the majority of students* and *programs that meet special needs*. To a large extent, the first category of programs can be characterized as "developmental" and the second category as "remedial." However, several key DI programs meet other needs that are not remedial in nature. These include "fast-cycle" programs designed to teach students at an accelerated rate and programs for English language learners (ELL), also known as English as an additional language (EAL) students in the United Kingdom.

All of the programs listed in this section meet the axioms outlined in *Rubric for Identifying Authentic Direct Instruction Programs*, discussed in chapter 2 of this book. Note that supplementary materials commonly used in DI classrooms are not listed in this section, such as the *Sentence Copying Program*, which is available through the NIFDI store (www.nifdi. org/store/category/20-instructional-materials.html). These supplemental programs are not described in this chapter because they do not meet the requirements of the rubric.

Additional information about the programs described in this chapter can be found in the programs tab of the website of the National Institute for Direct Instruction (NIFDI) (www.nifdi.org) as well as in the *Program Reference Chart*, which is also available through the NIFDI store. The

Program Reference Chart lists such critical information as the number of lessons in each level of the programs, the frequency of mastery tests, grouping guidelines, and the time requirements of the lessons.

Nearly all of the programs described in this chapter are available commercially through McGraw Hill Education (www.mheducation. com). Other vendors of DI programs include Voyager Sopris Learning (www.voyagersopris.com), *Funnix* (www.funnix.com), and Educational Achievement Publishing (www.eapublish.com). All of the programs described here can be purchased through McGraw Hill Education unless otherwise stated.

PROGRAMS FOR THE MAJORITY OF STUDENTS

The DI methodology has been applied to several of the main elementary school subject areas – reading, language arts, mathematics, history, and spelling – which has resulted in multi-level instructional programs designed for the majority of students. These programs are intended to serve as the *core instructional programs* for students and are not designed to be used as supplements to other curricula.

READING PROGRAMS

The main developmental reading program is *Reading Mastery*, a six-level comprehensive literacy program. There are several different editions of the program. The most widely used edition at the time of writing is the *Reading Mastery Signature Edition*, which has a reading strand and a separate language strand (discussed later in this section). As described in the previous chapters, the first two levels of the reading strand of the *Signature* edition teach students a modified orthography with 40 symbols that correspond to sounds made in the English language. Students do not need to possess prior knowledge of letter names to start the program. In the kindergarten level and early part of the Grade 1 level of the program, symbols are referred to as "sounds." Students learn the names of letters as the orthography transitions to the regular English alphabet in the Grade 1 level of the program.

The most recent edition of the program is *Reading Mastery Transformations*, which was released in 2021. The first two levels of the *Transformations* edition differ from the first two levels of previous editions, including the *Signature* edition, by adapting the content analysis and instructional sequence used in the *Horizons* and *Funnix* DI reading programs. In contrast to earlier editions of *Reading Mastery*, these programs are intended for students who either know their letter names or can learn them easily; they are designed to take advantage of students' knowledge of letter names to help them learn the sounds that letters make. Table 4.1 summarizes the way the two sets of programs teach sounds and letters.

Program	How sounds and letters are taught
Reading Mastery Signature and earlier editions of *Reading Mastery*	• Students do not need to know any of the letters of the English language to start the program. • Instead of letters, students learn a 40-character orthography with each character referred to as a "sound." • The regular English alphabet, including capital letters and letter names, is taught in the Grade 1 level of the program after students have learned the 40-character orthography and read words and stories written in this orthography.
Reading Mastery Transformations, Horizons and *Funnix*	• Students already know some or all of their letter names before starting the program. A 40-lesson pre-program is designed to teach students select letters and essential language skills. • The sounds letters make are taught through the letters of the English alphabet themselves. • The program uses the regular alphabet throughout with some minor modifications made to the alphabet in the K and Grade 1 levels for irregular sounding words, such as blue letters indicating that a letter is silent.

Table 4.1 How different DI reading programs teach sounds and letters.

The levels of both the *Reading Mastery Signature* and *Transformation* editions are designated by grade. The lowest level of each edition is kindergarten or Grade K with the highest level designated as Grade 5. Note that the grade-level designations provide only a rough guide for deciding which programs will be best suited to which students. Each level comes with a placement test, which should be administered to students before materials are purchased. The results of the placement test determine which level is best suited to each child's current skill level. If students attending Grade 3 or above place into the first two levels of the program, they may be best suited for *Corrective Reading*, a remedial DI reading program discussed later in this chapter.

In addition to the grade-level programs, the *Signature* edition of *Reading Mastery* includes a 35-lesson program called *Transitions* that provides a bridge between the Grade 1 and Grade 2 levels. *Transitions* is designed to provide extra practice in decoding and comprehension to students who are entering the program at the Grade 2 level or students who completed the Grade 1 level but are not ready for the content-rich material in the Grade 2 program. *Transitions* can also be implemented as a supplementary program for all students in Grade 2 to reinforce essential literacy skills. *Reading Mastery Transformations* does not include a program between Grades 1 and 2.

Although there are great differences in the first two levels of the *Signature* and *Transformations* editions, the content of the programs converges beginning in the third level of the programs. As described in the previous chapter, the first two levels focus on *learning to read* with a greater emphasis on decoding (although literal and interpretive comprehension activities are included). In the upper levels, the focus is on *reading to learn* with a heavy emphasis on building students' background knowledge.

Teacher materials in the *Transformations* edition are digital in contrast to previous editions of *Reading Mastery*, which are available as print programs only. *Transformations* student materials (textbooks and workbooks) are still available only in hard copy. Teacher presentation lessons in *Transformations* are accessible through an online account and streamed directly to users. Each instructor needs two devices to present *Transformations* lessons – a tablet and a display device (such as a projector, a laptop, or a smartboard). A class with two instructors running three groups (a common setup for DI in the lower grades, as discussed in section 2 of this book) requires four devices. After users log in, they have access to several different modes in the *Transformations* interface, including a planning mode and a teacher presentation mode. A notes function is available for teachers to record observations about student performance or other critical information about instruction.

Horizons is a four-level print reading program that uses the same letter-first approach in the first two levels of the program, Levels A and B, as is used in the first two levels of *Reading Mastery Transformations*. *Horizons Fast Track C-D* is an accelerated program that combines the equivalent of

Grades 2 and 3 of *Reading Mastery Signature* into one year. The program is often used with English language learners and with students who are getting a later start with reading. After completing *Horizons C-D*, students typically place into fourth-grade level material.

Funnix is a two-level, semi-automated, computer-based reading program based on the *Horizons* instructional sequence. Like *Reading Mastery Transformations, Funnix* is streamed directly to users. Unlike *Transformations*, the teacher presentation in *Funnix* is completely automated. An instructor does not deliver the lessons to students. The program has a built-in, software-driven presentation with dynamic audio and visual displays for every lesson. An adult user operates the mouse and clicks on buttons in response to students' performance to repeat exercises or proceed as appropriate. *Funnix* is designed for one-on-one or small-group instruction, although some teachers have used the program with larger groups by projecting the lessons onto a smart board. The automated presentation greatly reduces the amount of time needed for initial training in program delivery in comparison to other DI programs.

REWARDS (**R**eading **E**xcellence **W**ord **A**ttack and **R**ate **D**evelopment **S**trategies) *Intermediate* is one of several *REWARDS* reading programs available through Voyager Sopris Learning. All of the *REWARDS* programs teach the same strategy for decoding multisyllabic words by breaking words down into affixes and roots. *REWARDS Intermediate* is a 25-lesson program designed for students in Grades 4 through 6 who read at a third-grade level or above but have difficulty decoding multisyllabic words. The program also teaches students critical vocabulary and background information. This program can be used developmentally or remedially. (Other programs in the *REWARDS* family are discussed later in this chapter under "Programs that meet special needs".)

LANGUAGE AND WRITING PROGRAMS

As mentioned above, the *Reading Mastery Signature Edition* contains a reading strand and a language strand. The language strand of *Reading Mastery Signature* consists of six levels that correspond to the same levels as the reading strand:

- Grade K
- Grade 1
- Grade 2
- Grade 3
- Grade 4
- Grade 5.

As with the reading strand, students are placed at their performance level as determined by the program's placement tests, not by grade level.

The first two levels of the language strand are oral language programs designed to teach critical concepts, vocabulary, and language conventions that are needed for students to function well in an academic setting. Students learn the fundamental concepts needed to follow their teacher's directions, including the use of prepositions, pronouns, tenses, number (plural versus singular), part–whole relations (some versus all), and conditional rules (if/then statements). They also master higher-order concepts that lay the basis for more advanced learning, such as object classification, analogies, temporal sequencing, opposites, and synonyms. Sentence writing, story-related reasoning, and writing skills are introduced in the Grade 1 level of the program.

The Grade 2 level of the program serves as a transition from oral language to written language while students expand their mastery of fundamental reasoning skills. In the first half of Level 2 (Lessons 1–65), there is a strong emphasis on story grammar. Students predict what will take place when a familiar character appears in a new adventure based on the story grammar students learned in previous lessons. This activity lays the foundation for students to create new stories of their own by applying the same story grammar. In the second half of Grade 2 (Lessons 66–110), students learn how to write paragraphs that 1) tell the main idea of what occurred in an illustration, and 2) tell details that support the main idea. In addition, the second half of the program teaches critical writing-related skills, such as grammar, parts of speech, punctuating sentences, and editing passages that have errors.

As mentioned in chapter 3 of this book, students learn to write multi-paragraph compositions in the Grade 3 level of the program. In Grades 4 and 5, students continue to develop their expository writing skills as they expand their critical thinking skills. They analyze and rewrite sentences for clarity. More critically, they analyze arguments for faulty reasoning and construct counter-arguments based on evidence. They follow specific formats for creating counter-arguments in response to different types of logical fallacies, including contradictions, inadequate evidence, and improbable inferences.

The language strand of *Reading Mastery Transformations* contains much of the same highly effective material that is in the *Signature* edition with some critical additions and other changes. For instance, the Grade 5 level of the program provides a new approach to teaching tense consistency in sentences. Students focus on the first word in the predicate after the subject as the "key verb" in the sentence, which helps them handle difficult grammatical constructs, such as, "When they **win** all their games, he **will have proved** his point."

The biggest change in the language strand of *Transformations* is that writing occurs much earlier in Grades 2–5 of the program. Many of the narrative writing exercises that were in the Grade 3 level of *Signature* language have been moved to Grade 2. In addition, new writing, vocabulary, and grammar exercises have been incorporated into the Grade 2 level. These include new tracks on informational writing, opinion writing, describing personal experiences, and group research writing projects.

Until the *Signature* edition, DI language and writing programs were completely separate from DI reading programs. The DI language and writing programs are now part of the *Signature* and *Transformations* editions as a multi-level language strand. Earlier editions of *Reading Mastery – DISTAR Reading, Reading Mastery Classic,* and *Reading Mastery Plus* – were separate from the DI language programs. Several programs that helped form the basis for the language strand of the *Signature* and *Transformations* editions of *Reading Mastery* are still available for purchase separately. These include *Reasoning and Writing* as well as three of the "Language for" programs (*Language for Learning, Language for Thinking,* and *Language for Writing*). The "Language for" programs are three sequential, yearlong language programs. *Language for Learning* corresponds very closely to the Grade K level of *Reading*

Mastery Signature and *Transformations*, which are very similar to each other in content. *Language for Thinking* provides the basis for the Grade 1 level of *Reading Mastery Transformations*, which is substantially different from the Grade 1 level of the *Signature* edition in how certain concepts are presented to students. *Language for Writing* is the exception to the other two "Language for" programs in that it did not provide the basis for any of the language levels of either *Reading Mastery Signature* or *Transformations*. The upper grades of the *Signature* and *Transformations* editions incorporated material from the upper levels of the six-level *Reasoning and Writing* program, with major alterations occurring in the instructional sequence of the Grade 2–5 levels of the *Transformations* edition as described above.

Reasoning and Writing is designed to teach students higher critical thinking skills and how to express their reasoning clearly. Levels A and B of *Reasoning and Writing* teach students to attend to story grammar and the sequencing of events. When students finish Levels A and B, they can make predictions about story plots and anticipate the actions of characters. These skills provide a firm foundation for constructing clear sequences in their own narrative writing, which becomes the focus of the program beginning in Level C. In this level, students learn writing mechanics, grammar, and basic paragraph writing structured around a main idea and descriptions that report what happened. Levels D–F focus on writing that expresses clear thinking. In Level D, students complete exercises that require them to use evidence to support conclusions, identify misleading claims, use facts to contradict inaccurate comparisons, and write extended critiques. Level E introduces new writing elements, such as parallel sentence structure, while expanding the application of higher-order thinking. Students learn to vary word choice and sentence construction as well as recognize inconsistencies in their own writing and the writing of others. Level F extends the program into even more complex thinking and writing activities. Students examine writing for logical fallacies, and they use a variety of reference sources to develop convincing arguments. Separately published *Reasoning and Writing Extensions* accompany each level of the main program and provide students with additional practice applying the skills covered in the main program.

Students who finish the highest levels of *Reasoning and Writing* or the *Signature* or *Transformations Reading Mastery* editions can proceed onto *Essentials for Writing*, the most advanced DI writing program. *Essentials for Writing* is "designed to build the set of competencies that are measured in high-school exit exams and that are expected of high-school students" (Engelmann, S. and Grossen, 2010, 9). Students expand their knowledge of the mechanics of writing and editing, and they then apply what they've learned to different writing genres. Students write autobiographical sketches, descriptive essays, persuasive arguments, and position papers. They respond to literature in different ways: by answering literal questions about a narrative text, writing responses to study questions, citing textual evidence as they write interpretations, and creating stories on the same theme as a story they read as a class. Graduates of the program know how to compose a variety of critiques and arguments, which helps them become much more sensitive to attempts to manipulate their thinking through propaganda or advertising.

SPELLING PROGRAMS

As described in the previous chapter, *Spelling Mastery* is a six-level developmental DI spelling program that addresses the complexities of spelling in English by utilizing three different strategies: phonetic, whole-word, and morphemic. This sophisticated, highly effective spelling program enables students to apply coherent spelling rules to words rather than simply memorize weekly spelling lists.

The *Reading Mastery* programs have supplemental spelling programs built into them. Each level of the *Signature* edition has a separate Spelling Presentation Book with optional lessons that are designed to reinforce the decoding skills taught in the reading lessons. Because the spelling lessons match the reading lessons and build off them, students should not be presented with spelling lessons more advanced than their reading lessons.

In implementations of DI supported by NIFDI, students receive instruction in the first two levels of the spelling programs that are built into the Grade K and 1 levels of *Reading Mastery*, commonly referred to as "kit" spelling because they come with the *Reading Mastery* kit, and then transition to the *Spelling Mastery* program. After completing the *Reading Mastery* kit spelling, students test into Level B of *Spelling Mastery* or higher.

HISTORY PROGRAMS

Understanding U.S. History is a two-volume history text designed for middle-school students, although it can also be used for reading in a content area for advanced elementary students who have completed the *Reading Mastery* series. As mentioned in the introduction of this book, the program uses a problem-solution-effect structure to analyze historical events. Students learn that historical actors have options to choose from in response to problems – **a**ccommodating, **d**ominating, **m**oving, **i**nventing, or **t**olerating the problem. Students learn to apply this ADMIT model to past events, identify which option historical actors chose, and determine the consequences these choices had for future events and the choices taken by other actors. With this model, history becomes much more comprehensible to students as events are presented in the context of processes that transcend individual events.

As described in the previous chapter, science and social studies information has been incorporated into the upper levels of the *Reading Mastery* programs. Several elementary schools have implemented *Reading Mastery* only without additional science or social studies programs with very positive results.

MATHEMATICS PROGRAMS

Connecting Math Concepts Comprehensive Edition (CMC CE) is a six-level mathematics program (levels A–F). CMC CE, which is a revision of an earlier edition of the program, explicitly addresses the Common Core State Standards. To meet these standards, the program includes new material on money, geometry, measurement, word problems, data classification, and other topics. Other changes in CMC CE include more group oral practice on new concepts and skills by students before they work problems independently.

Essentials for Algebra is the most advanced DI mathematics program as it integrates pre-algebra topics with topics found in more traditional algebra courses. The program ensures that students have mastered fundamental mathematics operations and concepts, such as rounding decimal values to the nearest thousandth place or adding fractions with like denominators, before moving onto more advanced topics. The program teaches algebra operations involving fractions, exponents, straight-line equations on a coordinate system, word problems, and simultaneous equations. It employs a unique rate equation strategy that allows students to solve problems more easily and reliably by reducing the complexities of the computations involved in working algebra problems. *Essentials for Algebra* can be used either developmentally in middle schools or junior high schools, or remedially as an intervention to help students pass high school exit examinations.

DISTAR Arithmetic 1 is the most basic DI mathematics program. It is appropriate for students who do not have the skills to place into the lowest level of CMC CE, Level A. *DISTAR Arithmetic* systematically teaches the preskills that allow students to perform basic addition and subtraction operations, such as rote counting as a prerequisite skill for addition, and backwards counting as a prerequisite skill for subtraction. By the end of the program, students advance to more complex mathematics skills, including basic algebra operations and simple story problems. Students who successfully complete *DISTAR Arithmetic* Level 1 usually place into CMC CE Level B and do not need to go through CMC CE Level A.

Funnix Beginning Math is a single-level, semi-automated mathematics program that is part of the *Funnix* family of computer programs available through Funnix.com. Like *Funnix Beginning Reading* and *Funnix 2*, *Funnix Beginning Math* has a completely automated teacher presentation with lessons that are streamed directly to users. *Funnix Beginning Math* is designed for preschool or kindergarten children who do not possess basic mathematics skills, such as rote counting. It can also be used with older students who have not adequately mastered beginning math operations. The program download includes all of the student workbook pages. A bound student workbook is available for purchase separately. As with the other members of the *Funnix* family of computer programs, the automated presentation of *Funnix Beginning Math* greatly reduces the amount of time needed for initial training in program delivery in comparison to other DI programs.

PROGRAMS THAT MEET SPECIAL NEEDS

There are three categories of DI programs that meet special needs: 1) programs designed to accelerate students through the instructional sequence for teaching students at an accelerated rate ("fast-cycle" programs), 2) programs for English language learners, and 3) remedial DI programs.

FAST-CYCLE PROGRAMS

All of the DI programs can accelerate students' performance if teachers place students at their skill level and implement the lessons as written. In addition, there are various "fast-cycle" versions of programs to help accelerate the performance of students at an even quicker pace. Four hard-copy, fast-cycle versions of print programs are available for purchase:

- *Horizons* A/B, which combines Levels A and B of *Horizons*
- *Horizons* C/D, which combines *Reading Mastery Signature* Grades 2 and 3
- *Corrective Reading Comprehension* Level A (described later in this chapter), which condenses the regular 65-lesson program into 30 lessons
- *Corrective Reading Comprehension* Level B1 (described later in this chapter), which condenses the regular 60-lesson program into 35 lessons.

In addition, many DI programs have built-in acceleration schedules:

- Students can be fast-cycled through the first two levels of *Reading Mastery Signature* by following the acceleration schedule in the Assessment Handbook of the Grades K and 1 levels of the programs.
- Exercises that are part of the fast-cycle schedule in the *Reading Mastery Signature* Grade K language program are indicated by a yellow star in the teacher presentation book.
- In the second level of *Expressive Writing* (described later in this chapter), students can be fast-cycled by presenting every other lesson.
- Fast-cycle schedules are available in every module of *Corrective Mathematics* (described later in this chapter).

For a full list of fast-cycle options, see the *Program Reference Chart* (NIFDI, 2023).

PROGRAMS FOR ENGLISH LANGUAGE LEARNERS

The DI programs for English language learners (ELL) are differentiated by the target students' age and proficiency in their native language and English. *Direct Instruction Spoken English* (DISE) is a two-level oral language program available through Educational Achievement Publishing (EAP). DISE is intended for English language learners from any language background who possess the equivalent of a third-grade or higher understanding of their native language and little or no proficiency in English. In contrast to *Language for Learning* and the Grade K level of the language strand of the *Reading Mastery* editions, which systematically teach fundamental language concepts, DISE is designed for students who already understand the basic language concepts taught in the program but do not know how to express these concepts in English. DISE takes advantage of students' knowledge of their native language to teach them how to express concepts in English.

Lessons in the DISE program are accompanied by instructional display slides that teachers project on a screen and refer to as they teach the program. For students who start at the beginning of the program, the teacher may need to repeat initial lessons several times until students master each new convention of the English language that's introduced. The program uses both academic and social vocabulary to teach fundamental sentence structures. Often, students can complete the program in one year or less and emerge with functional receptive and expressive English language skills.

Español to English is a 40-lesson program designed to help Spanish-speaking students learn critical receptive and expressive language skills and transition to speaking English. In the beginning of the program, the teacher presents lessons in Spanish using a translation of *RMSE Language Grade K*. Students respond in English as the teacher models English-language statements and vocabulary. As students progress through the program, instruction gradually shifts to English until it is the sole language of instruction. *Español to English* is best suited for students who are in Grade 2 or below and have not yet mastered critical fundamental concepts in Spanish. Older students who understand fundamental language concepts in Spanish are best suited for *Direct Instruction Spoken English* (DISE), described previously.

REMEDIAL DIRECT INSTRUCTION PROGRAMS

DI remedial programs cover the major academic subject areas of reading, language and writing, spelling, and mathematics. They are appropriate for students in Grades 3 or 4 and above depending on the program. For younger students who have gaps in their learning, they should be placed in the level of the developmental program that matches their performance level.

Reading programs

Corrective Reading is a remedial reading program that contains two strands – *Decoding* and *Comprehension*. The strands are each divided into four levels: A, B1, B2, and C. The division of the program into two strands allows for flexibility in providing students with instruction that matches their performance levels. Students take separate placement tests for each strand to determine which level best matches their skills. Often, students place at lower levels of the *Comprehension* strand than the *Decoding* strand. For instance, a student may place into *Decoding* B2 and *Comprehension* A.

In the lower levels of *Decoding*, the focus is on accurate reading. The program is designed to eliminate guessing by making the word selection and sentence structure in stories unpredictable so students must pay close attention to the printed words. Level A is designed for students performing at the pre-primer level who do not have a clear understanding of the sound–symbol relationships necessary to decode simple words. In this level, students learn to decode short, phonetically spelled words and some irregularly spelled words accurately. By the end of the program, they can read selections composed of a few sentences containing these words. In Level B1, students expand their ability to decode phonetically spelled words with an emphasis on consonant blends and other letter combinations as well as compound words and word endings.

In Level B2, the focus starts to shift to fluency. New word types are introduced, and students must still demonstrate that they can decode words and passages accurately as in the previous levels. At the same time, the length and fluency requirements of the passages increase. Story length increases from about 600 words at the beginning of Level B2 to almost 900 words at the end of the level, and the expected fluency rate increases from 90 words per minute to 130 words per minute at 98% accuracy. By the time students finish Level C, they are able to read passages containing multisyllabic words at a rate of 150 words per minute at the sixth to seventh grade difficulty level at 98% accuracy. They read newspaper articles and other outside material, and they are able to summarize the content of the selections they read.

The *Comprehension* strand greatly expands students' ability to think clearly as well as comprehend the texts they read. Students learn to attend to details of the texts they read in the *Comprehension* programs through workbook exercises that require them to follow directions precisely. These directions change often from lesson to lesson, which requires students to pay attention to the exact wording that appears in all directions. Students also acquire a great deal of new vocabulary and common information in the *Comprehension* strand. In Level A, students learn the following information:

- Calendar (months, seasons, holidays)
- Poems (through memorization)
- Animals (definitions of mammals, reptiles, and other classes of vertebrae; felines, canines; herbivorous, carnivorous classifications) (Engelmann, S., Haddox and Hanner, 2008a, 7).

In Level B1, students learn the classes of different objects, and they learn how the major systems of the human body function. In Level B2, students learn basic rules of economics as well as more about the human body. In Level C, they learn how to use different sources of information, such as graphs, maps, and illustrations.

Perhaps the most unique skill that students acquire in the *Comprehension* strand of *Corrective Reading* is the ability to analyze arguments and produce written works based on their analysis. Students learn to analyze the passages they read for a variety of logical fallacies – false analogies, improper deductions, overgeneralized conclusions, and false dilemmas. In the Inference track in Levels B1 and B2, students explain the rationale behind their responses to questions on passages that incorporate vocabulary and information presented in other tracks. In Level C, they produce outlines based on their evaluation of specific reference material combined with information from other sources.

The *Decoding* and *Comprehension* strands each have a system for motivating students to apply themselves and succeed. Students earn points for meeting performance goals in different phases of the lessons. Here is a description of the system used in *Comprehension* A:

> It is possible for students to earn as many as 14 points for each regular lesson—5 points for Thinking Operations, 5 points for the lesson's Workbook Exercises, and 4 points for the Information part of the lesson. The criteria for awarding points are specified in the lesson and are based on student performance. (Engelmann, S., Haddox and Hanner, 2008a, 11)

The correct usage of this point system leads to improved self-confidence as students are able to see evidence of their progress and receive recognition for their efforts and accomplishments. These positive effects occur only if students are placed properly in the program and the programs are implemented with fidelity so the students can have a realistic chance of earning a high number of points. When implemented with fidelity, the program leads not only to the rapid closing of performance gaps but also to improved attitudes and confidence on the part of the students.

As mentioned earlier, the *REWARDS* (Reading Excellence Word Attack and Rate Development Strategies) family of instructional programs, available through Voyager Sopris Learning, is a highly effective group of remedial interventions for students who have difficulty reading multisyllabic words. *REWARDS Secondary* (20 lessons) is the original program of the family and is recommended for students in Grades 6–12 who read at a 2.5 grade level or higher. Students who successfully complete *REWARDS Secondary* or *REWARDS Intermediate* can progress to *REWARDS Plus Social Studies* or *REWARDS Plus Science*, which apply the *REWARDS* strategy for decoding multisyllabic words to the type of texts that students encounter in content courses at the secondary level. Each of the Plus programs contains six review lessons and 15 application units. In the Plus programs, students read selections on a range of social science and science topics, such as photosynthesis and United States citizenship. They also learn to use a variety of support material – graphs, illustrations, timelines, and maps – that they will encounter in content courses.

The *REWARDS* programs are often combined with *Corrective Reading* to provide a greater number of options for meeting the needs of remedial students. Students should master the skills at the end of *Corrective Reading Decoding* B1 or the equivalent to be considered for the *REWARDS* programs, and many teachers wait until students have completed *Decoding* B2 before considering them for *REWARDS*.

Writing programs

Although some writing occurs in the upper levels of *Corrective Reading*, the two-level *Expressive Writing* program is the main remedial DI writing program. *Expressive Writing 1* is designed for students who have not mastered fundamental writing skills and have difficulty constructing grammatically correct sentences or paragraphs with a clear, coherent focus. Students who complete *Expressive Writing 1* are able to:

1. write a paragraph that describes a sequence of related actions using simple declarative sentences
2. punctuate sentences correctly
3. begin sentences with a capital and end sentences with a period
4. write consistently in the simple past tense
5. include sufficient detail
6. stay on the topic. (Engelmann, S. and Silbert, 2005, 1–2.)

Expressive Writing 2 expands students' skills for simple paragraph writing, story writing, and editing. Students learn to:

1. write using clear pronoun referents with details necessary for clarity
2. write with a variety of sentences – sentences that begin with a dependent clause, sentences that contain a series, and some compound sentences

3. write what people say and form appropriate paragraphs of their conversations

4. edit passages for clarity, punctuation, paragraphing, and sentence structure. (Adapted from: Engelmann, S. and Silbert, 2005, 2.)

Note: the content of *Expressive Writing 1* and *2* overlaps considerably with the Grade 2 and 3 levels of the language strand of *Reading Mastery Signature Edition* respectively. Graduates of *Expressive Writing 2* often place into *Essentials for Writing*, which provides them with the opportunity to acquire more sophisticated writing skills at a rapid rate as described above.

Spelling programs

Spelling Through Morphographs is a single-level program designed for students in Grade 4 and above who understand the basic sound–symbol relationships of the English language but have difficulty spelling words that they cannot easily "sound out." As with *Spelling Mastery* (described earlier), *Spelling Through Morphographs* gives students the tools they need to "think their way through spelling" (Dixon and Engelmann, S., 2007b, 2) rather than simply memorize word lists. Unlike *Spelling Mastery*, which provides students with a blend of three types of strategies (phonetic, whole-word, and morphemic), *Spelling Through Morphographs* concentrates on morphemic strategies to teach students to spell words correctly. In the program, students master 750 morphographs (prefixes, bases, and suffixes) and rules for applying them. They learn that the spelling of some morphographs changes when they are combined in predictable ways governed by consistent rules. They also learn how morphographs transform words into different parts of speech. For instance, adding the suffix *-ion* produces a noun (*instruct + ion = instruction*), while adding the suffix *-ive* produces an adjective (*instruct + ive = instructive*). Upon completing *Spelling Through Morphographs*, students are able to apply the strategies taught in the program to spell between 12,000 and 15,000 words correctly – regardless of whether they have seen the words before (Dixon and Engelmann, S., 2007b, 6).

Mathematics programs

Corrective Mathematics is a seven-module program covering: addition; subtraction; multiplication; division; basic fractions; fractions, decimals and percentages; and ratios and equations. (Note: the highest module, ratios and equations, was not included in the latest revision but still retains the same look and instructional sequence from an earlier edition.) The program is designed to provide a firm foundation in fundamental operations and core concepts, rules, and mathematical reasoning to students in Grade 3 and higher. Each module contains between 50 and 70 lessons that are delivered in short instructional periods lasting 25–45 minutes depending on the module. The number of students in each instructional group should be 15 or fewer to allow for sufficient attention from the teacher.

The program is not intended to serve as a comprehensive mathematics program. Rather, it should be employed as a supplement to an effective comprehensive mathematics program to address students' learning deficits in specific mathematics skills. The modular approach, short length of the program, and relatively short time requirements provide users with great flexibility in implementing the modules in a wide variety of learning situations.

All of the programs mentioned in this chapter require the use of specific teaching techniques described in the next chapter of this book.

CHAPTER FIVE
TEACHING TECHNIQUES

The previous three chapters of this book have focused on critical aspects of the Direct Instruction programs. These chapters have described the design of the DI programs, provided examples of the application of the DI design principles to specific content, and outlined the scope of the programs that fully incorporate these design principles. This chapter summarizes the teaching techniques that DI instructors use to ensure that students are successful with the DI programs. All of these techniques promote the effectiveness and/or efficiency of instruction. If these techniques are implemented properly along with the structural prerequisites for the programs (summarized in this chapter and discussed in detail in section 2), virtually all students should succeed with DI. If they are not implemented properly, student success with DI cannot be guaranteed. Note that understanding the description of these techniques will not result in their successful execution. Teaching staff will need to undergo extensive training and practice with coaching before they will be able to implement these techniques with fidelity, as described in detail in section 2.

Here are the specific topics discussed in this chapter:

1. Structural prerequisites for implementing DI successfully
2. Following the script
3. Observing the students
4. Varying pacing and emphasizing keywords
5. Eliciting group responses

6. Using appropriate signals for group instruction
7. Modeling new tasks
8. Providing a leading step for students
9. Testing students' knowledge
10. Correcting all errors
11. Managing student behaviors positively
12. Applying skills and concepts beyond the programs.

STRUCTURAL PREREQUISITES FOR IMPLEMENTING DI SUCCESSFULLY

The following structural requirements of the programs must be met before teachers can be expected to deliver the DI programs successfully:

- All students have been placement tested to determine the level of the DI programs that correspond to their current skill level.
- Instructional groups have been formed that are homogeneous with respect to students' skills as indicated by the placement test results.
- The size of the instructional groups conforms to the program's requirements.
- Instructional materials that correspond to the students' placement have been purchased in sufficient quantities.
- Sufficient time has been scheduled daily for group instruction and student independent work.
- The physical arrangement of the classrooms has been set up to facilitate 1) the teachers' delivery of the program and 2) their monitoring of students during group instruction and independent work.

If any one of these requirements has not been met, the techniques listed throughout this chapter can be expected to have a limited positive effect on student performance. For instance, if the physical arrangement of a classroom does not allow students to see the displays on the screen or in the teacher presentation book, the positive aspects of the teacher's delivery of the program will be nullified; regardless of how well the teacher provides a signal for the students to respond or emphasizes critical wording in the script, their delivery will not result in students learning the content of the lesson because students cannot see the displays for the lesson. Failure by the teacher to implement any of the other techniques listed can also have a nullifying effect on otherwise positive aspects of a teacher's delivery.

FOLLOW THE SCRIPT

The first, most basic Direct Instruction teaching technique is for teachers to follow the instructional scripts precisely. This involves understanding all of the conventions and nomenclature that appear in the scripts. For instance, a common direction in the scripts is to "repeat until firm." Teachers must understand that this involves following the seven steps of the Part-Firming Paradigm (discussed later in this chapter) in response to all student performance errors. Following the scripts also involves administering the required assessments and implementing the remedies indicated in the teacher presentation books in response to errors that students make on the assessments.

With very few exceptions, adding extra words to the scripts or omitting any part of the scripts should be avoided. As mentioned previously, the scripts incorporate all of the sophisticated DI design elements that have been demonstrated to be highly effective in teaching students to mastery. The scripts have been tested and revised based on field tryouts to verify that students who meet the programs' prerequisites will learn the content successfully. If a teacher adds extra words, the students could get confused if the wording does not blend with the wording of the scripts, and their progress through the program could be delayed. If the teacher omits any part of the scripts, student mastery and progress through the program may also be adversely affected. For example, in many reading exercises, students identify a sound or part in a word before reading the whole word. If the teacher omits the step of identifying the sound or part, students may be unable to read the whole word correctly, which will cause the group to spend more time on the exercise by having to correct otherwise preventable errors and potentially increase the frustration of the teacher and the students.

There are some rare exceptions to the requirement that the DI scripts should be followed exactly. If students are not familiar with a key word that appears in the script, the teacher may quickly teach the word. For instance, if a student has a British background and is not familiar with the word "truck," the teacher may quickly insert that "truck is the word we use for lorry." She may also ask for confirmation from the student: "What is another word for 'lorry'?" If the student answers correctly, the teacher can return to the script.

Another example of going off script is when a student provides an answer that is correct but doesn't match the answer in the book. The teacher should acknowledge that the student's answer is correct and then ask the student to use the wording that appears in the program as the preferred response. Here's an example of this procedure from the *Reading Mastery Signature Edition Grade 1* language program:

> In a Parts exercise a child might call the point of a pencil a tip. You say,

> "Right. Some people call this part a tip. But it's also called a point. Let's use point. What part is this?" (Engelmann, S., Osborn and Davis, 2008, 10.)

Adding brief statements of encouragement to the scripts is another exception. As discussed later, teachers should reinforce students for their efforts and accomplishments. The scripts contain some reinforcing statements. Teachers should feel free to add additional positive statements as long as they do not interfere with the momentum or coherence of instruction. The teacher can also give students individual turns in addition to what's written in the scripts as long as items belonging to a single cognitive routine are not broken up but are given to a single student. For example, if an exercise involves identifying a sound or part in a word before reading the whole word, both of these tasks should be given to the same student in one individual turn.

OBSERVE THE STUDENTS

It is critical that teachers observe their students while delivering the lessons. Teachers must know the scripts well enough that they can visually monitor students. If they are not sufficiently familiar with the scripts, they may become "script bound" and won't know what their students are doing while they are reading the scripts. If a teacher cannot verify that her students are paying attention sufficiently, she will not know whether the students didn't understand a task when one of them commits an error or whether they simply weren't looking at the correct part of the display. Each type of error involves a different remedy to correct it so teachers must be able to determine precisely what type of errors occur.

Teachers must carefully monitor students' performance responses, both verbal and written. Students may give the appearance that they are responding fully during group instruction, but some of them might be mimicking other students. Some students "coat-tail" on the response of other students by waiting a split second to respond. In fact, some students do not respond fully; they simply mouth words instead of producing a response. These behaviors constitute a very serious threat to the fidelity of the implementation as they reduce the instructional activities to parroting instead of genuine learning by all students. The teacher must be attuned to these possible types of errors, which is only possible if they can devote their attention to observing students and not allow their attention to be consumed by reading the script.

VARY PACING AND EMPHASIZE KEYWORDS

Following the script means more than reading the scripts accurately. The overall goal is to proceed through the lessons as quickly as the students can demonstrate that they have mastered the content, which requires a fast overall presentation pace by the teacher. This is a challenge to teachers who do not know the scripts well, so it is important that they practice the scripts to gain fluency. A fast overall pace is also conducive to keeping students' attention. However, varying the presentation pace is the best way to retain students' attention, which is a critical prerequisite of any type of direct teaching.

Varying the pace is also necessary for the teacher to underscore the most critical elements of the task at hand. To do this, teachers should "pause and punch" keywords. For example, "not" and "is" are two words in the early lessons of the beginning language programs that often need emphasis in such sentences as, "This *is* a vehicle" and "This is *not* a tool." Another example in the early language program is when students are learning plurals and articles. Teachers should emphasize "*an* apple" and "*an* airplane" in exercises requiring students to discriminate between the articles "a" and "an." They should also emphasize the ending of the following sentences to show that plurals do not require articles: "A wagon *has a handle*" and "A wagon *has wheels*." Students may not be able to recognize these key discriminations if teachers simply deliver the lesson in a monotone or at a rate that students can't follow (too fast or too slow).

Providing sufficient think time for students to formulate a response after a teacher presents a task is an important element of pacing. For every item during group instruction, the teacher presents a direction or a question and then pauses for a moment to give students time to think before signaling students to respond as a group. Think time during these pauses varies between one and three seconds depending on the difficulty of the task. Simpler items and items that are familiar to students generally require less think time than items that are complex or new to students. Thus, it is critically important that a teacher *customizes the think time* to her students and *takes into account any items that have been difficult for them in the past.* If a teacher does not give her students enough time to think about a task before she signals them to respond chorally, some of the students will make mistakes or not respond, which will cause the teacher to repeat the task, thereby slowing down the progress of the group. Providing just an extra second or two of think time allows groups to go slower on a task but go faster on the lesson overall by avoiding unnecessary student performance errors.

ELICIT GROUP RESPONSES

Choral responses are a key part of the DI approach for group instruction because they allow for much more efficient instruction. Watkins and Slocum identify three ways in which choral responses are efficient:

1. All students get high-quality practice on every item because they provide their own response and cannot echo other students.
2. All students are busy learning the material and are less likely to become distracted.
3. Teachers can assess the skills of all the students in an instant and be well informed about their skills. (Watkins and Slocum, 2004, 45)

Conversely, if a teacher relies exclusively on individual student responses, she will receive potentially inaccurate information about what her students know. Suppose that a teacher asks a student, "What's seven plus four?" and the student answers correctly, "11." If the teacher then asks another student the same question and they answer correctly, the teacher has no way of knowing whether the second student already knew the answer or was just repeating what the first student said. With choral responses, students must produce their own responses instead of copying the responses of others.

As mentioned before, the teacher needs to be able to determine that students are, in fact, producing their own responses during group instruction, and she needs to be able to discern what those responses are. This may involve the teacher physically repositioning herself during instruction so she can monitor student responses closely, especially with larger instructional groups. The teacher may also call on subgroups – students by row, right half/left half of the classroom, etc. – to determine whether all students are producing their own responses. If the teacher suspects that a student may be leading the group, the teacher can ask the student to listen silently for an item or two as the other students respond.

USE APPROPRIATE SIGNALS FOR GROUP INSTRUCTION

To ensure that students know when to respond together, teachers must provide a consistent signal that elicits a unison response for every oral item during group instruction. As mentioned above, if one student leads the group and produces a response before the other students, the teacher will not be able to determine whether the other students produced their own responses or simply mimicked the response of the leading student.

The type of signals used in the DI programs varies greatly depending on the instructional task. For example, an *audible signal* is used when students are focused on written material and cannot look at the teacher. A *point-and-touch signal* is used when directing students to visual representations in the teacher presentation book or board displays. The number and type of signals vary greatly across the different program levels as the programs transition from primarily oral instruction in the lower levels to primarily written instruction in the upper levels. The broadest range of signals is used in the lower levels of the programs, which are designed to teach students a wide range of fundamental skills. For instance, the kindergarten level of the *Reading Mastery Signature Edition* reading strand involves the use of seven major signal types with additional signal combinations (see Table 5.1).

Types of Signals	Use
Continuous Sound Signal	For students to produce a continuous sound in response to a written symbol.
Stop Sound Signal	For students to produce a discontinuous sound in response to a written symbol.
Pronunciation Signal	For students to repeat sounds orally without a written symbol prompt.
Say-It-Fast Signal	For students to say or read a whole word.
Sound Out Signal	For students to blend sounds orally as they decode a series of written letter symbols in a word.
Audible Signal	For directing students while they are engaged in reading and worksheet activities.
Point-and-Touch Signal	For students to read isolated sounds or sounds that are contained in a single word separately.
Hand Drop Signal	For students to respond to a question or task when looking at the teacher rather than at a written prompt.

Table 5.1 Types of signals used in *Reading Mastery Signature Edition Grade K*. Adapted from: Engelmann, S. and Bruner, E. C. (2008b). *Reading Mastery Signature Edition Teacher's Guide Grade K*, pp. 18–40.

In contrast, the Grade 5 level of the program involves the use of a single signal (see Table 5.2).

Type of Signal	Use
Audible Signal	An audible signal for directing students while they are engaged in reading and worksheet activities.

Table 5.2 Type of signal used in *Reading Mastery Signature Edition Grade 5*. Source: Engelmann, S. et al. (2008d). *Reading Mastery Signature Edition Teacher's Guide Grade 5*, p. 24.

The broad range of signals used is one indication of the comparative difficulty of teaching the lower levels of the DI programs, as discussed more thoroughly in the next section of the book. Teachers must receive training and coaching on their signals as this is a unique aspect of DI that teachers will not have encountered previously in their careers. Mastering the use of signals requires that teachers practice the signals with expert feedback.

MODEL NEW TASKS

Teachers model all new tasks for students as specified in the lesson scripts, which ensures a high rate of initial correct student responses, a critical prerequisite for teaching to mastery. Modeling new tasks can involve providing a *direct model* of the specific response that is expected of students, such as, "This sound is /a/" when students will be asked to produce /a/ in the exercise. Or it can involve *modeling a rule, strategy, or process* that students are supposed to follow, such as blending words together, counting from a number other than one, or determining whether two fractions can be added by examining their denominators. Sometimes the model step follows a review of relevant information that is already within the students' repertoire. For instance, the teacher asks students to *count lines in a group* in steps a through c in the following exercise in Lesson 15 of *Connecting Math Concepts Comprehensive Edition* (CMC CE) *Level A*, a task that students already mastered in previous lessons.

EXERCISE 9: COUNTING SEPARATE GROUPS

a. (Display page.) [15:9A]
Here are two groups of lines.
(Point to first group of lines.) Here's one group.
(Point to second group of lines.) Here's another group.

b. You're going to count the lines in each group.
• (Point to first group.) Count the lines in this group. Get ready. (Touch lines.) *1, 2, 3, 4, 5.*
• How many lines are in this group? (Touch.) *5.*

c. (Point to second group.) Count the lines in this group. Get ready. (Touch lines.) *1, 2, 3, 4.*
• How many lines are in this group? (Touch.) *4.*

d. I'm going to count the lines in **both** groups.
(Point to first group.) I'll count the lines in this group. Then I'll just keep on counting. Watch.
(Touch lines in first group.) 1, 2, 3, 4, fiiive, 6, 7, 8, 9.
• Do it with me. (Touch lines in first group.) *1, 2, 3, 4, fiiive.* (Touch lines in second group.) *6, 7, 8, 9.*

e. This time I'll do the first group. Then you'll keep on counting.
• (Touch lines as you say:) 1, 2, 3, 4, fiiive. (Touch lines in second group.) *6, 7, 8, 9.*
(Repeat step e until firm.)

f. How many lines in both groups? (Signal.) *9.*

Figure 5.1 Model, lead and test steps in a beginning mathematics exercise. Source: Engelmann, S. and Engelmann, O. (2012a). *Connecting Math Concepts Level A Teacher Presentation Book 1*, p. 178, © McGraw Hill.

In step b above, the students count the lines in the first group. In step c, they count the lines in the second group. Both of these tasks review what the students have already done successfully in past exercises – count lines that are part of a single group. In step d the teacher then models the new skill of counting lines in both groups without stopping:

> **d.** I'm going to count the lines in **both** groups.
> **(Point to first group.)** I'll count the lines in this group. Then I'll just keep on counting. Watch.
> **(Touch lines in first group.)** 1, 2, 3, 4, fiiive, 6, 7, 8, 9.

Providing students with a precise model of the new behavior is much more efficient than simply asking students to do something they have not seen before. In the exercise above, if the teacher were to ask students to count the number of lines in both groups together without the teacher first providing a model, some students might count only the first group of lines because stopping after counting the first group conforms to the tasks they've been doing up to this point in the program. Providing an explicit example of the expected behavior ensures a much higher initial success rate in performing the new task. Some students may still not perform new tasks correctly initially even with a model, but the number of students who perform successfully on their first try is much higher with an explicit model than it would be without a model.

LEAD STUDENTS AS NEEDED

Teachers can provide a *leading step* for students if they think students might have difficulty producing the expected response in an exercise. A "lead" is any type of assistance that the teacher provides to students to help them form a response. S. Engelmann defined a lead as follows:

> When you lead, you prompt the response or help the learner produce it. (Engelmann, S., 2018, 73)

Often, a lead involves saying the expected response together with the students, and some of these leads have been incorporated into the published scripts. In the second bulleted part of step d in the counting exercise in Figure 5.1, the teacher counts the lines together with the students as the teacher touches the lines:

- Do it with me. (Touch lines in first group.) *1, 2, 3, 4, fiiive.* (Touch lines in second group.) *6, 7, 8, 9.*

Leading is often used to help students produce complex responses. For example, in the kindergarten level of the *Reading Mastery Signature Edition* language program, students are introduced to the following statements in a single exercise on Lesson 71:

- A dentist is a person who fixes teeth.
- A dental assistant is a person who helps a dentist.
- A city is a place with lots of people. (Engelmann, S. and Osborn, 67–68)

Students often experience difficulty saying these definitions in their entirety the first time they encounter them, and they must repeat them several times before they can say them completely. Having the teacher accompany the students as they say the sentences can help students memorize the sentences more quickly, especially if the teacher emphasizes critical parts that are difficult for students, such as, "A dentist is *a person who* fixes teeth."

Leading is often accompanied by chunking or chaining – breaking down more complex responses into shorter responses that the teacher practices with students separately before they attempt to produce a complete response on their own. In the first target sentence above, the teacher can firm up the segments "a dentist is a person" and "who fixes teeth" separately until students are at mastery on both segments before asking them to say the complete sentence. As students improve their performance, they should receive positive reinforcement for closer approximations of the desired response. (For specific guidelines on shifting the criteria of different levels of reinforcement as students make closer approximations of the desired outcome behavior, see S. Engelmann and Carnine, 1991, pp. 308–9.)

Many students may experience a different production challenge – knowing *when* to produce different responses. They may be able to produce complete responses, but they may not know which response relates to which item. For example, in the language exercise about dentists, students are supposed to respond to the task "say the whole thing about a dentist" as follows:

A dentist is a person who fixes teeth.

However, some students may erroneously give this same response to the question, "What do we call a person who helps a dentist?" because this question ends in "dentist" as does the direction to "say the whole thing about a dentist." Students often cue off the final two words of the question ("a dentist") rather than respond to the whole question. Their confusion can be reduced by the teacher:

1. giving them an additional cue by emphasizing "what do we call *a person who helps* a dentist?" when asking the question
2. voicing over (leading) the response "a dental assistant"
3. repeating this process until students answer correctly.

Note that these two types of errors should be addressed separately. Engelmann and Carnine caution that teachers should "initially use separate teaching for *when* and for shaping the response, then put them together" (Engelmann, S. and Carnine, 1991, 310). Indeed, if a teacher tries to firm complex production responses while they try to address which response is correct, students may make so many errors that the teaching interaction can become unproductive and frustrating for both the teacher and the students.

When students are able to produce a response but do not know when to produce it, a useful strategy is to have another adult act as a "shill" to give the learners a model of the correct response. A shill is a second adult who responds with the students while the teacher is teaching. Using a shill is particularly helpful if students experience difficulty understanding personal pronouns and matching verb forms. For instance, if students have difficulty correctly differentiating between "You are touching your ear" and "I am touching my ear", a shill can help accelerate student learning by voicing the correct response to the matching prompt. Otherwise, the teacher and students can get caught in an endless loop of corrections as the teacher attempts to teach the students to distinguish between the times when the word "you" refers to her and the times when the word "you" refers to the students. Using a shill can be particularly helpful teaching pronouns and their usage to English language learners.

A student who responds correctly can, in effect, act as a shill. The teacher can use individual students as models for students who are struggling with difficult tasks. She can ask all of the other students to listen as that student responds. Then, she can ask the other students to respond along with the student. In this way, the teacher is actually promoting a type of coat-tailing, but only until the other students can respond correctly on their own.

With all leads, it is critically important to remove prompts over time. Leads should be faded as soon as students demonstrate that they can perform a task independently. Otherwise, students can become reliant on prompts and may not be able to perform tasks independently without assistance. When removing prompts, it is important to recognize that performing independently may be difficult for some students at first; otherwise, there would not have been a need for the prompts in the first place. The teacher can present tasks as a challenge in recognition of how difficult they may be for the students to perform successfully:

> "Let's see if you can say that whole sentence without any help from Mrs. Daniels."

Then, when the students successfully perform a task, the teacher can be very reinforcing:

> "Look at you! You all said that whole sentence without any help.
> It was a long sentence, but you all said it correctly on your own!"

In some cases, students' performance may require prompts in some form for days or even weeks before they can be faded completely depending on the performance of the students. However, teachers should not consider students to be at mastery on any items that involve a lead or prompt. Items should be repeated until all students can perform independently at mastery, which may require that students practice items for short periods of time several times a day outside of the formal instructional period. If students are not at mastery on all tasks or at least require only minor assistance, they may not have a sufficiently strong foundation for learning new material.

Note that leads are used very selectively in the published DI programs because the lead step requires additional time. Students who are properly placed in the program should be able to produce most of the targeted responses based only on their teacher's model of the correct response. If students are capable of producing a complete and correct response without a prompt, the teacher should not insert a lead step and proceed directly to the test.

TEST STUDENTS' KNOWLEDGE

The instructional format of DI is the opposite of the lecture format, which involves long periods of one-way communication between an instructor and learners before the instructor provides a check on understanding. *The DI approach involves testing students' knowledge immediately after a concept or skill has been presented.* This ensures that students do not develop misapprehensions of the targeted skill or concept, the remediation of which requires several additional repetitions of correct responses by the students for each error.

The test step follows the lead step – or the model step if the teacher does not provide a lead. The test step is a check on understanding. Test items involve the direct application of the targeted concept or skill; they do not initially involve applications outside the parameters of the concepts presented in the model or lead steps. Additional applications are included over time as discussed in the example of counting that appears later in this chapter.

Testing students' knowledge can take several forms: group choral responses, individual turns, independent work, and tests that are part of the full error correction procedure (discussed shortly). Group choral responses are the most common form of tests that occur in the DI programs, which are specified in the lesson scripts. In the counting exercise mentioned earlier in the chapter, steps b and c test students' knowledge of counting lines in separate groups.

Individual turns are often specified in the DI programs. The procedure for conducting an individual turn is for the teacher to *first say the item and then call on an individual student.* This ensures that all students pay close attention to the teacher's directions for the task because their name might be called. Teachers may also use individual turns at any time to verify that students understand the content. It is critical that students demonstrate that they can perform every task to a criterion. So *if a teacher has any doubt about whether an individual student has mastered a task during group instruction, they can call on that student to respond individually.*

During story reading, the teacher should use a system for randomly calling on students to read a couple of sentences at a time, such as pulling popsicle sticks with students' names written on them from a basket. If the teacher doesn't have a system for randomly calling on students and simply asks them to read in a set order, some students may not pay close attention and follow along in their reader because they know they only need to be prepared to read at predictable junctures. If the teacher uses a randomized system, students don't know when it will be their turn to read, which means they must pay attention and be ready to read at any moment.

CORRECT ALL ERRORS

To ensure students master every task in the lessons, teachers should correct all errors that students make. If errors are not corrected, students will not develop a firm foundation for incorporating additional skills and concepts into their repertoire. All errors should be remediated as soon as the teacher recognizes them. If errors are not corrected immediately, the likelihood that the students will remember incorrect answers increases, which will be harder to undo over time. In general, the more times students practice or hear an incorrect response, the more difficult it will be for them to learn and remember the correct response.

In every exercise, the scripts contain such directions as:

(Repeat step __ until firm.)

Repeating until firm means correcting student performance errors and redoing the missed items until all students demonstrate they can perform all tasks in an exercise to mastery.

There are specific formats that teachers should follow when correcting errors. Most of the teacher presentation books contain specific scripts for correcting errors that students commonly make on new tasks when they are first introduced. For instance, the following box appears in Lesson 1, Exercise 4 of *Reading Mastery Signature Edition Grade K*.

> **To Correct**
>
> **(If the children do not say *aaa*:)**
>
> 1. aaa.
> 2. (Touch the first ball of the arrow.) Say it with me. Get ready. **(Move quickly to the second ball of the arrow. Hold for two seconds. Say aaa with the children.)** *aaa*.
> 3. **(Touch the first ball of the arrow.)** Your turn. Get ready. **(Move quickly to the second ball of the arrow. Hold for two seconds.)** *aaa*.

Figure 5.2 Sound correction format. Source: Engelmann, S. and Bruner, E. C. (2008c). *Reading Mastery Signature Edition Grade K Teacher Presentation Book A*, p. 1, © McGraw Hill.

The error correction procedure provides another chance for the teacher to teach the students the skill by following the same model-lead-test procedure of the original teaching presentation. In the "to correct" procedure in Figure 5.2, the teacher:

1. presents the original model, aaa, in step 1
2. provides a lead as she says the sound with the students – "Say aaa with the children" – in step 2
3. tests the students on the task in step 3: Your turn. Get ready.

In this way, DI error corrections involve repeating the original teaching format to provide additional opportunities for students to acquire critical skills and receive reinforcement for their efforts and accomplishments.

Specific error correction scripts appear for a lesson or two in new formats, after which they are discontinued for two reasons. First, the authors assume that teachers will *remember these specific error correction procedures*. Second, discontinuing the correction scripts saves space. If the directions for every possible specific error correction procedure were included in every lesson, the length of the teacher presentation books would increase to the point of becoming unwieldy. Because later lessons incorporate the content of earlier lessons, the scripts of possible error corrections would greatly exceed the rest of the lessons in length by the end of each program level. If teachers have difficulty remembering critical error correction procedures, they can *practice the error corrections as part of their daily lesson preparation.* They can put a "sticky note" or other page marker in the teacher presentation books so they can more easily refer to the lessons where the "to correct" scripts of key correction procedures appear.

Some DI programs do not spell out specific error correction procedures for different formats. Instead, they rely on teachers to apply a generalized correction procedure to different types of errors that appear in the programs. The National Institute for Direct Instruction uses the Part-Firming Paradigm as the generalized correction procedure for teachers to follow when remediating errors (see Figure 5.3).

Correction Procedures for Verbal Tasks:

Every time an error in an exercise occurs:

1. Give the answer (tell, show, or show and tell).
2. Repeat the task (statement or question).
3. Go back and repeat the part. (If you can't figure out what the "part" is, go back at least two things: two sounds, two words, two pictures, or two problems.)

(Repeat steps 1-3 until the whole part is 100% firm—no errors are made)

4. Go to the next part. Repeat parts until all parts are firm.
5. Go back to the beginning of the exercise, if it is a short exercise. In lengthy exercises, go back to those tasks or parts where errors occurred.
6. Give individual turns.
7. Provide a delayed test at least 2 more times (e.g., after the next exercise, at the end of the lesson, in line in the hallway, before lunch).

Figure 5.3 The Part-Firming Paradigm. Reproduced with permission from the National Institute for Direct Instruction.

Step 1 in the Part-Firming Paradigm is a repetition of the model step, during which the teacher demonstrates the correct answer. This is important to do right away rather than withholding the answer and using an alternative strategy, such as asking the student for the answer again, cajoling the student that they should know the correct response, or asking another student to provide the correct answer, which is not a reliable strategy because the second student may provide an incorrect answer. The quickest, most efficient and reliable way to communicate the correct response is for the teacher to model it *immediately*.

Note that there can be some variation in the first step if there is a rule or strategy that the students need to apply. In this case, the teacher should not simply provide the answer; the teacher should refer the students back to the rule or strategy they learned. If the teacher does not prompt students to apply the relevant rule or strategy, students may not learn it, and they may become reliant on the teacher for the correct answers. For instance, if students learn the rule that *two fractions can be added or subtracted only if they have like denominators*, the teacher should prompt students to apply the rule when they commit an error on tasks that ask whether a specific pair of fractions can be added or subtracted.

Suppose students have learned this rule, and they are presented with the following problem:

$$\frac{3}{4} + \frac{5}{4} =$$

When the teacher asks the students, "Can I add these fractions?" some of the students may answer incorrectly, "*No.*" If the teacher uses the simple correction of modeling the answer and then asking the question again (the first two steps in the Part-Firming Paradigm in Figure 5.3), she will say something like, "Yes. I can add these fractions. Can I add these fractions?" When the students repeat the answer and say, "*Yes,*" the teacher has no indication that the students know *why* it is possible to add the fractions as written. So there is no indication that the students won't commit the same or a similar error again in the future. To them, whether fractions can or can't be added or subtracted may seem to be a random chance occurrence because they are not being referred to a rule they can apply.

Here are the first two steps of *a strategy-based correction* for the same error in which the teacher references the relevant rule:

Are the bottom numbers the same?

Yes.

So can I add these fractions?

Yes.

Now the teacher has a strong indication that the students know *why* it is possible to add the fractions as written, and they will be less likely to commit a similar error again in the future. If students make a mistake on either of the questions, the teacher will be able to determine whether a) students don't understand the rule or b) they are not firm on when to apply the rule, which will enable the teacher to correct the specific source of their misapprehension.

In the remaining steps of the Part-Firming Paradigm, the teacher provides additional tests of the missed item and inserts distractors (items different from the missed item) between tests of the missed item. These steps help students remember the correct answers of items they missed. Step 3 provides at least two distractors for the students to respond to. Then the missed item is repeated as part of Step 3. If the student responds correctly, the teacher proceeds to Step 4 and presents the rest of the exercise, which contains more distractors. In Step 5, the teacher provides individual turns *to any of the students who missed the original task.* In Step 6, she gives the class and/or individual students "delayed tests" after two or more minutes have passed. Note that the teacher returns to Step 1 and goes through the entire Part-Firming Paradigm if students make any errors during any of these steps.

If the students answer correctly during each of the test steps indicated in the Part-Firming Paradigm, the probability is high that they will retain the correct information. At the beginning of the next DI lesson and possibly for a day or two thereafter, the teacher can provide a quick test of the items that were difficult for students in order to provide additional practice on the items and ensure that students have mastered the material. Some teachers reserve a part of the whiteboard to write down items that have been difficult for their students, which they review several days in a row.

Correcting student performance errors on verbal tasks across multiple class periods requires the teacher to remember which students committed which errors on which tasks. Teachers can keep a written record of information on students' errors, which can be a formidable undertaking if there are many errors. To keep errors to a minimum, it is important to ensure that students are placed appropriately in the programs. The more that students are placed over their heads in material that is too difficult for them, the more errors there will be for the teacher to track.

In addition to errors on verbal tasks, errors on independent work should be corrected. In the DI approach, the teacher reviews and corrects the work of younger students. Once students are capable of correcting their own work, the teacher reviews the correct answers with students as a group. Students use a red pen to mark their papers and write the correct answers. Monitoring is critical to catch errors and reinforce correct answers in a timely manner. The teacher should scan the workbooks of students while they are engaged in independent work activities so she can intercede as soon as she notices individual errors or a trend of errors among a quarter or more of the students. *If more than 25% of the students make an error on any single independent work item, the teacher reteaches that item to the group.*

Teachers must understand what constitutes an error before they can remediate errors effectively. For most group verbal tasks, the teacher presentation books contain specific wording that students are expected to say in their responses. But for many exercises, the scripts provide a more general indication of what students should say. Open-ended responses are indicated by the word "idea" in the scripts along with a suggestion for acceptable student responses. For instance, consider the following excerpt from the Literature Guide for Grade 4 of *Reading Mastery Signature Edition* as the teacher prepares students to read the story *Hans in Luck*:

> "Hans in Luck" is a type of story called a folktale. Many folktales are old stories that people told aloud. Parents would tell these stories to their children, and when the children became parents

themselves, they would tell the same stories to their own children. Some stories were passed on in this way for hundreds of years without ever being written down.

In the early 1800s, two brothers from Germany named Jacob and Wilhelm Grimm began listening to folktales and writing them down. The folktales they collected were from Germany and other countries in Europe. Many of these folktales were hundreds of years old.

How did people pass on the folktales without writing them down? (Idea: Parents told them to their children.)

About how long ago did the brothers Grimm begin collecting folktales? (Idea: About 200 years ago.)

Where did these folktales come from? (Ideas: Germany; other countries in Europe.) (Engelmann, S. et al., 2008e, 8.)

In this exercise, the students *do not need to produce the exact wording* that appears in the teacher presentation book as long as they convey the general idea indicated in the script. So it would be an error for the students to say that the folktales collected by the Brothers Grimm came from South America, but it would not be an error for them to say that the folktales came from "different parts of Europe" or similar answers that convey that general meaning. Making students repeat the phrase "other countries in Europe" would not only be inefficient, but it would also discourage students from expressing their thoughts in their own words, which is an important part of the learning process.

Note that teachers might want to include other criteria for acceptable responses to open-ended questions. For instance, some teachers require students at this level to answer questions in complete sentences. They consider a response containing only a sentence fragment to be an error, and they ask students who answer in incomplete sentences to answer again in a complete sentence.

Note also that there is another class of errors that doesn't relate to incorrect answers. This class has to do with behavioral "errors," the most common of which is the signal violation, discussed later in this chapter.

MANAGE STUDENT BEHAVIORS POSITIVELY

Managing student behavior is an integral part of Direct Instruction. Students must be motivated to focus their attention for long periods of time, respond frequently, and repeat material to mastery. To prompt students to try their best, teachers should use techniques that reinforce behaviors that facilitate instruction.

The goals of behavior management in the DI approach are closely tied to the overarching goal of accelerating the performance of every student through efficient and effective instruction. A successful behavior management system maximizes:

1. the amount of time devoted to *on-task* instructional time daily
2. the level of student effort.

These two goals of behavior management are usually complementary, although there can be a trade-off between maximizing the amount of instructional time and encouraging students. An excessive amount of time spent on reinforcing activities can slow lesson progress. In general, teachers should favor quicker types of reinforcement that maintain the momentum of instruction as much as possible.

There are several different levels of instructional time. Two of the most important are *allocated instructional time* and *on-task instructional time*. Allocated instructional time – the amount of time scheduled in the timetable for a particular subject – does not equal the amount of time during which teaching actually takes place, which can be characterized as on-task instructional time (also known as *engaged time*). The difference between these two categories of time includes any off-task behavior as well as transitions that occur into and out of activities in the instructional setting.

During transitions between instructional activities, students perform several steps in succession. These may include:

- putting away materials used in the prior activity (or coats and hats if students are coming from outside)
- forming the proper student groupings required for the new activity, which may involve walking to another classroom

- taking assigned seats for the new activity
- accessing appropriate materials for the new activity
- locating the proper place within the materials
- turning their attention to the teacher.

The speed with which each of these steps occurs translates into a higher percentage of allocated instructional time that is on-task time. Time students spend finding their seat, searching for materials, thumbing through pages to find today's lesson, etc. reduces the amount of on-task time. Teachers can increase this speed by challenging students to be ready in less time than they took yesterday and praising them for a fast transition time.

During instruction, students' attention should continue to be on the lesson in order to maximize on-task time. Otherwise, small delays can add up to large amounts of time over the course of the day, which is compounded over weeks and months to constitute a significant amount of learning time. Just six minutes a day lost to transitions or inefficiencies during instruction can have serious implications for students' success in the long run. Six minutes a day adds up to half an hour a week, two hours per month, 20 hours per year, or 120 hours that could have been spent on instruction for a student who started DI in kindergarten by the end of Grade 5. In several DI programs, teachers have been able to complete or nearly complete a full level of the program in 120 hours of instruction. So for many students, losing just six minutes a day could mean the difference between performing at grade level and performing significantly below grade level. For similar reasons teachers should teach "from bell to bell" for the full amount of allocated instructional time. If teachers finish a lesson but have time left in the period, they should use the remaining time to firm students on critical parts of the lesson or proceed to the next lesson in the program. Otherwise, students could lose critical academic learning time at the end of instructional periods.

The amount of engaged time can be maximized by establishing efficient routines and expectations for students. To be most effective, teachers should teach each of the steps in a routine separately and then combine the steps once the students have mastered each step. Teachers should briefly model each step explicitly with negative as well as positive examples. For example, when a teacher demonstrates the step of *standing up from a table and pushing the chair in*, the teacher can provide a negative example of pushing the chair in part way so it's askew or being very noisy, then end with a positive model of pushing the chair in correctly. The teacher should narrate what she is doing and explain how one demonstration meets her standards and the other demonstration does not. Then, students should practice each step separately to mastery within a time limit. While they are doing this, the teacher should give feedback to students with an emphasis on specific praise for fast and efficient behavior. The brief amount of time devoted to these practice sessions during the first week of school can pay great dividends later as students move easily and quickly from one activity to another with positive feedback from their teacher.

The National Institute for Direct Instruction has translated several of the most important instructional behaviors into a "bank of games" with teacher scripts and directions. Here is the "Pencils Up/Pencils Down" game:

Pencils Up/Pencils Down: (1 minute round)

- Play game for 1 minute (after attendance, before reading or before starting a group activity).
- Make sure all students have a pencil.
- Determine a place or spot on the desk where the pencil is to remain when not in use. You can say the pencil is **"parked."**
- **Say: "Boys and girls, it's time to play the Pencils up/Pencils down game."**
- **"Please park your pencil and then listen for my directions."** Continue once all pencils are parked.
- **"Pencils up."** Wait 5 seconds – scan for pencils in air. **"Pencils down."** Scan for "parked" pencils.
- Play at least 3 times awarding students points (per the Teacher/ Student game) each time all students follow directions completely.

- Add a writing direction to the final practice. **Say: "Pencils up, write your name, pencils down when done."**

- After introducing students to the game, shorten the 5-second scan. The goal is to have students consistently complete the task in 1-2 seconds.

Reprinted with permission from the National Institute for Direct Instruction.

The second-to-last step in the "game" above can be expanded to include more complex activities in addition to students writing their name. After students have played this game several times over a few days with adequate reinforcement, instructional sessions involving writing or workbooks will go much smoother. As with all of the instructional games, separate practice sessions may be needed after breaks or holidays to maintain student performance at a high level.

The Teacher/Student game is mentioned in the third-to-last bullet in the set of directions above. Unlike the "Pencils Up/Pencils Down" game, the Teacher/Student game is not related directly to a routine. Instead, it is a point system used to reinforce appropriate behaviors and eliminate or reduce behaviors that interfere with instruction. This point system complements the point systems built into *Corrective Reading* and other programs to reinforce students for successfully meeting specific performance criteria described in the teacher presentation books. For the Teacher/Student game, the teacher awards points to herself when students don't adhere to a rule or follow a direction, and she awards points to the students for working hard, following the rules, and successfully accomplishing tasks. Points are always awarded; they are never erased or taken away. Once the teacher or student earns a point, it remains part of their total score until the game is ended, which can be at the end of the instructional period or the end of the day. An overall objective is for the students to earn more points than the teacher so the instructional sessions are reinforcing to them. The teacher can even challenge students to get 10 points more than the teacher for a special reward. At the same time, the teacher can shape unwanted student behaviors, such as answering before the teacher signals the group to respond, to make the instructional sessions more conducive to student learning.

The Teacher/Student game scoring chart should be readily accessible to the teacher during instruction so they can add points or direct the students' attention to the chart easily. The T/S game can be "played" on a whiteboard or sticky note, or projected on a screen as long as the teacher doesn't need to move far or reach awkwardly to add points. It should be displayed so the students as well as the teacher can see it. If it isn't within the view of the students, they can't see how well they are doing in the game.

For the game to be effective in reinforcing behaviors selectively, the teacher should narrate very specifically why they are awarding points. If the teacher awards points silently without indicating why, the students will not know what they are doing that meets or doesn't meet the teacher's expectations, which would prevent the game from functioning as an effective communication tool. It is also ineffectual for the teacher to award points accompanied by general comments, such as "you earned another point," or "another point for me," if the students do not know why the points are being awarded. Instead, the teacher should *accompany the awarding of each point with the specific reason why it's being awarded.* For instance:

"You said every sound on that page correctly. Two points for you!"

Or

"I need to see everyone's eyes on the book. Point for me!"

Critical behaviors can be translated into a set of rules or procedures that can be posted where the teacher and students can see them. The rules should be simple so students can memorize them easily. One common set of rules for younger students during group instruction follows the STAR acronym:

- **S**it tall
- **T**alk big
- **A**nswer together
- **R**espect others.

Similar rules can be established for independent work. These rules help reduce the amount of explanation that the teacher needs to provide when awarding points. If the students meet all the criteria for the STAR set of rules, instead of listing each behavior separately, the teacher can simply say, "Three points for the group for meeting all of the STAR rules!"

Note that the STAR rules are stated positively, not negatively. In his book, *Teaching Behavior: Managing Classrooms Through Effective Instruction*, Terrance M. Scott explains the rationale for wording rules positively about what students *are* expected to do instead of what they are *not* expected to do:

> Effective rules are taught in a positive manner. That is, we teach the student what we want him or her to do as opposed to what we don't want. While this seems reasonable, rules for behavior are very often written in [a] negative manner: no running, no talking, no hitting. This is not the way we teach academics. We would never see a teacher say, "on the board are 10 incorrect answers to this problem. Memorize them all." It makes far more sense to simply tell students what we want them to do. (Scott, 2017, 81)

When providing feedback to students on their performance, the overall ratios of positive-to-negative statements and points should be overwhelmingly positive. A widely accepted minimum ratio for effectively reinforcing students is 4:1, although Marchand-Martella, Blakely and Schaefer cite a ratio of about 9:1 for DI programs (Marchand-Martella, Blakely and Schaefer, 2004, 319). Many of the lessons in the DI programs have built-in specific, affirmative praise statements, such as the following excerpt from Lesson 14 of *Connecting Math Concepts Comprehensive Edition Level A*:

> How many pennies were in the cup? (Signal.) 8.
>
> You counted the pennies as I dropped them into the cup.
>
> Good for you.
>
> (Engelmann, S. and Engelmann, O., 2012a, 166)

These built-in praise statements can serve as models to teachers for giving additional praise to students. In order to reach the minimum of four positives to one negative, teachers may need to generate many additional positive statements in each exercise, and the number of positives must increase if students make errors. Because error corrections, however nicely executed by the teachers, are negative statements, teachers need to generate more positive statements to compensate for every error students make to maintain a 4:1 ratio. (If the Part-Firming Paradigm is followed, there will be several opportunities for additional positive feedback for each error as students perform correctly on delayed tests.) For this reason alone, it is critically important that students should be placed at their performance level. If students are placed in material that is too difficult for them, the number of errors will make it impossible for the teacher to provide students with sufficient positive feedback, and students' motivation to work can be expected to diminish as the group spends a higher-than-expected amount of time working on remediating student errors.

Completion of a lesson can be further delayed if students do not adhere to basic behavioral expectations of group instruction. Instructional material needs to be repeated if students cannot produce a full choral response. If a student does not respond on signal and does not answer along with their peers, for example, this is an error. The remedy is for the teacher to communicate the error and have the group repeat the task. Then the teacher starts the exercise over from the beginning or at least backs up a couple of items to introduce some distractors. For instance, if a student answers before the signal on a math addition problem, the teacher might say, "Oh! Everyone needs to wait for my signal! Let's do that again. What is 5 + 8? That's right, 13. Okay, starting over." It is most efficient for the teacher to *focus on these "signal violation" errors early in the school year to ensure that students can perform as a cohesive instructional group as soon as possible*. Otherwise, students' progress through the program can be hampered throughout the school year as the teacher is forced to repeat material because students don't produce consistent choral responses.

To help encourage students, and to help achieve proper praise ratios, teachers should *praise students for improvements in their performance*. If students were only able to count by fours to 16 yesterday but are able to count by fours to 24 today, the teacher should reinforce the students for improvement. This is especially important for the teacher to do when students have been struggling with a task. The more students have been struggling, the more the teacher should recognize their accomplishments when they finally perform the task successfully. Reinforcing students for effort helps motivate them to persevere in the face of adversity. This approach can be applied to signal violations, too. When students respond as a group to the teacher's signal, the teacher can say, "Look at how you answered together on all of the words on this page! Two extra points for you!"

To help improve students' behavior as well as achieve the 4:1 positive-to-negative feedback ratio, teachers should "catch kids in the act of being good," a slogan made popular by Wesley C. Becker, co-founder of Direct Instruction. Directing attention toward the desired behavior and away from inappropriate behavior serves the dual purpose of reinforcing the former and reducing the latter. As Becker, S. Engelmann, and Thomas explain:

> *Make the misbehavior of one child the signal to find and praise another child who is behaving well.* For example, if Johnny is out of his seat when he should be sitting working on an assignment, the teacher might say, "I see Jimmy is in his seat and doing a good job working on his arithmetic." This may prompt Johnny to return to his seat and begin to work, at which time the teacher might say, "Johnny, Carol and Mike are being good workers." Making the *misbehavior* the signal to praise someone else does two things: first, it immediately takes the teacher's attention away from the misbehavior; and second, it gives the misbehaving child a gentle prompt as to what he should be doing. If the teacher is praising Jimmy, she can't be criticizing Johnny. Thus, if the teacher follows this rule, she will praise more and criticize less. (Becker, Engelmann, S. and Thomas, 1975, 70–71)

In general, the teacher should praise the desired behaviors that are incompatible with the problem behaviors that caused the teacher to earn a point. If the teacher got a point for a signal violation, the group should receive points when they answer on signal. If the teacher got a point for "eyes not on me," the group should then get points when their eyes are "on the teacher."

Teachers may find it motivating for students to have medium- and long-term goals they are working for with celebrations to match the goals. A goal can be for students to finish a storybook or a level of the program or for all of the students to complete their mastery tests without any errors. Teachers can use a thermometer chart system for independent work and establish goals themselves at regular intervals for students to meet. (Information on thermometer charts is available at www.nifdi. org/services/training/in-service-training/video-in-services.html.) When students meet the goals, there should be a celebration. Table 5.3 lists some examples of celebrations that are educational versus recreational.

Ideas for intermediate goal celebrations (about 10-15 minutes)	Ideas for final goal celebrations (up to a whole class period long)
Educational— • teacher reads a story • trip to the library • spelling (or trivia) bee • construct homework notebooks • pencils, bookmarks or other school supplies • read to another class • Mad Libs *Non-educational—* • popcorn, ice cream, fruit roll-ups, or other snack • prize ribbons, buttons, grab bag • sing/have radio on • Hangman, BINGO, 7-Up, Simon Says, or other game • puzzles, coloring • secret message from the teacher for class to decode • extra recess	*Educational—* • write and perform a short skit • write and perform a song/rap • help design/post a bulletin board • free choice reading • activity centers • instructional video *Non-educational—* • pizza party • ice cream sundae party • work together in hobby groups • magic tricks/experiments • movie • lunch in the classroom • board game party (with favorites brought in from home) *Note:* • any of the ideas for intermediate goals, but for a longer period of time.

Table 5.3 Intermediate and end-goal celebration ideas. Reprinted with permission from the National Institute for Direct Instruction.

Celebrations should not be overlong. In many cases, accomplishing the goal and the positive attention from the teacher are sufficient to reinforce students for their work. Celebrations only need to last long enough for the students to feel a sense of satisfaction and accomplishment. They shouldn't last so long that behavioral problems might develop. If behavioral problems are a concern, the celebration can take the form of a structured game with clear roles for students to fulfill. Mini-celebrations lasting just a few seconds to half a minute can be inserted throughout a lesson to celebrate the completion of difficult exercises and the attainment of smaller goals. Imitating peeling a banana, setting off fireworks, or riding on a roller coaster while still seated in the instructional setting are examples of quick ways of reinforcing students for working hard while taking only a short break in academic learning.

In many well-implemented DI classrooms, the motivation of students seems to grow year after year. As teachers become more familiar with the DI programs, they anticipate which exercises or concepts might be the most difficult for students to master. They present these exercises as positive challenges to students and provide praise and encouragement for every successful step toward mastery. Experienced teachers also know the major benchmarks in the program – when students have been introduced to all of the sounds, when they complete their first word problem, when they have learned all of the months of the year or days of the week – and they use the instructional groups' attainment of each benchmark to celebrate student success. The teacher builds up students' anticipation of future lessons by giving them hints about the stories they will read and the great things they will learn in the coming weeks. Students look forward with confidence to whatever the teacher presents to them. They feel they can learn anything in the program or any outside material that comes their way.

APPLY SKILLS AND CONCEPTS BEYOND THE PROGRAMS

The DI programs are carefully designed to prevent "stipulation," the incorrect conceptualization by students that can develop if the range of examples presented in the program is too narrow and does not represent a broad application of a skill or concept. The initial setup for teaching a new skill or concept in the DI programs is carefully controlled to help students focus on the relevant variables as examples are expanded to indicate the full range of the applicability of the skill or concept. For example, the very first lesson of *Connecting Math Concepts: Comprehensive Edition Level A* uses a broad range of examples to introduce students to two important aspects of counting – counting to a number from one and counting objects. In steps a through d in Exercise 1 shown in Figure 5.4, the teacher models counting the cardinal numbers from one and ending at different numbers: three, six, five, and four. This prevents students from stipulating that "counting" involves ending at a certain number, like three or 10. (In later exercises, students practice starting from different numbers to prevent students from stipulating that counting always starts with the number one.) In step g, the teacher models how to count objects by touching and counting the images of four identical tigers. In Exercise 5 of the same lesson, shown in Figure 5.5, students are presented with similar tasks to those in Exercise 1 except that they count skunks instead of tigers, which prevents students from stipulating that counting is an action applicable only to a particular type of object.

Lesson

EXERCISE 1: ROTE COUNTING—*Count to 4*

Note: (Do not display the page until step g.)

a. Listen to me count: 1, 2, 3. I ended up with 3.
 • Once more: 1, 2, 3. What number did I end up with? (Signal.) 3.
 Yes, 3.
 (Repeat step a until firm—children's response is correct and on cue)

b. Listen: 1, 2, 3, 4, 5, 6. What number did I end up with? (Signal.) 6.
 Yes, 6.

c. Listen: 1, 2, 3, 4, 5. What number did I end up with? (Signal.) 5.

d. Listen again: 1, 2, 3, 4. What number? (Signal.) 4.

e. Let's all count and end up with 4. Every time I tap, you count. Get ready. (Tap 4 as you say with children) 1, 2, 3, 4.
 (Repeat step e until firm.)

f. Your turn: Count and end up with 4. Get ready. (Tap 4.) 1, 2, 3, 4.
 (Repeat step f until firm.)
 • Do it once more, and I'll show you a picture of 4. Count and end up with 4. Get ready. (Tap 4.) 1, 2, 3, 4.
 • (Display page.) [1:1A]

g. Here's a picture of 4. The picture shows 4 tigers.
 What are these 4 things? (Signal.) *Tigers.*
 Yes, these 4 things are tigers.
 • Listen: I know how many tigers there are. 4.
 I'll count them. (Touch and count) 1, 2, 3, 4.
 • Everybody, how many tigers? (Signal.) 4.
 (Repeat step g until firm.)

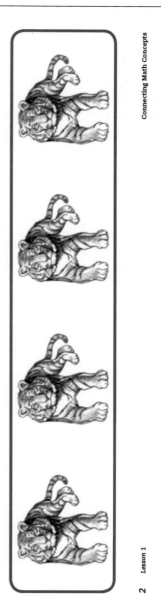

Connecting Math Concepts

2   Lesson 1

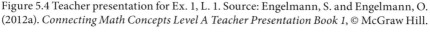

Figure 5.4 Teacher presentation for Ex. 1, L. 1. Source: Engelmann, S. and Engelmann, O. (2012a). *Connecting Math Concepts Level A Teacher Presentation Book 1*, © McGraw Hill.

177

EXERCISE 5: ROTE COUNTING—*Count to 5*

Note: (Do not display the page until step g.)

a. Listen to me count: 1, 2, 3, 4, 5. I ended up with 5. Once more: 1, 2, 3, 4, 5. What number did I end up with? (Signal.) *5.*
   Yes, 5.
   (Repeat step a until firm.)

b. Listen: 1, 2, 3, 4, 5, 6. What number did I end up with? (Signal.) *6.*

c. Listen: 1, 2, 3, 4. What number did I end up with? (Signal.) *4.*

d. Listen: 1, 2, 3, 4. What number did I end up with? (Signal.) *4.*

e. Let's all count and end up with 4. Every time I tap, you count. Get ready. (Tap 4 as you say with children) *1, 2, 3, 4.*
   (Repeat step e until firm.)

f. Your turn: Count and end up with 4. Get ready. (Tap 4.)
   1, 2, 3, 4.
   (Repeat step f until firm.)

   • Do it once more, and I'll show you a picture of 4. Count and end up with 4. Get ready. (Tap 4.) *1, 2, 3, 4.*   [1:5A]

g. (Display page.)
   Are these tigers? (Signal.) *No.*

   • These are skunks. What are these 4 things? (Signal.) *Skunks.*
   Yes, they are skunks.
   Did you ever smell a skunk? Stiiinky.

h. Listen: I know how many skunks there are. 4. I'll count them. (Touch and count) *1, 2, 3, 4.*

   • Everybody, how many skunks? (Signal.) *4.*
   (Repeat step h until firm.)

Connecting Math Concepts

6   Lesson 1

Figure 5.5 Teacher presentation for Ex. 5, L. 1. Source: Engelmann, S. and Engelmann, O. (2012a). *Connecting Math Concepts Level A Teacher Presentation Book 1*, © McGraw Hill.

The range of the types of objects is expanded in subsequent lessons. Here are the numbers of different objects that students count in the first six lessons of the program:

Lesson and Exercise	Objects Counted	Terminal Number
L. 1, Ex. 1	tigers	4
L. 1, Ex. 5	skunks	4
L. 2, Ex. 1	noses	3
L. 2, Ex. 4	tables	4
L. 3, Ex. 1	tails	3
L. 3, Ex. 5	ears	5
L. 4, Ex. 1	feet	5
L. 4, Ex. 4	cars	2
L. 5, Ex. 1	pigs	4
L. 5, Ex. 4	dogs	5
L. 6, Ex. 3	birds	4
L. 6, Ex. 3	birds	5

Table 5.4 Counting exercises in Lessons 1–6 of *Connecting Math Concepts: Comprehensive Edition Level A.*

As Table 5.4 shows, the first six lessons of the program involve students counting a wide range of objects (animals, inanimate objects, human body parts, animal body parts) with a variety of numbers of objects (2–5) to help prevent students from developing a misunderstanding about the nature of counting. In addition, in Lesson 6, the students learn to *count objects in a different order* – first from left to right, and then right to left – which prevents them from developing a misrule that counting is an action that only applies to objects in a particular order. Students also learn to count events, such as the number of times the teacher claps, which further expands their conceptual understanding of counting.

Teachers can help ensure that students generalize their learning to different examples beyond the DI programs. For beginning mathematics, teachers can ask students to count different objects when they are lining up to go to lunch or during a short break. They can count the number of desks in a row, the number of windows in a classroom or the number of times the teacher points at the ceiling. The teacher should make sure that the students can count to the terminal number, and she should be prepared to correct any errors the students might make by repeating the counting until all students can perform to mastery.

For language arts, extra practice outside of the program facilitates students' acquisition of new vocabulary words. Different applications of the same word in different contexts can help students consolidate their understanding of the meaning of words. Taking advantage of "teachable moments" can be an effective strategy for building students' vocabulary. If "envelope" is a vocabulary word in the reading lesson and a student walks in from the office with a large envelope, the teacher can take a moment to show everyone that the word "envelope" applies to large envelopes as well as small ones. Teachers can also plan for extra practice in critical vocabulary or information. When they do, they should make explicit connections between new information and information students have already mastered. If students are going to see a short film on France, for instance, the teacher can show where France is located on a globe in relation to the countries that Herman the Fly visited in the Grade 2 level of the *Reading Mastery* program. By activating prior knowledge that students have acquired in the DI program and relating new learning to it, the teacher can help students solidify their knowledge base as they expand their understanding of the subject matter.

The DI reading programs offer several vehicles for students to apply the knowledge they acquire in the programs to outside activities. The reading track of the *Reading Mastery Signature Edition* includes a set of five research projects for each level of the program in Grades 2–5. The projects are designed to help students develop their research skills as they build on the knowledge they acquire in the main program. Each project contains specific objectives related to content covered in the main program. Here is the research objective for *What's Bugging You?*, the second project of the Grade 2 level of the program:

Objective:

Many insects experience several stages of life. Just as Herman began life as an egg, emerged as a worm/maggot, then changed into a fly, other insects also go through life stages. Using a variety of resources, find out about other insects that experience several life stages. Use visual aids, such as models or cartoons, to show the life stages of the insect you have chosen to study and share what you have learned with your classmates. (*SRA Research Projects Grade 2*, 2008, 8)

Each research project comes with blackline masters that students use to organize their research and to evaluate their presentations, which are based on their research. Because each project builds upon specific content of a lesson in the main program, the projects should be introduced *after* students have completed the designated lessons.

The *Corrective Reading Decoding* programs come with additional activities that are part of the *Core Resource Connections*, a supplementary resource that includes leveled passages "designed to help students improve their overall comprehension and vocabulary and to give students additional practice applying reading strategies and skills" (*SRA Core Resource Connections Decoding B1*, 2013, 1). There are numerous passages for each level of the program, and each passage is accompanied by comprehension questions requiring multiple-choice, fill-in-the-blank, or short-answer written responses.

Some levels of the language strand of *Reading Mastery Signature Edition* also offer extension activities. In the *Story Construction* track of the Grade 2 language program, for example, students work cooperatively in mixed ability groups to write stories or plays involving characters from stories in the program. The exercises in this track provide students with a set of prompts that they follow when composing stories or plays. This structure can provide a model for the students to follow if the teacher assigns additional cooperative activities for the students to do as extensions of the stories in the program.

Whether teachers use the extension activities that are provided as part of the DI programs or create other opportunities for students to apply their knowledge outside of the program, teachers will need to be mindful of their wording and example choices and use effective instructional practices that lead to successful outcomes for all students. The next chapter addresses these practices as it describes the distinction between authentic Direct Instruction and lower-case direct instruction techniques.

CHAPTER SIX
UPPER-CASE DI, LOWER-CASE DI, AND EXPLICIT INSTRUCTION

INTRODUCTION

The information in the preceding chapters provides a basis for addressing the differences between authentic or upper-case Direct Instruction (DI) and lower-case di, also known as *explicit instruction*. The main difference between the two is that capital DI involves instruction using the published DI programs, which incorporate the design elements discussed in the previous chapters of this book. These design elements are also described more fully in *Theory of Instruction* (Engelmann, S. and Carnine, 1991) and *Rubric for Identifying Authentic Direct Instruction Programs* (Engelmann, S. and Colvin, 2006). Lower-case di and explicit instruction do not involve the implementation of published DI programs and so do not incorporate many of the design elements inherent in the programs. Instead, lower-case di emphasizes the teaching practices that are integral to the delivery of the DI programs without using the programs themselves. In other words, lower-case di involves implementing a specific pedagogy, not a specific program that involves a similar pedagogy.

The actual usage of the terms doesn't always follow this clear-cut distinction. For example, in a recently published article in the *National Review*, Baker A. Mitchell, Jr. uses the term "direct instruction" to describe the teaching methodology employed at four charter schools in southeastern North Carolina involving two published DI programs, *Language for Learning* and *Reading Mastery* (Mitchell, 2020). Conversely,

Sarah Barker, assistant headteacher in Bristol, England, uses the term "Direct Instruction" in upper case when she refers to techniques such as *brain dumps* ("students ... write down everything they know about an element of previous learning") and *think-pair-share* (students contemplate answers to a question related to previous learning, share their ideas with a partner, and then report back to the class), which are not used in the DI programs (Barker, 2019, 112). This variation in the way the terms are used has the potential to lead to confusion about the precise instructional methodology that is being used.

This chapter describes the differences between the terms DI and di/ explicit instruction with the purpose not of establishing an orthodoxy of definitions but to provide a suggested nomenclature that can facilitate practitioners' discussions of instruction, student learning, and educational reform. It is important for practitioners from the same school or district to establish a common nomenclature before adopting a new instructional approach or reform model. Without a common vocabulary, it is very difficult for a group of practitioners to select and effectively implement an instructional reform model. This chapter outlines the origins and early development of DI/di to establish the context for defining the terms. It then compares the specific practices of DI with the practices described in two of the most prominent sources on lower-case direct instruction: Barak Rosenshine's "Principles of Instruction" (Rosenshine, 2012) and *Explicit Instruction: Effective and Efficient Teaching* (Archer and Hughes, 2011). This chapter also addresses the implications to teachers of implementing di versus DI, and it provides recommendations on the appropriate role of lower-case di in classrooms that are implementing the published DI programs.

SIEGFRIED ENGELMANN'S DIRECT INSTRUCTION

Rosenshine indicates that "the term direct instruction has been used for over a century to refer to any academic instruction that is led by the teacher" (Rosenshine, 2008). The use of "direct instruction" in this manner implies direct teaching but does not imply a systematic approach to instruction. The first known use of the term to refer to *a specific system of instruction* in contrast to simply teacher-led instruction was by Carl

Bereiter and S. Engelmann in *Teaching Disadvantaged Children in the Preschool*, published in 1966, to describe the approach they used in their groundbreaking preschool program at the University of Illinois. (The positive effect of this preschool program was discussed in chapter 1.) So although S. Engelmann is best known as the developer of upper-case Direct Instruction, he was also a pioneer in developing lower-case di. In *Teaching Disadvantaged Children in the Preschool*, the authors explained some of the benefits of the "direct-instruction approach" vis-à-vis less structured approaches to improving the academic outcomes of at-risk preschoolers:

> The direct-instruction approach ensures that every objective can at least be attended to, and it gives the teacher better day-to-day control over pupil progress so that she will know what objectives need additional attention. (Bereiter and Engelmann, 1966, 51)

In the Bereiter–Engelmann preschool, the instructors did not use scripts or published programs to deliver instruction. Instead, they followed 18 teaching strategies to provide instruction to the preschool children:

1. Work at different levels of difficulty at different times.
2. Adhere to a rigid, repetitive presentation pattern.
3. Use unison responses whenever possible.
4. Never work with a child individually in a study group for more than about 30 seconds.
5. Phrase statements rhythmically.
6. Require children to speak in a loud, clear voice.
7. Do not hurry children or encourage them to talk fast.
8. Clap to accent basic language patterns and conventions.
9. Use questions liberally.
10. Use repetition.
11. Be aware of the cues the child is receiving.
12. Use short explanations.
13. Tailor the explanations and rules to what the child knows.
14. Use lots of examples.

15. Prevent incorrect responses whenever possible.

16. Be completely unambiguous in letting the child know when his response is correct and when it is incorrect.

17. Dramatize the use value of learning whenever possible.

18. Encourage thinking behavior. (Bereiter and Engelmann, 1966, 120)

The authors cautioned that:

> Each of these apparently simple rules requires a considerable amount of skill if it is to be executed successfully ... The actual skill can only be acquired through disciplined experience. (Bereiter and Engelmann, 1966, 120)

As mentioned previously in this book, teachers who attempted to learn the direct instruction approach from S. Engelmann experienced great difficulty in constructing coherent and effective instructional sequences with appropriate examples as they taught, which led Engelmann to develop scripts that provided the examples, directions, and specific wording that characterize the DI programs today.

This list can be considered a first draft of recommended teaching strategies as it differs in many ways with subsequent lists of effective strategies discussed later in this chapter. However, there are some items that appear in later lower-case di lists, such as #9 "use questions liberally" and #14 "use lots of examples." As Bereiter and Engelmann explain in *Teaching Disadvantaged Children in the Preschool*, successful teaching involves not just using a lot of examples, but examples that are selected and arranged to convey the intended meaning faultlessly which, as indicated in strategy #15, would "prevent incorrect responses whenever possible."

The last two strategies in the list are critical for motivating students, yet they are often omitted from later definitions of direct instruction. Strategy #17 – "dramatize the use value of learning" – involves the teacher establishing tasks that they know students can perform accurately as being difficult and then exhibiting surprise at students' success. To implement this strategy, a teacher presents a task as something that is very challenging that only smart students can accomplish. The teacher expresses doubt that the students can actually perform the task correctly because it is so "tough." She says statements such as:

"This is really tough stuff"

or

"This is something that kids in the next grade up are doing."

Then, when the students successfully perform the task, the teacher indicates that this is an impressive accomplishment. She says statements like:

"You got it correct the first time! That's unbelievable!!"

The students, being logical learners, conclude that they must be smart. If the task can only be accomplished by someone who's smart, and they performed the task correctly, then they must be smart students. This affirmation of their abilities encourages them to work hard in the future and succeed.

This strategy (#17) involves realizing the obvious fact that learning new skills and concepts can be difficult for students even if they appear easy to accomplished learners. From an adult's perspective, learning to decode simple words or count to 50 may seem like simple tasks, but from the perspective of a learner who has not mastered these skills, these tasks are, in fact, quite challenging. Strategy #17 prompts the teacher to view instruction from the students' perspective. In contrast, the opposite strategy can be devastating to students' self-esteem. If the teacher says that a task is easy, but then the students aren't able to perform the task, the logical conclusion is that they are less-than-capable learners.

The last strategy in the list, #18 – "encourage thinking behavior" – is also critical for students' motivation. This strategy involves reinforcing students for trying to apply what has been covered in past lessons even if they don't get the correct answer. For instance, if students attempt to set up an equation from a word problem, but they use the wrong operation (addition instead of subtraction, for example), they should be reinforced for trying to apply what they've learned about setting up equations despite using the incorrect operation, especially if they have shown improvement in setting up equations over time.

Both of these strategies indicate that, from the outset, the DI approach was very sensitive to students and very humane – not robotic as some have claimed. The method's creators focused on the emotional as well as intellectual development of children, both of which are critical to their academic success.

Just a few years after publishing the first list of teaching strategies, S. Engelmann generated another list of strategies that appeared in *Preventing Failure in the Primary Grades*. This list retained some of the strategies of the former list but made significant changes as the approach was being refined:

1. Group the children in a way that will make it possible to work with them effectively.
2. Teach children in a way that provides maximum feedback on what they are learning and where they are having difficulty.
3. Make use of the feedback.
4. Gear the presentation to the lowest member of the group.
5. Don't be afraid of looking bad.
6. Make maximum use of study periods; reduce homework to a minimum.
7. *Learn to isolate the concepts.*
8. *Don't use complicated demonstrations; always seek the simplest form in which to present a concept.*
9. *Don't correct the child by appealing to his intuition or his thinking habits – program rules for thinking.*
10. Preserve the child's self-image, but tell him when his answers are wrong.
11. Give the children ample evidence that they are capable of learning.
12. *Structure the teaching sessions so that the children work for no more than 5 to 8 minutes on a particular series of tasks.*
13. *Use fun examples in tasks with a payoff.*
14. *Concentrate on those aspects of the curriculum that can be accelerated.* (Engelmann, S., 1969a, 41–60)

The continuity of the list of strategies is not always apparent from their titles. For instance, strategy #17 from the first list – "dramatize the use value of learning" – is incorporated into strategy #11 from the second list – "give the children ample evidence that they are capable of learning."

Strategy #5 from this later list is a unique appeal to teachers and support staff. "Looking bad" doesn't have to do with physical appearance, such as hairdos or clothing styles. Instead, this strategy is an admonishment to teachers and support staff to realize that students may not always perform perfectly, and that instruction involves students making errors and learning from them. The strategy calls on teachers to correct errors and repeat steps no matter who is observing because that's what's best for children. If teachers avoid correcting student errors just to make a positive impression on observers, they lose the opportunity to provide the instruction that the students need in that moment to advance their understanding of the skills and concepts addressed in the lesson. Ignoring mistakes and omitting corrections may give a more positive impression of the instruction taking place in the classroom to some observers, but providing this impression is to the long-term detriment of the students. Instead, the long-term benefit of the students should always be the main orientation of teachers and support staff. Coaches and other school leaders should recognize that effective classroom instruction does not always mean perfect performance by the students. In fact, if students never make any errors, the material is not challenging enough for them, and students should be presented with more advanced lessons so they have the opportunity to learn skills and concepts they haven't mastered yet.

Several of the strategies in the lists were incorporated into the DI programs when they were published starting in the late 1960s. This includes all of the items concerning the use of questions, short explanations, and numerous examples in the first list. It also includes all of the italicized items in the second list: numbers 7, 8, 9, 12, 13, and 14. With the published programs, teachers no longer need to: select the tasks to present and figure out how many lessons the tasks should appear in; determine the order in which to present the tasks; identify the specific examples that are used to present skills and concepts; construct specific corrections for different types of response errors; or decide how and when student mastery should be assessed and how to remediate students based on their performance on these assessments. The printed instructional programs ensure that these strategies are in place as long as the teachers faithfully follow the lessons' directions. This is a critically important advantage of the scripts. Published programs that incorporate these and other design elements relieve the teacher of being an instructional designer, which allows them to concentrate on their delivery of the program and their response to students' performance and behavior. Teachers using the scripted programs still have plenty of aspects of teaching they need to focus on to ensure that instruction is effective for all students.

FROM LOWER-CASE DI TO UPPER-CASE DI IN SIEGFRIED ENGELMANN'S WORK

The success of the Bereiter–Engelmann preschool at the University of Illinois in the mid-1960s provided an impetus for expanding the application of the direct instruction approach. The opportunity to expand the number of schools implementing the method was given a big boost when it was selected as one of the models to participate in Project Follow Through (1968–77), the largest educational experiment in the history of the United States (see Topic Brief 8). S. Engelmann and colleagues were faced with an existential problem: how could the number of teachers who were capable of implementing the approach be increased to support a rapid scale-up of the number of implementations? The solution was to develop scripts that detail all aspects of the presentation and corrections inherent in the approach.

The lists that appeared in *Teaching Disadvantaged Children in the Preschool* and *Preventing Failure in the Primary Grades* were not sufficient for teachers to learn and implement the methodology effectively. When teaching, S. Engelmann formulated the instructional sequence mostly in his head on the fly, which was extraordinarily difficult to train other teachers to do. Teachers had great difficulty using terms consistently and selecting examples that illustrated new concepts clearly while reinforcing students for paying attention and working hard. He was able to train a few teachers in the methodology, but it required months of side-by-side coaching for them to be able to create effective instructional sequences on their own as they taught children. If this methodology was going to be adopted by anything but a small cadre of instructors, he needed to find a way to train other teachers more efficiently so he could scale up the approach.

The idea of scripting instruction developed in several discrete stages in response to specific needs. The notion of creating teaching scripts did not stem from a single decision but rather evolved over time. The first stage was to develop a list of examples for teachers to follow. In his memoir, *Teaching Needy Kids in Our Backward System*, S. Engelmann described this initial stage of script evolution:

> At first, we thought it might be sufficient to provide trainees with a list of the examples they were to present. With this change, the trainees did not have to make up examples or create sequences of examples. They would just refer to the list and present the next example listed. (Engelmann, S., 2007, 18)

The list of examples helped the most experienced trainees, but the list was not sufficient to improve the performance of less-experienced trainees who still had difficulty producing consistent and precise wording:

> Even with the list of examples, these teachers talked too much, used clumsy wording that was not consistent from one example to the next, and presented labored corrections. (Engelmann, S., 2007, 18)

The remedy was to provide scripts that detailed all of the wording that teachers were to follow, including procedures for correcting student performance errors on different types of instructional formats:

> Because lists of examples were not sufficient, we programmed simple, consistent wording and consistent and manageable correction procedures. ... We could train them in presenting the script verbatim, possibly memorizing the wording for the critical and frequently-used tasks, and teaching standard correction procedures that were tightly referenced to the script. (Engelmann, S., 2007, 19)

The use of the scripts allowed teachers to become effective instructors much more quickly than they had prior to the development of the scripts. Again, from *Teaching Needy Kids in Our Backward System*:

> The scripts were successful because they permitted the teacher to teach, not to be both an instructional designer and a teacher. Because the scripts relieved the teacher of the technical design

details, the teacher was able to concentrate more on presenting the material efficiently and providing corrections. The introduction of verbatim scripts did not make the teachers flawless presenters; it simply limited the number of details they had to learn before they were effective. With scripts, we were able to teach new trainees more in two weeks than we had previously been able to teach in more than four months. (Engelmann, S., 2007, 20)

The year 1968 serves as the date when the methodology created by S. Engelmann started to be referred to as upper-case "Direct Instruction" as this term appeared in title caps as part of the name of the first published DI programs – *Direct Instruction Systems for Teaching and Remediation* or DISTAR for short. The methodology was no longer referred to as lower-case "direct instruction" because the term was now part of the title of several DISTAR programs:

- *DISTAR Reading*
- *DISTAR Language*
- *DISTAR Arithmetic.*

There were at least two levels of each of the DISTAR programs. The first two programs listed – *DISTAR Reading* and *DISTAR Language* – have become part of the *Reading Mastery Signature Edition* with some modifications. As mentioned in chapter 4, the first level of *DISTAR Arithmetic* is still available in the same form today.

BARAK ROSENSHINE'S LISTS OF DIRECT INSTRUCTION STRATEGIES

Starting in the late 1960s, others adopted the term lower-case "direct instruction" to describe teaching strategies that conform to several aspects of the original lower-case direct instruction pioneered by S. Engelmann and colleagues. The main figure in defining lower-case di was Barak Rosenshine, who arrived at the University of Illinois from Temple University in 1971 after S. Engelmann and most of his DI colleagues left for the University of Oregon. Before coming to the University of Illinois, Barak Rosenshine visited several sites where S. Engelmann implemented his teaching methodology.

Unlike S. Engelmann, who developed the DI methodology and programs through intensive interaction with students in the classroom, and unlike Anita Archer, who has worked with many teachers on di techniques and modeled the use of these techniques in live classrooms as part of the professional development she offers, Rosenshine didn't teach elementary or secondary level students, implement his own teaching strategies directly, or train or coach teachers. Instead, he played an important role as a synthesizer and compiler of effective teaching strategies that he observed or read about, much as John Hattie has played an important role in compiling meta-analyses on different topics in education.

The number of strategies, functions, or principles that appear in Rosenshine's lists varied over the years. In fact, his article that appeared in the *American Educator* in 2012 "presents 10 research-based principles of instruction" (Rosenshine, 2012, 12), yet it also has a box with a list of 17 principles of effective instruction that "overlaps with, and offers slightly more detail than, the 10 principles" that are the focus of the main article (Rosenshine, 2012, 19). Rosenshine's first description of effective teaching strategies was published in 1986, 20 years after Bereiter and S. Engelmann published their list of strategies employed in the Bereiter–Engelmann preschool. In putting together his list of strategies in 1986 (together with Robert Stevens, also from the University of Illinois), Rosenshine didn't refer to either of the lists that S. Engelmann developed in the 1960s but instead drew from an article published in the *Harvard Educational Review* in 1977 by Wesley Becker, who was the co-sponsor along with S. Engelmann of the DI model in Project Follow Through (Rosenshine and Stevens, 1986). Becker's article in many ways was actually a better source than the earlier lists because, as mentioned above, several items from earlier lists were assumed by the published programs.

In addition, Rosenshine drew from several other sources unrelated to the work of S. Engelmann, Bereiter, or Becker in compiling his lists of teaching strategies. In the article that appeared in the *American Educator* in 2012, he identified three categories of sources for the strategies: "(a) research in cognitive science, (b) research on master teachers, and (c) research on cognitive supports" (Rosenshine, 2012, 12). He asserted that "there is *no conflict at all* between the instructional suggestions" that come from each of the sources he used to compile his list of teaching strategies

(Rosenshine, 2012, 12). Here are the 10 research-based principles of instruction Rosenshine identified:

1. Begin a lesson with a short review of previous learning.
2. Present new material in small steps with student practice after each step.
3. Ask a large number of questions and check the responses of all students.
4. Provide models.
5. Guide student practice.
6. Check for student understanding.
7. Obtain a high success rate.
8. Provide scaffolds for difficult tasks.
9. Require and monitor independent practice.
10. Engage students in weekly and monthly review. (Rosenshine, 2012, 12)

Although the DI programs were published well before Rosenshine's first list appeared, these principles are reflected in the DI programs (along with the other principles described in chapter 2 of this book). Here is how the DI programs address each of these principles:

1. *Begin a lesson with a short review of previous learning.*

    In the DI published programs, the review of previous learning plays a much more prominent role than just beginning a lesson. As discussed in chapter 2, new parts of a lesson account for only 10–15% of all of the material in a lesson. Review and application of skills and content introduced previously in the program make up the remaining 85–90% of the lesson material. The implications of this design (if correctly implemented) are that:

    - Students can master the new skills and content if they are placed properly in the program because there is such a small amount of new material that is introduced daily.
    - They achieve high levels of fluency or automaticity with the rest of the lesson because they are already at least partially familiar with its content. As a result, they develop a very strong

knowledge base, which prepares students for learning more advanced skills and concepts.

- As they proceed through the DI programs, students anticipate that they will learn everything that the teacher presents to them. They understand that they will be able to master new material; if they don't learn it completely the first day, they know they will practice the material on subsequent days until they master it fully.

2. *Present new material in small steps with student practice after each step.*

In all of the DI programs, exercises are coordinated so that new material is presented clearly in isolation with practice and feedback designed to promote student mastery. An example of a small step in learning can been seen in Figure 6.1. When working problems that involve carrying in column addition, many students often write the correct numerals in the incorrect spots. To prevent this from occurring, the addition module of *Corrective Mathematics* provides explicit scaffolding that directs students where to write each numeral during column addition in isolated steps (starting in Lesson 28). They are provided with the sum of the numbers in the ones column. In the example in Figure 6.1, the sum of the ones column is 25, which is written to the side and circled. Students are also provided with a box indicating where they are supposed to write the number of tens that are being carried. So at this stage of the program, all the students have to do is write the five below the line in the ones column and the two in the box at the top of the tens column, nothing more.

Figure 6.1 First steps in column addition.

Once students have mastered these steps, the circled sum of the ones column is faded, but the box at the top of the tens column is retained for several lessons. Eventually, that box is removed too, and because of the structured practice they had writing the numerals in the correct spots for several lessons, students know where to put each numeral reliably.

3. *Ask a large number of questions and check the responses of all students.*

   In DI, teachers ask students questions frequently and check their responses. The most efficient way of doing this is through choral responses, as described in chapter 5. Instead of just hearing what one student knows in response to a question, choral responses allow the teacher to verify whether *all* students know the answer to *every* question. The teacher can always ask students individually if there is any doubt whether some students responded correctly to a question asked of the whole group.

   The rate of questions asked by the teacher depends on the complexity of the task and the familiarity of the students with the material. Simple rote tasks that involve short answers, such as identifying the counting numbers or the letters in a word, do not require as much time for students to process as the application of rules, such as the difference between lizards and amphibians. In general, students require more think time to formulate answers on material that is complex or that they are less familiar with, which has the effect of slowing down the rate of student responses until students become more familiar with the material.

4. *Provide models.*

5. *Guide student practice.*

6. *Check for student understanding.*

   Principles 4–6 correspond to the classic teaching paradigm of *Model, Lead, Test* in DI as described in chapter 5, which corresponds directly to the *I Do, We Do, You Do* strategies espoused by Anita Archer (Archer and Hughes, 2011, 29–39). As mentioned in chapter 5, providing students with a precise model of new behaviors is much more efficient than simply asking students to do something they have not seen before. In DI, the teacher provides a lead step only if students have difficulty producing the expected response. Testing occurs immediately after the model step (or the lead step if a lead is needed) to verify that students can produce the expected response. In addition to tests that immediately follow models and leads, the program incorporates various delayed tests over time to ensure that the students master new skills and concepts fully.

7. *Obtain a high success rate.*

   Students obtain a high success rate in the DI programs if (and only if) they are placed in the programs at lessons that match their individual skill levels and are taught with fidelity according to the program's requirements, which include correcting all errors immediately as they occur. Students are considered to have completed a lesson successfully if they are at mastery on all components of the lesson, which means they can respond correctly to any task in any exercise in the lesson. Mastering all components of today's lesson provides a firm foundation for students to master the next day's lesson. In-program assessments ensure that students achieve a high success rate as 90% correct is the minimum passing criterion for mastery tests.

8. *Provide scaffolds for difficult tasks.*

   The DI programs provide several forms of scaffolding, including leads, which are described as part of Principle 5. As discussed in chapter 5, leading is often accompanied by chunking or chaining: breaking down more complex responses into shorter responses that the teacher practices with students separately before they attempt to produce a complete response on their own. In this manner, errors that are corrected a part at a time constitute an important form of scaffolding in DI.

   Prompts that make it easier for students to respond correctly are another form of scaffolding that occurs in the DI programs. Here's an example of a scaffold in the form of a prompt from *Reading Mastery Signature Edition Grade 1*.

EXERCISE 2

Words with underlined parts

a. First you're going to read the underlined part of each word in this column. Then you're going to read the whole word.

b. (Touch the ball for **easy**.) Read the underlined part. Get ready. (Tap the ball.) *eee*.

• Read the whole word. (Pause.) Get ready. (Slash.) *Easy*.

c. (Repeat step *b* until firm.)

d. (Repeat steps *b* and *c* for each remaining word in the column.)

e. (Repeat the column until children read all the words in order without making a mistake.)

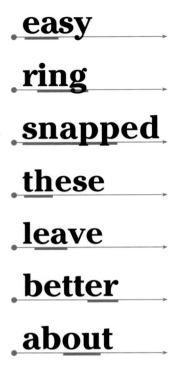

Figure 6.2 Prompts in reading a word list. Source: Engelmann, S. and Bruner, E. C. (2008a). *Reading Mastery Signature Edition Teacher's Guide Grade 1*, © McGraw Hill.

For each word, students read an underlined part and then read the whole word. For instance, they read "ea" and then "easy," "ing" and then "ring." This procedure helps direct students' attention to critical parts of the words that they may otherwise misread or mispronounce. In previous lessons, students would have already been taught the sounds associated with these word parts. At this point of the program, they can successfully apply this knowledge in a more complex context: a mixed set word list containing different types of words. It is a "mixed set" because the words don't all have the same sound spelled the same way, such as /eee/ spelled e-a, which would be easier for students to read because they would all be the same word type. Yet even though this is a mixed-word set, the students can read the list accurately because of this word-part scaffold. Successfully completing this exercise provides a firm foundation for students when they encounter these same words later in stories. Note that this scaffold is removed from word lists later in the program. Students are able to read all these words without any prompt or assistance by the end of this level of the program because they were taught using this prompt at a critical stage in their emergence as successful readers.

Chapter 3 of this book provides several other examples of scaffolds in the DI programs:

- A workbook exercise in *Spelling Mastery Level A* with irregularly spelled parts of words provided and regularly spelled parts missing.

- An exercise in *Spelling Mastery Level B* with groups of irregular word "families" that share a common spelling.

- Sequencing the introduction of letters in the *Horizons/Funnix/Transformations* reading programs according to which part of the letter names represents the sounds the letters make when they are read.

- Visual displays that illustrate selected content in the Grades 2–5 levels of *Reading Mastery*, such as a baseball diamond, a timeline, and a map.

- Vocabulary boxes and elements of composition "checks" for students in the Grade 3 writing program of *Reading Mastery Signature Edition* (RMSE).

There are many other examples of scaffolds in the DI programs that help students learn critical elements in different subject areas. These scaffolds are systematically removed as students master the skills and content taught in the programs.

9. *Require and monitor independent practice*

Independent practice is an integral part of the DI approach. The objective of teaching any skill or concept in DI is that students will be able to apply the skill or concept reliably and independently by the end of the program. To facilitate this goal, there is a direct correspondence and reinforcing effect between group instruction and independent work. Everything that is introduced in the DI programs is taught to mastery during group instruction and then incorporated into independent work.

As with other aspects of DI "tests" (independent work is a delayed test on material covered during group instruction), the passing criterion for independent work is high: 85%. To ensure total mastery of the material, students must fix all errors, which provides them with practice producing and seeing the correct answers. In addition, if more than 25% of students miss an item, it is retaught to the group. Thus, errors are an opportunity for the teacher to reinforce student learning regardless of whether they occur during face-to-face instruction or during independent work.

To ensure that students can complete independent work successfully, the lessons often contain one or more "teacher-directed" parts of the exercises that appear in the independent work. The teacher leads students as a group through an example or part of a task, which the students later complete on their own. During independent work time, teachers monitor students and provide feedback to them as needed. Except for rare instances in which students are required to copy the story title or other wording exactly, textbooks are closed to guarantee that the independent work accurately tests students' retention of skills and concepts covered in the program, not their ability to find information in the textbook.

10. *Engage students in weekly and monthly review.*

In addition to independent work, the DI programs contain formal assessments, the most common of which are mastery tests, which usually occur every 10 lessons with considerable variation depending on the program and level. All mastery tests address the skills and concepts covered since the last test. As described in chapter 2, the passing criterion for the mastery tests is 90%, which is realistic if group instruction and independent work procedures are implemented properly. As with independent work, students must fix all errors, and if more than 25% of students miss an item, it is retaught to the group. Mastery tests include remedy tables, which direct teachers to the specific exercises they should use to reteach missed concepts. Students are then retested on items that they missed.

Here's part of the remedy table for the first mastery test of *Connecting Math Concepts Level D*. There are nine parts in the mastery test, but only the first five parts are shown in Table 6.1. The remedy table directs teachers to the precise lesson and exercises for them to present to students for missed items. For instance, if more than 25% of the students or any individual student scores below 90% in "Part 1: Addition and Subtraction Facts", the teacher would reteach the following exercises:

- Lesson 3, Ex 3
- Lesson 4, Ex 1
- Lesson 5, Ex 1.

Part	Test Items	Remedy		Remedies Worksheet
		Lesson	Exercise	
1	Addition and Subtraction Facts	3	3	Part A
		4	1	Part B
		5	1	Part C
2	Number Families (Missing Number)	3	1	—
		4	4	Part D
		5	4	Part E
3	Comparison Sentences (More/Less)	7	2	Part F
		8	2	Part G
4	Expanded Notation	1	7	Part H
		2	4	Part I
		3	7	Part J
5	Count-by Problems	6	6	Part K
		7	7	Part L
		8	7	Part M

Table 6.1 Remedy table for Mastery Test 1 of CMC Level D. Source: Engelmann, S., Silbert, J., Engelmann, O. and Carnine, D. (2013). *Connecting Math Concepts Comprehensive Edition Level D Presentation Book 1*, © McGraw Hill.

As with group instruction and independent work, errors made during the in-program assessments provide another opportunity for the teacher to reteach critical content to promote students' mastery of the material.

LIMITATIONS STEMMING FROM ROSENSHINE'S LIST OF INSTRUCTIONAL STRATEGIES

Although Rosenshine's list contains descriptions of research-based instructional strategies, the list itself is often insufficient for teachers to use to provide effective instruction to students, especially highly at-risk students. The article that appeared in the *American Educator* in 2012 provides some examples of the different principles in action, which help the reader understand the principles, but the examples may not provide sufficient guidance for a teacher to actually apply the strategies to specific teaching situations. For instance, for Principle 6, "check for student understanding," Rosenshine provides the following examples:

> Effective teachers also stopped to check for student understanding. They checked for understanding by asking questions, by asking students to summarize the presentation up to that point or to repeat directions or procedures, or by asking students whether they agreed or disagreed with other students' answers. (Rosenshine, 2012, 16)

A teacher who is providing students with background information for a story that takes place in the Arctic, for instance, must determine how to apply the principle to the specific content they are teaching – when to ask comprehension questions, what questions to ask in which order, when to ask students to summarize the background information, etc. – which requires a great deal of thought and planning.

The same is true for the description of the other principles in the list. The examples that are provided help teachers understand the principles, but they may be insufficient to help teachers apply the principles to daily instruction. Moreover, for instruction to be effective, teachers must weave all of these principles together into a seamless whole, which requires balancing the requirements of the different principles. Teachers are directed by Principle 3 to "ask a large number of questions and check the responses of all students." It is unclear how many questions constitute a large number of questions. Moreover, it isn't clear how much time should be spent on asking questions versus reviewing previous learning (Principle 1), presenting new material (Principle 2), guiding students (Principle 5), and checking for understanding (Principle 6). Rosenshine concludes that:

> The most successful teachers spent more time in guided practice, more time asking questions, more time checking for understanding, and more time correcting errors. (Rosenshine, 2012, 17)

This conveys to the "average" teacher that they need to increase time spent on these strategies, but it doesn't suggest an upper time limit on any of these principles or the trade-off between time spent on one principle versus the other principles.

The published DI programs provide a solid basis for the balanced application of these strategies, as many of the principles have already been addressed by the program authors, including incorporating a review of previous learning, presenting new material in small steps, providing models of expected student work, checking for student understanding, providing scaffolds for difficult tasks, and reviewing past material regularly. Moreover, the DI programs incorporate other critical DI design elements that promote student success, especially:

- faultless communication
- incremental step design
- the track or strand structure of lessons.

All of these elements require a great deal of thought, time, and effort to incorporate into instruction, and college-level coursework may be needed to provide teachers with a full understanding of effective principles of instructional design. Upper-level college courses on instructional design have been devoted to teaching the intricacies of faultless communication and other design elements as described in *Theory of Instruction* (Engelmann, S. and Carnine, 1991) with university students required to produce sequences of examples and non-examples of targeted concepts or skills for different types of learning objectives. Incorporating an incremental step design – Rosenshine's second principle – requires making decisions as to what constitutes a learning "step," how this step should be articulated and differentiated from previously learned knowledge, and which order of the steps best leads to successful acquisition of the material by all students. This process is complicated further if lessons are divided into tracks or strands, as they are in the DI programs. As mentioned in chapter 2, DI lessons are composed of several exercises that represent different tracks (sequences of exercises that introduce and expand on a specific skill type over many lessons). Distributing skills over several lessons requires much more work on the part of the instructional designer. In contrast, most lower-case di lessons are devoted to a single topic, which is much easier to create than lessons that focus on several topics in a single lesson.

The difficulty involved in applying and integrating all of these components together to form coherent, effective instruction can be illustrated by section 3 of *Rubric for Identifying Authentic Direct Instruction Programs*, which covers over three quarters of the book (Engelmann, S. and Colvin, 2006, 24–108). The first two sections of the book address the empirical features of DI and the axioms that allow for effective instruction in DI programs. The third section consists of an application of the axioms to three lessons from an unpublished beginning grammar program. The program:

> ... has many of the features of a well-designed DI program. The lessons are sequenced; tasks have clear objectives; and DI procedures such as model, lead, and test are incorporated in the lessons. (Engelmann, S. and Colvin, 2006, 24)

Despite this superficial resemblance to DI programs, the grammar program does not adhere to numerous axioms critical to ensuring effectiveness and efficiency of instruction. The rubric devotes over 80 pages to explaining in detail how each of the axioms were not followed and how the grammar program could be rewritten to incorporate them to improve the instructional sequence substantially. This analysis of the grammar program demonstrates the difficulty in incorporating the deeper aspects of DI that lead to effective instruction.

RESOURCES FOR CONSTRUCTING EFFECTIVE INSTRUCTION

The two sources mentioned earlier, *Theory of Instruction* and *Rubric for Identifying Authentic Direct Instruction Programs*, are both key resources for teachers and curriculum specialists designing effective instruction. A couple of other resources, *Direct Instruction Reading* (Carnine et al., 2017) and *Direct Instruction Mathematics* (Stein et al., 2018), were co-authored by DI program authors. These resources involve adaptations or extended explanations of the approaches used in the DI programs. Many of the procedures that appear in *Direct Instruction Reading* were derived from the *Reading Mastery, Language for Learning,* and *Corrective Reading* DI programs. Similarly, many of the procedures that appear in *Direct Instruction Mathematics* were derived from the *DISTAR Arithmetic, Connecting Math Concepts, Corrective Mathematics,* and *Essentials for Algebra* DI programs. Each of these resources include dozens of formats that provide teachers with very specific models for teaching critical skills. Purchasers of the DI mathematics book have access to over 100 printable teaching formats for use in their classrooms (Stein et al., 2018, iv; a list of the math formats can be found on pages xiv-xvi).

Although the formats provide strong tools for designing instruction, teachers must do additional work to use them effectively. Teachers must select new items that fit the format and the teaching objective, determine the order for presenting the formats, and adjust the number of times to present the format in response to students' performance. They must also integrate the instruction developed through these resources with a core curriculum because both of these resources are designed to supplement a main instructional program. Guidelines on selecting, using, and modifying core programs are integrated into chapters throughout the DI reading book while the DI math book devotes a separate chapter to evaluating and modifying commercial mathematics curricula (Stein et al., 2018, 19–24).

Another resource for designing lessons is *Explicit Instruction: Effective and Efficient Teaching* (Archer and Hughes, 2011), which approaches the topic of effective instruction from the lower-case direct instruction perspective. Archer and Hughes use as their starting point Rosenshine's principles of effective instruction, which they expand upon to provide a comprehensive guide to teachers who are interested in incorporating these principles into their teaching. Roughly one third of this resource is devoted to applying Rosenshine's principles to designing lessons covering skills and strategies (chapter 2), vocabulary and concepts (chapter 3), and different types of rules (chapter 4). The bulk of the rest of the book addresses organizing and delivering instruction using positive examples as well as non-examples to help illustrate concepts to readers. Effective instruction principles are applied to various subject areas, including decoding, science vocabulary, spelling, mathematics, and persuasive writing. As with the DI reading and mathematics books, *Explicit Instruction* is a very useful tool for teachers as long as they understand that a great deal of additional work outside of the book will still be required to construct an effective instructional sequence.

A third resource, *The researchED Guide to Explicit and Direct Instruction: An Evidenced-Informed Guide for Teachers* (Boxer, 2019), is an eclectic resource on various topics related to the full spectrum of lower-case di and upper-case Direct Instruction. The guide contains examples of a wide variety of applications of effective instructional principles to different subject areas. It covers such diverse topics as the research base for the DI methodology, construction of DI lessons, and factors to consider when adopting a schoolwide reform program. One of the most unique chapters, titled "Electrolysing Engelmann," applies the principles described in *Theory of Instruction* to teaching chemical processes caused by introducing electric currents to a liquid or solution containing ions (Jones, 2019). As with the other resources listed above, *The researchED Guide to Explicit and Direct Instruction* provides examples of the use of the DI approach to different subject areas that can help readers better understand effective instruction, but readers must still perform the bulk of the work themselves to translate the DI theory into a usable program of daily instruction.

WHY TEACHERS SHOULD LEARN TO CONSTRUCT THEIR OWN DI LESSONS

Although time-consuming, there are several reasons why teachers should use one or more of the resources above to learn to construct their own lessons, even if they are using a DI published program. First, they gain better insight into the construction of the DI programs. By creating their own lessons, teachers can better appreciate the incremental design, the selection of examples and wording, the progression of the instructional tracks from basic to more advanced concepts, the synthesis of the tracks into more complex applications, the use of scaffolds, and many other design elements that have been seamlessly incorporated into the DI programs. Constructing their own lessons will reinforce how each component of the scripts plays an important role, and how the lessons must be delivered with fidelity so students can master the content in preparation for the next day's lesson.

Teachers should also learn to create their own lessons because during the course of the year they will need to teach topics that are not addressed in the published DI programs. Local history or culture, current events, recent scientific discoveries and innovations, and local flora and fauna are all important topics that may not be covered in the DI programs. To make sure that students understand these topics, teachers should apply the design elements that are described in these resources and tie the material into knowledge that the students have already mastered. By establishing explicit connections between what students have already learned in the DI programs and new material, teachers can effectively teach other topics not covered in the DI programs.

Given the great demands placed on teachers to deliver instruction effectively to all their students, teachers may find that the best instruction they can provide will follow this rule of thumb: *if there is a published DI program that addresses the content your students need, use that program. If there isn't a published program for the content needed by your students, apply effective instructional principles to design and deliver instruction that addresses your students' needs.*

TOPIC BRIEF 1: RESEARCH ON TEACHING EXPLICITLY VS. DISCOVERY LEARNING

Extensive research has shown that student learning is enhanced if initial instruction is done explicitly. An article in the Spring 2012 issue of the *American Educator*, "Putting Students on the Path to Learning: The Case for Fully Guided Instruction" by Richard E. Clark, Paul A. Kirschner, and John Sweller, describes the strong evidence base in support of teaching new content explicitly:

> Evidence from well-designed, properly controlled experimental studies from the 1980s to today … supports direct instructional guidance. In a very important study, researchers not only tested whether science learners learned more via discovery, compared with explicit instruction, but also … whether those who had learned through discovery were better able to transfer their learning to new contexts (as advocates for minimally guided approaches often claim). The findings were unambiguous. Direct instruction involving considerable guidance, including examples, resulted in vastly more learning than discovery. Those relatively few students who learned via discovery showed no signs of superior quality of learning. (Clark, Kirschner, and Sweller, 2012, 7–8)

The authors of the article explain that discovery methods should be used only when students are applying skills or already understand the subject matter. If used with students when they are first introduced to a skill or topic, discovery methods can lead to the following problems:

- First, often only the brightest and most well-prepared students make the discovery.
- Second, many students … simply become frustrated. Some may disengage, others may copy whatever the brightest students are doing—either way, they are not actually discovering anything.
- Third, some students believe they have discovered the correct information or solution, but they are mistaken and so they learn a misconception that can interfere with later learning and problem solving. Even after being shown the right answer, a student is likely to recall his or her discovery—not the correction.

- Fourth, even in the unlikely event that a problem or project is devised that all students succeed in completing, minimally guided instruction is much less efficient than explicit guidance. What can be taught directly in a 25-minute demonstration and discussion, followed by 15 minutes of independent practice with corrective feedback by a teacher, may take several class periods to learn via minimally guided projects and/or problem solving. (Clark, Kirschner, and Sweller, 2012, 8)

The authors emphasize that using discovery methods for initial instruction has the potential to be especially harmful to at-risk students. Their analysis indicates that:

> ... *minimally guided instruction can increase the achievement gap* ... a number of experiments found that less-skilled students who chose or were assigned to less-guided instruction received significantly *lower* scores on posttests than on pretest measures. For these relatively weak students, the failure to provide strong instructional support produced a *measurable loss of learning*. (Clark, Kirschner, and Sweller, 2012, 8, emphasis in the original)

With such strong evidence that explicit instruction is much more effective in teaching initial skills and concepts, why are discovery methods still so much more popular than Direct Instruction? The authors indicate two probable reasons: 1) confusion between constructivism as a theory of knowledge acquisition versus constructivism as a teaching methodology; and 2) the prevalence of constructivism as a teaching methodology in colleges of education. They suggest that:

> ... many educators confuse "constructivism," which is a theory of how one learns and sees the world, with a prescription for how to teach ... Many educators (especially teacher education professors in colleges of education) have latched on to this notion of students having to "construct" their own knowledge, and have *assumed* that the best way to promote such construction is to have students try to discover new knowledge or solve new problems without explicit guidance from the teacher. Unfortunately, this assumption is both widespread and incorrect ... In fact, the type of active cognitive processing that students need to engage in

to "construct" knowledge can happen through reading a book, listening to a lecture, watching a teacher conduct an experiment while simultaneously describing what he or she is doing, etc. Learning requires the construction of knowledge. Withholding information from students does not facilitate the construction of knowledge. (Clark, Kirschner, and Sweller, 8, emphasis in the original)

The authors conclude that explicit instruction should be used for teaching new knowledge with a reduction of guidance after students master new skills and concepts. This is precisely what happens in the Direct Instruction programs. New knowledge is introduced explicitly with careful, teacher-led models and explanations of new skills and concepts. After several lessons of highly structured exercises addressing a new skill or concept, scaffolding is gradually reduced. As students demonstrate mastery of the content, these skills are integrated into more advanced material. At various junctures, there are open-ended applications of the skills and concepts that students have mastered. In this way, discovery is not used for initial teaching in the DI methodology, which would discourage those students who don't have the background knowledge to "discover" the object of the open-ended activity. Rather, students apply what they know *after* they demonstrate that they have mastered targeted skills and concepts.

In DI, the question is not *whether* discovery and open-ended activities should take place. The question is *when* they should take place. The answer is *after* students' performance indicates that they will be successful in open-ended activities, which can then serve to reinforce their knowledge acquisition and cognitive growth while they build their self-confidence.

TOPIC BRIEF 2: WHO WAS SIEGFRIED "ZIG" ENGELMANN?

Siegfried "Zig" Engelmann, 1931–2019, father of the author of this book, was the creator of Direct Instruction (DI), professor of education at the University of Oregon, senior author of the DI programs, and founder of the National Institute for Direct Instruction (NIFDI). (See Topic Brief 3 for more information on NIFDI.) Along with Dr. Carl Bereiter, he started the Bereiter–Engelmann preschool, where he developed the principles that laid the foundation for the DI approach. A maverick in the field of education, he closely observed the interaction between what he and other instructors presented to students and the minute-by-minute performance of the students. He held to the simple yet profoundly impactful philosophy that if a student didn't learn the content presented by the instructor, the teaching had to change. He coined such well-known sayings as "all students can learn," and "if the students haven't learned, the teacher hasn't taught," which reflected this philosophical orientation.

Adhering to this approach, S. Engelmann established an unmatched standard for creating instructional programs that are effective with a wide range of learners. He pioneered procedures and techniques for developing and field-testing programs designed to ensure that all students who meet the programs' entrance requirements learn 100% of the programs' content in a timely manner. A key step in program development was field-testing new programs and revising the programs based on the results of the field tests. An example is the development of the *Reading Mastery* program in the 1970s. S. Engelmann and his colleagues discarded three drafts of the *Reading Mastery* program during its development and continued to revise and test the program until it met the high standard he established for program effectiveness.

S. Engelmann was a prolific author. He wrote over 100 instructional programs covering a wide range of subject areas and grade levels, from beginning reading to pre-algebra and earth science, and instructional programs intended for home use. In addition to the DI programs, he is best known for his many publications on educational practices, theory, and reform, including the following books:

- *Teaching Disadvantaged Children in the Preschool* (1966)

- *Give Your Child a Superior Mind* (1966)
- *Conceptual Learning* (1969)
- *Preventing Failure in the Primary Grades* (1969)
- *Your Child Can Succeed: How to Get the Most out of School for Your Child* (1975)
- *Theory of Instruction: Principles and Applications* (1982)
- *War Against the Schools' Academic Child Abuse* (1992)
- *Inferred Functions of Performance and Learning* (2003)
- *Rubric for Identifying Authentic Direct Instruction Programs* (2006)
- *Teaching Needy Kids in Our Backward System: 42 Years of Trying* (2007)
- *Could John Stuart Mill Have Saved Our Schools?* (2013)
- *Successful and Confident Students with Direct Instruction* (2017).

S. Engelmann's published research spanned a wide range of topics. In one study, he taught deaf children to identify words by sensing vibratory patterns through their skin using a device he invented (a "Tactual Vocoder"). In another study, he accelerated the learning of low-income high school students who had been identified as demonstrating potential for college-level studies. Some of his earliest experiments demonstrated the limitations of Piaget's set stages of development by teaching 6-year-old children concepts such as specific gravity, which were supposed to be too advanced for children of that age to understand (see S. Engelmann, 1967).

In 1970, S. Engelmann co-founded the Engelmann-Becker Corporation along with Professor Wesley C. Becker to support and coordinate the work of DI authors as they conceptualized, wrote, and tested DI programs. With only a bachelor's degree in philosophy from the University of Illinois, he became a full professor of education at the University of Oregon in 1974. In 1995 he founded the Engelmann Foundation, which provides small grants to educators to implement and promote effective instructional practices. As of September 2022, the foundation had awarded 112 grants worth more than $729,000.00 (http://engelmannfoundation.org/).

In 1984 S. Engelmann received an honorary doctorate degree from Western Michigan University. In 1994 the American Psychological

Association awarded him the Fred Keller Award of Excellence. In 2000 he was named one of the 54 "most influential people" in the history of special education in the November/December issue of *Remedial and Special Education,* and in 2002, he received the Council of Scientific Society Presidents' Award of Achievement in Education Research.

S. Engelmann was a man of diverse talents and interests. He loved riding motorcycles and painting watercolors. More information on "Ziggy" and access to several unpublished works are available on his personal website, www.zigsite.com.

TOPIC BRIEF 3: WHAT IS NIFDI?

The National Institute for Direct Instruction (NIFDI) was founded by Direct Instruction creator Siegfried "Zig" Engelmann (see Topic Brief 2) in 1997. NIFDI's primary focus has been to support schools and districts as they implement the comprehensive DI model schoolwide with DI programs used for core instruction in reading, language/writing, math, and spelling. S. Engelmann wanted to establish an organization that could provide complete training and implementation support to schools to help transform them into demonstration sites showcasing the degree to which DI can accelerate the performance of all students. Since its founding, NIFDI has worked with schools in such diverse places as: Gering, Nebraska; the Rio Grande Valley, Texas; the island of Guam; Native American tribal schools in the Pacific Northwest; the Midlands of England; and Western Australia. Several of the schools that NIFDI has supported have received widespread recognition for improving student performance, including City Springs School in Baltimore.

NIFDI provides a thorough training program in the DI methodology for coaches and teachers. Before school starts, teachers attend a four-day "preservice" training program in which they learn to deliver the specific exercises that they will present to students in the first few weeks of school. Teachers receive ongoing in-service training throughout the year on delivering the exercises that students will encounter later in the school year. Coaches attend these training sessions and receive additional multi-session training on coaching techniques specific to the DI programs. School leaders' capacity for managing the DI implementation is enhanced through weekly data analysis and problem-solving sessions that are led initially by the NIFDI implementation manager but are gradually taken over by the school-based coaches over time.

Over the years, NIFDI has expanded its focus beyond training and implementation support. It has sponsored and participated in research studies, and it offers free access to an extensive database of abstracts of research publications on Direct Instruction through its website, www.nifdi.org. It sponsors open-registration events on DI that are attended by teachers and school leaders from across the US and beyond.

NIFDI has become a leader in remote training and support as it offers a wide variety of virtual sessions for teachers, coaches, and administrators, including sessions on adapting DI for distance learning. NIFDI provides free access to videos and other resources on its website for school leaders who may be interested in implementing DI, including a nine-part *Introduction to Direct Instruction* video series. See www.nifdi.org/services/getting-started.html for resources on getting started with DI.

SECTION 2
HOW TO IMPLEMENT DIRECT INSTRUCTION SUCCESSFULLY

INTRODUCTION TO THE SECTION

The previous section addressed the key conceptual underpinnings of Direct Instruction (DI) as it discussed the design of the programs, the rationale behind each component of the programs, and the strategies and procedures teachers use to "deliver" the programs with the goal of accelerating the performance of all students. The purpose of this section is to provide a roadmap for teachers and school leaders to implement DI successfully. This section describes the steps needed to ensure that the DI programs are implemented with fidelity and that all students who receive DI are highly successful. If you have skipped right to this section without reading the previous section, I strongly advise that you go back to section 1. Successful implementation involves understanding the design and rationale for DI and not just following the steps described below.

As much as possible, this section is organized chronologically. The steps for implementing DI are presented in the order that they need to be addressed by teachers and school leaders for the school to be successful with DI. The implementation steps are divided into four broad categories that are executed by a school's leadership team:

- Preliminary steps – building the culture, consensus, and behavioral orientation that is necessary for a successful and well-defined implementation of DI.

- Setup – a school's leadership team sets expectations for the staff and establishes the structure for the successful implementation of DI.

- Monitoring – once the DI implementation has been set up properly, the leadership team monitors it to ensure that it is executed with fidelity.

- Responding actively – when a problem of implementation is identified through observations or data analysis, the leadership team takes appropriate steps to ensure that the problem is solved. Responding also involves celebrating success. Any problem should eventually lead to reinforcement when it has been resolved. So a successful implementation of DI is frequently punctuated by teachers' and school leaders' recognition of the accomplishments of students.

By definition, setup occurs at or near the beginning of an implementation while monitoring and responding actively occur later during the course of an implementation. The relationship between monitoring and responding is iterative: monitoring the implementation generates data that are analyzed by the leadership team to formulate a response. The effect of the response must then be monitored to determine whether it has led to a resolution of the problem. If the problem has not been resolved, new data must be analyzed by the leadership team to formulate a modified response. This back-and-forth between monitoring and responding continues until the problem has been resolved. In general, monitoring occurs before responding so monitoring is addressed before responding in this section, and setup occurs before either of these, so it is addressed before them.

Note that one form of response can be to reset expectations. For example, if one of the expectations of the teaching staff is for them to adhere to established schedules/timetables and teach "from bell to bell" five days a week for a set amount of time, but observations show that one of the teachers is not following this expectation, the response would be to reset expectations with the teacher regarding the time commitment for delivering DI.

The first step in the journey of implementing DI is for the school's leadership team to take a series of pre-implementation steps that provide the foundation for defining the role of DI in the school.

CHAPTER SEVEN
PRE-IMPLEMENTATION STEPS

Before Direct Instruction (DI) can be implemented successfully, there are several preliminary steps that must be taken first. Some of these steps link directly to the implementation of DI, including deciding the scope of the implementation in terms of the staff, students, and subject areas involved. Other preliminary steps should address broader changes that facilitate or support a successful implementation of DI, such as installing a positive behavior management system and building a culture and consensus among the staff in support of implementing DI effectively. These steps may or may not occur in a set order, as developments in different areas may overlap with each other and continue after DI has been adopted. Many of the foundational steps of culture and consensus will need to be maintained or revisited several times in order for the implementation of DI to be successful.

DEFINE THE DI IMPLEMENTATION FOR YOUR SCHOOL OR DISTRICT

The first step toward implementing DI is to define the scope of the implementation, or at least the initial scope of DI with the understanding that it could expand over time. DI programs are conducive to a variety of different types of implementations, ranging from a schoolwide, "full-immersion," comprehensive implementation with DI programs as the core curricula in all major subject areas, to a single teacher in a resource room using a DI program as an intervention to help students with special needs. The involvement of the staff and leadership team will differ depending on the type of implementation of DI. Their involvement may change over time if the initial implementation leads to a significant increase in student performance. If the students of a solitary teacher excel with DI, other staff members and the school's leadership may want to explore expanding the implementation to other students in the school.

The following questions should be discussed and addressed thoroughly by the school's leadership team or the lead adopters of DI in a school before taking the first steps toward implementation:

- *Who* will be involved in the DI implementation?
- *What* specific subject areas are going to be addressed?
- *When* will the implementation commence?
- *How* will the DI implementation fit into the school's mission and goals?

The question of *who* will be involved in the implementation should center on the needs of the students first and foremost, which will drive decisions on selecting staff to teach DI. The scope of the implementation should be defined clearly with respect to the grade levels of the students and specific populations within different grade levels. DI can be used to close gaps in student performance in comparison to national norms, or it can be used to accelerate student performance beyond national norms. Limiting the implementation to a specific grade level or year is a workable option as long as the instructional groups that are formed can accommodate the performance levels of the students selected to receive DI. As discussed elsewhere in this book, students are placed and grouped at their skill level in the DI programs, and their placement may or may not correspond to their nominal grade or year. In the upper grades, the variation in skills among students is usually greater than the variation in the lower grades. So the upper grades may require more instructional groups – and more staffing for the groups – to cover the wider range of student performance. An option that limits the number of staff involved is to avoid the intermediate and upper grades initially because of the great variation in student skill levels there, and start the implementation of DI in the lowest grade levels at the school (preschool/reception or kindergarten/ Year 1), where virtually all students can be placed in the same program: the kindergarten level of the *Reading Mastery* language program.

By starting the implementation of DI in the lowest grades first, the school can take advantage of "the cohort effect," which requires fewer staff to accommodate a smaller number of instructional groups in the long run. As the cohort of students who start DI progress through the grades, they bring higher performance with them over the years. If DI is implemented with fidelity in the lowest grades, a high proportion of students who exit these grades will be performing at grade-level expectations or higher. This wave of higher achievement greatly reduces the need for remediation in the intermediate and upper grades when the original cohort reaches those levels, as only continuing students with severe disabilities and students who transfer into the school will be performing below grade-level expectations (with the possible exception of continuing students who are absent for extended periods of time). Thus, the demand for staff will be lower using the cohort-effect strategy because there will be less need for remediation in the intermediate and upper grades when DI is extended into those grades.

Students with severe disabilities will need to be considered when deciding on the scope of the implementation of DI. These students may not be able to participate in the published DI programs initially and may be better served by more customized instruction that follows the methods and procedures described in *Strategies for Teaching Students with Severe and Low-Incidence Disabilities*. As Caitlin Rasplica Khoury and Jean Stockard explain in the preface to the book:

> Students with severe developmental disabilities often do not have the skills needed to benefit from the lowest levels of the DI programs – such as understanding simple requests, responding to questions, or working in a group. But all of these skills can be taught. (Engelmann, 2018, vii-viii)

A low student–teacher ratio will be needed to accommodate these students. Groups with only a couple of students or one-on-one teaching should be expected, as neither the skill set nor the learning rate of students with severe disabilities will match those of other students in the school. Staff members who work with students in these groups will need extensive training on effective instructional practices and positive behavioral management techniques.

At the other end of the learning spectrum, some high-performing students may place into program levels that are above their nominal grade level. These advanced students can join instructional groups that are composed of students from higher grades. However, if a student places higher than all of the other students in the school, the options are either 1) arranging one-on-one instruction that matches the student's skill level or 2) adding the student to the next highest performing group in the school. If the second option is selected, the student should also be assigned more advanced supplementary material that matches their skill level. The teacher may be able to draw on the highest levels of the DI programs, which teach secondary-level skills in mathematics (*Essentials for Algebra*) and writing (*Essentials for Writing*) as described in chapter 4 to accommodate these exceptional students. Because schools usually cannot spare a staff member to provide an individual student with one-on-one advanced instruction, adding the student to the next highest performing group in the school may be the next best option.

For school staff, the question of *who* should be involved in the DI implementation pertains to program delivery as well as coaching and support. Program delivery can and should involve certified teachers, but it does not need to be limited to them; instructional assistants can also deliver DI effectively if they receive initial training in the DI methodology and regular feedback from experienced DI coaches. In fact, we have experienced that some teachers may require more coaching and support than instructional assistants, as they may initially resist implementing the practices inherent in delivering the DI programs because the DI approach contradicts the content of the coursework they took for their college degrees or teaching certifications. Instructional assistants who have not taken courses that depict DI in a negative light are more likely to adopt the DI approach without hesitation.

Instructional assistants usually teach the language program to children who place into the kindergarten and first-grade levels of the programs while certified teachers teach reading. These beginning levels of the programs are the most difficult to teach effectively, to low-performing students in particular, as many children who are new to school lack fundamental skills and concepts that make learning easier, such as knowledge of pronouns and verb tenses. These students require a great deal of positive reinforcement and repetition to achieve mastery, which in turn requires considerable skill on the part of the instructors. The discrepancy between the demands on instructional assistants in a DI implementation and their compensation can be a source of tension, as assistants are given some of the most difficult teaching assignments, yet they receive far less compensation than certified teachers. To resolve this discrepancy, some school systems have found ways of increasing instructional assistants' compensation. The IDEA Schools charter school network headquartered in Texas, for instance, has established a more elevated position of co-teacher, which involves higher compensation for teaching DI language groups.

In addition to teaching assistants, specialist teachers who are certified, but not certified in the subject area that is the focus of the DI implementation, can also teach DI groups effectively. In schoolwide implementations at the middle-school level, instructors whose area of specialization involves providing immediate feedback to students on their performance, such as music or physical education, have been very effective in teaching remedial literacy DI programs, such as *Corrective Reading*.

The number of staff involved in the DI implementation will vary according to the level of the programs the students place into. DI programs can be divided into those requiring small groups of students and those that can be delivered to larger groups consisting of a whole class. The student–teacher ratios of the first two levels of the programs are usually small, with the largest groups not to exceed 12 students and smaller group sizes recommended (four or even fewer) for lower-performing students. In contrast, groups can number 25 students or higher in the upper levels of the programs as long as all students are grouped homogeneously and placed at their skill level. To maintain low student–teacher ratios for the first two levels of the programs, a sufficient number of staff must be involved in the implementation and fully trained in the DI methodology. As mentioned earlier, the first two levels of the language program are usually taught by instructional assistants (under the supervision of certified teachers). Students who place in these levels require two instructional periods a day, as discussed in more detail later in this section, which influences how these positions are structured. Full-time assistants are preferable to part-time assistants in these grades so students in the language groups can receive consistent instruction from the same instructor across the school day.

Accommodating students who transfer into a school that has successfully implemented DI for years can present a staffing challenge to school leaders. If a school has fully implemented DI so that the initial cohort of students who started at the earliest grade level have now advanced through the upper grades, the average performance of these students should be more advanced than their nominal grade level. Most of the continuing fourth- and fifth-graders should be performing at the fifth- or sixth-grade levels or higher, respectively, which is usually greater than the average performance of students from surrounding areas. When new students transfer into the school, they may be performing one or more levels below grade level. To accommodate these students, the school will need to establish "gateway" groups that teach the students at their performance level. These groups should consist of a small number of students as they familiarize transfer students with the format and expectations of Direct Instruction, as well as provide them with the fundamental skills and concepts that other students in their grade level mastered years earlier. In reading, many of the fourth- or fifth-grade students who transfer into the school can be expected to require instruction in *Corrective Reading* while the continuing students in these same grades will receive instruction in the highest level of *Reading Mastery* or a more advanced DI program, such as *Understanding U.S. History*, as discussed in chapter 4.

While fully implemented DI schools will need gateway groups with a single instructor for students who transfer into the school, they may also need to provide one or more instructors for English language learners (ELL). The size of these groups and the quantity of staff involved will vary according to the number of ELL students in the school, their grade level, and their performance level. If these students all have the same native language, it is beneficial to place them with a teacher who speaks that language.

Staff members responsible for managing the DI implementation should be identified in the planning stages, with clear responsibilities articulated for ensuring that the steps outlined in this section are taken: building culture and consensus, setting up the expectations for the staff, meeting the structural requirements of the program, monitoring the DI implementation, and responding actively to student performance. The most immediate steps for the managers are to ensure that the *structural* requirements of the program (those that apply to scheduling, material ordering and storing, instructional group size, classroom configuration, placement and grouping, and data collection) and the *training* requirements (those that apply to placement testing, program delivery, and data recording) are met.

The involvement of the principal as the instructional leader of the school should be established early in the planning stage of the DI implementation. Even if many of the critical decisions can be made by a grade-level lead or the special education team lead, the school's principal should be aware of the requirements of the DI programs and the steps that need to be taken to meet these requirements. Many of the steps described in this section can be delegated to others, but the principal should monitor the implementation in specific ways and intervene as needed to ensure a successful implementation of the programs. If more than one school is participating in the DI program adoption, the appropriate personnel at the district level should also be involved in setting up the implementation of DI, determining the criteria for success, monitoring the implementation, and intervening as needed to ensure that obstacles to the programs' success are removed in a timely manner.

What will be implemented (*which specific subject areas* are going to be addressed in the DI implementation) depends on the needs of the students, which may involve more than one subject. If you identify needs in mathematics, social studies, or science, the students may also have literacy needs that should be addressed first. Students who struggle in mathematics may have difficulty reading the directions to problems, or they may not understand the word problems they read. Students who struggle to express their thinking in history class will benefit from a systematic program focusing on language or writing before addressing gaps in understanding history itself.

To address literacy needs first, a common approach is to implement DI language and reading programs the first year and add mathematics and spelling the second year. This has the advantage of allowing teachers who teach all subjects (usually at the elementary school level) to concentrate just on DI language and reading programs initially. In this scenario, teachers continue to use the mathematics and spelling programs that they were already using previously while they implement DI language and reading during the first year of the DI adoption. When schools implement DI just to address literacy, they often see an increase in mathematics performance because students are more able to access their grade-level math texts and follow the directions of their teachers.

In brand new schools that do not have pre-existing mathematics or spelling curricula, however, the DI implementation cannot be limited to literacy as students need to receive instruction in all major subject areas. If leaders of newly founded schools want to implement DI in stages over a couple of years, they would have to purchase another math program that would be used for only one year, which is impractical and financially unsound. It is most economical for new schools to implement DI across the board starting the first year, even though this approach is more stressful on the staff and school leadership as it increases the demand on teachers to learn several DI programs at once. Implementing DI in all major subject areas at once pushes up the cost of materials and initial program (preservice) training in the first year of implementation, but the overall cost to the school in the long run is less than implementing non-DI programs to be used for only one year.

As indicated earlier, a critical staffing decision for implementing DI is the assignment of subject areas and instructional groups to teachers, which can be accomplished in two different ways. Teachers can teach all of the subject areas involved in the implementation (literacy, spelling, and mathematics), or teachers can specialize, with language arts teachers teaching reading and language, and mathematics teachers teaching math. Specialization will work if the implementation of DI is on a small scale. However, if the DI adoption involves a schoolwide implementation, low student–teacher ratios will require the participation of teachers who do not specialize in teaching language arts or mathematics. In this way, the scale and scope of the implementation should be considered in deciding whether to specialize or not. At the secondary level, where teachers commonly specialize, a schoolwide implementation implies that teachers will need to teach subjects out of their area of specialization, as mentioned previously. If there is a perceived need to upgrade the literacy levels of most or all students at a middle school, for instance, all of the instructors may need to participate in the implementation of DI and teach reading or writing groups. This presents a challenge for building consensus and support for the implementation among the staff, as they will be required to teach students basic literacy skills – something they were not trained to do at university.

An example of teachers' hesitancy at the secondary level to teach subjects outside of their area of specialization can be seen in the remarks of a teacher from Gering, Nebraska, who participated in a schoolwide DI literacy implementation in the early 2000s at the local junior high (covering Grades 7 through 9). The teacher's remarks were recorded as part of the video, *Closing the Performance Gap: The Gering Story*, which is available from the website of the National Institute for Direct Instruction:

> When this whole process started, I had real mixed feelings. Part of me selfishly thought, *Why should I, being a Math teacher, spend a class period every day teaching out of my field, teaching reading.* I felt very inadequate. But I found that the kids responded and I began to see kids' creativity. I began to see them read better. My 'aha' moment came in the middle of one of the stories when I had to discipline kids for trying to read ahead because they wanted to know what was going on. (Weitzel, 2012, 16–17)

The principal of the school expressed how other staff members were initially hesitant until they saw that students were successful with the DI methodology:

> It was really a big change to/for our teachers since they had not had any reading instruction in their prior college instruction. So this was foreign to them. After we got some of the results back and they felt more comfortable with it and could see where it was going, they embraced it and were glad that we did it. I think our results show that. (Weitzel, 2012, 16)

As the Gering example indicates, staff at the secondary level may be more likely to support a schoolwide implementation of DI if they know that their students will be successful with the new approach and that they will only need to teach outside their area of specialization for a limited time. If DI is implemented only at the secondary level, there will be a perennial need for DI schoolwide at the secondary school, as significant percentages of students from the feeder schools will continue to perform below grade level. However, an implementation of DI that accelerates the performance of all students at the elementary school level will obviate the need for a large-scale implementation of DI at the secondary level, as only students who transfer into the junior high from outside the district, along with students with severe disabilities, will be performing below grade-level expectations.

The implementation of DI in Gering, Nebraska in the early 2000s provides a successful example of a temporary dual-level approach at both the elementary and secondary levels concurrently. Located in the northwest corner of the state, the Gering school district implemented a schoolwide literacy program with *Reading Mastery* at the four elementary schools, which covered kindergarten through sixth grade, and *Corrective Reading* at the sole junior high school. After five years of implementing DI, the performance of students graduating from the elementary schools improved dramatically. The percentage of fourth-grade students who scored in the *proficient* category on the statewide writing assessment increased from 57% in 2005 before DI was implemented to 95% in 2008. The Gering fourth-grade scores surpassed the state average, which increased from 83% to 91% in the same time period (NIFDI, *Closing the Performance Gap*, 2). As a result of the effective implementation of DI at the elementary schools, the need for DI at the junior high school dropped dramatically. After just two years, only teachers who were literacy specialists continued to use DI at the junior high. The rest of the teachers went back to teaching their normal subject areas. (Access the video, *Closing the Performance Gap*, at www.nifdi.org/videos/nifdi-schools.html.)

An important consideration is *when* the implementation of DI should commence. As depicted in Figure 7.1 and discussed in later chapters, initial steps for implementing DI should take place in a specific order (placement testing, forming instructional groups, ordering instructional materials, and training instructors in program delivery) before classroom teaching begins, as the results of each step determine the next steps to take. If these steps are not followed sequentially, or if any single step in the chain is not executed with fidelity at the proper time, the launch of the implementation will be adversely affected. If DI is scheduled to start in the fall, this process should start the previous spring and extend through the summer.

Theoretically, this process can start at any time of year, but the timing of the implementation is usually constrained by restrictions on scheduling the preservice program training. Because teachers should receive the equivalent of two full days of training per program level during preservice, the most practical time to hold the preservice training is after teachers have returned from the summer holiday but before students arrive at the beginning of the school year. The timing of the preservice drives the scheduling of the preliminary implementation steps, which should occur in the spring before the training so students will already be placed and grouped according to their skill level, and the materials that match the students' placement will arrive before training is completed so instruction can start the first week of school.

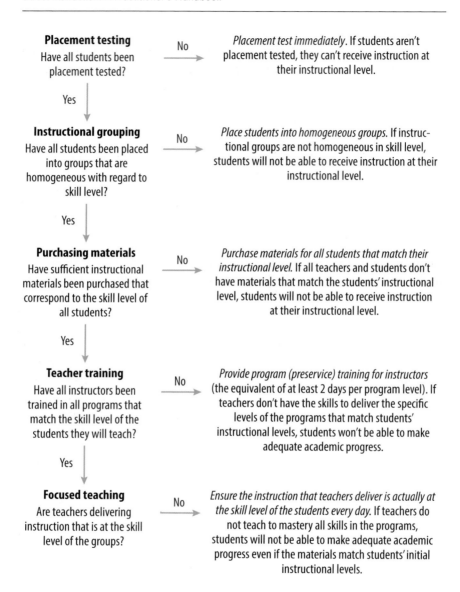

Placement testing
Have all students been placement tested?

No → *Placement test immediately.* If students aren't placement tested, they can't receive instruction at their instructional level.

Yes ↓

Instructional grouping
Have all students been placed into groups that are homogeneous with regard to skill level?

No → *Place students into homogeneous groups.* If instructional groups are not homogeneous in skill level, students will not be able to receive instruction at their instructional level.

Yes ↓

Purchasing materials
Have sufficient instructional materials been purchased that correspond to the skill level of all students?

No → *Purchase materials for all students that match their instructional level.* If all teachers and students don't have materials that match the students' instructional level, students will not be able to receive instruction at their instructional level.

Yes ↓

Teacher training
Have all instructors been trained in all programs that match the skill level of the students they will teach?

No → *Provide program (preservice) training for instructors (the equivalent of at least 2 days per program level).* If teachers don't have the skills to deliver the specific levels of the programs that match students' instructional levels, students won't be able to make adequate academic progress.

Yes ↓

Focused teaching
Are teachers delivering instruction that is at the skill level of the groups?

No → *Ensure the instruction that teachers deliver is actually at the skill level of the students every day.* If teachers do not teach to mastery all skills in the programs, students will not be able to make adequate academic progress even if the materials match students' initial instructional levels.

Figure 7.1 Start-of-the-year flow chart. Source: the National Institute for Direct Instruction (NIFDI).

If school leaders decide to start the implementation of DI at another time of year, they need to take into account the time requirements for preservice training. As mentioned above, training a single program requires the equivalent of two days (12 hours). So one approach to starting a DI implementation midyear is to focus on a single program and schedule a two-day preservice training in conjunction with a preset professional development day. By scheduling a preservice around a "kid-free" in-service day, substitutes will only need to be hired for one day for teachers participating in the training. This is a less expensive way of releasing the staff who will be involved in the implementation of DI than hiring substitutes for two consecutive days at some other time of year. The least expensive option is to schedule the preservice at the beginning of the school year before students arrive as described above.

In addition to the factors indicated in Figure 7.1, the timing of the start of the implementation may also be affected by the amount of consensus-building that needs to take place (discussed later in this chapter). The staff at schools that have been implementing positive behavior management practices and/or lower-case direct instruction techniques can be expected to be more receptive to and excited by the prospect of implementing authentic DI. In contrast, teachers who have only experienced discovery and cooperative learning methods might require more convincing that DI will be effective and more appropriate for their students. Thus, the optimal amount of time devoted to consensus-building and investigating the DI approach will vary considerably by the experiences of the instructional staff. For example, the leadership of Park Elementary in Great Bend, Kansas devoted an entire year to investigating DI before implementing it in the early 2000s. Another option is to start a pilot of the program on a small scale to provide a local demonstration of the efficacy of the DI approach to help build understanding of and support for DI among the staff before launching a broader implementation. These steps need to be factored into the timing of a DI implementation.

Many of the questions regarding *who* will be involved in the implementation of DI, *what* specific subject areas are going to be addressed, and *when* the implementation is going to commence, will logically flow from *how* the DI implementation will fit into the school's mission and goals. It is critically important that a school's leadership team determines specific goals for the implementation of DI that conform to the overarching goals for the school. For instance, if part of an elementary school's mission is to ensure that all students leave an elementary school with the skills needed to access content at the middle school level, the goal of the DI implementation may be to close performance gaps in fourth and fifth grade in reading, which would require the implementation of *Corrective Reading* with students who perform below established norms to bring their literacy skills up to grade-level expectations. If, however, an elementary school's mission is to ensure that all students leave an elementary school with the skills needed to *excel* at the middle school level, the goal of the DI implementation may be to accelerate student performance beyond grade-level proficiency starting with the earliest grade level, which would require a comprehensive implementation of DI in all major subjects (*Reading Mastery*, *Connecting Math Concept*s, and *Spelling Mastery*) involving all students in all grades to ensure that their literacy, numeracy, and reasoning skills exceed grade-level norms.

The goals a school establishes for implementing DI – and the answers to *who*, *what*, and *when*, which stem from the goals – may change over time. Many teachers or school leaders may initially seek out DI to help close achievement gaps in the upper grades, but after DI has been implemented successfully for a couple of years, school leaders may seek to prevent achievement gaps from forming in the lower grades, which then leads them to redefine the goals and the scope of the implementation. If DI is used as an intervention for students who are behind, school leaders may note that some of these students not only close the performance gap but also start to outperform grade-level expectations. This observation can prompt leaders to revise the goal to raise the achievement level of all students and implement DI schoolwide as a core program.

Note that the expansion of the goals of an implementation will only occur if the DI approach is implemented with fidelity. If the DI programs used in an intervention are not implemented with fidelity, the performance of students will not improve markedly, and school leaders will not have an incentive to use DI more broadly at their schools.

Once the goals of the implementation have been established, the next step is to establish specific criteria for success. These criteria can be purely academic, or they can be broader in scope. For academic criteria, school leaders should determine whether there are specific measures that match the students' expected skill acquisition if DI is implemented with fidelity. To demonstrate students' academic growth, it is important to identify a measure that captures their baseline performance and is sensitive to improvement of performance over time. If students are properly placed in the DI programs, the in-program mastery tests should capture the academic growth students experience in the programs. An external measure can also be used to capture this growth, which will usually be more convincing to others than a measure that is built into the DI programs. However, if students perform far below grade-level expectations before starting DI, grade-level external measures may not capture their academic improvement over time. Very few seventh-grade students who perform at the second- or third-grade level before starting DI will perform well on grade-level assessments after one year of instruction, even if they acquire skills at a markedly faster rate than they did in previous years. Other measures should be identified beforehand that can be expected to capture their skill acquisition over the course of the year.

Other effects of the implementation can be captured by surveys, interviews, and in-class observations. Potential topics of surveys include:

- students' attitudes toward school in general
- students' attitudes toward specific subject areas
- teachers' assessment of the school's climate
- teachers' assessment of their own ability to improve student performance.

In-class observations can include the amount of time students are on task during instruction of different subject areas. Administering these surveys and conducting observations should occur before DI is selected and then at regular intervals as DI is implemented, which can provide a more complete picture of the changes that occur at the school, rather than simply relying on academic measures.

If the initial implementation of DI is a pilot, decision points for expanding or discontinuing the pilot should be established beforehand. These should include a definite time frame as well as specific criteria for determining whether the pilot is a success, which can involve academic and non-academic measures.

BUILD CONSENSUS IN SUPPORT OF THE DI IMPLEMENTATION

As mentioned earlier, a critically important step for the school's leadership team is to build consensus among the staff in support of implementing DI. Many staff members may not have heard of DI, while others who have heard of it may be influenced by prevalent, negative myths about the DI approach. In either case, school leaders can expect that at least some staff members will be resistant to implementing DI or consider it to be appropriate only for students with special needs. It is important to address the staff's concerns thoroughly before starting the implementation to achieve broad "buy-in" from the staff. Hannah Stoten, also known as "Quirky Teacher" on social media, cautions school leaders that "the fact that DI is so very different from what people are used to means that you need to be even more careful when introducing it for the first time" (Stoten, 2019, 119). She recommends several steps that can build staff consensus in support of DI:

> … if there is capacity, you could consider creating a small team of early investigators and adopters who are interested in evidence-informed practice and who can see the wisdom in tackling fluency in a systematic and equitable way; they can be entrusted with the task of helping to iron out problems that may arise. Winning hearts and minds is crucial, and visiting other schools … reading research tasks, and a discussion group should start to build enthusiasm prior to the whole-school introduction. (Stoten, 2019, 120)

The NIFDI web page on getting started with DI (www.nifdi.org/services/getting-started.html) lists several steps that school leaders can take to inform their staff about the DI approach and build consensus for a DI implementation. Here are some of the steps listed there and on other pages on the NIFDI website:

1. *Watch videos on Direct instruction.* The NIFDI website offers a wealth of videos on DI, including the *Introduction to Direct*

Instruction Video Series, an online tutorial on implementing the comprehensive DI model, and several videos portraying the experience of schools implementing the DI model. By watching these videos, the staff can become more familiar with DI and the critical factors that need to be considered to make the implementation of DI a success. The site also offers written guides that accompany many of the videos, which can be used to lead staff in a discussion of the most important themes portrayed in the videos.

2. *Access information on the evidence base in support of DI.* The NIFDI website contains a searchable database of over 200 abstracts of research articles and other publications on the efficacy of the DI approach. The website also contains bibliographies of publications on DI that are organized by subject area.

3. *Read and discuss books on fundamental aspects of DI.* The webpage on getting started with DI has information on *Clear Teaching*, a book by Shepard Barbash that was commissioned by the Education Consumers Foundation (ECF). This book is designed to provide an accessible introduction to the basics of the Direct Instruction methodology to anyone who is new to DI. NIFDI has created a guide to help lead staff through a discussion of the book's major themes. The NIFDI store also offers a more in-depth resource on critical concepts undergirding the DI approach: *Successful and Confident Students with Direct Instruction*. NIFDI has developed a discussion guide for group study on this important resource, too.

4. *Review DI program resources.* The NIFDI website offers sample lessons, correlations with the Common Core State Standards, placement tests, and links to the publishers' websites for more information on DI programs. The *Program Reference Chart*, a compilation in tabular form of critical information on the major DI programs, is available in the free downloads section of the NIFDI website at www.nifdi.org/resources/free-downloads/programs/program-reference-chart.html.

As Hannah Stoten indicates, visiting a school that is implementing DI successfully can be a very powerful tool for helping build consensus among the staff. Viewing videos about schools that have implemented

235

DI can answer some of the questions the staff may have, but a visit to a school will allow the staff to explore the implications of adopting DI more fully. An effective format for the visit is to start with observations of instruction in several classrooms followed by a question-and-answer session with teachers and school leaders experienced in implementing DI. The direct connection between the staff of a school investigating the DI methodology and the staff of a school implementing DI can be enhanced by the use of email and video conferencing, so questions that arise before or after the visit can be addressed. Through visits and remote communication, the new school's leaders and staff can learn how another school has addressed such potentially difficult changes as deploying teaching assistants, forming instructional groups, and allocating sufficient time for instruction in daily schedules.

The power of these visits arises not just from the information that is gleaned by the visitors but also from the cohesion that develops among the visiting staff. Traveling together, staying in the same hotel, observing another school that shares similarities to the visitors' school, and debriefing after visits provide opportunities for the staff to develop a strong bond among themselves and attain a higher trust level, which can help facilitate a transition to a new teaching methodology. Some school leaders have institutionalized annual visits to other schools implementing DI and made them a regular part of the orientation of new staff members. For example, for several years Bernice Whelchel, the principal of City Springs Elementary in Baltimore, led a group of new teachers and other staff members on an annual trip to Houston to visit Wesley Elementary, which served as a model school for implementing DI with highly at-risk children in Texas in the 1980s through the early 2000s.

After the staff have had a chance to review information on DI and visit a school implementing DI programs successfully, a decision whether to implement DI at the school needs to be made. From the outset, school leaders should clearly communicate to the staff what the decision-making process will be, and what role a vote by the staff will play, if any. In some cases, the decision is made entirely at the district level. In other cases, it is a school-based decision. Even when the staff does not have an official role in deciding whether to implement DI, holding a discussion and a vote by the staff can help foster group cohesion. If the staff does not feel that they have been given a voice, their support for DI may be diminished even if they are otherwise in favor of implementing DI.

If DI is piloted on a small scale as a preliminary step for deciding whether to implement it on a larger scale, the leadership should revisit the criteria for success that were established before the pilot commenced and make a decision based on whether those criteria were met. A common threshold for deciding in favor of DI – or any schoolwide model – is 80% in a secret ballot (Herman et al., 1999). This threshold indicates overwhelming support among the staff and will likely lead to better outcomes because of the high level of support. At any threshold level, school leaders should clarify to the staff that they will all be expected to implement the program with fidelity regardless of their vote if the threshold in favor of implementing the program is reached. Staff members who vote against adopting DI will still be required to follow the program's precepts, accept feedback from coaches and incorporate it into their teaching, follow prescribed schedules, complete required data forms, and implement all of the other aspects of the DI methodology as outlined in this book and other sources, including the teacher's guides for the different program levels.

Many of the teachers who have initial doubts about DI may become strong advocates for it after they observe that the DI approach has positive effects on their students' performance. Often, this change in attitude occurs within the first few months of school if DI is implemented with fidelity. However, school leaders should be prepared for some teachers who vote against implementing DI to "self-select" out of the implementation if the school moves to adopt DI. These teachers may request to be moved to another grade, or they may leave the school entirely. It is important that the leadership accommodates any requests to be moved to a grade level that is not implementing DI, if possible. Asking a teacher to implement a program or approach that they do not support can lead to resentment and a decrease in enthusiasm for the new program, which can have a negative, rippling effect among the staff. If DI is implemented with fidelity, and the school experiences some "early wins" in terms of improving students' performance and attitudes toward school, teachers who were originally opposed to DI may warm up to DI. They can be brought into the fold over time as the DI implementation is expanded to other grade levels and other subject areas.

MAP THE DI CURRICULA AGAINST STATE AND NATIONAL STANDARDS

An important preliminary step to implementing DI is to map the coverage of the DI programs against state and national requirements to determine which standards the DI programs do and do not address. This curriculum mapping can be done in two stages. The first stage can consist of a broad assessment of the alignment of the DI programs with standards as part of the school leadership's initial research efforts on DI to inform the staff of critical information they should consider before voting whether to adopt it. The second stage can occur after DI has been approved for adoption by the staff and school leadership. Then, a more thorough mapping can take place as a means of determining in more detail the specific types of content that teachers will need to cover in addition to the content covered in the DI programs. This more thorough curriculum mapping should be followed by a plan on how to address standards that are not covered by the DI programs. This plan can be revisited and updated annually in response to the staff's experience supplementing DI to meet state and national standards.

Note that very little supplementing of DI will need to take place in the case of the Common Core State Standards (CCSS) as there is a high degree of alignment between the DI programs and the CCSS. The latest edition of *Connecting Math Concepts* was redesigned to incorporate the CCSS completely with 100% alignment. *Reading Mastery Signature Edition* (RMSE) was revised to address nearly all of the standards according to an analysis performed by the National Institute for Direct Instruction. The analysis shows that the standards not met by the RMSE program can be met easily through other means:

> Overall, *RMSE* met 95% of the ELA Standards prescribed in the CCSS. Only 23 out of 427 standards are not covered by the program. Moreover, the standards that are not covered by *RMSE* can be met through lessons and activities teachers regularly promote in their classrooms. For example, the following Kindergarten standard is not met through *RMSE*: "With guidance and support from adults, explore a variety of digital tools to produce and publish writing, including in

collaboration with peers." Teachers routinely introduce digital tools, such as computers and word processing, to their students within other subject areas and contexts during the school day. (NIFDI, *DI and the Common Core State Standards*)

Interestingly, evidence indicates that students who receive instruction in DI score well on a variety of assessments – if they get far enough in the programs at mastery – even if the DI programs have not been revised to align with the assessments. Dr. Jean Stockard examined the relationship between a) elementary grade students' progress (at mastery) through two DI programs (*Reading Mastery Signature Edition* and *Connecting Math Concepts: Comprehensive Edition*) at three different sites in the US (in Texas, Colorado, and an inner city on the East Coast), and b) the students' score on external measures of achievement: the State of Texas Assessments of Academic Readiness (STAAR), the Transitional Colorado Assessment Program (TCAP), and the Measures of Academic Progress (MAP) developed by the Northwest Evaluation Association, respectively. Dr. Stockard found that:

> … students who were at or approaching mastery at their assigned grade level in *RMSE* and *CMCCE* had a strong probability of scoring at the proficient level on state assessments, while far fewer students who were at lower levels in the program were found to be proficient. … In most cases, on average, over four-fifths of the students who were at or near mastery at their grade level placement scored at the proficient level. The only exception involves mathematics for the students in Colorado, where the definition of "near target" included any student who was in the third grade level of the program. Half of those students scored at the proficient level, compared to only 10 percent of those below that level. (Stockard, 2014, 21)

The reason why students who progress through the DI programs at mastery perform well on a variety of assessments is that they acquire grade-level content that provides a strong basis for addressing content that is not taught explicitly in the DI programs. If DI is implemented with fidelity, progressing through the programs involves students mastering a set of skills and knowledge in contrast to mere exposure. With a relatively quick introduction to the format of tests and some specific content that students haven't seen before, *these students will be able to apply the knowledge they've mastered in the DI programs to other contexts.* Other programs that may nominally align well with standards and assessments on paper, but do not require students to actually master the material covered, should not be expected to result in high student achievement on these assessments.

ENSURE THE POSITIVE MANAGEMENT OF STUDENTS' BEHAVIOR

In DI, the demands put on students regarding their engagement and effort during instruction are generally much higher than the demands required by other instructional approaches. As mentioned in previous chapters, students in DI must respond on signal at a high frequency to their teacher's questions and directions, repeat material until they demonstrate mastery as a group, answer questions individually, pay attention as other students respond individually, apply the skills and concepts covered during group instruction to independent work, and retain what they have learned at a high criterion (90% or higher) in order to pass in-program assessments.

In keeping with these high demands on students, there is a corresponding need for positive behavior management by teachers and school leaders. Students need to receive positive feedback at a high rate that communicates to them that they are meeting or exceeding academic as well as behavioral expectations. To prepare the staff to provide a positive environment for students, schools should implement schoolwide management procedures that clarify and reinforce behavioral expectations *during the year prior to implementing DI.* If the staff have a whole year to refine positive behavioral management procedures, the implementation of DI will go much smoother the following year.

As described in chapter 5, successful management systems include a clear set of routines, procedures, and expectations for student behaviors in classrooms as well as in common areas, such as school buses, the cafeteria, the playground, hallways, and bathrooms. Teachers should devote time to instruction around behavioral expectations in common areas early in the school year. They should demonstrate and practice with their class the specific behaviors that are expected of students and then watch and give feedback as students practice these behaviors. As with other aspects of DI, teachers should repeat the model-and-test-with-feedback cycle until students demonstrate consistent mastery.

The same process should take place in classrooms for transitions that occur in the instructional setting. As described in chapter 5, these transitions may include:

- putting away materials used in the prior activity (or coats and hats if students are coming from outside)
- forming the proper student groupings required for the new activity, which may involve walking to another classroom
- taking assigned seats for the new activity
- accessing appropriate materials for the new activity
- locating the proper place within the materials
- turning their attention to the teacher.

For all of these transitions, teachers should have students practice expectations and reinforce them for appropriate behavior.

There are many resources on positive behavior management practices that teachers and school leaders can access. Chapter 5 provides an example of a simple procedure for practicing and reinforcing following directions in the form of the "Pencils Up/Pencils Down" game. For a more comprehensive set of behavior management tools, visit the website of such organizations as Safe and Civil Schools (www.safeandcivilschools.com). Onsite training and coaching on positive behavior management systems can ensure that students and teachers are ready for the demands of DI.

With the scope of the DI implementation clearly outlined, a consensus established among the staff in support of implementing DI, the coverage of the DI programs mapped against state and national standards, and teachers well practiced in positive behavior management practices, the school is ready to take the main steps toward implementing DI successfully.

CHAPTER EIGHT
SETTING UP THE IMPLEMENTATION

A schoolwide implementation of Direct Instruction (DI) requires a school's leadership team to fulfill three functions that promote students' success. As depicted in Figure 8.1, these three functions are:

1. to set expectations for staff regarding the DI approach and ensure the setup of all aspects of the DI instructional model
2. to monitor the implementation of the DI approach in classrooms
3. to respond actively to students' performance and the staff's implementation of DI.

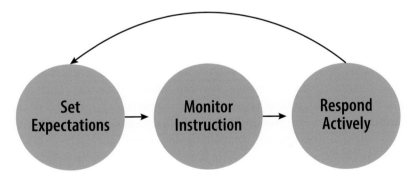

Figure 8.1 School leadership functions related to instruction.

In the figure, the two short arrows pointing right indicate that the functions occur sequentially from left to right for the most part. Expectations of the staff (the first leadership function) need to be established before monitoring (the second leadership function) takes place. If expectations are not set, and the staff is not aware of the details of the DI model, monitoring will most likely reveal that the DI model is not being implemented with fidelity, which will require the school's leadership team to communicate the expectations to the staff. Setting expectations as a proactive first step saves time and leads to an implementation that is much closer to fidelity than just providing general information on DI. Monitoring instruction, in turn, needs to take place before school leaders can respond actively (the third leadership function) because only through monitoring can problems of student performance and instruction be identified. If school leaders do not have a clear understanding of the state of the DI implementation through observations and data analysis, they won't know what to respond to and how to respond. Responding actively can involve a resetting of expectations with the instructional staff, which is depicted by the curved arrow pointing to the left at the top of Figure 8.1.

Although the relationship between the three functions may appear to be cyclical based on Figure 8.1, the relationship should be *iterative* for the implementation of DI to be successful. Instead of a constant or static cycle of *expectations setting, monitoring, and responding* with the same items discussed repeatedly, the specific items that are the focus of the school leader's attention should shift over time to more advanced aspects of the DI model with successive iterations, with each approximation closer to an ideal implementation. An implementation that shows promise of reaching full fidelity is one in which the focus of the leader's attention transitions from fundamental structural factors, such as scheduling sufficient instructional time and distributing materials, to more advanced factors, such as the delivery of complex instructional formats. However, if the same problem is identified and responded to by the school's leadership several times in a row – such as teachers not completing data forms correctly – this is an indication that the implementation is not likely to achieve a sufficiently high level of fidelity to ensure that students will be successful with DI.

This chapter addresses setting expectations with the instructional staff and other forms of setup of a successful DI implementation. These expectations include the following steps:

1. Assessing each student's skills by administering placement tests

2. Forming instructional groups based on the results of the placement tests

3. Ordering teacher and student materials that match students' performance levels

4. Scheduling sufficient time in the programs for each instructional group

5. Establishing the roles of staff members involved in the DI implementation

6. Establishing end-of-year goals for each instructional group

7. Providing initial training in the DI methodology

8. Arranging for ongoing training and coaching support

9. Configuring classrooms for efficient instruction

10. Establishing positive behavior management practices with all students.

These steps should be implemented in the order they appear above for the most part. To discuss each of these setup steps, this chapter takes as its initial point of reference a schoolwide, full-immersion implementation of DI as core instruction for all students. Practitioners who plan on implementing DI more narrowly can simply apply the requirements of a full-immersion implementation to a subset of students at their schools.

ADVANTAGES OF A SCHOOLWIDE IMPLEMENTATION OF DI

A full-immersion, schoolwide implementation of DI involves using DI programs for core instruction in reading, language, mathematics, and spelling for all students who place into the programs. As mentioned above, DI programs are usually implemented in stages so as to not overwhelm the staff with too much new learning at once. Reading and language are typically introduced in the first year of implementation, and mathematics and spelling in the second year with other DI programs introduced in the third year of implementation. In the full-immersion version of DI, *other instructional materials provide additional practice only* and do not involve instruction in these subject areas, *even if the programs are used before or after school.* The rationale for providing instruction in DI only is that, regardless of when students receive instruction, the strategies taught must be consistent with those of the DI curricula being implemented. Students may get confused when presented with more than one strategy. For instance, *Reading Mastery Signature Edition* refers to symbols as sounds and not letters in the first two levels of the program, while *Reading Mastery Transformations* refers to letter names from the beginning of the program. Using both programs with the same children has the potential to confuse them and delay their acquisition of critical literacy skills. (Meeting state or national standards sometimes presents an exception to using only DI materials for instruction. If the DI programs do not meet a standard that teachers are required to meet, they can use other materials to meet the standard.)

In addition to using DI for core instruction for all students, all interventions are done through the DI programs in a full-immersion, schoolwide implementation. Students are not pulled out for instruction in another program. Instead, intervention takes the form of remedies and additional practice that are implemented through the DI programs themselves. The exception would be for those students who perform too low for any of the DI published programs. These students would receive instruction described in *Strategies for Teaching Students with Severe and Low-Incidence Disabilities* (Engelmann, S., 2018). However, after these students have received instruction using these strategies for a time and are able to place into one of the DI programs, they would transition to receiving instruction in the DI programs exclusively.

The advantages of a schoolwide implementation of DI are several:

- *Forming instructional groups can be easier when the implementation of DI is schoolwide.* When all students in a grade level or school participate in a DI implementation, all instructional staff can be assigned DI groups. This increases the number of instructional groups, which increases the chance that the groups will be able to accommodate all students' skill profiles. In contrast, if only a single teacher implements DI in their classroom, their students may place into a wide range of program levels. Yet, they will find it difficult, if not impossible, to have enough time in the day to teach all of the groups that would correspond to each student's skill level. The greater the number of teachers included in the implementation, the greater the number of instructional groups the school can offer to accommodate a wider range of student skill levels.

- *Teachers don't have to employ multiple instructional approaches.* The DI methodology requires teachers to learn a different way of presenting, monitoring, and responding to student performance than they have used in the past. Once teachers become familiar with teaching a DI program, it is easier for them to learn other DI programs because the DI methodology has many consistent features across programs, such as homogeneous grouping, signals, choral responses, and immediate error corrections. (These features are discussed in previous chapters of this book.) A schoolwide implementation of DI obviates the need for teachers to employ several different instructional methodologies in the same day for core instruction.

- *Students have consistent expectations across their instructional day.* Students who are used to a "discovery questioning" approach with the freedom to call out answers during part of the school day may have difficulty waiting for their teacher's signal during DI. A schoolwide implementation of DI provides consistent expectations across the school day, which is especially helpful for highly at-risk children as "extroverted and highly articulate children are used to dominating the discourse of the lesson by calling out, finishing teachers sentences etc." (Stoten, 2019, 125). The DI method ensures that all students have an equal opportunity to respond and be heard.

- *Data decision rules for determining when a second program is used, for how long, and with which students can be complex.* If more than one program covering the same subject area is being implemented in a school, a set of rules needs to be developed that determine which students receive instruction in which program, and under what circumstances students' instruction will be switched to another program. The school's leadership team must set the decision points for making these changes and then monitor the implementation to determine when these decision points have been reached. School leaders should then communicate to teachers when students are supposed to be switched to the other program and conduct follow-up monitoring to ensure that the implementation has been modified as stipulated by the decision-making rules. Managing the implementation of the decision-making rules can be especially complex when two programs or instructional approaches are not designed to be taught together, such as DI and a "discovery questioning" approach. Using DI programs for both core instruction and remedial instruction alleviates this potential issue.

Using the schoolwide implementation as a reference point allows us to determine whether the students in a partial implementation of DI (in a resource room or for a single grade, for instance) are receiving adequate instruction. Students participating in any type of DI implementation should receive everything that students in a schoolwide implementation of DI would receive – instruction at their skill level with sufficient time in the programs daily by an instructor who delivers the program with fidelity and makes decisions based on student performance in the programs. If DI is only going to be implemented in a single classroom in a school, those students should receive the same type of instruction with the same effectiveness for the same duration as they would have received if DI were implemented schoolwide.

Note that most DI programs are designed to be implemented for core instruction, but some programs are meant to be implemented as interventions to bring students who are performing significantly below their cohort quickly to grade-level expectations. *Corrective Mathematics*, for instance, is designed to be "used to support a high-quality core mathematics program" (Engelmann, Carnine, and Steely, 2005, 1). Students who place into these programs could also receive instruction in the core math program that other students in the school receive if time and staffing resources allow it. Students from the same school who do not place into these programs would only receive instruction in the core math program as they would not need an instructional intervention in math.

ASSESSING EACH STUDENT'S SKILLS BY ADMINISTERING PLACEMENT TESTS

The first step in setting up a DI implementation effectively is to administer placement tests to all students who are being considered for DI. Placement testing is an integral and very important first step in implementing DI that is sometimes overlooked. A misstep on this first step can send the implementation on very different trajectories as proper placement is one of the cornerstones of the DI method (along with mastery and time-efficiency). As described previously, if students are not placed at their skill level, they will not be able to progress through the program at mastery. In addition, they may become discouraged if they have to repeat material several times because it is too advanced for them, and their discouragement can spread to the instructional staff and school leaders. However, if students are placed properly in the DI programs and other aspects of the program are implemented with fidelity, DI will likely be a success. So from the beginning of the implementation, the staff needs to commit to being responsive to their students' performance with DI – with placement testing being the first opportunity to demonstrate this commitment.

Every student who has been identified for participation in the DI implementation should be given placement tests in all DI programs they may receive instruction in. This allows the staff to determine the specific level – and starting point within the program levels – that corresponds to each student's skill level, which may be different than their grade level or age. All students new to DI should be tested in the spring before school ends so instructional materials that correspond to the students' placements can be ordered in time for the materials to arrive before school starts. Based on the results of the placement tests, students are grouped for instruction. The groups should be flexible in membership so they can be adjusted throughout the school year in response to student performance in the programs. This flexibility ensures that students' placement matches their skill levels as precisely as possible all year long, which allows them to take advantage of the small-step design that is essential to the DI approach, as described in section 1 of this book. This is especially important for beginning reading instruction.

As mentioned in chapter 1, each DI program comes with a placement test that can be used to determine the optimal starting point in the program that matches each student's instructional level. The placement tests consist of several different components: directions for administering the test, a script that testers follow exactly when administering the test, student material for the test items, an answer key, and a form for recording the results of the tests. The source of the placement tests varies by program. They may be found in the teacher's guide or the series guides of the programs.

For some tests, there are only two possible results – students can test into the program and start the program at the beginning (Lesson 1), or they do not have sufficient skills for the program and should be tested for a lower-level program. Each of the levels of *Corrective Reading Decoding* as well as *REWARDS Intermediate* and *REWARDS Secondary* fall into this category as Lesson 1 is the only starting place in the different levels of these programs. For other programs, there are multiple possible starting lessons. Table 8.1 displays the possible starting lessons for the different levels of *Connecting Math Concepts Comprehensive Edition* (CMC CE). As the table shows, there is only one starting point for Level A (Lesson 1) while there are two starting points for each of the other levels (Lesson 1 and another lesson).

Program level	Possible starting lessons
A	1
B	1, 16
C	1, 11
D	1, 26
E	1, 31
F	1, 16

Table 8.1 Potential starting points in *Connecting Math Concepts*. Source: Engelmann, S. et al. (2014). *Connecting Math Concepts Comprehensive Edition Series Guide*, pp. 188–220.

The program with the most possible starting points is *Reading Mastery Transformations Grade K* with seven different possible placements: Lessons 1, 15, 71, 101, and 131 as well as a pre-program with two entry points for students who haven't acquired sufficient skills to start at Lesson 1.

It is helpful to conceive of the placement tests, not as isolated assessments for the different levels of the programs, but as a series of assessments that allow for an adaptive process of identifying the best starting points for each child. For each part of every placement test, an individual student's performance determines the next step in the testing process. After a student completes a test, the tester decides whether a student's score should result in a) stopping the testing process and assigning a starting lesson to the student or b) continuing testing.

For example, the placement test for *Corrective Reading Decoding* has four parts, as indicated in Table 8.2. Testing could stop for students after the first part, or it could continue for a maximum of three parts of the test.

For Part I, the first test given, students who read the test passage with 12 to 21 errors in more than two minutes are placed at Lesson 1 of Level A, the lowest level of the program, and testing ends. Students who read the Part I test passage with 0 to 11 errors in more than two minutes are placed at Lesson 1 of Level B1, the next lowest level of the program, and testing ends. All other students are given additional parts of the test until their optimal starting points in the *Corrective Reading* series are found.

ERRORS	TIME	PLACEMENT OR NEXT TEST
PART I		
22 or more	-	Administer PART II Test
12 to 21	more than 2:00	Level A, Lesson 1
12 to 21	2:00 or less	Administer PART II Test
0 to 11	more than 2:00	Level B1, Lesson 1
0 to 11	2:00 or less	Administer PART III Test
PART II		
41 or more	-	No **Corrective Reading** placement; use a beginning reading program
8 to 40	-	Level A, Lesson 1
0 to 7	-	Level B1, Lesson 1
PART III		
16 or more	-	Level B1, Lesson 1
6 to 15	more than 2:30	Level B1, Lesson 1
6 to 15	2:30 or less	Level B2, Lesson 1
0 to 5	more than 2:30	Level B2, Lesson 1
0 to 5	2:30 or less	Administer PART IV Test
PART IV		
9 or more	-	Level B2, Lesson 1
4 to 8	more than 1:30	Level B2, Lesson 1
4 to 8	1:30 or less	Level C, Lesson 1
0 to 3	more than 1:20	Level C, Lesson 1
0 to 3	1:20 or less	Doesn't need **Corrective Reading** Decoding program

Table 8.2 Decoding placement schedule. Source: Engelmann, S. et al. (2008f). *Corrective Reading Decoding, Level B1 Teacher's Guide*, p. 49.

Although it is easiest to visualize this adaptive testing process in placement tests that have been organized around a program series, such as *Corrective Reading*, the same type of process occurs when placing students in DI programs that have separate tests for each level. The National Institute for Direct Instruction (NIFDI) has developed assessment flow charts that indicate the options for students by their grade level for different subject areas.

Table 8.3 shows the reading and language assessment guidelines for students entering fourth grade. Most of the steps shown in the table involve different levels of the reading track of *Reading Mastery Signature Edition* (RMSE), but other programs are also indicated as options for students depending on their performance on the RMSE placement tests. For example, students who do not pass the *RMSE Reading* Grade 3 placement test (the first test given to all fourth graders new to DI) are tested in *Corrective Reading Decoding* and follow the flow chart shown in Table 8.2. Students who pass the Grade 3 reading test are given one or more placement tests for *RMSE Language* (Grade 4 or 5 depending on their performance).

Placement Tests	If	Then
Give Signature Reading Grade 3 Test (passing criteria: part 1 - 2:00/0-6 errors; part 2 - 5:00/0-2 errors)	not passing...	Give Corrective Decoding test. (See Table 8.2.)
	passing...	Give RMSE Grade 4 test.
Give Signature Reading Grade 4 Test (passing criteria: part 1 - 2:00/0-6 errors; part 2 - 7:00/0-2 errors)	not passing...	Stop testing. Place in RMSE Grade 3, lesson 1. Give Language Grade 3 Story Writing test.
	passing...	Give RMSE Grade 5 test.
Give Signature Reading Grade 5 Test (passing criteria: part 1 - 2:00/0-6 errors; part 2 - 7:00/0-2 errors)	not passing...	Stop testing. Place in RMSE Grade 4, lesson 1. Give Language Grade 4 Story Writing test.
	passing...	Stop testing. Place in RMSE Grade 5, lesson 1. Give Language Grade 4 Story Writing test and give Language Grade 5 test. Follow 5th grade guidelines.

Table 8.3 Literacy assessment and placement guidelines for students entering fourth grade. Source: adapted from placement guidelines provided by the National Institute for Direct Instruction.

Because it is essential to get an accurate assessment of students' current skills, the first test students encounter in the testing process should be one they will likely pass. Success on the first test boosts students' confidence that they will be able to do well on other tests and motivates them to perform at their best. In contrast, if the first test intimidates students, they are unlikely to perform at their best on subsequent tests, and any placement based on their performance may not accurately reflect their actual skills. For the developmental programs, the first test should be the test that corresponds to the *next lowest grade level of the students*. As shown in Table 8.3, the first test given to fourth graders is the third-grade test. For *Corrective Reading Decoding*, the first test (Part I) is the second least difficult of the placement tests, which allows most students to feel confident as they go through the testing process.

Because there are many different paths the testing process can take in response to students' performance on the tests, the amount of time students require to complete the testing process varies according to the number of tests each student takes. Testers should make sufficient copies of all tests they might need for the students before they start to administer the tests so they can easily move from one test to the next. *Copies of the tests should be in color to show the blue lettering in the testing scripts.* (If testers make copies in black and white, they should prep the copies of the tests by highlighting the wording in the script they will say before starting the testing process.)

Testers should also become familiar with the format and setup requirements for each of the relevant tests as *some tests are group administered, and some are administered individually.* For instance, *Corrective Reading Comprehension* has three tests. The first test is administered to the whole class, and it is used to determine which of the remaining two tests the students receive. The first *Comprehension* test involves multiple-choice responses from students and requires no more than 10 minutes. The second test is administered individually (to students who make more than seven errors on the first test), and it requires about 10 minutes per student. The third test is administered as a group to all students who make seven or fewer errors on the first test. It also requires about 10 minutes to administer (Engelmann, S., Hanner and Johnson, 2008, 251–53). For the third test, students "underline sentence parts, write answers to questions, and indicate correct responses to multiple choice items" (ibid., 253).

Testers should be discreet in how they mark errors in front of the students. For many of the programs, the tester will score the test in real time as each student responds individually. It is important to make sure that students cannot see when the tester is marking errors as this could be distracting to the students.

Placement testing is a skill that requires about two to four hours of training, depending on the program levels involved and the familiarity of the testers with the programs. During the training, participants learn how to:

1. follow the placement test scripts and directions fluently
2. recognize what constitutes an error in order to develop inter-tester reliability
3. record errors in real time, including noting the specific types of errors students make in place of the correct answers
4. observe how students perform, especially while solving a math problem
5. motivate students to perform at their highest level.

During the training, it is important that participants simulate scoring different types of errors that students may make. For instance, the trainer can simulate how some readers "self-correct" by saying an incorrect word during reading but then quickly saying the correct word. For upper-level language programs, the trainer can share different passages to help testers come to a common understanding of what types of written responses are acceptable and what types are not acceptable. For all tests, it is important that the tester records the type of errors students make as well as the quantity of errors. A student making a single error multiple times may be much easier to correct than a student making many different types of errors. In reading, students who make errors on articles and prepositions will require a different type of instruction than those who make errors only on multisyllabic words. These differences should be taken into account in addition to the raw numerical score to make instructional groups as homogeneous as possible. For this reason, it is important that testers *save the original protocols* with marks indicating very specific information on the students' performance on the placement tests.

Placement testing may be the first opportunity for leaders to establish a schoolwide culture that is a fundamental prerequisite for success with the DI model – accepting the actual performance of students. As with all DI assessments, the focus of the placement tests should not be on whether students "pass." Rather, the purpose of the tests is to provide information that can inform teachers and school leaders on the type of instruction that can benefit students the most. In this way, student performance on placement tests should not be seen as evaluative of the testers or the teachers of the students. There should be no negative judgment or recrimination toward teachers whose students place low on the tests. All involved should accept that getting an accurate read on students' skills is a necessary first step to improving students' performance going forward.

Note that it is essential for testers to understand the importance of capturing first-time correct performance – a critically important concept in other phases of DI. If a student makes an error or has difficulty of any kind with an item, the tester should not give any hints to students regarding the correct answer. The students' first response without any assistance is the response that should be recorded.

To make sure that the results are completely objective, it may be best to avoid deploying teachers as the testers of students they have taught. Testers who are not the students' teachers are much less likely to have an emotional attachment to the performance of individual students and are therefore much less likely to prompt students or allow seemingly minor errors to go unrecorded. Regardless of whether teachers participate as testers in the placement testing, all teachers should attend the training on placement testing so they understand the assessment process and criteria for placing students and know how to administer placement tests to students who arrive after the beginning of the school year. Understanding the placement testing process will also help the staff administer other DI assessments, such as mastery tests. In addition, participating in the placement test training may help underscore that the instructional groups established initially through the placement testing process are temporary and will change throughout the year to accommodate differential changes in the performance of individual students.

Note that program lesson placement may differ for students who have been through a prior DI program in comparison to the placement for students who are brand new to DI. For example, if students have completed *Decoding A* at mastery, they can skip the first seven lessons of *Decoding B1* and start at Lesson 8 (Engelmann, S. et al., 2008g, 2). Similarly, students who have recently completed *REWARDS Secondary* at mastery can skip the review lessons in *REWARDS Plus*, which are intended for students who are unfamiliar with the *REWARDS* conventions and approach. Instead of review lessons, there is a 10-lesson pre-program for students who place into *Expressive Writing II* and did not receive instruction in the first program of the series, *Expressive Writing I*. Students who complete *Expressive Writing I* at mastery do not need to receive instruction in the pre-program but instead can start on Lesson 1 of *Expressive Writing II*.

As soon as the placement test results are checked and collated, the school can start the process of forming homogeneous instructional groups. It is important that a DI coordinator verifies the results to make sure that the testing process has been completed for all students. The most common error is for testers to stop testing too soon. The coordinator should double-check that the correct scores are recorded on a spreadsheet for each test for every child and verify that every child received all tests needed to find their optimal starting point in the DI programs. If there are students whose skill repertoire is such that they are not able to place in even the lowest levels of the DI programs, they should receive instruction that follows *Strategies for Teaching Students with Severe and Low-Incidence Disabilities* by Siegfried Engelmann (2018) as mentioned earlier.

FORMING INSTRUCTIONAL GROUPS WITH STUDENTS PLACED AT THEIR SKILL LEVELS

Forming homogeneous instructional groups can take place as soon as placement testing is completed for all students. Optimally, this should occur in the spring before the DI implementation is scheduled to start to allow time for the instructional materials to be ordered and arrive before the beginning of the school year. As mentioned previously, placement test results provide a starting point for students, but the groupings must be flexible to accommodate students' differential learning rates.

Some students will acquire different skills faster than other students who initially place at the same lesson in the program, although much of this variability in performance stems from differences in attendance. Other students will require more practice on different types of material to master it. Both of these types of students must be accommodated for them to proceed through the program at their optimal learning rate, which can change over time. Thus, an important part of the school culture must be to support and facilitate group flexibility by recognizing that the responsibility for students' learning rests with the school as a whole as well as with individual staff members. The school's leadership must monitor students' performance closely so adjustments to grouping can be made in a timely manner, as described in the next chapter.

OPTIMAL SIZE OF GROUPS

There is a clear difference in the optimal size of groups based on the level of the DI programs being implemented. Lower levels of the programs require smaller student–teacher ratios than higher levels of the programs, which can be taught to whole classes. Inexperienced or fragile learners who place into the lower levels of the programs need more attention, feedback, and adjustment of instruction than established learners, who place into the higher levels of the programs. For these reasons, the lower program levels should have a maximum of 12 students per group with smaller groups as needed according to the performance of the students. Table 8.4 shows the grouping guidelines for selected DI programs. As the table indicates, lower-performing students in the first two levels of *Reading Mastery* (reading and language) and *Connecting Math Concepts: Comprehensive Edition* (CMC CE), as well as *DISTAR Arithmetic 1*, should be in groups no larger than six. In the upper levels of *Reading Mastery* and CMC CE as well as all levels of *Spelling Mastery*, instructional groups can be much larger in size – up to 25 students or more – as long as the groups are homogeneous with respect to students' skill repertoire and the teacher is able to maintain students' attention on instruction. Student–teacher ratios for the upper levels of the programs can be whole-class, but smaller groups at these levels, though not required, can be beneficial as they allow the teacher to provide more attention to each child in the group.

Program	Program Level	Grouping Guidelines by Performance Level (no. of students per group)
Developmental programs		
Reading Mastery Signature Edition (reading and language)	Grades K & 1	Low: 6 or less Medium: 8-10 High: up to 12
	Grades 2 and above	Homogeneous whole-class or small groups
Spelling Mastery	All levels	Homogeneous whole-class or small groups
DISTAR Arithmetic	Level 1	Low: 6 or less High: up to 12
Connecting Math Concepts: Comprehensive Edition	Level A	Low: 6 or less Medium: 8-10 High: up to 12
	Level B and higher	Homogeneous whole-class or small groups
Remedial programs		
Corrective Reading: Decoding and Comprehension	Level A	6 to 8
	Level B1	15 or less
	Levels B2 & C	Homogeneous groups of any size
Expressive Writing	Levels 1 & 2	15 or less or individuals
Corrective Mathematics	All modules	15 or less or individuals
Programs for English Language Learners		
Direct Instruction Spoken English	Levels 1 & 2	No more than 10 recommended
Secondary School Programs		
Understanding US History	Levels 1 & 2	Homogeneous whole-class or small groups
Essentials for Writing	(One level)	Homogeneous whole-class groups or individuals
Essentials for Algebra	(One level)	Homogeneous whole-class groups or individuals

Table 8.4 Grouping guidelines by program level and performance level of students for selected Direct Instruction programs. Adapted from: NIFDI. (2023). *Program Reference Chart.*

There is a similar pattern of optimal group sizes for remedial students. For the lowest level of the *Decoding* and *Comprehension* tracks of *Corrective Reading Level A*, the optimal group size is six to eight students. Group sizes can be smaller to allow for even more attention from the teacher to students in Level A, who perform at the pre-primer level. For the rest of the programs listed in the remedial section of Table 8.4, the recommended group size is 15 or less. The exceptions are Levels B2 and C of *Corrective Reading Decoding* or *Comprehension*, which can support whole-class, homogeneous instructional groups.

For English language learners who place into *Direct Instruction Spoken English* (DISE), instruction can be whole-class, but a recommended maximum ratio is 10:1. Any ratio larger than 10:1 may result in students not getting sufficient practice in this highly interactive, oral language instructional program.

DI programs intended for secondary students can be taught whole-class, although the programs can also be used with students in small groups and in one-on-one tutoring settings. As described in chapter 4, these programs include *Essentials for Algebra* and *Essentials for Writing*. They are intended for core coursework that addresses the needs of the majority of students in middle school or high school. As with other DI programs, the groups must be homogeneous with respect to students' skill repertoire. All members of the group must meet the entry requirements for the programs, and they must receive instruction at the specific lesson that matches their skill level for the programs to be effective.

The implication of the grouping guidelines is highly significant for staffing the DI implementation as there is a direct connection between the placement results and group size. Since staffing and teaching assignments are determined to a large degree by the distribution of where students place in the programs, it is preferable to administer the placement tests, analyze the results, and form the instructional groupings sufficiently early in the spring. This allows time for any additional staff hiring or reassignment that may need to occur to accommodate the optimal instructional group configuration for a DI implementation.

Although all of the programs can be used in one-on-one teaching or tutoring settings, group settings are preferred for many reasons. It is often easier to motivate students to follow rules and work hard when there are several students in the group whom the teacher can set as a positive example for other students. Also, there are some items in the programs that require more than one student, such as exercises in the beginning language program that teach the pronouns "he," "she," "we," and "they." And conversations in response to comprehension questions in the reading programs can be much livelier when there are several opinions about the motivation of characters and a variety of predictions about what is going to occur in the stories.

COPING WITH GROUPING CHALLENGES

Placement test results may not always perfectly match the DI programs' guidelines as the number of students who place at any particular starting point may exceed the guidelines' limits. So, although a wide variety of possible starting points help to match students' skills with the lessons they initially receive, practical limits in staffing – and hence practical limits in the number of groups that can be accommodated – may prohibit the school from matching all students precisely with their optimal starting points in the DI programs. In these cases, school leaders need to make compromises on grouping with the goal of accommodating as many students as possible. If choices need to be made between staffing levels at different grades in a school, a priority should be made to allocate sufficient staff to accommodate students who place into the beginning DI reading programs as that will foster the greatest improvement in student performance in the long run.

A general rule to follow in making grouping compromises is to place students lower rather than higher in the DI programs. It's best to err on the side of placing students in material that is too easy for them initially, especially if they are not used to DI expectations and conventions. If students are evenly split in their placement test results, the whole group should be placed at the lower placement lesson. For instance, the results from placement testing students in *Reading Mastery Transformations* (RMT) Grade K that are shown in Table 8.5 require compromises in grouping students for instruction.

Lesson	Number of students
1	3
15	3
71	6
101	7
131	5

Table 8.5 Sample of initial placement of children in a single kindergarten classroom in *Reading Mastery Transformations* (RMT) Grade K.

The table shows a single class of 24 kindergarten students in RMT Grade K with seven different possible placements: Lessons 1, 15, 71, 101, and 131 as well as a pre-program with two entry points for students who haven't acquired sufficient skills to start at Lesson 1. For each kindergarten class, the standard practice is to divide students into three groups that rotate through reading and language as described later in the chapter in the discussion about schedules (timetables). The distribution of the students depicted in Table 8.5 allows for groupings that would meet the guidelines described in Table 8.4 through different compromises. By moving students lower, children who placed at Lesson 15 can be moved to Lesson 1 to form a group of six students that start the year there. In this example, it would not be possible to move the students from Lesson 101 to Lesson 71 because the size of the combined group would be larger than the limit in the guidelines (13 instead of 12 students). So the next lowest performing group could be formed by moving the students who placed at Lesson 131 to Lesson 101 and form a group that would start the year there. Note that if the students who placed at Lesson 131 were left to form a group by themselves, it would consist of only five students, which would result in the highest performing group having the least members and violate the guideline that the lowest performing group should have the smallest student–teacher ratio. Instead, the highest performing group should have the highest student–teacher ratio, which it would if it is combined with the students at Lesson 101 to form a group of 12 students.

The example in Table 8.5 accommodated moving students to lower starting points in the program because the number of students who were moved in each case was equal to or less than the number of students they were combined with. However, what should happen if just one or two students out of a larger group place lower than the other students? In this case, school leaders can try to put the students at the higher placement provisionally with the understanding that the lower-placing students may need additional monitoring and support. The lower-placing students would need to receive instruction at the lesson where they placed in addition to receiving instruction with the rest of the group at the higher lesson. In this way, the lower-placing students can cover the lessons that correspond to their initial skill level until they close the performance gap with the rest of the students in the group.

The example in Table 8.5 underscores the importance of employing cross-class grouping (and cross-grade grouping within a grade level for students in first grade and higher) to provide as many options as possible for forming homogeneous instructional groups. For this example, if there are other kindergarten classrooms with students who test into a range of initial placements in the K level of *Reading Mastery Transformations*, more homogeneous groups can be formed than the ones listed in Table 8.5. If, for instance, another kindergarten classroom has several students who place at Lessons 1 and 15, separate groups can be formed at each of these placements, which would help ensure that the instruction the children receive matches their skill repertoire. To accommodate these groups, the rosters of the classrooms can be adjusted to conform to the placement test results, or students can "walk to read" – i.e. their homeroom can be different from their reading group room. If these assignments are made in the spring, the homeroom assignments can accommodate the groupings without the need for students to walk between classrooms at the start of the school year. However, groups should be flexible as some students may need to walk to read later in the school year if data and observations indicate that there is another group in a different classroom that better accommodates their reading skill repertoire.

The size of the school can be an influential factor in cross-class and cross-grade grouping. Forming homogeneous instructional groups can be extremely challenging in very small schools (e.g. elementary schools with less than 100 students) where the low number of students per grade severely limits grouping options. In contrast, large schools, such as elementary schools with more than 100 students per grade level, allow for great flexibility in forming initial groups and for moving students between groups as their performance indicates throughout the year. Large schools present a different challenge – organizing and managing a large number of fluid groups – but if there is a staff member devoted to managing DI, the school can take advantage of the large number of students to form highly homogeneous groups. Still, for schools or implementations of DI of any size, if placement results do not result in clear-cut homogeneous groups, school leaders will need to form the most homogeneous groups possible and make adjustments as needed throughout the school year based on student performance.

Student behavior and teachers' effectiveness in managing student behavior can also play a role in decisions about group size. In general, the size of groups should be inversely related to the number of disruptive behaviors and other behavior management problems that can be expected. If students have demonstrated frequent disruptive behaviors, the group should be smaller in size than the general recommendations. At the other extreme, a larger-than-recommended group size can be considered if students are extremely well-behaved and attentive. With larger group sizes, the teacher would need to be very mindful of monitoring each student's performance through individual turns during group instruction as well as during independent work to ensure that all students master each day's lesson.

ASSIGNING GROUPS TO TEACHERS

After initial groups have been formed, they need to be assigned to specific instructional staff members. The instructors do not need to be certified teachers if they are able to follow the requirements of the program and implement it with fidelity. Once an initial layout of teaching assignments has been made, it may become apparent that more staff members are needed than were originally expected. This often occurs when a larger-than-anticipated number of students place into the lower levels of the program. For example, if leaders of a secondary school anticipated that most students would place into the upper levels of the *Corrective Reading* program (Levels B2 and C), but a larger-than-expected number placed into the lower levels of the program (Levels A and B1), the school would need to provide lower student–teacher ratios for the students, and hence include more teaching staff in the implementation than originally planned.

Initial test results may prompt school leaders to expand the scope of the implementation if students' skill deficits are greater than expected. For example, if the leaders of a school implementing *Corrective Reading* originally tested only sixth graders and found out through the test results that their performance was much lower than anticipated, the school leaders may decide to test seventh and eighth graders to determine the extent to which they would benefit from receiving instruction in *Corrective Reading*.

Conversely, test results can also prompt school leaders to contract the scope of the DI implementation. Since schools' budgets are constrained by limited resources, the leadership may decide to focus the implementation of DI on students with the highest need – those who place into the lowest levels of the program – if the test results reveal that students' skill deficits in the school are greater than expected. School leaders may be able to allocate funds from other sources to accommodate a more extensive implementation of DI in the long run, but in the short run, they may be forced to make the difficult decision of prioritizing DI for smaller segments of the student population than the full scope of students who would benefit from DI.

When assigning specific groups to teachers, it is important to consider the teachers' experience in providing intensive instruction to lower-performing students. If teachers have used lower-case direct instruction techniques or intensive behavior modification in the past, they may be well prepared to learn how to implement upper-case DI techniques. An important consideration is the role of instructional assistants. At the elementary school level, instructional assistants teach DI language (under the supervision of the teachers) to students who place into the first two levels of the language program. Many of the assistants can become highly effective in delivering DI if they receive initial training and ongoing coaching, as described later in this chapter.

Teachers with a demonstrated track record of improving the performance of lower performing students using other instructional strategies should be considered for the lowest performing groups. If none of the staff members has a superior track record of success with low performers, each of the teachers can be assigned groups with different performance levels so all teachers can experience how the program works with a range of students. Indeed, it is beneficial to share the experience of working with the lowest performing students so that the school does not become too reliant on any one teacher for the success of the program. Moreover, a staff member may get "burnt out" by always being responsible for improving the performance of the lowest performing students. Instead, it is most beneficial for all teachers to acquire the skills to be able to deliver DI to a wide variety of students, which provides greater flexibility for the implementation to accommodate all students' needs.

INSTRUCTIONAL GROUP COHESIVENESS AND IDENTITY

In addition to serving as instructional units, DI groups are social units that can be a source of great enjoyment and encouragement to students and teachers. At the elementary school levels in particular, instructional groups are assigned names that are designed to encourage students to learn, as in the case of naming instructional groups after colleges or universities, or to simply serve as a source of enjoyment and pride. The teacher can generate the names of the groups (the bluebirds, the tigers, the panthers, etc.), or the teacher can let the students decide the name of their group themselves (within reason).

Once an instructional group has been formed, it provides a new identity for the students. Students who don't already have high self-esteem can take pride in the accomplishments of the group as a whole. The existence of the group simplifies motivating and reinforcing students as the teacher can refer to the group instead of individuals or the class as a whole. The group is where students experience the bulk of their success and encouragement each day. It is the locus of frequent, short-lasting mini-celebrations during instruction, while larger, less-frequent celebrations occur at the level of the classroom, grade, or school as a whole. Groups can facilitate behavior management as the teacher provides positive reinforcement to students in the group who meet expectations, which can serve as a strong motivating force for other students in the group who might otherwise misbehave if they were left to work on their own. In order for the instructional groups to function well, the teacher must establish rules of fairness and reinforce students for following these rules.

ADJUSTING THE COMPOSITION OF INSTRUCTIONAL GROUPS

As mentioned several times in this chapter, instructional groups are formed on the basis of initial placement test results, but they are not intended to be static over the course of the year. Students are not on permanent tracks based on the placement tests. Rather, placement test results simply provide a starting point for grouping students at their current skill levels. The composition of the instructional groups is intended to be flexible in response to changes in performance as students demonstrate a consistent trend over time.

It is important to establish consistent, schoolwide guidelines for adjusting groups with explicit and consistent criteria based on student performance data. Although teacher recommendations are important for identifying students as candidates for changing groups, objective data must be used as the basis for all grouping decisions. Students can be moved to another group after a consistent trend for three weeks. If a student fails to pass mastery tests three weeks in a row, for instance, the student should be considered for a lower-performing group after other remedies have been attempted to address their skill deficits and keep them in their current group. Or if a student posts perfect scores on the mastery tests three weeks in a row, they should be considered for a higher-performing group. More frequent adjustments to the group composition are difficult to manage, and they may not represent consistent trends in students' performance. In addition to ongoing adjustments to the instructional groups, a comprehensive regrouping should occur at least three times a year. The performance of all students on in-program assessments and independent work should be analyzed, and new groups might need to be formed on the basis of this quarterly analysis across the school. For schools starting to implement DI for the first time, the first regrouping should occur early in the school year – within three or four weeks of school starting – to accommodate students who respond quickly to the DI format and performance expectations.

The effect of all changes to the composition of the groups should be closely monitored through student performance data analysis and direct observations during instruction. Some students who move to a higher group may require more attention and support initially from their teacher than other members of the group so they can perform well at a more demanding lesson. Students who move to a lower group may require more attention and support than other members of their new group for different reasons – they may get discouraged that they are repeating material that they already covered earlier in the school year. In this case, the teacher needs to emphasize to these students that they are mastering the retaught material successfully, which means they will be ready to learn new material in the future.

If multiple classrooms are implementing DI, the school leadership must ensure that any regrouping is coordinated and directed at the school level. The expectations should be made clear to the staff that the building coordinator will make decisions on regrouping as they have the broadest viewpoint across the DI implementation and can identify which adjustments would serve the greatest number of students.

ORDERING TEACHER AND STUDENT MATERIALS

After placement tests have been administered to students and the initial instructional groups have been formed, the proper configuration of program materials can be ordered. If materials are ordered before students have been placed in the program and grouped into homogeneous groups, there is a significant risk that the materials will not match the needs of the students or the availability of staffing that best supports the students' needs. If the materials don't match students' needs, they will need to be exchanged for materials that do match the students' needs. The time required to return materials to the publisher and receive replacements can delay the onset of the implementation with negative implications for student progress through the programs. Ensuring that the material order is placed several months before the targeted start of the implementation should allow sufficient time for the materials to arrive at the school for a successful DI launch. Putting together the daily schedule, discussed later, may lead to some adjustments in staffing and grouping. It is therefore advisable to complete the bell schedule for the upcoming school year for all classrooms with DI as soon as possible in the spring or summer.

Each DI program comes with separate materials for teachers and students. The most important of these for teachers are the teacher presentation books (TPBs), which contain the precise scripts that teachers should follow when presenting the lessons. (For *Reading Mastery Transformations*, teacher presentation materials come in the form of digital files rather than a physical book.) The TPBs may contain other support material, such as planning pages for groups of lessons. Other teacher materials may include:

- assessment guides containing mastery tests
- answer keys for in-program assessments
- a teacher's guide, which explains key aspects of the program level
- a series guide, which explains key aspects of the program series
- a literature guide for outside reading
- computer displays that accompany the teacher's presentation.

Typical student materials include:

- workbooks
- textbooks
- storybooks
- blackline masters for additional independent practice.

Specific materials vary by program. For most DI programs, teacher materials represent a onetime purchase while student materials are a mix of consumables that need to be purchased annually for each student who participates in the implementation (workbooks) or a onetime purchase (textbooks, storybooks, and blackline masters). However, *Direct Instruction Spoken English* (DISE) does not involve any student materials of any kind as it is a completely oral language program. *Reading Mastery Transformations* and *Funnix* have digital teacher presentations instead of hard copies that are purchased in the form of an annual subscription. The cost of materials published by McGraw Hill Education can be found at mheducation.com while the cost of other materials can be found on the websites of the respective publishers.

The configuration of students' placement can change the total cost of instructional materials. If all other factors remain constant, the broader the scope of the implementation, the greater the range of teacher materials that will be needed for a successful implementation. For instance, if students only place in the B1 and B2 levels of *Corrective Reading*, the total material cost will be less than if the same number of students place into all four levels of the program – A, B1, B2, and C – because more teacher presentation books must be purchased to cover all four levels of the program. Also, if students place disproportionately into the A and B1 levels of *Corrective Reading* instead of the B2 and C levels, student-teacher ratios will be lower and more groups will be needed, which may require more staff members and, hence, the need for more teacher materials. Scheduling restrictions can also play a role in determining the cost of the materials. If there is only a single time slot that is reserved for DI, such as a 90-minute block in the morning, more teachers may need to be recruited to accommodate multiple groups of a particular level, and each teacher will need their own teacher presentation book. In contrast, if a single teacher teaches different groups of students throughout the day, the school needs to purchase only one teacher presentation book for each level of the program.

If there are still some students who need to be placement tested, it is best to be conservative in terms of the level of the programs to order. For instance, if the general trend of the placement test results indicates that most of the students place one level below their grade level, it is best to order materials that are in keeping with that general trend. The materials can be returned as long as the school's stamp has not been put on them.

Materials can take several weeks to arrive after the order has been placed, but there is considerable variation in delivery time depending on the location of the school, the backlog of orders, and other factors. For this reason, it is recommended that you place the order in the late spring or early summer before the implementation is scheduled to start. For schools in larger districts, the purchasing department may require weeks or months to process and place the order, which reinforces the recommendation to place the materials order as soon as placement testing and grouping have been completed.

When the materials arrive, it is important to have a system for organizing and storing the materials for ready access throughout the year. The materials needed by students can be expected to change as they progress through the lessons. Many of the DI reading programs have multiple storybooks, workbooks, or textbooks in each level. It is important that these materials are distributed to the classrooms *before* the students reach the lessons that require the new books. The old storybooks and textbooks should be taken from the classrooms and stored until they are needed by another instructional group.

The types of materials involved in a DI implementation, and hence the cost of materials, may change drastically over time for a school or district that implements the DI comprehensive model with fidelity. In many of the schools that NIFDI has supported, virtually all second graders require small-group instruction as they place into the kindergarten or first-grade levels of the program at the start of the implementation. This results in initial high material costs because each instructor requires a teacher presentation book for the program(s) they teach. After a couple of years of faithful implementation of DI, only transfers into the school and continuing students with severe special needs still receive instruction at the kindergarten or first-grade levels of the program. This means the material cost per grade level declines as students move into programs that are taught to whole classes of two dozen students or more rather than small instructional groups.

Over time, an even larger drop in material costs occurs when DI is implemented across elementary and secondary schools with fidelity. As discussed in chapter 7, the scope of the DI implementation at the junior high school in Gering, Nebraska in the early 2000s contracted from involving all staff at the seventh grade, including non-literacy specialists teaching DI groups, to only literacy specialists using DI after just two years. This contraction was accompanied by a precipitous drop in the need to purchase *Corrective Reading* consumables at the junior high as most students no longer needed the program.

If there is a cluster of schools implementing the same programs, schools may be able to share materials to help reduce costs. This is especially true if they have a staggered start to the implementation. As the need for lower levels of the programs drops in schools after a couple of years, these materials can be transferred to schools that are just starting to adopt DI. This type of exchange can be facilitated by district-level personnel, or it can occur through direct school-to-school contacts.

SCHEDULING SUFFICIENT TIME IN THE PROGRAMS

One of the most challenging aspects of implementing DI is to schedule sufficient time for the programs. Often school leaders and teachers want to implement multiple programs using a variety of approaches with the hope that students who are exposed to more instructional approaches will achieve better performance outcomes than those who receive instruction in only one approach, such as DI. School leaders and teachers also often want all students to partake in the same set of electives and enrichment activities even when it is apparent that some students do not possess the prerequisite skills to participate fully in the electives and enrichment activities. It is critically important that school leaders and teachers *prioritize the instruction that is most critical for students' long-term success,* which may involve students forgoing some of the electives and enrichment activities *now* as they build up their skills and background knowledge as a prerequisite to participating in these courses and activities *later.*

School leaders play a key role in ensuring that sufficient time in DI is scheduled for all students. Except in the case of DI being used in a single classroom, scheduling requires the direct involvement of the school's leadership to ensure that 1) there are common instructional times for each grade level so cross-class grouping can occur, and 2) the amount of time scheduled for each instructional group meets the program guidelines, which may vary considerably by instructional level.

As discussed previously, the kindergarten and first-grade levels of the reading and language programs require small groups that are taught concurrently by different staff members. For these levels of the programs, DI should take place for 90 minutes in the morning (with a three-group rotation of 30 minutes each) and 60 minutes in the afternoon (with a three-group rotation of 20 minutes each). If the number of students is small and their placement allows for two homogeneous groups per classroom, the 90-minute block can be separated into two 45-minute periods, and the 60-minute block can be separated into two 30-minute periods. The option of having longer instructional periods can help accommodate an implementation of *Reading Mastery Transformations,* as lessons in the lower level of the program may require more than 30 minutes to complete.

Table 8.6 shows the three-group rotation that is typical of the comprehensive DI model for students who place into the kindergarten or first-grade levels of the beginning reading and language programs. During the rotation, the teacher teaches reading while the teaching assistant teaches language to a different group, and a third group engages in independent work that is tied directly to the DI programs. The order of the rotation differs depending on the performance level of the students. In Table 8.6, Group C should be the highest performing group because the highest performing students will be most able to start their day with independent work instead of face-to-face instruction.

	Time	Teacher	Teaching Assistant	Independent Workers
Morning	8:15–8:30	Opening routines		
	8:30–9:00	Group A: RM Reading K*	Group B: RM Language K	Group C: Quiet independent work
	9:00–9:30	Group C: RM Reading K*	Group A: RM Language K	Group B: Quiet independent work
	9:30–10:00	Group B: RM Language K*	Group C: RM Language K	Group A: Quiet independent work
	10:00–1:30	Other kindergarten activities: recess, science, social studies, spelling, lunch, math, PE, art, etc.		
Afternoon	1:30–1:50	Group A: Continue RM Reading K*	Group B: Continue RM Language K	Group C: Quiet independent work
	1:50–2:10	Group C: Continue RM Reading K*	Group A: Continue RM Language K	Group B: Quiet independent work
	2:10–2:30	Group B: Continue RM Language K*	Group C: Continue RM Reading K	Group A: Quiet independent work

* Instead of reading, the teacher teaches language in these time slots until students finish at least 40 lessons of *Reading Mastery* language, Grade K, to ensure that the students can follow the teacher's directions during the reading lessons.

Table 8.6 Sample schedule for full-day kindergarten implementing *Reading Mastery* (RM) in a classroom with one teacher and one teaching assistant.

Teachers should not commence reading instruction until students have mastered at least the first 40 lessons of the language program, as indicated by the asterisk in the table. This requirement can be higher (60 or 65 lessons) for English language learners. Students with a solid language base will be able to respond quickly and correctly to the directions involved in the reading lessons, which will go much more smoothly once students have mastered some of the fundamental language content in the program. So, in Table 8.6, Group B should not yet have reached Lesson 41 of the *Reading Mastery* language program because they are getting "double dosed" in language by the teacher and the teaching assistant. The other two groups (Group A and Group C) should be farther in the language program than Lesson 40 as they are receiving reading instruction from the teacher.

For all groups, instructors should carry on from the exact spot where the students finished at the end of the last instructional period. For example, if Group A in Table 8.6 completed Exercise 4 of Lesson 52 of RM Language in the morning, the teaching assistant would start Exercise 5 of Lesson 52 of RM Language in the afternoon. If the teaching assistant completed Exercise 2 of Lesson 38 of RM Language with Group B at 9am, the teacher would start Exercise 3 of Lesson 38 of RM Language with Group B at 9:30am.

	Time	Teacher
Morning	8:00–8:15	Opening routines
	8:15–9:45	Reading – RM Reading 2
	9:45–10:00	Recess
	10:00–11:00	Language – RM Language 2
	11:00–12:10	Math
Afternoon	12:10–12:40	Lunch
	12:40–1:30	Science, social studies, or PE
	1:30–2:30	Reading – Most of another RM Reading 2 lesson*
	2:30–2:45	Clean-up and dismissal

Required for students who perform below grade level.

Table 8.7 Sample schedule for second grade, third grade, or fourth grade groups that are in RM Reading/Language Grade 2, and no teaching assistant.

Continuing instruction from the precise spot where students ended during the previous period requires a simple and reliable system of communication so the next instructor knows where she is supposed to start. Using a paper clip can be effective for indicating the correct spot, but a sticky note also allows the first instructor to note that the next instructor might need to review specific items before continuing in the program. Note that there may be some exceptions to continuing from where the students last left off if they struggled with specific items, which the afternoon instructor should repeat before proceeding with the lesson.

The schedule for teaching literacy changes dramatically when students reach the Grade 2 level of the programs. While children in the first two levels of *Reading Mastery* rotate through two instructors and three "stations" (reading, language, and independent work), students in the

Grade 2–5 levels of the programs are taught in a whole class by a single teacher, who teaches both reading and language. As shown in Table 8.7, the morning reading block is 90 minutes in length with no rotation. The lessons are much longer than lessons from the first two levels of the program as they involve considerable writing and higher-order tasks. Language instruction occurs during a separate hour (10:00am to 11:00am in Table 8.7). An afternoon reading period of an hour in length is necessary for students who perform below grade level, which is defined as *not being on track to finish the program that corresponds to their grade level by the end of the school year.* Instruction for these students in the afternoon should carry on from the exact spot where the students finished at the end of the morning instructional period, just as it occurs for students in the Grade K and Grade 1 programs. For students in the Grade 2–5 levels of the programs who are on track to finish the DI program that corresponds to their grade level, the afternoon reading period is optional. It can be used to continue with DI, or it can be used for other activities. Because of the extensive information on science and social studies in the Grade 2 and 3 levels of *Reading Mastery* and the highly enriching literature in the Grade 4 and 5 levels of the program, it is highly recommended that teachers use the afternoon period to continue with DI for all students. (For information on the content covered in these levels, see Woolfson (2014) and NIFDI (2013).)

Spelling instruction requires additional time for students when they have had sufficient experience reading connected text. For the first two levels of *Reading Mastery Transformations*, spelling is integrated into the daily lessons and doesn't require any extra time. The spelling track starts at Lesson 25 of the Grade K level of *Transformations* with students writing words that are dictated. The spelling track continues through the end of the Grade 1 level of *Transformations*. However, 10 additional minutes per day should be scheduled for spelling for students in *Reading Mastery Signature Edition* (RMSE) when instructional groups reach Lesson 50 of RMSE, Grade K. Spelling in RMSE is taught from a separate booklet that comes with the kit (hence the nickname, "kit spelling"). According to procedures developed by the National Institute for Direct Instruction (NIFDI), RMSE Grade 1 kit spelling starts at Lesson 1 and continues until Lesson 84 when students are tested for *Spelling Mastery. Once students* reach the Grade 2 level of RMSE, an additional 25 minutes per day should be reserved for students to receive instruction in *Spelling Mastery*. RMT has its own spelling lessons included in the subscription so there is no need to add time for lessons in *Spelling Mastery*.

Program	Grouping	Daily Time Requirements (in minutes)
DISTAR Arithmetic I	Two or more small groups of 12 students or less per classroom	30–35 minutes per group for teacher-directed work plus 20–30 minutes for independent work
CMC CE A	Small groups of 10 students or less	30 minutes per group for teacher-directed work plus 15 minutes per class for independent work
CMC CE B	Whole class	40 minutes for teacher-directed work plus 10 minutes for independent work
CMC CE C	Whole class	50 minutes for teacher-directed work plus 20 minutes for independent work
CMC CE D	Whole class	45–50 minutes for teacher-directed work plus 15–25 minutes for independent work
CMC CE E	Whole class	50 minutes for teacher-directed work plus 20 minutes for independent work
CMC CE F	Whole class	50 minutes for teacher-directed work plus 20 minutes for independent work

Table 8.8 Daily time requirements for *DISTAR Arithmetic* and *Connecting Math Concepts Comprehensive Edition* (CMC CE) (minutes per instructional group). Sources: *DISTAR Arithmetic Teacher's Guide*; *CMC CE teacher's guides*; *Program Reference Chart*.

As shown in Table 8.8, scheduling requirements for developmental mathematics are similar to the requirements for the different levels of the developmental literacy programs. Small groups with a rotating schedule of approximately half an hour characterize the lowest level of DI math. Instruction becomes whole-class with larger lengths of teacher-directed work time starting in Level B of *Connecting Math Concepts Comprehensive Edition* (CMC CE). For levels C–F of CMC CE, school leaders should schedule 50 minutes for teacher-directed work plus 20 minutes for independent work with some flexibility in scheduling for Level D.

Fluency with math facts becomes increasingly important as students progress through the different levels of the math programs. Fact accuracy and fluency can determine how quickly students master the lessons. Students who take a great deal of time to perform basic computations may slow down a group's lesson progress. For this reason, *NIFDI recommends that schools schedule an additional 10 minutes of fact practice daily for all students who are in CMC CE levels C–F.* Fact practice and review can be used as a "warm-up" for students to start the math instructional period, or it can be scheduled at any other time of the day as it does not need to occur in conjunction with the rest of the teacher-directed instruction or independent work.

Daily time requirements for the remedial DI programs vary considerably by program and level. Completing a lesson in *Decoding* Level A requires 30–45 minutes depending on the size of the instructional group. For Level B1, the time required to complete a lesson is 45–50 minutes per lesson. In general, the time required will be on the lower side of the range if the program is used one-on-one with a student in a resource room or similar setting. However, *90 minutes is recommended daily for the A and B1 levels of the programs so students can complete two lessons per day* (see Table 8.9). Students who place into these levels of the programs are so far behind their peers in reading that the extra time is necessary to close the performance gap. Students who place into *Decoding* A and B1 cannot access grade-level material, so their time is much more productively spent receiving instruction at their performance level instead of their grade level. In fact, putting these students into grade-level material can be counter-productive, as participating in grade-level activities can be punishing to them until they acquire basic literacy skills. It is far more beneficial to release students who perform at the A and B1 levels from content courses so they can spend more time in *Corrective Reading* rather than having them spend time struggling with grade-level history or science texts. Once students get far enough in the program – through Level B2 at least along with completion of the *REWARDS* programs – they are more likely to be able to access grade-level content and participate successfully in class activities, depending on their grade level.

Program Level	Decoding	Comprehension
A	90	30–45
B1	90	45–55
B2	45	45–55
C	35–45	45

Table 8.9 Daily time recommendations for *Corrective Reading Decoding* and *Comprehension* (minutes per instructional group). Source: NIFDI. (2023). *Program Reference Chart*, p. 3.

The time allocation for *Direct Instruction Spoken English* (DISE) is the same as the time allocation for the lower levels of the *Decoding* program for similar reasons. Just as students who place into Level A or Level B of *Decoding* can't read grade-level content material, and hence their time is much more productively spent acquiring fundamental literacy skills, students who place into DISE Level 1 can't understand spoken English and express themselves in English with sufficient clarity to be able to participate in grade-level discussions. So their time is much more productively spent acquiring fundamental English oral language skills. Once these students achieve basic oral language proficiency, the time devoted to DISE can be reduced. For these reasons, the recommended time for students who place into DISE Level 1 is 90 minutes while the recommended time for students who place into DISE Level 2 is 50 minutes (see Table 8.10).

Level 1	Level 2
90	50

Table 8.10 Daily time recommendations for *Direct Instruction Spoken English* (DISE) (minutes per instructional group). Source: NIFDI. (2023). *Program Reference Chart*, p. 11.

In contrast, *Expressive Writing* time requirements are consistent across the two levels. As Table 8.11 shows, teacher-directed instruction takes about 45 minutes per day while independent work takes 10–20 minutes per day. However, if schools prioritize writing over other subjects, students can be double-dosed in this program, too.

Teacher-directed instruction	Independent work
45	10–20

Table 8.11 Daily time recommendations for *Expressive Writing*, Levels 1 and 2 (minutes per instructional group). Source: NIFDI. (2023). *Program Reference Chart*, p. 10.

Spelling Through Morphographs, the remedial DI spelling program, requires 20–30 minutes daily for students to complete a lesson (Dixon and Engelmann, S., 2007b, 1). As with other DI remedial programs, an option is to double-dose *Spelling Through Morphographs* so students can complete two lessons per day.

Balancing the time requirements for the remedial DI literacy programs can be challenging. Dr. Bonnie Grossen has put together the REACH Higher System to help guide school leaders as they select and implement the DI remedial literacy programs in a comprehensive intervention. Dr. Grossen created a single placement test for the programs, which greatly simplifies the assessment and grouping processes. In the REACH Higher System, not all of the remedial programs should be taught at the same time. For example, students who place into *Decoding* Level A read at the pre-primer level, so they will need to receive a daily double dose of the program until they complete Level B1 before they have the skills to successfully participate in activities that require reading. Students should not start *Spelling Through Morphographs* until they have completed *Decoding* B2 so their reading skills are at a high enough level to allow for spelling instruction to occur effectively.

Table 8.12 shows the REACH Higher System, which presents prioritized recommendations for schools depending on the skill level of students and the amount of time that is available for DI. Schools that have just one or two instructional periods of 45–55 minutes each to devote to DI should teach the "main" programs of *Corrective Reading* shown in the first two rows of the table. For schools that have more than two periods, one or more of the "optional" programs listed in the next four rows can be implemented.

Note that there is not a one-to-one correspondence between the different levels of the programs in the REACH Higher System. Students who place into *Corrective Reading Decoding* Level A are placed into *Comprehension* Level A, but students who place into *Decoding* B2 may also be placed into *Comprehension* Level A, too. Also, the table should be used as a rough guide only. Individual students may progress faster through some programs than others. For instance, students may reach Level C in *Decoding* yet still need instruction in *Expressive Writing* instead of the upper levels of *Reasoning and Writing.*

Program Type	Program	Levels				
Main	Corrective Reading Decoding	A	B1	B2	C	
	Corrective Reading Comprehension	A	A	B1	B2	C
Optional	Reasoning and Writing	B	C	D	E	F
	Expressive Writing		1	2		
	Spelling Mastery	A	B	C		
	Spelling Through Morphographs				Teacher Presentation Book 1	Teacher Presentation Book 2

Table 8.12 Correspondence of Direct Instruction programs in the REACH Higher System with periods ranging from 40 to 90 minutes in length. Adapted from: SRA/ McGraw Hill. (2008). *The REACH Higher System: System Guide,* p. 3.

The time requirements for the *Corrective Mathematics* series vary considerably by level (module). As shown in Table 8.13, the time requirements for the four operations modules (levels), which cover addition, subtraction, multiplication, and division, range from 25 to 45 minutes in length (Engelmann, Carnine, and Steely, 2005, 3–4). The lower end of this range provides enough time for the instructional group to complete the face-to-face parts of the lessons. The upper end of this range allows for students to work in small groups for the "fact game," during which they practice math facts. The upper range also provides enough time for the students to complete all of their daily independent work and for the teacher to conduct a "work check," which involves reviewing the problems and the answers orally with the students.

Module(s)	Daily Time Requirements (in minutes)
Operations modules	25–45
Basic fractions	20
Fractions, decimals, percents	30
Ratios and equations	25

Table 8.13 Daily time recommendations for *Corrective Mathematics* (minutes per instructional group). Source: Engelmann, S., Carnine, D. and Steely, D. (2005). *Corrective Mathematics Series Guide*, pp. 3–5.

The time requirements for the upper levels of *Corrective Mathematics* – which cover basic fractions; fractions, decimals, and percentages; and ratios and equations – are set for each module and do not allow for a range of times. The short time requirements (20–30 minutes) facilitate the program's use as a supplement to a core mathematics program or as a temporary replacement core. Again, students can be double-dosed in the modules if sufficient time is available.

The two "essentials" DI programs (*Essentials for Writing* and *Essentials for Algebra*), which are intended to be used at the secondary level, have been designed to fit into the typical high school schedule of 55 minutes per period (NIFDI, 10 and 15). Students of *Essentials for Algebra* spend approximately another 45 minutes per day on independent work, which can be assigned as homework. The authors of *Essentials for Writing* suggest combining reading and writing at this level. They recommend "a 90-minute block with half of the block dedicated to instruction in SRA Essentials for Writing and the other half dedicated to reading instruction using SRA Corrective Reading, Decoding Level C" (Engelmann, S. and Grossen, 2010, 10).

Note that for any instructional schedule involving DI programs, sufficient time should be allotted for transition time between activities. If students change classrooms for DI, time should be allowed for students to walk down the hall to the DI classroom, get to their desks, pull out the relevant materials and open them to the appropriate pages. If students stay within the same classroom but there is a transition between different DI programs, such as reading and language, the transition time should be accounted for so the actual instructional time meets the requirements of each of the DI programs.

ESTABLISHING THE ROLES OF STAFF MEMBERS INVOLVED IN THE DI IMPLEMENTATION

For DI to be successful in a school, it is essential that the staff understand the roles they will play in the DI implementation, with specific expectations for teachers, coaches, and school leaders. Ideally, the core of these expectations will be communicated to the staff before DI is adopted, as described in chapter 7. The expectations should be restated and described in more detail once the decision to adopt DI has been made.

The role of teachers changes with the implementation of DI as each teacher becomes part of an integrated system dedicated to helping all students succeed. In this system, each teacher has their individual responsibilities, such as following the scripts precisely, teaching to mastery, recording and submitting data, and acquiring essential delivery and correction skills. At the same time, each teacher also works as part of a larger team in which *many aspects of instruction are decided by the school's leadership.* Teachers must recognize that:

- Students' placement and grouping will be flexible to accommodate different rates of students' learning, which may involve moving students between classrooms for instruction.

- The school's leadership will consider teachers' input on placement and grouping, but school leaders will decide when and where to move students between groups or change the placement of an intact group based on observations and data.

- Teachers will receive in-class, real-time coaching from DI experts and will be expected to incorporate the feedback of anyone who serves as a coach.

- Schedules/timetables will be determined by the school's leadership, and teachers will be expected to follow the schedules precisely as they teach "bell-to-bell" to maximize students' instructional time.

The term "teacher" can be used to refer to anyone who teaches an instructional group. For implementations of DI in the primary grades, this includes instructional assistants, who teach the language program while the teacher teaches the reading program during the DI instructional blocks (as mentioned earlier in the discussion on scheduling). Although the school's instructional assistants may have had some teaching responsibilities in the past, the requirements of teaching DI can be expected to exceed the requirements of their previous experience. Instructional assistants should attend all training sessions, receive in-class coaching, teach instructional groups, and record data (with the input of the classroom teacher as needed). The teacher should monitor the assistant's group and their progress through the programs and be prepared to help implement any solutions that the school's leadership has designed for addressing student performance and problems of instruction with the assistant's groups.

For implementations involving more than a couple of teachers, a staff member should be designated to be the DI building coordinator. Optimally, the coordinator should already have some experience with DI, explicit instruction, and/or positive behavior management before the DI implementation begins. The coordinator helps establish the setup items discussed in this chapter (testing students, forming initial instructional groups, arranging schedules/timetables with sufficient time in the programs for each instructional group, etc.). The coordinator also acts as the head DI coach after attending specialized training that prepares them to provide feedback to teachers on data completion and program delivery. To build up the school's capacity to provide support to teachers, the leadership should identify and train lead teachers to fulfill the role of grade-level coaches who can provide feedback to their peers on data completion and program delivery. Teaching DI daily can help build the expertise of the peer coaches in specific levels of the DI programs in combination with coaches' training.

In order for the building coordinator to be successful, they should be freed from all other duties so they can devote themselves full-time to supporting DI if the implementation is schoolwide, unless the student population of the school is small – less than a hundred students – in which case the coordinator may just need to be available to support DI part-time. If the coordinator does not have prior experience teaching DI, *they should build time into their schedule to teach at least one group regularly several times a week for a semester or more.* Getting experience teaching DI will allow them to provide coaching support to the teachers at a deeper level than if they have no DI teaching experience. If they don't have experience teaching DI, the coordinator's support for teachers will be much more superficial than if they gain insights into the programs by teaching them.

The school principal or director should assume the role of chief decision-maker and problem-solver. Implementing DI schoolwide sometimes involves making difficult choices regarding staff assignments, grouping, schedules, and other aspects of instruction. It is important that the principal 1) receives timely information on potential problems of instruction, 2) observes instruction in the classroom, and 3) makes decisions that are communicated clearly to the staff along with the rationale for the decisions.

It is essential that the school's leadership explain the rationale for monitoring instruction closely through direct observation and data analysis. Teachers should understand that the purpose of the leadership's monitoring is evaluative only to the extent that it identifies what teachers can do to improve student performance. DI should not be seen by the staff as a Procrustean approach demanding uniformity for its own sake – a common misconception about the DI method. The leadership should stress to the staff that if students are successful, nothing needs to be changed in the classrooms, even if the teachers' application of DI techniques is unorthodox. For example, if a teacher has an unusual signal but all of the children respond in unison at the appropriate time on cue, the signal does not need to be changed. Or if a teacher employs unorthodox, quick routines for reinforcing students for successful work and the students are motivated by these routines, they do not need to change. If a teacher's method of selecting and calling on students for individual turns is different from the method used by other teachers, the teacher's practice should not change as long as the use of individual turns allows the teacher to verify that students have mastered the material successfully. Instead of seeking to change unorthodox elements, the school's leadership should provide positive feedback to teachers whenever students are successful. The leadership should make clear that coaches and leaders are there to help teachers deliver DI effectively, not police them unnecessarily or require them to conform to a set of uniform practices for the sake of conformity.

It is especially important that the school's leadership explains to the teachers and paraprofessionals the specific procedures of in-class coaching. When one or more persons fulfilling the role of the coach visit the classroom, the teacher should continue to teach the lesson unless otherwise directed by a coach. Coaches will position themselves where they can see and hear each student, which means they may reposition themselves several times during a classroom visit. The coaches may interrupt instruction if there is a problem or to provide specific praise to students, and they may use hand signals or other prompts that have been established ahead of time to communicate specific actions to the teacher (as described in chapter 10). At the beginning of the school year, the teacher should discuss with the students that other adults will visit the class to observe them and perhaps teach part of a lesson. The students should answer "big" for the visitors and show how smart they are!

When planning for the implementation of DI, it is important to determine what will take place when teachers are absent from the building; if a teacher is out, who will teach DI to their students? There are two solutions: have another staff member teach the class, or bring in a substitute teacher. In either case, it is essential that the replacement teacher is trained in DI and has critical information on each instructional group they will be teaching. The building coordinator may be able to take over some of the teaching load when teachers are absent, but the more that the coordinator teaches groups, the less they are available to support the implementation elsewhere in the school. To build teaching capacity, many schools that have been successful with DI "overtrain" staff by training counselors, librarians, physical education instructors, and other staff in the DI methodology, as well as substitute teachers who can be called upon when a teacher is absent. The replacement teachers may not be quite as effective as the regular teacher in delivering the program, in which case classroom teachers may need to repeat some exercises after they return to the school, but the instructional groups will not have to repeat every part of every exercise, which is often the case when completely untrained substitutes fill in during teachers' absences.

Note that the specific title of the staff member who fulfills a particular function is far less important than ensuring that the function gets fulfilled. It is not necessary that instructors be certified teachers, as described earlier. In fact, instructional assistants may acquire DI skills at a faster rate than teachers who are resistant to adopting the DI approach due to negative exposure to DI in their university studies. Assistants are far less likely to have taken coursework that paints DI in a negative light, which allows them to be more receptive to DI, especially when they see the positive effect DI has on students' performance and self-image. Regarding leadership functions, different staff members can fulfill the role of building coordinator, such as a teacher on assignment (TOA), or an assistant principal of instruction (API). The role of instructional leader and ultimate decision-maker has been assumed successfully in some schools by an assistant principal. In some cases, the principal has been the instructional leader and combined that function with other functions. In the Arthur Academies, a small network of public charter schools in the greater Portland area in Oregon, the position of principal and kindergarten teacher were combined into one position for several years. For half of the school day, the principal fulfilled all of the leadership duties associated with the position. For the other half, the principal was in the classroom and served as a kindergarten teacher in every way – teaching instructional groups, motivating students, recording data, etc. This unique arrangement allowed the charter schools to have leadership in every building while the instructional needs of their youngest students were met – on a limited budget.

ESTABLISHING END-OF-YEAR GOALS FOR EACH INSTRUCTIONAL GROUP

An essential goal for the school is to maximize the skills and knowledge that each student learns through the DI programs, which provides a firm foundation for future learning. At the beginning of the school year, the leadership should establish specific end-of-year goals for each instructional group based on placement data and communicate the goals to each teacher. The end-of-year goals serve as a guidepost for assessing the success of DI in each classroom throughout the school year. Each group should have its targeted end-of-year lesson, which students can be expected to complete *at mastery*. If the students reach the targeted lesson but do not master the content, they will have to repeat parts of the program, so they will not have actually attained the end-of-year goal.

A common goal for students in the developmental programs is to complete at least one level of a DI program at mastery per year. Most students who are placed appropriately and taught to mastery every day for the required amount of time should be able to reach or exceed this goal. So most students who place into the first lesson of the Grade 2 level of *Reading Mastery* should be able to finish the program by the end of the year at mastery and be ready for the Grade 3 level of the program the following year. Some students, in fact, will be able to go much further in the program and finish both the Grade 2 and Grade 3 levels in a single year if they follow a "skip schedule." At the other extreme, some students who place into the Grade 2 program may not be able to complete it by the end of the school year, in which case they will need to complete the program during the summer or the next school year.

An alternative and usually more demanding goal for students in the developmental programs than completing a level per year is to finish a lesson a day. In this case, the end-of-year goal will equal the number of instructional days at the school if students place at Lesson 1, which may involve students starting the next highest level of the program before the year's end. For example, the number of lessons in the different levels of the reading track of the *Reading Mastery Transformations* (RMT) program ranges from 140 lessons in Grades 3–5 to 160 lessons in Grades K and 1. So if all students in a school using RMT place at Lesson 1 and complete a lesson a day at mastery, students in the programs for Grades 3–5 will finish their levels earlier than students in the lower levels of the program.

Higher initial placement of students within each level will push out the end-of-year expectations. As mentioned in Table 8.5, the RMT Grade K reading program provides seven different possible placements: Lessons 1, 15, 71, 101, and 131 as well as a pre-program with two entry points for students who haven't acquired sufficient skills to start at Lesson 1. Students who place at later lessons of the kindergarten program can be expected to finish one level of the program and get much farther into the next level of the program by the end of the school year than students who place into Lesson 1 or Lesson 15.

For students in the DI remedial programs, the number of levels covered over the course of the school year should, in general, be higher than the number of levels covered by students in the developmental programs due in part to the shorter length of most of the remedial programs. For example, Levels A, B1, and B2 of the *Corrective Reading Decoding* program as well as Levels A and B2 of the *Comprehension* program contain 65 lessons apiece. Students in the remedial programs should be able to cover at least two of these shorter levels per year if they are placed properly in the programs initially, they are taught to mastery every day, and the schedules provide sufficient time for instruction in the programs. As with the goals for students in the developmental programs, many students in the remedial programs will exceed these goals, especially "undertaught" students who do not have a learning disability but have simply never received sustained, systematic instruction in the subject matter.

For students with severe learning disabilities, these goals may need to be modified based on actual student performance. Instead of starting the year with preset end-of-year goals, the goals for these students can be determined after a few weeks of instruction based on their rate of progress through the program since the beginning of the school year. Specific goals for these students can be determined by projecting the same rate of lesson completion (at mastery) for the rest of the year – by multiplying the number of days remaining in the school year by the average daily rate of lesson completion to date. For schools in their first year of implementing DI, the rate of lesson progress at mastery may increase over time as students and staff acclimate to the structure and requirements of DI. The end-of-year goals can be adjusted later in the year through a recalculation of expectations based on the higher rate of lesson progress. These revised end-of-year goals can serve as the default expectations for students with disabilities in subsequent years as they are based on the actual performance of similar students in the school during the initial year of implementing DI.

PROVIDING INITIAL TRAINING IN THE DI METHODOLOGY

A common misconception about DI is that it must be easy to teach because it is scripted. According to this line of thought, anyone should be able to pick up a teacher presentation book and deliver the program, especially a certified teacher who has completed a university-level program. However, delivering DI successfully requires a teacher to utilize a unique set of skills according to the content and structure of each lesson – and in response to the performance of the students to that content and structure. Many of the DI skills will be new to teachers because they weren't covered in their university program or, if they were, the focus was theoretical rather than practically applied to teaching specific subject areas. As described in chapter 5, a teacher delivering DI must:

1. follow the scripted directions of each lesson precisely
2. vary the pacing of the presentation and emphasize keywords
3. elicit group responses
4. monitor students' performance responses closely
5. use appropriate signals for group instruction
6. employ a model-lead-test approach for delivering content and checking for students' understanding
7. follow DI correction procedures to correct all student performance errors and firm lessons part-by-part to mastery
8. manage student behaviors positively
9. apply skills and concepts outside the DI programs as appropriate.

For teachers to be successful with DI, they need to receive training that specifically addresses these skills in the context of the program they will be delivering to their students. The training should provide sufficient practice in the DI delivery skills until they become second nature to teachers. To be highly effective with DI, teachers must be fluent in presenting the scripted material and only glance at the script occasionally so they can direct most of their attention to the students. After they signal the students to respond to an instructional task, they must determine whether all students answered together, whether they answered correctly, and if not, which student(s) made which type of error. Teachers need to respond immediately with a correction that addresses the error or proceed in the program with positive praise interjected at strategic moments. They must remember the error pattern of all of the children on a given day's lesson so they know which items require delayed tests during the lesson and at other times during the school day. They must recall how the program presents each new skill because they may need to present the skill later in the program as a review if any student had difficulty with material that was presented earlier.

Teachers usually require three to five years of teaching the same program with expert training and coaching support before they are highly fluent in DI presentation, correction, and motivation techniques. The first time teachers present a DI program, it can feel very unusual to them, and it may take several months before teachers start to implement all aspects of a lesson effectively. During the second year of implementing DI, teachers have a better sense of how all of the pieces of the program fit together, how the program builds students' skills incrementally, which learning "steps" might be the most difficult for students, and which actions to take to help students master these difficult learning steps. By the third year of teaching the same DI program, teachers can start to refine their delivery of DI, hone their observation skills of students' performance, and anticipate the specific problems individual students can be expected to encounter throughout the school year. With more years teaching the same program, teachers' delivery, correction, and motivation techniques become more and more fluent, and the script becomes a familiar guide that the experienced teacher can navigate easily. They administer assessments efficiently, remediate specific performance problems, and motivate students with hints of what they will learn later in the program. At this point, experienced teachers are prepared to receive advanced training to become a coach or trainer so they can help other teachers who are new to DI acquire the skills and knowledge they need to help their students succeed.

The first step to becoming an effective teacher with DI is to attend a "preservice" program training with the goal of being well prepared to start to teach the specific levels of the program that students place into. To ensure that the levels the teachers receive training in correspond to the program levels the students place into, *preservice training should occur only after students have been placement tested and grouped for instruction based on the placement test results.* Training usually takes place the week before school starts in the fall, which should allow for the instructional materials to arrive in time for the start of school if placement testing and grouping took place in the spring. Scheduling the preservice before students arrive is much more cost-effective than scheduling the training after school starts as substitutes must then be hired to free up the staff for training. Scheduling the preservice close to the start of school facilitates teachers' acquisition of essential DI delivery skills as there is only a small gap of time between preservice and the time teachers start to implement the teaching techniques covered during training.

Preservice can take place on site or it can be provided remotely. Remote training is far less expensive as it eliminates the trainers' travel and lodging costs. However, remote training has some drawbacks because trainers are more limited in what they can present and observe through distance conferencing. Another option is for teachers to receive training in the most popular DI programs at the National Direct Instruction Conference, which is held annually during the third week of July in Eugene, Oregon.

Preservice training should include separate sessions for different DI programs with each session lasting the equivalent of two days per level. Some levels of the DI programs can be combined because of highly similar content and teaching techniques. *Reading Mastery Signature Edition* (RMSE) Grades 2 and 3 can be combined into a single training session as can RMSE Grades 4 and 5. Table 8.14 shows a sample preservice training schedule that combines these four levels of the programs into two sessions. It is organized into morning and afternoon sessions with reading in the morning and language in the afternoon. A one-day training on routines and expectations is scheduled for all day Monday for all participants. An onsite training with more than three trainers would require a preservice organizer to come on site before the training takes place to prepare the site for the five training sessions. This would require access to the training site on the weekend or, if this is not possible, on the Friday before the training takes place.

In elementary schools with a high percentage of at-risk students, there may not be any students who place into levels 4 and 5 of the reading program as all students may place into lower levels of the program. For this reason, the preservice training schedule of a school that is in its first year of implementing DI may not include the language and reading programs for Grades 4 and 5. These levels may also be excluded if the leadership decides to limit the implementation of DI initially for financial or other reasons. In either of these cases, Trainer 4 in Table 8.14 would not be necessary as the preservice training would require trainers for *Reading Mastery Signature Edition* (RMSE) Grades K through 3 only.

The preservice training can be shared by more than one school as long as the participant numbers are kept low enough for trainers to provide sufficient attention to each participant. The limit for in-person training is 25 participants per session, and for remote training, the limit is 12 participants per session because of the relative ease of monitoring and providing feedback in person in comparison to remote training. If the number of participants exceeds these limits for any level of the program, additional trainers should be added until the proper ratios have been reached.

It is important that the number of participants in each session conforms to these limits so they can achieve mastery on the skills covered in the preservice. Unlike other types of professional development that are more theoretical in nature, effective DI preservice training involves a great deal of application of the skills and concepts introduced by the trainer. Only about a third of the preservice involves "trainer talk," during which the trainer explains concepts and provides rationale and background information on the skills addressed in the training session. The remaining time is devoted to practicing key exercises in the program. To build participants' capacity to deliver specific exercises in the program, there is a set progression of activities for each instructional format that is introduced during the preservice:

1. The trainer plays the role of the teacher and teaches the exercise as the participants play the role of students who respond as a group without errors.

2. Participants play the role of the teacher and teach the exercise in unison as the trainer plays the role of a student who responds without errors.

3. Participants practice in small groups as they take turns playing the role of the teacher and students who make no errors.

4. The trainer plays the role of the teacher and reads the exercise as the participants play the role of students who respond as a group *with* errors, which requires the trainer to do a correction.

5. Participants play the role of the teacher and teach the exercise in unison as the trainer plays the role of a student and responds *with* errors, which requires the participants to do a correction.

6. Participants practice in small groups as they take turns playing the role of the teacher and students who make pre-selected errors, which the "teacher" corrects.

Morning sessions: Monday–Friday AM 8:00–11:30

Trainer	Monday	Tuesday	Wednesday	Thursday	Friday
Trainer 1	Routines and expectations	RMSE K Reading	RMSE K Reading	RMSE K Reading	RMSE K Reading
Trainer 2	Routines and expectations	RMSE 1 Reading	RMSE 1 Reading	RMSE 1 Reading	RMSE 1 Reading
Trainer 3	Routines and expectations	RMSE 2–3 Reading	RMSE 2–3 Reading	RMSE 2–3 Reading	RMSE 2–3 Reading
Trainer 4	Routines and expectations	RMSE 4–5 Reading	RMSE 4–5 Reading	RMSE 4–5 Reading	RMSE 4–5 Reading

Afternoon sessions: Monday–Friday PM 12:30–4:00

Trainer	Monday	Tuesday	Wednesday	Thursday	Friday
Trainer 1	Routines and expectations	RMSE K Language	RMSE K Language	RMSE K Language	RMSE K Language
Trainer 2	Routines and expectations	RMSE 1 Language	RMSE 1 Language	RMSE 1 Language	RMSE 1 Language
Trainer 3	Routines and expectations	RMSE 2–3 Language	RMSE 2–3 Language	RMSE 2–3 Language	RMSE 2–3 Language
Trainer 4	Routines and expectations	RMSE 4–5 Language	RMSE 4–5 Language	RMSE 4–5 Language	RMSE 4–5 Language

Table 8.14 Preservice training schedule for an elementary school implementing *Reading Mastery Signature Edition* (RMSE) Reading and Language.

The same principles of incremental learning that are infused in the DI programs are applied to preservice training. Steps one and two above involve no errors so participants can get used to the specific wording of key formats and become familiar with the types of signals required as well as the expected student responses. Participants should be able to present the format successfully without errors before proceeding to step three. Steps four through six should incorporate a range of behavioral and response errors, such as not responding on cue (behavioral error) and responding with an incorrect answer (response error).

By design, preservice training concentrates on the first 25–30 lessons of the programs. The positive effect of concentrating on the first 25–30 lessons during preservice was discovered by accident. The very first DI training sessions for new teachers included extensive rationale and practice on lessons "from the beginning, middle and end of each instructional program" (Engelmann, S., 2007, 86). However, providing training on lessons from all parts of the program was not possible at a training that took place in Tupelo, Mississippi in the 1960s due to problems with shipping. Just the first five lessons arrived at the training site, so the participants were limited to practicing only these lessons for the entire week of training. As S. Engelmann recounts:

> The material for reading that was sent to Tupelo, Mississippi didn't arrive in time for the workshop. Through recurring foul-ups, Tupelo did not receive these lessons during the entire week. All the trainers had were the first five lessons of the program. So the trainers provided some description of the later parts of the program, but the only exercises they could use for practice were from lessons 1 to 5. So teachers worked on presenting all parts of these lessons. Every teacher taught the entire sequence of lessons several times during the week.

> When we observed the performance of teachers during the first few weeks of school, we discovered that those in Tupelo performed better than those in other sites. The reason had to be that teachers in the other sites … had spent too much time working on tasks that they would not teach to children for months. In contrast, the Tupelo teachers became quite familiar

with everything they would present during the first week of school ... We modified our original procedures, not so radically that teachers worked only on the first five lessons, but almost exclusively on the first 25 lessons (Engelmann, S., 2007, 87–88).

On the last day of the preservice, the teachers go through a skill assessment called a "checkout." Since the goal of the preservice is for each participant to be ready to teach the program starting the first day of school, the participants are "checked out" on their presentation and correction skills by the trainer to ensure they've mastered essential DI teaching skills. If the participants cannot demonstrate that they can present lessons fluently and correct basic performance errors with other participants playing the role of students making pre-planned errors, the likelihood is low that they will be able to teach the program effectively in an actual classroom setting with real students making unpredictable errors. Teachers' initial effectiveness with the Direct Instruction programs in the classroom at the start of the school year will be greatly enhanced if they can successfully check out on the practice exercises. The more teachers learn in preservice, the more comfortable and successful they'll be during actual classroom instruction. If teachers do not experience success with DI initially, they can turn against the program, which has the potential to undermine the schoolwide consensus in support of implementing the DI methodology. Just as the students will become more receptive to DI if they are successful with it, teachers will become more supportive of DI if they feel successful delivering lessons starting on the first day of implementation.

For the checkout, the participants are set up into small groups as they role-play a DI lesson. While they are in the small groups, the trainer assesses the following presentation skills of the participant playing the role of the teacher:

- following the script
- use of appropriate signals
- use of appropriate pace
- looking at students
- transitioning quickly between tasks.

The trainer also assesses the following correction skills. In response to an error, they note whether the teacher:

- gave the correct answer
- repeated the task
- went back at least two items to repeat the part
- provided individual turns to students who made the error
- provided two delayed tests of the missed item.

On a specialized form, the trainer records a plus sign (+) if the teacher's skills are "on target" or writes "NP" if the participant "needs more practice." The participants take turns playing the role of the teacher as the trainer observes, provides feedback, and records plusses and NPs. Teachers who have been assessed as needing more practice are expected to practice their skills with their peers and get re-checked. If they pass the re-check, the trainer circles the "NP" that was recorded the first time the participant was observed. If they don't pass during the re-check, or the trainer does not have time to re-check all of the participants who received NPs, arrangements need to be made for the participants to continue to practice after preservice is over and get re-checked at a later date. This can be done by the DI trainer remotely or by a local coach who has already been trained in DI. If a teacher has several NPs, they should attend a make-up training session and practice the exercises until they can demonstrate mastery of essential presentation and correction skills.

Administrators, building coordinators, and district staff supporting the DI implementation should participate fully in the preservice training, including the checkouts. Acquiring fundamental presentation and error correction skills will help school and district leaders understand what to look for when they go into classrooms, and they will have a better understanding of how to ensure that teachers are successful with DI. If any staff members have received prior training in DI, they may be able to serve as assistants to the trainer and help monitor and facilitate small-group practice.

Near the end of the first year of implementation, school leaders should begin planning a preservice training for the second year of implementation. For the second year, teachers who are new to DI should receive a preservice training of the same length and structure as teachers received in the first year of implementation. Participants in a second-year preservice should include teachers who are new to the school, teachers who are being reassigned from grades with no DI to grades in which DI is being used, or teachers who are continuing in their assignment from the previous year but will need to learn DI because the implementation is expanding into the grade level they teach. As mentioned above, a long-term approach to DI is to start the implementation in select grades (such as kindergarten and Grade 1) and expand the implementation to other grades as the cohort of students who receive DI advances through the grade levels.

Over time, the school can build its capacity to provide its own preservice training. In addition to program training, the National DI Conference offers in-depth institutes for coaches, trainers, and school leaders. The Institute on Becoming an Effective DI Trainer, which requires an application for admission, prepares experienced DI teachers to become trainers. Participants who successfully complete the institute can provide initial program training to their peers on site at their schools with little to no support from outside DI experts.

ARRANGING FOR ONGOING TRAINING AND COACHING SUPPORT

Preservice training is just the start of teachers' process of learning DI. Ongoing training and coaching should be a regular part of a DI implementation during the school year so teachers can improve and expand their repertoire of skills consistently over time. Since preservice training concentrates on the first 25–30 lessons of the program, there needs to be regular in-service training and practice sessions that address later lessons in the program. The practice sessions should be supervised with a specific focus for each session. As with preservice training, the emphasis of the practice sessions should be on the practical application of skills instead of discussing aspects of the program. Rationale should be provided for the techniques and the design of specific instructional formats, but discussion should be kept to a minimum so that teachers spend most of the time practicing essential skills that will help improve student performance in their classrooms.

Stages	Focus	30 min. session	60 min. session
Part 1: Large Group	Model of correct execution of formats and procedures	7 min.	15 min.
Part 2: Small Group	Teacher rehearsal of upcoming formats and procedures	18 min.	35 min.
Part 3: Large Group	Questions and answers	5 min.	10 min.

Table 8.15 Schedule for 30-minute and 60-minute format practice sessions. Source: The National Institute for Direct Instruction (NIFDI).

Practice sessions should take place at least twice a week for the first year of implementation and more often as needed. They can be reduced in frequency in subsequent years of implementation as the instructional staff demonstrate mastery of essential teaching skills. However, when new teachers are hired, they should receive the same DI practice regime as the other staff experienced during their first year of teaching DI. Table 8.15 shows the schedule of practice sessions of two different lengths – 30 and 60 minutes – that incorporate large- and small-group professional development activities. The practice sessions are divided into three stages. In the first stage, a trainer models the skills that participants will practice (part 1 of the session in Table 8.15). Participants then break into small groups and practice the targeted skills as the trainer provides feedback to the participants (part 2 in Table 8.15). Small-group rehearsal takes up more than half of the total time of the practice session. After the participants have practiced the formats and skills, they reconvene into a larger group to address any questions they may have (part 3 in Table 8.15).

Note that in-class coaching should not be seen as a substitute for training. Since training involves pulling together multiple staff members on the same topic to address a potential problem of student performance *before* it occurs, training is more efficient than coaching. If a school relies exclusively on coaching, similar problems will exist across many classrooms, which the coach can try to resolve through individual coaching sessions. However, it will take some time for the coach to 1) get into all of the classrooms, 2) have the opportunity to identify specific problems of instruction through observation, and 3) debrief with each instructor individually to ensure they understand how to address the problems. In the meantime, classroom instruction will be negatively impacted until these problems are addressed. *It is much more efficient to pull the staff together to address common problems in the form of an in-service training* rather than attempt to address them through individual coaching sessions. It is most efficient to provide in-services of potential problem areas *before problems develop in the classroom* if they can be anticipated. Potential problem areas can be anticipated based on years of DI teaching or coaching experience.

Although coaching cannot be a substitute for training, training without coaching will not lead to an optimal implementation. Without coaching, teachers cannot be expected to implement targeted skills with fidelity for the simple reason that teachers will not be able to correct a problem if they do not know it exists. For example, a teacher who is learning to deliver DI may unknowingly mouth out the words students are supposed to say as students are sounding them out, which, in effect, gives students the answer if they look at the teacher's mouth rather than reading the letters and blending the sounds. Another example is when a teacher holds the teacher presentation book (TPB) at an angle that does not allow all of the students to see it clearly. Or a teacher may not notice that the students don't all answer chorally to the signal. An expert DI coach can observe these problem areas of the teacher's delivery and prescribe practice regimes to address each of these problems.

In an effective DI implementation, training and coaching exist in coordination with each other. Training sessions can provide a basis for what coaches should look for when they visit classrooms, and coaching can provide a basis for the types of problems to address in the training sessions when the same problems are observed in multiple classrooms.

In terms of expectations for staff, the school leadership should convey to teachers that they are expected to preview the lessons they will teach daily and rehearse them orally during their planning time in addition to attending the supervised practice sessions. Because the programs contain everything that a teacher will need for the lessons, there is very little planning that needs to take place with DI. Instead, teachers should concentrate on becoming fluent with the scripts, especially corrections, and anticipate where students may experience difficulty, especially with new content.

In addition to regular practice sessions that focus on delivering upcoming lessons, school leaders should arrange for other in-service sessions that address specific skills that support the implementation of DI. Here is a list of in-service topics broken into four categories that should be addressed in a school's first year of implementing DI:

Setup

- Physical arrangement of classrooms and materials.

Behavior

- Specific, positive praise
- Transitions
- Teacher/Student game
- Thermometer charts
- Good work ticket system (a token-based system)
- Routines and expectations
- Give me five (a procedure for getting students' attention within five seconds).

Program delivery and monitoring

- Correction procedures for verbal tasks
- Pausing and punching bold words
- Pacing in Direct Instruction
- Keeping kids from droning
- Individual turns
- Active monitoring of independent work
- Conducting teacher-directed work checks
- End-of-year/start-of-year procedures – to be reviewed before the second year of implementation.

Data and assessment

- Conducting mastery tests and checkouts, including providing remedies
- Lesson progress charts (LPCs)

- Student test summary (STS) forms
- Data analysis
- First-time correct mastery.

The in-service on *setup* prepares teachers to configure classrooms for efficiency with the goal of maximizing instructional time. The in-services on *behavior* also prepare teachers to improve the efficiency of instruction by motivating students to pay attention, follow directions, and work to the best of their abilities. The in-services on *program delivery and monitoring* prepare teachers to implement critical aspects of the DI lessons effectively and determine in real time the degree of effectiveness of their instruction. The in-services on *data and assessment* prepare teachers to assess the efficiency as well as the effectiveness of their instruction by analyzing objective data on student performance.

To provide training and ongoing support, schools need to contract with an expert DI coach, such as those provided by the National Institute for Direct Instruction (NIFDI). The coach should be an experienced DI teacher who has taken advanced training on coaching. They should be able to:

- assist with placement, grouping, and program selection
- provide advice on schedules, room configurations, material management, data collection, and other structural aspects of the DI implementation
- conduct a variety of in-class observations and intervene during instruction to demonstrate key DI presentation and correction techniques
- identify problems of student performance and potential remedies that address specific problems observed
- analyze student performance data for potential problems and opportunities for accelerating students through the program
- provide written summaries of observations and recommendations for improving the implementation of DI
- suggest a regime of practice sessions and in-service training for the year.

NIFDI has created several resources that provide support for conducting effective in-service training without the need to hire an outside consultant. The NIFDI video in-services, which are available for purchase online at www.nifdi.org/store/category/19-training-materials.html, provide expert guidance on implementing the following aspects of a DI implementation:

- Critical phrasing (how and when to emphasize specific wording to help students focus on critical parts of a DI lesson)
- How to correct discrimination errors (errors that involve incorrect answers)
- How to correct signal violations (errors that involve students not answering chorally at the appropriate time)
- Thermometer charts (a system for reinforcing students for high achievement on independent work).

The online in-service packages come with a facilitator's guide, videos containing expert rationale on specific procedures for an effective DI implementation, clips of examples and non-examples of these procedures, participant materials, and a form for school leaders to use to conduct follow-up observations to verify that the staff incorporate all procedures addressed in the in-service. The videos are interactive with places for the facilitator to pause the video so participants can practice a technique or discuss a specific topic. Because so much training expertise is built into the video in-service packages, they can be led by a coach who is relatively inexperienced in DI. The video in-services can also provide a model to school and district leaders on how to construct effective training sessions that lead to teachers' mastery of critical skills – how to sequence examples and non-examples and include a range of activities that promote teachers' mastery of targeted skills.

The run time of the videos without pauses ranges from 20 to 47 minutes. The total time for the in-services can be expected to range from about half an hour to over two hours to incorporate time for the activities. The longer in-services may need to be broken up over two or more sessions to accommodate the availability of the instructional staff.

CONFIGURING CLASSROOMS FOR EFFICIENT INSTRUCTION

As indicated above, there are ways of arranging a classroom physically that can improve the efficiency of instruction. In a DI classroom, the most efficient arrangements differ by the level of the program being implemented. The lower levels of the programs require smaller instructional groups than higher levels of the programs, and they require a different classroom setup. Children in the lower levels of the programs should be seated in chairs in a semicircle in close proximity to the teacher so they can see the presentation book or instructional display and the teacher can monitor them. The children should not be seated on the floor because they may shift their positions over time and interact with each other instead of focusing on instruction. They should also not be seated at desks for group instruction as this increases the distance between the teacher and the children and adds a potential distraction (the desks themselves) to the children during instruction. The students can, however, be seated at desks during independent work, and students in the remedial programs, such as *Corrective Reading Decoding A*, can be seated at desks or at a table – as these are generally more mature students than the children in the lower levels of the developmental DI programs – unless the desks prove to be a source of distraction during instruction.

Figure 8.2 shows the optimal seating configuration of a group with seven students. The teacher sits near the center of the semicircle facing the students. Even though students have been grouped for instruction as homogeneously as possible, the performance level of the students in the group can be expected to vary, and this variation should be taken into account when assigning seats to students. Lower-performing students are seated directly in front of the teacher so she can give them extra attention. Higher-performing students are seated on the periphery as they don't require to be monitored as closely as lower performers. Middle-performing students are seated in the other chairs. If the group is large, a second row of students can be formed that consists of middle- and higher-performing students seated in the gaps between students in the first row so they can see the teacher presentation book. Lower performers should not be seated in the second row as this will reduce the monitoring and support that the teacher can provide for them.

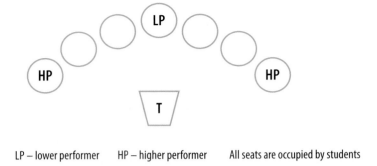

Key

T – teacher   LP – lower performer   HP – higher performer   All seats are occupied by students

Figure 8.2 Optimal seating for small-group instruction.

The positioning of the group within the classroom during instruction is important for reducing the distractions for the children. The teacher's back should be against a wall or corner of the room so the students can just see the teacher and the wall(s) behind her, while the teacher can survey the rest of the classroom at a glance. If the students' backs are against a wall or corner, and the teacher is facing the wall(s) behind them, she won't be able to see what's taking place in the classroom behind her, and the students are more likely to get distracted by people or objects in the rest of the classroom. Students who are engaged in independent work can be seated at individual desks (or tables if they need to share materials, such as crayons) that are located closer to the center of the classroom and some distance away from the instructional groups so as not to distract them.

For large-group instruction, students sit at desks or at small tables arranged so that all students are facing forward toward the front of the room with enough space for the teacher to walk around and monitor every student. Arranging the desks into rows and columns is best for monitoring. The desks or tables should not be arranged into clusters with students facing each other. Clusters or "four square" arrangements can be conducive to collaborative group work, but these arrangements are not conducive to most activities called for in the DI programs. However, when students are engaged in collaborative activities in DI, such as paired reading or writing activities, the furniture can be moved to facilitate these activities.

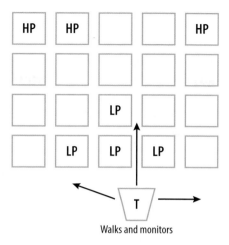

Walks and monitors

Figure 8.3 Optimal seating for large-group instruction.

Figure 8.3 shows the optimal seating configuration for a group of 20 students who are receiving DI. As with small-group seating arrangements, lower-performing students in large groups are seated directly in front of the teacher so she can give them extra attention. Higher-performing students are seated on the periphery as they don't require monitoring as closely as lower performers. Middle-performing students are seated in the other chairs with desks. As the figure indicates, the teacher spends some of her time at the front of the room, but most of the time she walks and monitors to ensure that students are on task and answering correctly during instruction.

For both small- and large-group instruction, the teacher will need some type of display (a projected computer screen, a whiteboard, or a chalkboard) upon which to mark points for the Teacher/Student game. The game needs to be readily accessible to the teacher, and it needs to be large enough and positioned so the students can see the points. Awarding points should become a fluid part of the teacher's presentation, and as such, the Teacher/Student game should be *convenient* for the teacher to access as well as *visible* to the students.

For all types of instruction, it is important that the teacher establishes efficient procedures for materials distribution. For younger children, the teacher should have all materials ready before instruction in a place that's convenient for them or the children to access. To accommodate these materials, students' chairs can be fitted with back-of-the-chair pockets where workbooks, storybooks, and other materials are stored for quick access, while remaining out of the way during times when they are not needed. Another option is for these materials to be stacked below the chairs or put into a hard case next to each chair. With older students, materials can be kept in individual desks or stored in a set location in the classroom. A different student can be designated each week to hand out the materials, or each student can get their own in an orderly way. Procedures for materials distribution and transitions between activities should be practiced to mastery at the beginning of the school year. As part of these practice sessions, students should be taught to use bookmarks appropriately so they can find their place quickly and not delay instruction by searching needlessly for the proper page. The teacher can reinforce students for fluent transitions between activities and for accessing materials quickly, in an orderly fashion, as described in chapter 5 of this book.

ESTABLISHING POSITIVE BEHAVIOR MANAGEMENT PRACTICES

In chapter 5 of this book, specific positive behavior management practices were discussed along with their rationale. These practices are necessary prerequisites for maximizing the effect of DI with all students. As discussed in chapter 7, it is optimal that schools implement schoolwide management procedures that clarify and reinforce behavioral expectations *during the year prior to implementing DI*. If this is not possible, positive management practices should be established very early in the school year when DI is first introduced – optimally from the moment the students step on campus for the first time. The start of the school year will go much smoother, and student performance will improve much more rapidly, if all students understand the expectations and the consequences of following or not following these expectations. If they learn that following expectations will be much more reinforcing to them than the alternative, many behavioral incidents will be avoided. If school bus drivers can be included in a training on behavior management, they can implement positive behavioral techniques while students are on the bus, which can help ensure that students arrive on campus ready to participate in effective instruction.

If school leaders and teachers try to ease students into the school environment by laxly explaining and enforcing behavioral or procedural rules at the start of the school year, students may become confused when the rules are tightened up later in the school year. Students surmise relatively early in the school year what is permitted or expected, what is not permitted or expected, and what consequences there will be for their actions. The longer the delay in communicating clearly to students the rules and expectations of the school and the consequences of specific behaviors, the more entrenched students' early interpretation of the school's requirements will be, and the more difficult it will be to correct their misinterpretation. If students understand from the first day what's expected of them at school and how meeting these expectations will be reinforcing to them, the higher the likelihood that the school year will start smoothly, and the more progress students will make over the course of the school year in acquiring critical skills. If there is a successful start to the school year, including the implementation of the setup items discussed in this chapter, students will progress through the DI programs at mastery. As they do, their positive image of themselves as successful students will be reinforced, which in turn will increase their willingness to follow the school's expectations and procedures, setting off a virtuous cycle of positive instructional outcomes and school climate.

CHAPTER NINE
MONITORING THE IMPLEMENTATION

The previous chapter described the main steps that school leaders should take to establish a schoolwide implementation of Direct Instruction (DI). This chapter is devoted to describing the second major function of school leaders – monitoring instruction. DI does not involve a "one and done" approach to changing instruction. Instead, it requires monitoring and follow-up by the school's leadership to ensure that continuous improvement in instruction is occurring in all classrooms across the school. Monitoring instruction helps communicate to the staff that the school's leadership is committed to ensuring that DI has a positive effect on student outcomes. Experienced teachers may have seen educational initiatives come and go before with very little lasting effect on instructional practices at their school, so they may assume that the expectations around DI are optional or temporary. By closely monitoring classroom instruction, leaders communicate to the staff that DI procedures will be implemented across the school with fidelity and without exception.

The need for monitoring is high in a DI implementation due to the incremental design of the programs. If students are misplaced in the program or not taught to mastery, students cannot be expected to progress through the program successfully. The greater the mismatch between the students' skill levels and their instructional level, the greater the difficulty students will experience in mastering the current lesson, which will have a negative implication for their ability to master the next lesson. In DI, it is imperative for a smoothly functioning implementation to be able to identify problems of placement, mastery, and other aspects of the program as soon as possible. The leadership should strive for ways to collect accurate information on the state of each instructional group and the performance of each individual student. A saying that applies to successful monitoring is that "a problem can't be solved if it is not identified."

This search for problems may represent a tectonic cultural shift for school staff as it is uncommon in many schools for leaders to monitor instruction closely with the goal of identifying problems of instruction so they can be resolved as soon as possible. Leaders will need to explain the rationale for monitoring instruction closely and review the specific types of monitoring that will take place at the school as part of the setup stage (discussed in the last chapter). This is especially true in schools with a history of teachers operating largely as independent practitioners in their own classrooms with very little involvement from the school's leadership.

The timing of monitoring is essential for an effective implementation. The leadership should check that each step described in the previous chapter is actually being taken when it is supposed to occur. For each type of DI training, school leaders should have a system for verifying that all of the staff members who are supposed to be at the training are present and contacting them immediately if they are not present. Leaders should track who has successfully completed a required training and passed the appropriate check on understanding to ensure that they've acquired the skills and content of the training. Ongoing monitoring throughout the year helps the leadership assess how successful training and coaching efforts have been and what types of remedies need to take place to improve the effect on student performance.

This chapter addresses the following aspects of monitoring that help ensure a successful implementation of DI:

1. determining what constitutes a problem of instruction
2. developing reliable sources of information on student performance
3. describing problems of student performance
4. monitoring instruction through direct observations
5. monitoring instruction through data analysis
6. assessing school leaders' support of the DI implementation.

WHAT IS A PROBLEM OF INSTRUCTION?

As mentioned previously in this book, a situation should only be considered to be a problem in DI if there is a problem with student performance. If a teacher employs some unorthodox routines, for instance, but the students are progressing through the program at an acceptable rate at mastery, there are no problems of student performance with the instructional group. Usually, though, one or more problems can be expected to occur in the classroom at any one time. When problems of student performance have been identified, the next level of monitoring is to observe the teacher's behavior to see if they are taking steps to address the problem and, if so, how they are addressing the problem. A situation in which the teacher is taking steps to address a problem has different implications for school leaders concerning how they should respond in comparison to situations in which the teacher doesn't take action to address a problem. The goal of monitoring is to understand the layout of student performance as well as the distribution of problems of instruction across the school at both the student and teacher levels. This allows the leadership to allocate its time and resources effectively to address the most critical problems in the school.

At the student level, there are two main categories of potential problems: mastery and lesson progress. *All problems at a school can be defined in terms of their impact on lesson progress or mastery.* For example, if students take a long time to find their place in their workbooks, this has negative implications for lesson progress. If the teacher does not correct student errors consistently, this has negative implications on student mastery of the lesson. Of these two categories, *problems of mastery should take precedence over problems of lesson progress* because of the incremental step design of the DI programs. If students have not mastered the content of a lesson, progress through the program should be delayed until they have mastered the content. If the students do not master the content and are "dragged" through the program without understanding it, they will not be successful because all future lessons are predicated on students' understanding of the content of previous lessons. A saying that captures the primacy of mastery in DI is: "lesson progress without mastery is not progress at all."

Mastery can be defined in several ways. According to one common definition, students are at mastery on a task if they can perform the task successfully as easily as they can say their own name. So a student is at mastery on something if they can respond correctly, fluently, and consistently when presented with a given prompt, such as, "What is your name?"

An important concept in assessing mastery is the *first-time correct* response, which refers to how successfully students respond the first time they encounter a task during an instructional period before the teacher corrects any performance errors. First-time correct rates on specific tasks capture the degree to which students are able to perform accurately and demonstrate the skills they have brought with them into the instructional setting on a given day. Rates of successful performance after students have received corrective feedback from their teacher are important, too, as students should respond completely correctly on all tasks by the end of a lesson. Student performance before corrections (first-time correct performance) indicates whether they are placed correctly in the program, whereas performance after corrections indicates whether they are "at mastery" and ready to proceed to the next lesson in the program.

Lesson progress (at mastery) is the second category of measuring success in the DI programs. Mastering the skills and content contained in the lessons is essential but insufficient as a criterion of success with DI. Students should not only master lessons but also proceed through the lessons at a rate that will allow them to learn at least one grade's worth of material in a year. The expected rates of progress differ according to the level of the program taught as well as the skill level of the students. Student progress through the lower levels of the programs (the first two levels) should meet the following guidelines *if there is sufficient instructional time allocated daily* as described in the previous chapter:

- High-performing groups should achieve eight to nine lessons a week at mastery
- Middle-performing groups should achieve seven to eight lessons a week at mastery
- Low-performing groups should achieve five to seven lessons a week at mastery (source: the National Institute for Direct Instruction).

For example, kindergarten students who place at Lesson 1 of the language track of *Reading Mastery Signature Edition* (RMSE) should be considered to be low performers and should only be expected to complete five to seven lessons a week (at mastery). However, kindergarten students who place at Lesson 41 of the language track of RMSE should be considered to be high performers and are expected to complete eight to nine lessons a week (at mastery).

Students in higher levels of the programs (higher than the first two levels) should be expected to complete only a lesson a day (at mastery) because of the longer length and greater complexity of the lessons.

Note that these rates should be considered to be long-term expected averages over several weeks of instruction or longer. Some instructional groups may need to spend more time on specific exercises that are difficult for them and repeat lessons to ensure mastery. Week-to-week variation in the actual lesson progress of the groups is inevitable as teachers respond to student performance and customize the length of time spent on specific items to ensure mastery. If lower-than-expected lesson progress continues for several weeks, however, there may be a serious problem with such factors as the daily schedule of instruction, program delivery, behavior management, or students' placement in the program, which will need to be addressed to ensure adequate lesson progress by the students.

School leaders should keep these two categories of problems in mind – problems of mastery and problems of lesson progress – when monitoring instruction. When observing instruction in the classroom or analyzing student performance data, the ultimate criterion for deciding whether a problem exists is whether students are progressing through the programs at mastery at the expected rate. If they are, there is no problem. If not, there is a problem, and the next level of monitoring is to determine what has caused the less-than-ideal levels of mastery and/or lesson progress.

SOURCES OF INFORMATION ON STUDENT PERFORMANCE

Monitoring instruction involves data in the broadest sense of the word: information on how students perform and how teachers deliver the program. There are three main sources of data in a DI implementation: direct observation, documentation of structural details, and written data.

With DI, the teacher has access to a continuous stream of data on student performance during live instruction, as every skill or concept is verified through an explicit written, oral, or kinesthetic task (such as touching a part of a worksheet) that can be observed directly. Teachers who monitor their students' performance closely during the face-to-face phase of instruction and independent work can anticipate with great accuracy how well each student will perform on the in-program assessments. Teachers who are not able to monitor their students' performance closely during instruction are not able to anticipate how well each student will perform on in-program assessments.

Successful monitoring of live instruction involves a great deal of focus and effort by teachers and coaches, as every student's response on every item is critical for determining whether all students have mastered each lesson. If a student makes an error that the teacher does not notice, and she proceeds to the next item, the student may make errors on similar items in the future and on content that presumes mastery of the item. Coaches must monitor the performance of the students, as well as the actions of the teacher in response to the students' performance, to determine which skills the teacher has mastered and which require additional support. Successful monitoring of DI also involves skill and experience as well as focus and effort. For instance, teachers and coaches must learn to detect when some students lag in their responses ("coat-tail"). Successful monitoring requires training and experience applying critical observational skills, just as successful delivery of DI requires training and experience applying instructionally critical skills.

A challenge for leaders of a DI implementation is how to get as much useful information on student performance and teacher delivery as possible without getting overwhelmed. As mentioned earlier, each teacher has access to a continuous stream of information on each student's performance during live instruction. School leaders can access this information, too, by observing instruction themselves if they have been properly trained. However, school leaders can only be in one classroom observing one instructional group at a time during live instruction. In the meantime, they are missing out on instruction that is taking place with all other instructional groups in the school – including those that are in the same classroom. So relying on in-person observations, which has great potential for revealing the state of student performance and teacher delivery, must be allocated judiciously across all of the classrooms during the times that the leadership is available to monitor instruction.

Video technology can help increase the monitoring potential of a school's leadership. By setting up cameras in multiple classrooms, the leadership can monitor instruction across the school asynchronously, which is particularly helpful when DI is restricted to a single instructional block at the same time across classrooms in a school rather than spread across the school day. If it is recorded, the leadership must still find time in their day to review the videos so they must be selective in what to watch. It's technically possible (but may seem Orwellian to the staff) to have cameras in all classrooms so the leadership can view all instruction as it takes place throughout the school simultaneously from a single office. However, school leaders can still only pay attention to one instructional group at a time with live instruction.

The leadership can recruit staff members to help with monitoring. One approach is to ask teachers to self-monitor and self-assess their instruction. It is most helpful for the staff to take videos of their own instruction and then receive feedback from an experienced coach after they self-assess. If the leadership relies simply on self-reports from teachers without a video review, there is the risk that the teachers won't be aware of errors in their delivery. For instance, a common error is for teachers to mouth the pronunciation of a word when the students are sounding out a word from the teacher presentation book or display. These teachers are unaware that they are providing the students with a contextual cue by mouthing out the words, which the students may use to figure out the word rather than actually applying the decoding strategies they've been taught. A teacher who has developed the habit of mouthing out words may require repeated feedback from an observer, along with guided practice, before they can extinguish this behavior.

Another approach to increase monitoring of instruction is to develop a system of peer coaches who can assist the building coordinator, as mentioned in the previous chapter. Peer coaches or lead teachers are instructional staff members who are either early adopters of DI or have demonstrated a knack for acquiring essential DI delivery and correction techniques. With the proper training and release time, peer coaches can act as another set of eyes and ears for the building coordinator, further extending the ability of the school's leadership to gather critical information on the status of the DI implementation. The building coordinator and peer coaches can also fulfill a screening function of identifying complex problems that need to be observed by the external support provider when they come on site.

In addition to direct observation of classroom instruction, structural details provide another source of useful data on a DI implementation. These include the number of students per group, the schedule/timetable of the instructional periods, and the inventory of DI materials broken down into relevant categories (program, level, and teacher vs. student material). Having accessible and clear rosters, bell schedules, and an inventory of materials can greatly facilitate the leadership's ability to identify potential problems of implementation caused by misconfigured structural factors.

Another critical source of information on a DI implementation is data on lesson progress and in-program assessments. Monitoring instruction through data can be a very powerful complement to in-class observations. These written data, which are discussed in more detail later in this chapter, allow school leaders to formulate weekly snapshots of important aspects of instruction across classrooms. Weekly data analysis is one of the most effective ways of expanding the eyes and ears of the school's leadership. Through it, the leadership can determine the extent to which each instructional group is meeting critical performance benchmarks without going into classrooms. The leadership can then channel the school's coaching resources to instructional groups that appear on paper to be struggling. In this manner, the analysis of the written data can act as an initial screener to help the leadership identify problems of student performance, after which the leadership can conduct in-class observations to get a clearer, more detailed description of the problems of instruction in classrooms of concern.

Before any form of data – observational or written – can be used for decision making, the sources of data must be verified to be reliable.

Staff involved in monitoring should successfully complete a training session on specific monitoring techniques, after which the trainer can shadow the trainees as they conduct in-class observations. After each classroom visit, the staff individually report on what they observed, and the trainer provides feedback. This process of "monitoring the monitors" should continue until the staff who are responsible for conducting in-class observations consistently notice the essential aspects of classroom instruction that each specific observational tool is designed to capture. Once the coaching staff reliably report data generated from a specific observation type, they are ready to proceed to the next most sophisticated observation type.

Sources of written data should also be subject to verification before they can be considered reliable. They may be unreliable for various reasons:

- *The data are incomplete.* The DI data forms are not intuitive to all teachers. They need to be trained on the type of data asked for in each category. Learning how to fill out the data forms is addressed briefly in the preservice (program) training, but the topic should be addressed in a longer in-service session after school starts. Even after teachers go through the training, they may require feedback from an experienced practitioner or a trainer on how to fill out the forms correctly.

- *Teachers do not fill in accurate information.* Inaccurate data entry may be due to a lack of understanding of each category of information on the data sheets, which is addressed during an in-service training session. Inaccurate data entry may also occur due to a lack of commitment to reporting exactly what occurs. A common error for recording the results of checkout data is for teachers to round the time it took a student to read a passage down to the next minute if the student exceeds the time limit by a just few seconds. However, a few seconds may make the difference between a student passing and not passing the checkout. If checkout data include several results that have been recorded as ending precisely on one or more minutes with no seconds remaining, those results may be suspect because of the rare chance (one in 60) of students finishing a passage exactly on the minute mark.

- *Test results do not represent the students' actual abilities because the teacher prepped the students for the test.* In some schools, teachers task-analyze the next mastery test that their students will encounter and ensure that the students can perform well on the specific tasks that appear on the tests when they encounter them in the lessons leading up to the mastery test. Although this approach may increase the chances of students passing the next mastery test, it does not ensure long-term success in the program *unless the students are brought to mastery on all of the content of the lessons leading up to the mastery test.* If students have not mastered parts of the exercises that are not covered in the test, they will not be ready to advance in the program. If a group needs a great deal of preparation outside of their normal lessons to pass the mastery tests, the group may be misplaced in the program and should be moved to earlier lessons that correspond more closely to their skill level. An example of inadvertently prepping students for an assessment occurs when students reread the same passage several times for a checkout. Sometimes, students will memorize all or part of a passage after repeated exposure, in which case they are not reading but reciting what they know, which diminishes the reliability of the checkout as an accurate measure of the students' reading skills. A rule of thumb is that a student who fails to pass a checkout repeatedly should not reread the same passage more than three times. Instead, the teacher should select a different passage from the same story for the student to read for additional checkouts as needed.

DESCRIBING PROBLEMS OF STUDENT PERFORMANCE

When conducting observations or describing problems, coaches and school leaders should start with the students first. They should:

1. describe precisely what they saw the students doing
2. describe what the teacher was or wasn't doing that is relevant to the student performance problem
3. come up with one or more remedies.

The logic behind this order is ironclad. As mentioned above, a situation should be considered to be a problem only if student performance is adversely affected. So if the first step of observing students is skipped, the next two steps may not be necessary. For example, an observer who notices that the teacher has an unusual signal should look at the students to determine if they are all answering together at an appropriate time before determining whether the unusual signal is a problem. If an observer follows the first step but skips the second step of observing the teacher, the observer may not know which remedy to apply. For example, an observer who notices that several students in a group are coming in late with their responses during letter identification tasks should not conclude that a teacher needs to increase the amount of think time for the students (a standard remedy) until the teacher's delivery is observed, because there may be other factors, such as the teacher's signal or the teacher's positioning of the teacher presentation book, which are causing the students to respond late. As discussed in the next chapter, describing problems should follow this same "student-first" order that monitoring instruction follows.

TYPES OF IN-CLASS OBSERVATIONS

Table 9.1 lists some of the most common types of observations that occur in a DI implementation. The different types vary in terms of the duration of the observation, the focus, and the skill level required by an observer. They are listed in a generally sequential order for use by the school leadership and external support providers over the course of a school year. The monitoring of preservice checkouts should occur first before school starts, followed by observations conducted at the beginning of the school year, and then observations that the leadership conducts throughout the rest of the school year. These observations are discussed later in the chapter in the order they appear in the table. For all observations, *it is critical that observers position themselves so they can see and hear the responses of all students.* Only then can observers determine whether a problem of student performance exists.

Observation	Duration	Type of data collected	When the observation is used
Preservice checkout	Five to 10 minutes	Basic teacher delivery and correction skills	After the preservice program training and before the start of the school year
Two-minute	Two minutes	Student engagement	Start of the school year; after breaks
Five-minute	Five minutes	Structural aspects and basic instructional delivery	Start of the school year; after breaks
Script fidelity	Five minutes up to an entire instructional period	Adherence to or deviation from the DI scripts and their conventions	Start of the school year; after new staff members have been hired
First-time correct	Two minutes up to an entire instructional period	Mastery percentages of students on new material and material introduced in previous lessons	Whenever needed to confirm placement and mastery of instructional groups
In-service follow-up	Ten minutes up to an entire instructional period	Implementation fidelity of techniques covered during in-service training sessions	After staff members have participated in an in-service training session
Pacing	Ten minutes up to an entire instructional period	Rate at which an instructional group completes one or more exercises	After the instructional staff has demonstrated script fidelity and basic delivery techniques consistently
Positive-to-negative feedback	Ten minutes up to an entire instructional period	Ratio of positive-to-negative feedback that students receive	After the instructional staff has demonstrated script fidelity and basic delivery techniques consistently
Show-off lesson	Usually an entire instructional period	Mastery data, error corrections, and other instructional components	To determine areas of improvement for teachers whose students have been struggling
Follow-up to problem-solving sessions	Usually less than an entire instructional period	Confirmation that individual instructional staff members have implemented specific requests by the leadership team	After the weekly problem-solving sessions

Table 9.1 Types of observations conducted in Direct Instruction classrooms.

PRESERVICE CHECKOUT VERIFICATION

One of the first opportunities that school and district leaders have to monitor the DI implementation is verifying the preservice checkout results. As described in the previous chapter, a key prerequisite to success with DI is for all instructional staff members involved in the implementation to demonstrate that they are ready to start teaching the DI programs effectively. Teachers should attend a preservice (program) training, during which the trainer "checks out" each participant on their delivery and correction skills. If the teachers do not pass all aspects of the checkout, they should practice the skills covered in the training and get re-checked on the delivery or correction skills that need improvement. The re-check can take far less time than the original checkout if a teacher needs improvement on only one or two skills. If, however, the teacher needs improvement on several skills, the re-check can take as long or nearly as long as the original checkout because many of the skills are embedded in procedures that include other DI presentation or correction skills.

Table 9.2 shows the preservice checkout summary form that the National Institute for Direct Instruction (NIFDI) uses to track the performance of teachers on their preservice checkouts and re-checks. The specific exercise of a lesson used for the checkout of each individual teacher is indicated in the second column. The next six columns address delivery skills, and the last five columns address correction skills. An additional column has been added in some versions of the form for assessing the mastery of participants in identifying and producing the sounds that correspond to the symbols students read in the *Reading Mastery* program (a "sounds checkout").

During the checkout, the trainer puts a plus sign (+) if a participant successfully demonstrates a skill or "NP" (needs practice) if the participant does not successfully demonstrate a skill. Teachers practice items with NPs and get re-checked on those items. The trainer circles the NPs if a participant successfully demonstrates proficiency in a skill during the re-check. (The original NP stays on the form; the circle is added.) Preserving the original NP allows the trainer and school leaders to see where the teacher originally struggled. The re-checks continue until all NPs have been circled, even if weeks are required to re-check all teachers on all items.

Teacher Name	Exercises	Followed script	Used appropriate script	Used appropriate signals	Looked at students	Transitioned quickly between tasks	Individual turns	Corrections: Gives answer	Repeats task	Goes back	Individual turns	Delayed test
1												
2												
3												
4												
5												
6												
7												
8												
9												
10												
11												
12												
13												
14												
15												
16												

Key: NP (needs practice)   + (on target)   ◯ (passed on retest)

Trainer comments: _____

Table 9.2 Preservice checkout summary form. Source: The National Institute for Direct Instruction (NIFDI).

The form greatly facilitates the ability of the leadership to monitor the effectiveness of the preservice training. The leadership does not need to be present at the preservice to determine which teachers have acquired the skills they need to start teaching DI. (However, it is highly recommended that the leadership attend some or all of the preservice for other reasons – to demonstrate that the training is important and to learn essential DI teaching skills themselves, which will greatly enhance their ability to coach and support teachers successfully.) The leadership only needs to look at the completed preservice checkout summary to determine which staff members require more practice and training before they can start teaching the program.

TWO-MINUTE AND FIVE-MINUTE OBSERVATIONS

Once the school year starts, school leaders should conduct quick screening observations in classrooms to assess the state of DI across the school. It is critically important that school leaders conduct classroom visits daily for the first few months of the school year for a new implementation of DI and as often as needed throughout the rest of the school year. NIFDI uses two different observations that allow for a quick assessment of instruction – the two-minute and five-minute observations. These observations are short so that school leaders can realistically visit all classrooms in the school in a day. They are conducted at the start of the year, after holiday breaks, and at other times as needed to verify that fundamental aspects of DI remain in place throughout the school year. Through the two-minute and five-minute observations, school leaders identify classrooms that might require more support to be successful, which helps determine the allocation of the school's coaching resources. These observations may also identify problems that require more investigation. The leadership can follow up the two-minute or five-minute observation with more advanced observations as needed to identify the causes of problems identified through these initial observations.

The two-minute observation focuses on one of the most important indicators of successful instruction – student engagement. For DI to be effective, students must be engaged in the appropriate activity at all times. Activities range from oral group responses to independent work. If students are not engaged in the targeted activity, the teacher will not know the extent to which they can perform correctly on instructional tasks, and the teacher will need to repeat the tasks. The teacher may need to repeat several tasks if a student isn't engaged in the targeted activity, which can slow lesson progress considerably.

School: _____   Date: _____

Teacher/Assistant Name	Start time of the observation	Is the teacher/assistant teaching? Y/N	Activity or program	Number of students in the instructional group	Approximate number or % consistently engaged	Comments:
1						
2						
3						
4						
5						
6						

Table 9.3 Two-minute observation form. Source: The National Institute for Direct Instruction (NIFDI).

Table 9.3 shows the form used by NIFDI for the two-minute observation. During the observation, the observer determines the extent of on-task behavior for each instructional group in a classroom (i.e. whether each student is engaged in the intended activity). The objective is to capture the approximate percentage or number of students that are following the teacher's instructions consistently. The observer doesn't need to stay in the classroom for the full two minutes. Rather, the observer needs to stay just long enough to determine how many of the students are on task.

This form has several advantages over other, more complex forms:

1. *It is simple.* The form can be used by an observer with little training. A new user of the form usually only needs to accompany an experienced observer a few times until they can determine when students are engaged fully and when they might be coat-tailing or mouthing the words to an oral task rather than responding fully.

2. *It is brief.* The observer can cover a lot of classrooms quickly. This is important for a district administrator, principal, coordinator, or coach who has a short time window for conducting observations. The two-minute observation can be used in some classrooms by a coach who also uses more extensive observations in other classrooms.

3. *It is not Direct-Instruction-specific.* Because the form is generic, the two-minute observation can be used to gauge the on-task behavior of students in any instructional situation. Data on student engagement during DI periods can be compared with data on engagement during other types of instruction to help inform the leadership and the staff of the differential effects of using DI in their school.

Lack of student engagement during instruction can be an indication of a more profound student performance problem. If students are not engaged, they are not involved in instruction by definition and shouldn't be expected to benefit as much from DI as they would if they were fully engaged. The reasons for a lack of student engagement may run the gamut from problems that are easily corrected to those that are more profound.

Students may:

- not be able to see the teacher presentation book
- be placed in material that is too difficult for them
- be placed in material that is too easy for them, so they're bored with the lesson
- be distracted by something in the setting
- not be sufficiently motivated to pay attention
- have difficulty understanding or paying attention to the teacher due to the pace of instruction and the teacher's intonation.

Some of the problems identified during the two-minute observation may be easily solved on the spot, such as moving furniture so that all students can see the teacher presentation book. The solution of other problems will require more time to fix and may involve repeated coaching and observation sessions.

The five-minute observation is designed to provide a quick assessment of a broad array of essential features of a successful DI classroom. It focuses on structural aspects of a DI implementation and basic instructional delivery techniques as well as student engagement. When five-minute observations are conducted across all classrooms, the leadership can get an overall picture of the state of the DI implementation at the school. The leadership can focus on classrooms with the highest need of support, or they can identify common problems across classrooms and address them in an in-service training shared by several teachers.

Although the five-minute observation can be conducted during any five-minute time block during an instructional period, the first five minutes of instruction provide the best opportunity to see how the teacher starts the lesson: how they get the students' attention, call them into the proper physical location, and provide praise to students who attend to directions. The last five minutes of an instructional period are also a prime time for conducting the five-minute observation as some teachers may stop instruction early if they have completed all exercises in a lesson. If a group finishes a lesson before the end of the period, the teacher should go on to the next lesson or review parts of the lesson where students made errors.

Figure 9.1 shows the five-minute observation form used by NIFDI. The items can be addressed sequentially, or they can be covered in a different order by different observers over the course of five minutes. The first three items address structural factors that affect instruction (which lesson is being taught, number of students, and physical arrangement). The next four items address essential aspects of group instruction (student engagement, teacher fidelity to the script, error corrections, and behavior management). The next three items address independent work – whether independent workers are on task, if errors on independent work have been corrected, and whether the work is neat and organized. The last three items address organization – of materials, student performance records, and the thermometer chart system of reinforcing students engaged in independent work. (Information on thermometer charts is available at www.nifdi.org/services/training/in-service-training/video-in-services. html.)

If an item is observed, the observer records a plus mark or check mark. If an item is not observed, the observer leaves the space blank. However, if an item is not applicable, the observer records "NA." For example, when students are in Grade 2 material or higher, the instructional group is the whole class, and there are no students engaged in independent work during group instruction. So the observer would record NA for the eighth item on the five-minute observation form: "students doing independent work are on-task."

The items in italics at the bottom of the form address how the observation fits into the teacher's professional development. These items indicate when the observer will meet with the teacher regarding the observation, how well the teacher demonstrated that they have mastered the skills that were the focus in previous observations, and the remedies that the observer recommends.

School: _____ Name: _____ T TA

Grade: _____ Date: _____

Start time: _____ Program/Level: _____

During a five-minute observation, watch for the following:

_____ The subject and lesson you were expecting to see is being taught.

_____ Number of students in group is appropriate.

_____ Physical arrangement allows students and teachers to see and hear all parts of the lesson.

_____ Students receiving group instruction are attentive and engaged.

_____ Teacher follows the script as written.

_____ Teacher corrects when students make errors.

_____ Teacher relies on positive techniques to manage student behavior.

_____ Students doing independent work are on-task.

_____ Independent work is corrected and students have done fix-ups.

_____ Student work is neat and well organized.

_____ Teacher and student materials are organized and accessible.

_____ Written records of student performance are posted or accessible.

_____ Thermometer charts are posted and implemented correctly.

Time and date of conference: *Follow-up from last visit:*

Date and procedure for follow-up: *Specific structural or training solutions:*

Signature:

Figure 9.1 Five-minute observation form. Source: The National Institute for Direct Instruction (NIFDI).

Note that some items on the five-minute observation form require that the observer has background knowledge on specific aspects of DI. The observer will need to understand what constitutes the following to be able to record their observations accurately: full student engagement in the DI context; basic program delivery techniques; error correction procedures; positive behavioral management techniques; procedures for correcting and fixing up student work; and the different types of data records used in DI. As such, an observer will need training in these areas as well as practice conducting five-minute observations before they can be expected to conduct these observations effectively.

School: _____   Date: _____

Teacher	Time	Program being taught/lesson number	Subject and lesson expected	Number of students appropriate	Physical arrangement appropriate	Students attentive and engaged	Teacher follows script as written	Teacher corrects when students make errors.	Behaviour management positive	Students on-task, working independently	Independent work corrected & fix ups done	Student work neat and organized	Teacher & student materials are organized & accessible	Written records accessible	Thermometer charts posted & implemented correctly.
1.															
2.															
3.															
4.															
5.															
6.															
7.															
8.															
9.															
10.															

Table 9.4 Five-minute observation summary form. Source: The National Institute for Direct Instruction (NIFDI).

NIFDI records the results of the five-minute observations on a summary form (see Table 9.4). Teachers are listed on the left side of the form, and the same items that appear in the regular five-minute observation form appear across the top. The group summary form allows the leadership to look down the columns to determine common areas of accomplishment (which areas teachers are implementing successfully) and common areas of need (which areas require additional training and support). In this way, the summary form allows the leadership to arrange in-service training sessions that address the common needs for professional development in the school. For example, if students in several classrooms are off task during independent work, a coach or the external support provider can provide an in-service on effective methods of increasing student engagement during independent work to the teachers of those students.

Several of the items on the five-minute observation form may require further investigation beyond what is possible in five minutes. More extended observations may be needed to fully assess how well the classroom is functioning in terms of teachers' fidelity to the script, error corrections, positive behavior management, and independent work.

SCRIPT FIDELITY OBSERVATIONS

After the basic structural components are in place in the classrooms, as verified through five-minute observations, the external support provider and support staff can focus more thoroughly on 1) student performance, and 2) the teachers' delivery of the program. The first, most fundamental aspect of teachers' delivery is script fidelity: are teachers following the teacher presentation book (TPB) as written? Inserting different wording and examples during the model-lead-test steps of the presentation may compromise the integrity of the program and undermine the positive effect the program can have on student performance and confidence. As discussed elsewhere, teachers can insert wording required to state behavioral expectations and give feedback to students on their behavior. The only other time that teachers can go off script is to correct student performance errors. Instructional wording and examples that are not scripted have the potential to confuse students and delay their progress through the DI programs. Omitting tasks or built-in assessments can result in students not being adequately prepared for future lessons. Failing to provide full error corrections when the script indicates that the teacher should repeat the instructional tasks "until firm" can also lead to students not achieving mastery on critical tasks that lay the basis for future lessons.

To verify teachers' script fidelity in real time, it is best that the observers have a copy of the teacher presentation book or its electronic equivalent in hand and open to the lesson being taught. Teachers can post the expected lesson for each instructional group for the day on the board or on the door outside of their classroom so observers don't need to ask the teacher which lesson she's teaching. The electronic versions of the lessons (which are accessible through the ConnectED platform of McGraw Hill Education (MHE), the publisher of most DI programs) have a couple of advantages over hard copy TPBs:

1. With the electronic versions of the lessons, observers only need to carry one device when visiting multiple classrooms instead of different TPBs for observing instructional groups at different levels of a DI program.

2. The observer can make notes on the electronic versions of the lessons.

Users can make PDFs of most of the programs that are available on MHE's platform and then mark on them using one of several note-taking, computer-based applications. The online service for *Reading Mastery Transformations* (RMT) does not allow users to make PDFs, but it does allow them to take notes that are retained as part of each user's account. Observers can share the notes easily with the teacher during a debriefing session on the observation.

After basic script fidelity, coaches can focus on other aspects of delivery that enhance the effectiveness of the program, such as providing appropriate think time (giving students sufficient opportunity to formulate a response to an instructional item), critical emphasis (pausing before keywords and "punching" them with more volume), error corrections (using a seven-step procedure to bring students to mastery on items they answer incorrectly), and varying the schedule of reinforcement to the students. Having access to digital versions of the lessons during observations greatly facilitates monitoring these other aspects of program delivery.

MONITORING STUDENT MASTERY DURING INSTRUCTION

Once observers verify that teachers are presenting the DI lessons as written, they can devote themselves to monitoring perhaps the most critical aspect of a DI lesson: student mastery of the material. As discussed elsewhere in this book, student mastery of each item in every lesson is essential before students can progress to the next lesson because of the step-by-step mastery design of the DI programs. There are several measures that can be applied to in-class observations as well as to in-program data to assess students' mastery of the lessons. The concept of *first-time correct* plays an essential role in all of these measures of mastery. First-time correct simply refers to student performance the first time they encounter an instructional task today before the teacher has corrected any performance errors. The extent to which students can respond correctly the first time they encounter instructional tasks during an instructional period reflects what they learned from previous lessons. If the first-time correct percentage of items is low, the students have not retained a sufficient amount of what was taught on previous days to be expected to master the current day's lesson. If the first-time correct percentage is high, they have retained enough from previous lessons to provide a solid foundation for mastering the content of the current day's lesson. So first-time correct measures have profound implications for the success of today's lesson. The more that students have retained material covered in previous days, the stronger the base of knowledge they have to build on during today's lesson, and the better the prospect that they will be successful in mastering the content of today's lesson. Conversely, the less that students have retained what was covered in previous days, the less reliable the base of knowledge they have to build on during today's lesson will be, and the dimmer the prospect that they will be successful in mastering the content of today's lesson. Students who have retained a low proportion of previous lessons are apt to get confused when new concepts and skills are introduced, which may actually cause their knowledge base to contract instead of expand.

During in-class observations of DI lessons, there are several types of first-time correct thresholds that can serve as key indicators of mastery. Students should perform:

1. at least 70% correctly on anything that is being introduced for the first time in the program *before errors are corrected*

2. at least 90% correctly on the parts of the lesson that deal with skills and information introduced earlier in the program *before errors are corrected*

3. 100% correctly on all tasks and activities by the end of the lesson

4. with a sufficiently low rate of errors so the group can complete the lesson in the allotted time. (Adapted from: Engelmann, S., 2014, 25.)

The first two criteria can be used to assess the skills that students have retained from previous instruction and, as such, they serve as indicators of correct placement. All DI lessons are composed of material that students have never seen before as well as material that was introduced in previous lessons. As discussed earlier, in most lessons new material is modeled by the teacher before students are asked to respond. Occasionally, students are asked to perform a task without a model, but in those instances, students have already mastered all of the component skills necessary to perform the task perfectly. For instance, in Exercise 2 of Lesson 46 of the *Reading Mastery Signature Edition Grade 2* program, students read the following list of words without the teacher first providing a model:

1. se<u>ve</u>ral

2. <u>con</u>tinue

3. <u>cor</u>ners

4. <u>hair</u>y

5. <u>en</u>emy.

However, the students read the first syllable of each word, which is underlined, before they are asked to read the whole word (Engelmann, S. and Hanner, 2008, 35). This scaffolding allows students to read the words correctly the first time.

Because the teacher provides a clear model, or because new material is an extension of previously taught material, students should be able to perform at a reasonably high level of accuracy on new material the first time they encounter it – 70% or higher. For material that was introduced in previous lessons, students should be able to perform at an even higher level of accuracy – 90% or higher. This high expectation is justified if the third criterion listed earlier was met during previous days – that all student performance errors were corrected. It would be unreasonable to expect that students can perform perfectly (100% correctly) on all material that was introduced in previous lessons, but they should be able to perform correctly 90% of the time or higher the first time they encounter material today that they mastered in previous lessons.

These two criteria are very useful for *assessing the appropriateness of students' placement in the program.* Placement tests provide a snapshot in time of students' skills that is essential for placing students initially in the DI programs. First-time correct percentages can be used to assess the appropriateness of students' placement on an ongoing basis throughout the school year. To perform a rough calculation of first-time correct percentages, observers can count 10 tasks students encounter for the first time and keep track on their fingers how many times the group answered chorally with the correct answer and how many times they didn't. If students answer correctly as a group on at least seven out of 10 items on new material (criterion 1) and nine out of 10 on all other material in today's lesson (criterion 2), they are placed correctly in the program. If students answer correctly on fewer items, they may be placed in a lesson that is too difficult for them. This strategy of counting first-time responses on your fingers is easiest to apply to review items because the DI programs do not present 10 new tasks in a row due to the incremental step design of the programs. Note that observers should have access to the script while taking first-time correct data so they can determine which tasks are new and which tasks were introduced previously in the program.

The most common cause of low first-time correct percentages is that students are not fully engaged in instruction, which then doesn't give a clear picture of the appropriateness of the material for the students. If students do not respond chorally to the teacher's signal – if some of them respond too late or don't respond at all – that response is counted as an error, which drags down the group's first-time correct percentage. For this reason, it is important that the teacher ensures that all students are fully engaged, responding on signal, and answering chorally. If the first-time correct percentages are still lower than the thresholds indicated when they are answering chorally, the students may not have been taught to mastery on previous lessons, which, in turn, may be an indication that one or more program delivery essentials is out of place. To get at the root cause, longer observations should take place in classrooms where a quick finger-counting assessment indicates a problem with first-time correct mastery.

Note that students who perform correctly on all material (new and review) 100% of the time the first time they encounter it in the lesson may be placed too low in the program. Complete mastery on all items the first time indicates that the students already know the material. If students score 100% the first time throughout a lesson, they can be presented with mastery tests that occur later in the program to see whether more advanced lessons more closely match their skills. The students should be placed where their first-time correct percentages start to approach the 70–90% threshold.

In contrast to the first two measures of mastery, which indicate how much of the skills and content students have retained from previous lessons, the third measure (100% correct on all tasks and activities by the end of the lesson) indicates how much students have learned from the current lesson. In order to achieve 100% student mastery of all skills and content in a lesson, the teacher must correct all student performance errors and provide sufficient practice on missed items for students to demonstrate proficiency. Part of the error correction procedure is to provide individual turns. *Student performance on individual turns should be 100% correct* because individual turns are presented after students have been brought to mastery on a set of tasks within an exercise as a group. If the group as a whole has answered the items correctly, each student should be able to perform correctly on the same items when called on to respond individually. Individual turns should take place in the context of group instruction, but they can also take place in the form of delayed tests at other times during the school day. An effective method of verifying mastery is to ask a child a question related to a skill or concept outside of the instructional setting. If the child can perform correctly when they are outside the teaching context, the child has demonstrated a firm understanding that will allow the teacher to build on the skill or concept.

The last criterion, completing a lesson in the scheduled time, is also a measure of correct placement. If a group makes so many errors during instruction that it can't get through a lesson on time consistently, the group, or individuals within the group, may need to be placed lower in the program even if the other measures of mastery are met. Repeating the lessons may allow the students to make fewer errors, which will allow them to proceed through the lessons more quickly in the long run. However, *every effort should be made to keep a group where they are in the program before moving students back to earlier lessons.* If a teacher's delivery or error corrections are contributing to students' underperformance, putting students earlier in the program will just lead to students repeating the same lessons with the same low level of mastery in the end. An extended observation of the group with a special focus on the teacher's error correction procedures may reveal concrete steps that can be taken to bring students to mastery without changing their lesson placement. In this way, low first-time correct percentages may be an indication of problems of instruction that need to be addressed before student mastery of the lessons can be expected.

Note that these mastery criteria can only be applied to a program that incorporates an incremental design that allows students to be brought to mastery on each lesson and each instructional step within each lesson. If a program contains more than 10–15% new material in each lesson, it is highly unlikely that students will be able to master all of the skills and content of a lesson within an instructional period, and, therefore, they are highly unlikely to be able to perform at 90% or higher the first time on material they've encountered in previous lessons.

These percentages may seem high to those who haven't taught DI programs before, but achieving these percentages allows students to move through the programs with very little backtracking. Although some students may require repetition of difficult concepts to achieve these percentages at first, the need to repeat exercises should diminish over time if they are adhered to by the instructional staff. Eventually, students who are placed correctly and taught to mastery daily will start to sail through the program with few errors as instructional periods overwhelmingly become a time for them to show off what they know and receive reinforcement for their correct responses.

IN-SERVICE FOLLOW-UP OBSERVATIONS

The results of the observations described earlier may indicate that the skill repertoire of teachers needs to be expanded through in-service training. As mentioned in the previous chapter, there are four categories of in-service topics that should be addressed in a school's first year of implementing DI:

- classroom setup
- behavior management
- program delivery
- data recording and assessment.

One option for arranging in-service training is to set a schedule ahead of time for the in-services in all four of these categories. This option may help ensure that all of the topics are covered over the course of the school year. However, the preferred option is to select in-service topics as needed in response to classroom observations. There's no sense in having an in-service on correction procedures, for example, if all teachers have mastered these procedures. If only one or two staff members need to improve their corrections of student errors, one-on-one practice sessions can be arranged on this topic.

Since each of the in-services should be devoted to strengthening the staff's implementation of skills and concepts that can make a difference with student performance, it is important that all staff members demonstrate mastery of the skills in their classrooms after they have attended an in-service training. NIFDI has created follow-up forms that can be used by school leaders during classroom observations after the staff has attended an in-service session. Each follow-up form follows a similar format: the names of the teachers are listed on the side, and the components of the training are listed across the top. In the cells, observers mark whether they have observed the in-service components in each teacher's classroom, which informs the leadership on any additional steps that may need to be taken to ensure that all instructors consistently demonstrate the skills covered during the in-services.

Table 9.5 shows the active monitoring follow-up form, which is used by coaches and external support providers after staff members have attended an in-service on active monitoring. A teacher's active monitoring of students as they work independently is essential for ensuring that students are on task and that their responses are accurate. The components of active monitoring covered in the in-service appear in the column headings across the top of the table. A description of these components can be found in appendix 1 of this book. The form in Table 9.5 has been completed with mock data, which can be used to help familiarize school leaders with the follow-up forms. A plus sign (+) is recorded for classrooms where the component of the in-service is observed, and an "NP" is recorded for teachers who still need to practice the component before they can implement it with complete fidelity.

By comparing the results of the observations, three staff members (Daniels, O'Brien, and Rory) stand out as requiring significantly more support than other staff members. Based on the results of the observations, the leadership should prioritize providing in-class coaching to these three staff members. The leadership could also provide a follow-up in-service training that concentrates on the most prevalent components of active monitoring that were not observed. If the leadership provides a follow-up in-service on the first component of active monitoring (room arrangement facilitates effective monitoring) and the third-to-last component (teacher provides group correction when needed), the five staff members who need practice on these components should attend, including the three staff members identified as needing the most support. *School leaders should then conduct another round of in-class observations to verify that all staff members consistently implement all components of active monitoring.* When a staff member implements a component targeted by the follow-up observation, the observer circles the NP on the form.

School: Two Rivers Elementary   Observer: F. Gardner   Date:

Teacher Name	Room arrangement facilitates effective monitoring	Teacher actively monitors all students during IW	Teacher orally reinforces correct written responses	Teacher checks student work while monitoring	Teacher does not provide reteaching for individual students	Teacher provides group correction when needed	Tchr consistently reinforces appropriate behaviour	Teacher immediately corrects off-task behaviour
1. Daniels	NP	NP	+	+	+	NP	+	NP
2. Walker	+	+	+	NP	+	+	+	+
3. O'Brien	NP	+	+	NP	NP	NP	+	NP
4. Rivera	+	+	+	+	+	+	+	+
5. Allston	+	+	+	+	+	NP	+	+
6. Hernandez	NP	NP	+	+	+	+	+	+
7. Everhart	+	+	+	+	+	+	+	+
8. Davis	+	+	+	+	+	+	+	+
9. Thomas	NP	NP	+	+	+	+	+	+
10. Madison	+	+	+	+	+	+	+	+
11. Gutierrez	+	+	+	NP	+	NP	+	+
12. Rory	NP	NP	NP	+	+	NP	+	NP

Key: NP (needs practice)   + (on target)   O (passed on recheck)

Table 9.5 Active monitoring follow-up form. Source: the National Institute for Direct Instruction (NIFDI).

The leadership should wait to introduce a new in-service topic until all, or nearly all, of the teachers consistently display the critical components of the last in-service topic so they do not become overwhelmed with new learning.

MONITORING PRACTICE SESSIONS

Rehearsing the DI scripts is a major engine of teacher skill improvement. The more that teachers can become fluent in presenting each of the specific formats in the exercises and the error corrections that are specific to each format, the more they are ready to receive feedback on other aspects of DI, such as motivating students and providing more practice to students who are having difficulty with the lessons. To help teachers become fluent in delivering the lessons, supervised practice sessions should take place at least twice a week for the first year of implementation and more often as needed, as mentioned in the previous chapter. In addition to the supervised practice sessions, teachers should review the lessons daily during their prep time to be ready to teach the next day's lesson.

Monitoring practice sessions is relatively simple and straightforward. Teachers should sign an attendance sheet for each practice session, and leaders should review the attendance sheets weekly. Leaders should also drop in on the practice sessions to ensure that the session is following the general schedule outlined in Table 8.15 in the previous chapter of this book, with more than half the time devoted to practicing targeted instructional formats or skills. School leaders should ensure that the practice sessions are productive for teachers who have struggled with lesson delivery in their classrooms by following the practice sessions with in-class observations. Just as preservice checkouts and in-service follow-up observations ensure that participants have mastered critical skills covered during preservice and in-service training sessions respectively, in-class observations after practice sessions ensure that teachers have mastered the critical skills covered during the practice sessions. The building coordinator and coaches can then draw on these follow-up observations when designing the next practice session to address specific problems of instruction observed in classrooms.

EXTENDED OBSERVATIONS

Extended observations that focus on a specific aspect of instruction can help identify areas of delivery that need improvement. First-time correct measurements (described earlier) are extended observations essential to determining proper placement of students in the programs that school leaders and teachers should learn in the first year of implementation. As discussed previously in this chapter, correct placement is a necessary prerequisite for student success in DI, and measuring first-time correct responses during live instruction is one of the very best ways to determine whether students are placed in the program where they can master each lesson successfully. Other advanced observations address the pace of instruction and positive-to-negative feedback to students.

The term *pacing* can refer to the rate at which students complete lessons over a period of time, such as a week or year, or it can refer to the minute-by-minute rate at which students respond to a teacher's presentation during specific exercises in a lesson. The former definition, along with mastery, is one of the two most important measurements of success with DI. Taken together with measures of mastery, lesson pacing is a strong and reliable *indicative* measure of how much students have learned over a period of time. However, since many factors can contribute to lesson progress at mastery over a period of time, lesson pacing is not a very reliable *diagnostic* measure on how to modify classroom instruction to improve student learning. If lesson progress for a month is slow, the causes could stem from a range of factors, such as frequent student absences, an insufficient amount of time scheduled for DI, inadequate correction procedures, or behavioral problems that disrupt the flow of instruction.

The causes of a low number of student responses per minute during specific exercises are much more limited in their scope, and the remedies are usually much more apparent in comparison to the causes of slow lesson progress over a longer period of time, such as a week or a year. If the rate of student responses during face-to-face instruction is slow, the cause is usually:

- the teacher's lack of familiarity with the script or essential delivery skills

- students' placement in the program
- students' lack of attention and motivation to give their best effort.

If a coach or another teacher who is fluent in the script teaches the same lesson at an appropriate pace with sufficient reinforcement to the students ("You will get 10 points as a group if you can read all the words in this column correctly!"), the factor or combination of factors causing the low pace of student responses should become apparent.

To assess the pacing of instruction, an observer can count the number of student responses per minute for different exercises and record the results on a simple tally sheet. The rate of student responses can be expected to vary by how familiar students are with the material (whether it is a new exercise) and how complex the specific tasks are. Short, rote tasks with items that students have seen several times, such as symbol identification, should take only a few seconds. Because the teacher talk for these tasks is very short ("What sound?" or "What number?"), students should be able to answer at a rate of 12–15 responses per minute for these tasks. For more complex, unfamiliar tasks, students may only be able to answer at a rate of five to six responses per minute. These are general guidelines. The optimal rate varies by task, level of the program, and each learner's performance.

Note that a faster pace, while generally desirable because of its positive effect on student engagement and efficiency of instruction, is not always preferable to a slower pace if students are not given sufficient time to formulate a response. As mentioned in chapter 5, it is essential that each teacher customizes the think time to their students and takes into account any items that have been difficult for the students in the past. Therefore, *mastery observational data should be recorded in conjunction with pacing data during instruction to determine the optimal rate of student responses for different types of tasks for each instructional group.* If mastery starts to decrease when a teacher increases the pace of presentation beyond a certain point for specific tasks, the teacher should reduce their rate of presentation in order to maximize lesson progress at mastery for the students in the instructional group.

Another extended observation that can help diagnose instructional problems is the ratio of positive-to-negative feedback to students. DI requires students to focus on specific exercises and perform at their best for the full instructional period. To ensure that students are motivated to give their best effort, they should receive much more positive feedback from the teacher than negative feedback. Four-to-one is a common ratio of positives to negatives. Positive feedback can take the form of verbal encouragement, hand gestures (such as a high five), student points that are part of the Teacher/Student game, and other reinforcers. Effective positive feedback involves the teacher naming the specific behavior that is earning the praise. Negative feedback can take the form of verbal statements, gestures, facial expressions (such as eye-rolling), or other non-verbals that communicate disapproval, such as sighing.

Corrections of student performance errors should also be considered to constitute negative feedback. No matter how nicely error corrections are delivered to the students by the teacher, they can have a negative effect on the self-esteem of some students. Therefore, placement in the DI programs is critical for helping students generate a positive attitude toward instruction. When students are placed appropriately at a lesson that matches their skills, they feel much better about their abilities in comparison to how they feel about themselves when they are placed in material that is too difficult for them.

Like the results of pacing observations, the results of positive-to-negative observations can be recorded on a tally sheet. Unlike pacing observations, which usually last for a minute, the length of time of positive-to-negative feedback observations is flexible. The observer may want to start the observation so it corresponds to parts of the lesson that have been problematic for students in the past. Often, the beginning of an instructional period when students transition from a preferred, unstructured activity, such as recess, into the classroom setting can be problematic. The teacher who "catches kids in the act of being good" and praises students for following classroom rules as they transition from one instructional setting to the next (as described in chapter 5) will start the DI period with plenty of tallies on the positive side of the ledger.

Like the two-minute observation – which is used to assess student engagement – pacing and positive-to-negative feedback observations are not DI-specific and can be used with any instructional approach in any setting. As with other observations discussed previously, pacing and positive-to-negative feedback observations can be conducted across the school and the results compiled to help school leaders identify which classrooms require more attention than others.

SHOW-OFF LESSON OBSERVATIONS

Another type of extended observation is the show-off lesson observation. The term "show-off lesson" is used in two different ways in a DI implementation. During the preservice program training, a show-off lesson refers to a lesson that has been selected because it contains key exercises that provide a model to teachers of how to teach essential concepts in a DI program. In each level of every DI program, NIFDI has designated several show-off lessons for training, which contain key exercises that students encounter for the first time in the program. In many program training sessions, the very first lesson of the program is a show-off lesson. Teachers practice the show-off lessons as modeled, receive feedback, and are "checked out" on exercises during preservice to ensure they master critical teaching skills as described in the previous chapter.

The term "show-off lesson" can also be used to refer to a lesson that is used after the start of the school year to diagnose a teacher's delivery of a DI program. In this context, a show-off lesson is a lesson that has been practiced by a teacher for two days with students before it is observed by a coach or an external support provider. The teacher tells the students that they are going to showcase how well they know the material – that they are going to "show off" what they know to visitors – as rationale for repeating the lesson for two days. With so much practice, the lesson should run very smoothly when it is observed on the third day. The teacher's delivery should be flawless, and students should respond at a high level of mastery. Any problems of delivery or behavior management during the show-off lesson are problems that the teacher needs help to correct. Problems the teacher was able to remove with practice are problems the teacher will be able to eliminate with time. Problems that remain may be beyond the teacher's self-awareness or beyond the teacher's ability to correct without support, so coaching is necessary. Thus, observing show-off lessons provides coaches with a clear understanding of how to improve instruction in the classrooms.

During the show-off lesson, observers focus on student mastery of the exercises first and foremost. They take first-time correct data on the students and then track whether the teacher follows the full correction procedure for every student performance error. In addition, the observers take notes on specific performance problems and aspects of the teacher's delivery that are contributing to performance problems. In this way, the objective of show-off lessons is not just to collect data on student responses, but also to link those responses to causal variables that can be addressed so as to resolve specific student performance problems.

Individual teachers whose groups have been struggling can be asked to teach a show-off lesson to determine the causes of the students' performance problems, or all of the instructional staff can be asked to teach a show-off lesson during the same week. Involving all staff can help build group camaraderie and solidarity. It can also lead to a deeper understanding of common problems of instruction across classrooms, which can be addressed by bringing selected staff members together for practice sessions or in-service training sessions as described earlier. The use of show-off lessons may slow down lesson progress in the short run, but it usually leads to greater lesson progress at mastery in the long run as it helps the coaching staff build the skills of teachers, which allows for faster, sustained success with DI over time. It also often helps clarify to new teachers that their students can perform at a high level of responsiveness and mastery.

FOLLOW-UP TO PROBLEM-SOLVING SESSIONS

The outcome of the weekly problem-solving meetings described in the next chapter is a list of remedies and other actions that the building coordinator communicates to the instructional staff after the meeting. These remedies across the classrooms may range from retesting students to extending the think time on selected exercises. Before the next problem-solving session, the building coordinator should confirm that the remedies have been implemented, and if so, what the effect of the remedy has been on student performance. This confirmation often takes the form of visiting classrooms and conducting observations. The type of observation the building coordinator conducts is determined completely by the problem and remedy identified during the most recent weekly problem-solving session. So the amount of time of the observation varies according to the problem and remedy. For example, if the remedy was for a teacher to increase the think time for students on oral multiplication fact practice, the building coordinator would only need to spend a couple of minutes in the classroom to observe that exercise. However, if the remedy was to move students to a higher reading lesson, the building coordinator would want to spend more time observing the group to ensure that the more advanced lessons are not too difficult for the students who have been moved up.

Finding time for the building coordinator to conduct follow-up observations to the weekly problem-solving sessions can be challenging, especially in a large DI implementation. After the weekly problem-solving sessions, initially communicating to the staff the actions they should take to solve instructional problems can require a significant amount of time. Conducting follow-up observations to ensure that teachers have implemented the instructional remedies can take even longer. A solution can be to have a system of lead teachers or peer coaches who attend part or all of the problem-solving sessions and are responsible for communicating remedies to the rest of the staff. Then the building coordinator can concentrate on conducting follow-up observations.

MONITORING INSTRUCTION THROUGH DATA

In addition to in-class observations, the effectiveness of instruction can be monitored by analyzing student performance data. The DI programs offer several types of data that can be collected and analyzed to indicate student performance successes and potential problems. Three types of formal assessments are discussed in chapter 2 of this book – mastery tests, cumulative tests, and checkouts. The passing criterion for the mastery tests as a whole is 90% (or as close as mathematically possible to 90%), with separate passing criteria in many mastery tests for the individual parts of each test. Checkouts (informal reading assessments) each contain separate rate and accuracy passing criteria, which become more demanding as students advance through the programs.

MHE has an online data system for the DI programs called *SRA 2Inform*. DI practitioners can use the online system, or they can use paper-and-pencil or Excel versions of the data forms described below.

STUDENT TEST SUMMARY (STS) FORMS

An example of a student test summary (STS) form appears in Table 9.6, which shows the first page of the STS form used by NIFDI for *Reading Mastery Signature Edition Grade 2 Reading*. Teachers record the results of checkouts (COs) and mastery tests (MTs) from the beginning of the program through Lesson 85. They list the results of the COs and MTs for the remaining lessons on a second page of the form (not pictured). The checkouts, which occur every five lessons starting at Lesson 10, are listed first across the top of the form followed by the mastery tests, which occur every 10 lessons starting at Lesson 10. The checkouts have an error limit of two errors and a time limit of one minute for this level of the program. The error limit for mastery tests ranges from two to four errors depending on the specific mastery test.

For the checkouts, teachers test the decoding skills of each student individually as the student reads a passage from the instructional group's current lesson as designated in the teacher presentation book (TPB). After the student finishes reading the passage, the teacher records the results for each student as a fraction with the *time* it took for students to read the passage *over the number of errors* the student made. For the mastery tests, the teacher records the percentage of the items each student answered correctly. For both checkouts and mastery tests, the following scoring conventions apply:

1. The teacher retests each student who does not meet the passing criteria.

2. If the student passes on the second try, the teacher circles the original score.

3. If the student passes on the third try, the teacher draws a triangle around the original score.

4. If students are tested more than three times, the teacher places a slash through the box with the original score. (The slash does not necessarily indicate whether the student has passed. It just indicates that the student has been tested more than three times.)

Lesson	CO 1	CO 2	CO 3	CO 4	CO 5	CO 6	CO 7	CO 8	CO 9	CO 10	CO 11	CO 12	CO 13	CO 14	CO 15	CO 16	MT 1	MT 2	MT 3	MT 4	MT 5	MT 6	MT 7	MT 8
(Lesson)	10	15	20	25	30	35	40	45	50	55	60	65	70	75	80	85	10	20	30	40	50	60	70	80
Criteria — Errors	1	1	1	1	1	1	1	1	1	1	1	1	1	1	1	1	2	2	3	3	3	3	4	2
Criteria — Time	0-2	0-2	0-2	0-2	0-2	0-2	0-2	0-2	0-2	0-2	0-2	0-2	0-2	0-2	0-2	0-2								
Criteria — WPM	100	100	100	100	100	100	100	100	100	100	100	100	100	100	100	100								
Possible																	24	22	25	26	33	32	36	19

Name	Grade																							
1.																								
2.																								
3.																								
4.																								
5.																								
6.																								
7.																								
8.																								
9.																								
10.																								
# of Students Passed/Total Tested																								
Percent of Group Passed																								

Key: CO - checkout   MT - mastery test

Table 9.6 Student test summary for *Reading Mastery Signature Edition Grade 2 Reading*. Adapted from: the National Institute for Direct Instruction (NIFDI).

INDEPENDENT WORK

In addition to using the student test summary, school leaders can monitor students' independent work to assess student mastery, which provides a daily source of information on students' knowledge of skills and concepts covered in the DI programs. As described in chapter 2, there is a progression of the content and an evolution of formats in all DI programs as exercises proceed from more structured and teacher-led activities to more independent activities as part of the generalization process. Each DI program, starting from the earliest level, includes independent work assignments that provide practice in the material covered in the day's lesson and review material from previous lessons. (The only exception is the *Direct Instruction Spoken English* (DISE) program, which is a completely oral language program for English language learners. DISE does not contain any independent work as all activities are done orally, face-to-face between students and their teacher.) Students in the kindergarten and Grade 1 levels of the programs use a crayon or pencil (depending on the item), and the teacher or paraprofessional corrects their work. Students in the upper levels answer the items using a pencil and then correct their own work using a pen as the teacher reviews the items and provides answers orally. Before the teacher collects the students' work, they review the items as a group in a "work check" and then individual students rework or "fix up" any items that they missed.

The teacher should inspect students' workbooks daily to verify the accuracy of the students' corrections and to record each student's performance on their independent work. Students should perform correctly on at least 85% of their independent work. As with mastery test results, if more than a quarter of the students in an instructional group answer incorrectly on any part of the independent work, all students in the group should repeat that part of the lesson.

School leaders can examine students' independent work while making classroom visits. Assessing independent work is part of the five-minute observation, but leaders can examine student's written work at any time. One of the oldest and most reliable ways of judging mastery is to observe what the children can do independently through their written work. Students' independent work can also reveal the type of written feedback the teacher provides to the students and how closely they examine student work for correct answers and errors. Before relying on independent work to represent students' mastery of the DI lessons, it is important to observe the instructional groups engaged in independent work to ensure that the teacher does not provide extra assistance to them. Only then can the leadership rely on the accuracy of the independent work as representative of each student's performance.

The independent work summary chart shown in Table 9.7 can help teachers and school leaders analyze students' mastery of program content over time. The summary allows teachers to record the number of errors students make on their independent work for seven lessons. Teachers calculate and record the percentage of correct responses for each student. After students have fixed any errors, the teachers circle scores that are less than the 85% threshold. (Note that this use of circling differs from the use of circling on the student test summary (STS) forms, in which a circled score indicates that a student passed the retest.)

Teacher _____   Subject _____   Group _____

NAME	LESSON NUMBER																		
	E.	%	E.	%	E.	%	E.	%	E.	%	E.	%	E.	%	E.	%	E.	%	E.	%
1.																				
2.																				
3.																				
4.																				
5.																				
6.																				
7.																				
8.																				
9.																				
10.																				
11.																				
12.																				
13.																				
14.																				
15.																				
16.																				
17.																				
18.																				
19.																				
20.																				

Passing Criteria: 85%

Table 9.7 Independent work summary chart. Source: the National Institute for Direct Instruction (NIFDI).

For all assessments of mastery – mastery tests, checkouts, cumulative tests, and independent work – it is critical that the assessments are given to the students without any prior preparation. Passing the tests should not be a goal in and of itself. Rather, the tests serve as indicators of the degree to which the students have mastered the instructional material during the lessons and, thus, are reflective of the effectiveness of the instruction the students have received. If the instruction is altered to "prepare" students for the tests, then the tests cannot serve as a clear indicator of the effectiveness of instruction.

LESSON PROGRESS CHART (LPC)

Teachers summarize the results of the latest mastery tests and checkouts on the lesson progress chart (LPC), depicted in Table 9.8. The LPC is designed to give an overview of the performance of a teacher's instructional groups over the last week. The first five columns provide identifying information for each group (the names of the groups, the grades and numbers of students in each group, the subject and level of the programs being used) and a designation of the group's performance level (high, medium, or low). In the next five columns, the teacher records the lesson(s) completed each day (Monday–Friday). There are slots for recording the lessons covered during the morning (a.m.) and afternoon (p.m.). If a group doesn't complete a lesson, the teacher records the lesson number followed by a period and the exercise number. For example, if a group finishes up through Exercise 6 of Lesson 42 of a program, the teacher would record 42.6 for that day. The teacher would then start teaching Exercise 7 of Lesson 42 during the next instructional period. Following the columns for recording daily lesson completion, the teacher records the weekly lesson progress rate as a fraction (the number of lessons taught over the number of school days). *By examining this column, school leaders can quickly assess the progress of students through the programs for the week.*

Teacher _____   Start Date _____   End Date _____

School _____   Coach's Name _____

Group	Grade	# in Group	Subject/Level	Performance Level (H, M, L)		Lesson Progress					# lessons taught / # of school days	Test or √out	Mastery Test or Checkout Summary				
						M	T	W	T	F			# of students passing (A)	List names of students absent (B)	List names of students not passing (C)	List type of items missed	If √out, write time/errors
					a.m												
					p.m												
					a.m												
					p.m												
					a.m												
					p.m												
					a.m												
					p.m												
					a.m												
					p.m												
					a.m												
					p.m												

Comments: _____

Key: H - high-performing group   M - medium-performing group   L - low-performing group   √out - checkout

Table 9.8 Lesson progress chart. Source: the National Institute for Direct Instruction (NIFDI).

The teacher records the results of the in-program assessments in the remaining columns of the table: the type of assessment, the number of students passing, the students who were absent when the test was administered, and the type of items students missed. *By examining these columns, school leaders can quickly assess the extent to which students mastered the content taught during the week.* In this way, the LPC provides a single resource for summarizing the effectiveness and efficiency of instruction in a classroom. Comparing the LPCs of different teachers will help school leaders determine which classrooms should be given high priority in allocating coaching support across the school.

DATA BOARD

A data board or data wall can be used to help monitor the groups' progress through the program. A data board is a comprehensive display of information about each instructional group's current lesson and mastery that is kept up to date by the building coordinator or peer coaches. It usually takes up a large portion of one of the walls of the room where the weekly problem-solving sessions take place, such as a conference room. Typically, the data board contains the following information:

- the grade of the students
- the teacher's name
- the name of the instructional group
- the number of students in the group
- the program and level of the DI program for the group
- the current lesson
- the results of the latest mastery tests or checkouts.

A whiteboard is the most common medium used for the data board. Lines can be drawn to form a table with cells containing the information for the different categories. Some of this information, such as the teacher's name and the group's name, can be entered once at the beginning of the school year so that only the information that changes over time, such as the current lesson, needs to be rewritten weekly. The data can be written in different colors to indicate the level of priority the groups should receive. The color red can be used to indicate groups that are significantly below grade level in terms of their placement in the program, while green can indicate that a group is on track to finish the program at mastery by the end of the school year.

Among other uses, a data board facilitates making decisions about regrouping students. As mentioned previously, instructional groups should be flexible and responsive to the different instructional needs of students. If "the light bulb has gone on" for a student ("the penny dropped") and they are ready for more advanced material, the leadership should determine whether there's a higher-performing group at a lesson that matches the student's skill level. Conversely, if a student has been absent for an extended period or simply has not been able to master the content at the current group's placement, the leadership should determine whether there's a lower-performing group at a lesson that matches the student's skill level. These and other types of adjustments to the composition of groups can be decided much more easily using an up-to-date data board. The board is very useful in anticipating the merging of groups that occurs when the program transitions from small-group to large-group instruction, such as at the end of *Reading Mastery Grade 1*, *Corrective Decoding A and B1*, and *Connecting Math Concepts Level A*.

ASSESSING LEADERSHIP PERFORMANCE

As with the instructional staff, observing and providing feedback to school leaders on their performance can help lead to higher student outcomes. As discussed in section 3 of this book, which is devoted to describing potential pitfalls in implementing DI, it is difficult to overstate the role of school leaders in determining the success of DI. Optimally, a review of the leadership's contributions to the DI implementation should occur annually if not more often so school leaders can acquire additional skills they may need to support the DI implementation more effectively.

To help provide feedback to school leaders on their contributions to the DI implementation, NIFDI has developed two different tools: a principal support form and a coordinator support form, both of which are located in the appendix. These forms are designed to represent all of the major functions that principals and coordinators can fulfill to help ensure that the implementation of DI is successful.

The forms cover:

- conducting observations
- reviewing data and participating in weekly problem-solving sessions
- overseeing the implementation of instructional components
- facilitating visits by the external support provider (ESP)
- arranging for training as needed
- establishing essential policies with the staff
- following up problems until they are resolved.

School leaders receive points for the different items on the form depending on the frequency with which the items are observed (never, some of the time, usually). The items cannot all be observed in a single session but instead require ongoing knowledge of the state of the implementation and the specific actions school leaders take. Point allocation for the items on the support forms has been configured for a maximum possible score of 100, which allows for a percentage-like assessment of the effectiveness of the performance of principals and building coordinators. In a multi-school implementation of DI, the forms can be used by district leaders to compare the contributions of school leaders to the success of their students in the DI programs.

CHAPTER TEN
RESPONDING ACTIVELY TO PROBLEMS AND ACHIEVEMENT

As indicated in the previous chapter, the objective of monitoring is to determine the extent to which the components of DI are in place and having the desired effect on student performance. Components of a DI implementation that are having the desired effect should result in a positive response from the school's leadership, while components that are not having the desired effect should result in a corrective response from the leadership. Responses can involve a) reinforcing students and staff for their efforts or b) corrective action by the staff or school's leadership through the use of remedies. Reinforcement should take place whenever there's been improvement even if a problem has not been totally resolved. A situation should only be considered to be a problem in DI if there is a problem with student performance.

Responses can occur at the level of instruction, the level of management, or at both levels. At the level of instruction, teachers should reinforce students for their achievements and for putting forth consistent effort. They should also consistently correct students if they make an error. At the level of management, school leaders should reinforce students for their achievements and teachers for improvements in their implementation of DI. They should also correct problems identified across the school that prevent students and teachers from achieving their potential with DI, such as inadequate time allocated to DI in the daily schedule, inconsistent data collection and analysis, and insufficient in-class coaching support to teachers. The notion of "nested responsibility," which implies that teachers assume responsibility for the performance of their students and leaders assume responsibility for the performance of all students and teachers in their school, lies at the heart of any successful schoolwide implementation of DI.

The response time by the leadership to problems identified through observations and data analysis varies according to the specifics of each problem. The leadership should be prepared to intervene immediately in situations that undermine the integrity of the implementation or cause students to mislearn skills or concepts. For instance, if a child says a sound incorrectly during a *Reading Mastery* lesson, the teacher should immediately "voice-over" the child's response with the correct response and follow the voice-over with a full error correction. If the teacher does not voice-over the child's response, the school leader should model the expected procedure to ensure that the student hears the correct pronunciation and practices it immediately. Other leadership responses may not need to take place during instruction but can occur outside the DI period, such as discussing with a teacher the steps to take to help students who have been absent for several days to catch up to the rest of their instructional group. Some leadership responses may require much more time to implement fully with effects that stretch out over several years, such as building the school's capacity to provide training and coaching independently without any external support.

Responding actively may involve reiterating expectations (discussed in chapter 8) and monitoring the teachers (discussed in chapter 9) on the implementation of these expectations. In this way, a successful DI implementation involves *cyclical management* that requires school leaders to follow statements of expectations with in-class verification and an appropriate response of a) reinforcing students and staff, or b) taking corrective action as needed. Once a problem of performance or implementation has been identified, the management cycle should be followed until the problem has been fully resolved.

This chapter addresses several aspects of responding actively that help ensure a successful implementation of DI:

1. Identifying different types of remedies

2. Employing the principle of least obtrusiveness
3. Providing constructive feedback to teachers
4. Adhering to the coaching cycle
5. Managing the DI implementation through problem-solving sessions
6. Prioritizing problems using the Implementation Priority Pyramid
7. Celebrating student achievement and other accomplishments
8. Building the capacity of the staff to implement DI
9. Orienting new staff to the Direct Instruction implementation
10. Conducting quarterly reviews of the DI implementation.

TYPES OF REMEDIES

The term "remedy" can refer to a specific response to a student's error on an in-program assessment, or it can refer more generally to a solution to any problem. As described in chapter 2 of this book, mastery test directions include specific remedies for students who make errors on mastery tests. In addition to specific remedies for student errors on in-program assessments, school leaders and the instructional staff employ two different types of remedies to address problems of student performance: *structural* remedies and *training* remedies. Structural remedies are procedures that do not involve directly training teachers. They usually involve *moving something to change the structure, setup, or environment in which students and teachers operate*. Examples of structural remedies include the following:

- Rearranging the classroom furniture to allow the teacher to monitor student participation more easily
- Organizing books and using place markers to facilitate students finding a lesson
- Skipping part of a lesson that the teacher is not prepared to present to the students
- Regrouping students to more closely fit their performance levels
- Reassigning teachers in accordance with their ability to deliver the DI programs

- Backing students up to repeat a series of lessons
- Giving placement tests and accelerating students to the next level of the program (source: the National Institute for Direct Instruction).

In the examples above, physical objects are moved (furniture, books) as well as people (teachers, students) or students' placement in the program. Structural remedies are preferred over training remedies in several situations:

- When there is a structural element out of place (such as furniture or books)
- When problems of student performance are so serious in the moment that the teacher should not continue teaching part or all of today's lesson
- When students are so seriously misplaced in the program that they will not be successful at their current placement even if the teacher is further trained.

Structural remedies have the advantage of requiring little expertise in DI to implement, although they can require expertise to design or select. For instance, determining when and where to move students to a different instructional group requires considerable skill, but actually moving students may simply require notifying the students and the teachers and changing the rosters of the instructional groups, which does not require expertise in DI. Therefore, many structural remedies can be implemented successfully by a staff member with very little expertise in DI as long as they are directed by a DI expert.

The other main class of remedies involves training – *broadening or deepening teachers' skills and their knowledge of when to use the skills.* These skills can include specific delivery requirements of a program, correction procedures, motivating students, and an understanding of how to implement structural remedies correctly.

Training can take a wide variety of forms, including:

- in-service sessions outside the classroom for groups of teachers with similar problems

- individual training sessions with one-on-one rehearsals between a trainer and a teacher
- side-by-side coaching in the classroom with students present
- pairing a teacher with an expert teacher who can provide a demonstration of a lesson or part of a lesson.

An efficient method of side-by-side coaching is to arrange for several teachers to take turns teaching the same group of students while getting feedback from a coach. This allows the teachers to learn from the feedback that the other teachers receive during the coaching session. It also strengthens the bond between the teachers and helps them form a learning community among themselves in support of each other's delivery of DI.

It is difficult to overstate the importance of providing time for instructional staff to practice and receive feedback on their teaching skills outside of instruction without students present. If teachers cannot demonstrate mastery of critical procedures without students present, the chances are very low that they will be able to implement the procedures correctly while instructing students. Training and practice sessions with multiple teachers allow for the simulation of a wide range of classroom situations, which can help prepare teachers for actual teaching situations with students. If a targeted skill or procedure requires considerable practice, attempting to improve a teacher's delivery during instruction can consume precious instructional time and lead to behavioral problems as the coach provides detailed explanations of the procedure to the teacher. If there is an urgent need for the coach to intervene (discussed later), the coach can teach the problematic part of the lesson to the students and discuss the issue later with the teacher during a debriefing session.

Sometimes both a structural remedy and a training remedy can be implemented for the same problem. For example, a coach may ask the teacher to skip part of a lesson (a structural remedy) and arrange a practice session with the teacher on delivering the exercise effectively (a training remedy). In this way, the children can continue to receive instruction on the parts of the lesson that the teacher can deliver effectively in the moment without trying to address serious gaps in the teacher's skills with the children present, which could consume a considerable amount of instructional time.

As discussed in chapter 8, it is essential that the instructional staff understand that they will receive in-class, real-time coaching from DI experts and will be expected to incorporate the feedback of anyone who serves as a coach. During in-class observations, a coach with sufficient expertise can be expected to intercede during instruction to demonstrate correct procedures to the teacher. Coaches will position themselves where they can see the students and hear their responses. Coaches may interrupt instruction if there is a problem and ask the teacher to repeat part of the lesson while modifying the instructional delivery in some way. This interruption may be directed at students with wording that states their behavior, a change in the teacher behavior, and a challenge for a new student behavior. "Most of you did that perfectly. Let's see if *all* of you can do it perfectly if your teacher does that part again a little bit faster."

Coaches may interact directly with students, modeling the instruction for the teacher, or they may use hand signals or other prompts that have been established ahead of time to communicate specific actions to the teacher. It is helpful for teachers to inform their students at the start of the school year that a coach may intervene occasionally and teach part of a lesson. For a more in-depth discussion on setting coaching expectations, see www.nifdi.org/services/coaching.html.

During an observation, the coach must determine which problems require immediate intervention and which problems can be addressed later with the teacher during a debriefing or practice session. A rule of thumb is that immediate intervention is required if students are learning something incorrectly that will be difficult to unlearn. As mentioned earlier, if students are learning an incorrect sound for a letter, that should elicit an immediate intervention by the coach if the instructor doesn't intervene, who should model the sound correctly. If students are learning the concepts and skills correctly (the instruction is effective), but the exercise is taking more time than is optimal (the instruction is not efficient), that would generally not require immediate intervention unless there is an easy solution the coach can demonstrate to make instruction more efficient.

In addition to considering whether students are mislearning a critical skill or concept, the decision by the coach to intervene or not intervene can depend on:

- the relationship established with the teacher prior to the classroom visit
- the successful implementation of the teaching skills that the coach has already asked the teacher to focus on
- the teacher's progress and confidence in learning the DI teaching methodology.

Some staff members can be expected to feel more comfortable receiving feedback from coaches than other staff members. The coaching process may be stressful initially for those staff who have never received detailed feedback on their delivery of instruction. For others, the process may not be stressful if the feedback is limited to a couple of aspects of instruction, but it can be overwhelming to them if they receive too much feedback on their instructional delivery. To avoid overwhelming teachers with new learning, the coaches' feedback should be concentrated on those areas of delivery that will be easiest for the teacher to implement and have the greatest potential for improving student performance (the biggest bang for their buck). As the teacher's skills and confidence improve, the coach can add new foci, but the coach should not give the teacher feedback on any more than three foci at any one time. As with all learners, if teachers get overwhelmed with too much feedback, not only will their learning of new skills stall, but they may implement the techniques they had previously mastered with less fidelity.

Successful in-class coaching involves building up the capacity of the teachers to become their own coach. This involves teachers internalizing the process of observing students closely during instruction, identifying problems of student performance, modifying their own behavior, and observing how these modifications affect students' behavior and performance. Coaches can help teachers internalize this process by narrating their own coaching and asking critical questions of teachers in a debrief session. Many interventions a coach does can be in the format of a comment directed to students about the student performance (stating the problem), naming a change in teacher behavior and an expected different student performance. This way the coach focuses the teacher's attention on the link between their behavior and student performance during the coaching session.

THE PRINCIPLE OF LEAST OBTRUSIVENESS

When the coach intervenes, they should abide by the principle of using the *least obtrusive intervention* to remediate a problem. The use of the least obtrusive remedy is designed to address instructional problems in such a way as to minimize the involvement of the coach in instruction. The goal is to maintain instructional momentum with the least amount of interruption to the students while the coach addresses problems of delivery and student learning. To achieve this goal, the most obtrusive remedy should be reserved for problems that require the coach's immediate intervention to prevent students from mislearning essential concepts.

Observing in classrooms with practice at another time	• Assign a show-off lesson (teacher rehearses lesson with children for two days, then "shows off") • Rehearse lessons with the teacher without children present, then observe again in the presence of children
In-class prompting without demonstrating	• Use a hand signal agreed upon ahead of time to signal a known technique • Interact directly with children or voice-over the children • Prompt verbally (based on previous training or rehearsal session)
Demonstrating techniques during instruction	• Take over part of the teacher's job while the teacher does another part (e.g. reinforcing children) • Team teach – coach teaches, then teacher repeats the same exercise (sometimes arranged ahead of time) • Demonstrate a large part or all of the lesson (arranged ahead of time) • Interrupt to demonstrate a large part of the lesson (teacher knows this might happen but it has not been prearranged)

Table 10.1 Levels of intervention during coaching from the least obtrusive to most obtrusive interventions. Source: the National Institute for Direct Instruction (NIFDI).

Table 10.1 shows three levels of classroom intervention by coaches:

1. *Observing in classrooms with practice at another time.*

   In this case, there is no intervention during instruction. Instead, the coach addresses problems during a debriefing or practice session without students present. This option is appropriate for situations in which students are not practicing errors that will delay their acquisition of essential skills and content.

2. *In-class prompting without demonstrating.*

   A coach can use verbal prompts or signals to communicate to the teacher to take specific actions. Common signals coaches use include: pointing at a specific student to prompt the teacher to give the student an individual turn; drawing lines in the air to prompt the teacher to give students points as part of the Teacher/Student game; pointing the index finger toward the floor and rotating the wrist so the finger points up, which indicates that the teacher should repeat the exercise by going back to the top. The coach should explain these signals to the teacher before they are used during instruction, or else they will become a distracting pantomime rather than a quick, reliable form of communication that doesn't interrupt instruction. Prompting can also include the coach interacting directly with the students to modify their behavior, such as, "Oops! Someone didn't answer. We need to hear everyone. Let's do that again!"

3. *Demonstrating techniques during instruction.*

   This is the most obtrusive level of intervention, yet also the most potentially effective in providing teachers a clear model of what should be done. If teachers need to wait a long time until a debriefing session, they may forget some of the details of the situation and the specifics of the problem. In-class demonstrations provide an immediate model of correct procedures in response to specific problems. Because there are several different layers of obtrusiveness within this category, coaches should implement the least obtrusive intervention that addresses the problem successfully.

Although demonstrating techniques during instruction may be the most effective method for showing teachers correct procedures, overuse of demonstrations can reduce teachers' confidence in their ability to deliver the program. If a teacher suspects that the coach will intervene during instruction and take over teaching every time the coach visits the classroom, the teacher will anticipate that the coach will intervene and may become distracted by that anticipation. The teacher may deliver the lesson with hesitancy, which might prompt the coach to intervene, creating a self-fulfilling feedback loop of anticipation and intervention. For these reasons, the coach should emphasize teachers' independent delivery of the program as much as possible. If the coach can use a hand signal or other prompt to remind teachers about procedures they had already discussed, the teacher will be closer to delivering the program independently with fidelity. However, the coach should also limit the number of prompts that the teacher receives as this can also reduce the teacher's confidence in delivering the program.

Note that the second level of obtrusiveness, *in-class prompting without demonstrating*, may be more disruptive to some teachers than the third level, *demonstrating techniques during instruction*. Teachers new to DI may be so absorbed with following the script and observing their students that they may find it difficult to incorporate the feedback provided by the prompts as they continue to teach. For these teachers, having a coach interrupt instruction and demonstrate techniques is a less stressful process than trying to continue to teach while the coach provides prompts. While the main objective is for instruction to continue as normally as possible *for the students* during the coaching session, the coach should also keep in mind the effect coaching may have on teachers, especially teachers who are brand new to DI.

If a coach needs to interrupt instruction, the coach follows an eight-step procedure for reinforcing the students and teachers for their efforts before implementing a remedy to address the problem that prompted the interruption:

1. First, the coach tells the students what they've been doing well, such as, "Wonderful that you've all had your fingers on the right spot in the textbook, and you are answering together on signal!"

2. The coach tells the teacher what the teacher has been doing well.

3. The coach gives a short assignment to the students that pertains to the focus of instruction, such as, "I'm going to talk with your teacher for a bit. In the meantime, think of as many words as possible that end in 'at'."

4. The coach describes the focus of the interruption in terms of the students' performance and describes the remedy.

5. The coach returns to the students and asks them for their answers to the assignment.

6. The coach demonstrates the correct procedure or technique with the students.

7. The coach provides positive feedback to the teacher on implementing the remedy and asks the teacher to repeat the procedure until the teacher implements the procedure successfully.

8. The coach provides an encouraging, positive word or two to the students as she departs, such as, "Keep up the good work!"

PROVIDING CONSTRUCTIVE FEEDBACK TO TEACHERS

During an observation, the coach should provide positive feedback to the teacher even if it is nothing more than a quick "thank you" of appreciation at the end of the visit. The coach can also reinforce the teacher by providing specific praise to the students as the success of students reflects positively on their teacher. Specific, positive praise also reinforces students for behavior that's conducive to instruction, which helps strengthen their efforts to work hard and achieve success.

After a coach conducts an observation or reviews a video recording of instruction, the coach should meet with the teacher to review the observation. This debriefing session should be designed to improve the teacher's capacity to deliver the program with greater effectiveness and efficiency. As a result of the debrief, the teacher should gain new insights into the performance of the students and understand how instructional practices influence the students' behavior and academic performance.

The debriefing session should start with the teacher's self-analysis of their instruction. This will help the teacher become an active participant in their own development as a DI practitioner. If the self-analysis stage of the debriefing session is skipped, the teacher may become less thoughtful about their own delivery and more reliant on coaches to tell them what to do over time. Including self-analysis in the session prompts teachers to analyze student performance as it occurs and consider how their own teaching behavior affects student performance because they know they will need to share their thoughts later during the debriefing session.

To facilitate the self-analysis process, teachers should have a good idea of the possible foci of observations before they take place. If possible, it is helpful for coaches to inform teachers of the focus before they visit the classroom. If the teacher has been informed that an observation will occur as a follow-up to an in-service training session, the teacher will know the specific focus of the observation. Coaches will also be looking for teaching skills or procedures that had been the focus of previous training or coaching sessions, not just the most recent training session. Skills covered during the preservice training should serve as a default starting point for any observations. As noted in Table 9.2 in the previous chapter, the preservice training covers the following presentation and correction skills:

Presentation skills

- Followed the script for the lesson
- Used appropriate signals
- Used appropriate pace
- Looked at the students
- Transitioned quickly between tasks
- Provided individual turns.

Correction skills

- Gave the correct answer
- Repeated task
- Went back to repeat the part
- Provided individual turns
- Provided delayed tests until students demonstrated mastery of the concept.

During the self-analysis, the teacher should first describe the students' performance before analyzing their own teaching behavior. As mentioned previously, the performance of the students, by definition, determines whether there was a problem of instruction, which, in turn, influences whether the teacher needs to alter the classroom setup or modify their teaching behavior. Often, a careful and thorough description of the problem will directly imply a specific remedy.

After the teacher has shared their analysis of the teaching session, the coach should provide feedback on what went well and what problems of instruction were observed. The coach, too, should describe the students' performance before analyzing the teacher's behavior. The description of the problem should lead to a specific remedy for the teacher to implement. The remedy can involve a one-time structural change, or it can involve a new procedure that will require practice by the teacher to implement effectively.

Note that *the introduction of new procedures and skills should occur only as a teacher demonstrates mastery of the skills that were introduced previously.* As with any learner, it is impractical and counterproductive to introduce skills beyond the capacity of a teacher to master them. Consequently, there should not be an automatic ratcheting of demands on teachers by introducing new teaching skills and procedures before they master the skills and procedures introduced to them previously. As mentioned earlier, *the coach should limit feedback to a maximum of three areas of improvement for a teacher to practice and implement at any one time.* Indeed, sometimes it is best for a teacher's development to focus on improving just a single aspect of their instruction until they have mastered a specific procedure or technique, which will provide a solid foundation for further skill development. The remedies provided to the teacher should be those that:

- can be expected to make the greatest and most immediate positive impact on student performance
- the teacher is most likely to be able to implement successfully.

If multiple staff members and external support providers observe and coach the same teachers, it is important to coordinate the coaching effort to ensure that all coaches know what the specific foci are for each teacher and when the teachers are ready to be introduced to more advanced delivery techniques. This will require all coaches to have access to the observation forms recorded by the coaches through a system of electronic or hard copy folders for each teacher. Coaches can also share their observations of the teachers during the weekly problem-solving sessions (described later in the chapter). Through such measures, the negative effects of conflicting coaching directives on teachers' skill acquisition and confidence in their implementation of DI can be avoided.

The debriefing sessions should be customized to incorporate each teacher's progress toward acquiring the full range of DI-related teaching skills. The debriefing sessions should not be used by coaches to demonstrate how much they know. Sometimes, new coaches show off their expertise by discussing all of the ways in which a teacher's delivery can be improved. This is a very good exercise for new coaches to do in the presence of an expert support provider because it allows the support provider to further develop the coaches' skills without the teacher present. But a comprehensive listing of all of the problems of instruction observed in a classroom should not take place in the presence of the teacher who was observed because the teacher may get overwhelmed by the long list of improvements they need to make.

During the debriefing sessions, *it is important for coaches to stress the positive aspects of the teacher's delivery of DI* with a special emphasis on improvements made since the last coaching session. Like all learners, teachers need to receive positive feedback for their efforts. Teaching is very demanding work, especially teaching the Direct Instruction programs, as teachers must attend to and respond to the behavior of all of their students moment by moment throughout the DI period. Because it is unlikely that teachers received training on DI while at university, many aspects of the DI approach will be new to teachers and might be more difficult for some teachers than others. Just as learning to drive a car can be unusual and difficult at first, delivering DI can seem awkward and unusual in the beginning for many teachers. However, just as most adults become efficient and effective at driving with practice and coaching, virtually all teachers can become effective at delivering DI and confident in their ability to improve the performance of their students.

A standard formula for the debriefing sessions is for the coach to sandwich constructive feedback (areas for the teacher to improve, described as "grows" below) between positive feedback on the teacher's delivery:

Positive feedback + grows + positive feedback

With a focus on student performance, the coach first describes several aspects of instruction that went well during the observation. Then the coach addresses the areas of improvement and ends the feedback with one more aspect of what went well to end on a positive note. Following this formula ensures that the coach is providing enough positive feedback to encourage the teacher to keep improving their mastery of DI techniques. The formula is especially useful with teachers who are completely new to DI and with teachers who have not received intensive coaching before.

Once a teacher has received positive coaching for a while, coaches do not need to adhere to the formula so strictly. In fact, experienced teachers will often want the coach to jump right to the areas of improvement and not review what went well. The coach can comply with this request and only discuss problems and their remedies during the debriefing session, but the coach should make sure to provide positive feedback to the teacher at some other time outside of the debriefing session – a quick thumbs up in the hallway on students' independent work, for example – to make sure that the teacher receives positive feedback for their efforts. Of course, one of the most effective reinforcements for teachers is to see their students succeed. So schoolwide celebrations of student achievement, described later in this chapter, not only reinforce students for their accomplishments, but they also reinforce teachers for their efforts to improve student performance.

The debriefing session should include practice and feedback on skills the coach has identified as necessary to address the specific student performance problems that the coach observed. The teacher should practice the specific skills until they demonstrate mastery of them, which may require multiple sessions over time.

The debriefing session should end with the teacher articulating the next steps they will take. The teacher should describe what they will do differently in the future along with how and when they will practice any techniques or procedures discussed during the debriefing session. This ensures that the teacher understood the problems and the remedies the coach identified and that the coach and the teacher are on the same page regarding next steps. The coach should also provide a hard copy or electronic access to the form they completed for the observation, which will eliminate or greatly reduce confusion about the next steps the teacher should take. Before the end of the session, the coach should describe when they might visit the classroom again to conduct a follow-up observation. The timing of the follow-up visit will depend in part on the seriousness of the problem. If there were very serious problems of student performance, such as a complete lack of choral responses or frequent and disruptive student behaviors, the coach might schedule a follow-up visit for the very next day. However, if there was only one relatively minor problem of instruction, such as students not forming their letters fully when they write, the coach may schedule a follow-up visit for a week out or more. The timing of the coach's next visit will also vary according to the proven track record of the teacher to acquire and implement new teaching techniques. The coach will want to schedule frequent follow-up visits for new teachers who are inexperienced with DI. For experienced DI teachers who have demonstrated that they incorporate constructive feedback readily into their teaching practices, the coach can schedule visits less frequently.

In addition to the specific skills that teachers acquire through the coaching process, an integral goal of coaching is for teachers to understand the influence they can have on students' behavior and performance. Many teachers who are new to DI do not understand the full extent of their potential to affect students positively. They don't realize that what students do is usually directly related to what they, the teachers, do. Many teachers enter the profession with the misconception that student behavior is inevitable, that teachers have very little influence on student outcomes, and that problems of learning are inherent within the students as opposed to workable by changing the conditions in the classroom. In contrast, experienced teachers who have received extensive coaching in DI come to realize that everything they do – from the pacing of their presentation to the inflection of their voices to the frequency and form of reinforcement – can have a great effect on each student's behavior and rate of learning.

THE COACHING CYCLE AND PROBLEM SOLVING

Coaching and debriefing are part of a broader cycle of data analysis, problem solving, and iterative improvement in the implementation of DI as portrayed in Figure 10.1. An essential step in problem solving is to determine whether a problem exists, which is done by comparing what is expected in a DI implementation (Step 1, colored green in the figure) with what actually is occurring in the classroom (Step 2, colored yellow in the figure). Expectations are articulated in the form of documents, such as the teacher's guides for the DI programs or this book, or in rules that have been shared by the staff with the students, such as a procedure for students to access and store their workbooks. What is actually occurring in a classroom can be referred to as "data" in the broadest sense, which consists of information from observations or data on the performance of students on in-program assessments (independent work, checkouts, mastery tests, and cumulative tests). The comparison between what is expected in a DI implementation with what actually is occurring in the classroom occurs in Step 3, colored magenta. If there are no differences between what's expected and what's occurring in a classroom, then no problems of instruction exist (as represented by Step 3A in the figure).

If, however, there is a discrepancy between what's expected and what's occurring in a classroom (as represented by Step 3B), the school leadership should determine whether the information they have is sufficiently specific to enable them to formulate an effective remedy (Step 3C). For instance, information that several students failed a mastery test is insufficient for formulating a remedy. The leadership needs to know exactly which students failed which items on the mastery test and the specific type of errors they made. The leadership team may also need a second source of data on the problem before they can specify a remedy (Step 3D). If students miss items on a mastery test, for instance, the coach can visit the classroom when similar exercises are being taught so the coach can observe the performance of the students on these items. The coach can also observe the teacher's delivery as well as the correction of any student errors. These observations may indicate one of many different possible problems of instruction – from students not looking at the presentation book to the teacher not correcting errors that occur. Once the leadership team has sufficiently specific information on the problem, they can decide on the remedy and its implementation. This involves designating a staff member who will take agreed-upon actions by a specific time to address the problem (Step 4).

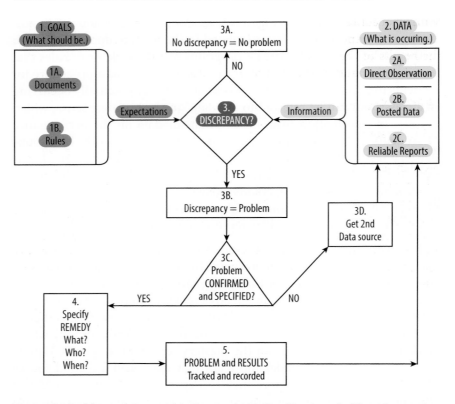

Figure 10.1 Problem-solving graphic. Source: the National Institute for Direct Instruction (NIFDI).

The communication of a remedy in Step 4 does not complete the problem-solving process. As indicated in Step 5, after the remedy has been communicated to the staff member who is expected to implement the remedy, the leadership must determine whether a) the remedy was fully implemented, and b) the remedy solved the problem that was identified. This is done by going back to Step 2 to access a new round of data and observations that can determine whether the problem still exists. In order for the problem to be considered resolved, the leadership should use the same source of information that was used to identify the problem in the first place. If the problem was identified through observation, someone from the leadership team must observe the same exercise or same procedure in the classroom again. If the problem was identified from assessment data, someone from the leadership team must examine the results of the same assessment again. Only then can the leadership team verify that the problem has been resolved.

PROBLEM-SOLVING SESSIONS

With the support of the school's external support provider, the leadership team addresses specific problems of instruction during a weekly problem-solving session, which is the main forum for managing the DI implementation. To be effective, problem-solving sessions should involve regular reviews of student performance data, observations, and expectations for each instructional group to identify problems of instruction and determine each problem's status on the coaching cycle. The status of all groups should be reviewed systematically and not just problems that immediately come to mind to the leadership team and other participants of the problem-solving session.

During the problem-solving sessions, the discussion should focus on problems at the level of individual instructional groups as well as problems that are common across several instructional groups or several classrooms. As mentioned previously in this chapter, problems that are specific to a single teacher are best addressed through individual coaching and training, whereas problems that are common across teachers are best addressed through in-service training followed by individual coaching sessions as needed.

For schools that are just starting to implement DI, problem-solving sessions should last about an hour, depending on the size of the school and the number and complexity of the problems of instruction. The sessions should occur weekly to ensure that all problems are being moved along the coaching/problem-solving cycle, which requires the participants to remember the status of each problem. After a school has been implementing DI for several years, the frequency of the problem-solving sessions may be reduced. However, if problems begin to accumulate or the leadership experiences difficulty tracking each problem, it is best to return to weekly meetings. A shorter weekly meeting that allows the leadership team to keep on top of all major problems of instruction in the school is preferable to a longer, less-frequent meeting that does not allow the leadership team to resolve problems quickly.

Weekly problem-solving sessions should not preclude mid-week discussions around specific problems. In fact, problem-solving sessions can be made more effective by supplementing them with mid-week check-ins. Many schools also implement a morning check-in to discuss the priorities for the coaching staff for the day and a quick review at the end of the day of the status of the major problems. This provides an efficient way to manage and resolve the most pressing problems of instruction at a school.

If possible, the weekly problem-solving sessions should occur at a time that is not scheduled for instruction, practice sessions, or training. The school leadership should visit classrooms as much as possible during instructional time to provide support to teachers and observe students. So problem-solving sessions should take place at a time when instruction is not scheduled to take place. Participants in the session should include all members of the leadership team: the principal, the building coordinator, and any peer (grade-level) coaches or lead teachers. The school's external support provider should lead the sessions until the school's leadership team has successfully completed the appropriate levels of coaches' training that prepare them to run the sessions. If the school is large, the call can be divided into two weekly sessions covering different grade levels. If DI is being implemented for literacy and mathematics in all grade levels in a large elementary school, for instance, the call can be devoted to kindergarten through second grade in the first half hour and third grade through fifth grade in the second half hour. This would allow any grade-level coaches to rotate in and out of the problem-solving sessions so they can attend to other school-related duties during the half hour they are not attending the sessions.

The leadership team may request that teachers also attend the problem-solving sessions on occasion. It can often be most efficient for teachers to provide information directly to the leadership team in addition to the coach observing and reporting information on the performance of an instructional group. An additional benefit of allowing teachers to participate in the call is that they can see how the leadership team *focuses on student performance as the criterion for determining whether a problem exists,* which can help build the confidence of teachers in the problem-solving process. Participating in the problem-solving sessions also reinforces the importance of accurate and complete data to teachers as they observe how the leadership team uses data to identify and resolve problems of student performance during the sessions.

For schoolwide implementations of DI, an hour of data review and problem-solving goes by quickly. For the problem-solving session to run smoothly and efficiently, all data sheets (or their electronic equivalents) should be collected and screened for completion beforehand. If the data are not complete, the status of a problem cannot be assessed. So the building coordinator should collect the data at least a day in advance and return uncompleted forms to the teachers to be completed before the problem-solving session takes place. All completed observation forms, observation notes, and student performance data should be made available to all participants and reviewed beforehand. Usually, these materials are ordered by grade level, which corresponds to the order in which the instructional groups are reviewed during the session.

During the problem-solving sessions, the leadership team should address the following:

- Follow-up from last week's session
- This week's review
- Accolades
- Redline and red-flag problems.

Reviewing the status of problems identified in the previous week's session ensures that appropriate follow-up has taken place and that these problems are being resolved. Following up on last week's session should take place before the leadership team reviews this week's data so that problems do not drop off the leadership's list of priorities without due consideration. In addition to analyzing problems, the leadership should reserve time during the session for accolades that recognize the accomplishments of students and staff.

Communication of persistent and serious problems should be more targeted depending on the nature of the problems. A "redline" designation indicates that a problem threatens to undermine the DI implementation. Examples of redline problems include a reduction in the amount of time allocated to DI or the introduction of a program that is designed to teach the same content as the DI programs being implemented in the school. A "red-flag" designation indicates that a problem has existed for three weeks or more without being resolved. Any problem can become a red-flag problem – even something so seemingly minor as a teacher's failure to retest students who failed a mastery test. The rationale for the "red-flag" designation is that any problem, no matter how minor, can have serious, negative effects on student performance if it is not resolved. If a student fails a mastery test and is not remediated, for example, that student has not built a sufficient foundation for further learning. If the problem is not remediated, the student will need to return to the lessons that were not mastered and receive instruction in the content that was missed, which can disrupt the lesson progress of the instructional group the student belongs to.

Each problem-solving session should be followed by a distribution of a summary of the problems identified and the next steps that specific staff members should take. The structure of the summary template used by NIFDI corresponds to the four phases of the meeting described above (follow-up of last week's session, this week's review, accolades, and redline and red-flag problems). Appendix 4 has an example of a blank problem-solving summary that can be updated weekly. After the problem-solving session, a completed summary should be distributed to the participants of the weekly session only. The building coordinator should then communicate to the instructional staff individually the next steps that are specific to each classroom.

PRIORITIZING PROBLEMS USING THE IMPLEMENTATION PRIORITY PYRAMID

An integral part of the problem-solving process is prioritization. In order for the implementation of DI to be most effective, school leaders and instructional staff must focus their attention on resolving problems that will lead to the greatest improvement in student performance over the course of the school year. Teachers prioritize problems at the level of individual students, instructional groups and their separate classrooms, while school leaders prioritize problems at these levels and at the level of maximizing student performance across the school. This system of *nested responsibility* is most effective if there is a common set of criteria for determining the priority for each instructional group and each classroom in the school.

As mentioned previously, identifying action steps that the staff are capable of implementing and have the greatest potential for improving student performance is a basic objective of prioritizing problems. But this objective of getting the biggest "bang" for a given amount of effort in and of itself is insufficient for successfully prioritizing problems. Effective problem solving also assumes that *certain types of problems are more fundamental than other types of problems* – that some problems can only be solved by resolving certain problems first. If these more fundamental problems are not addressed and resolved first, more complex problems cannot be resolved.

A simple example of a fundamental problem is when students cannot see the teacher presentation book. If there are other problems of student performance – such a lack of choral responses or a lack of students' mastery of the lesson content – these problems cannot be addressed successfully until all students are able to see the teacher presentation book. Once this problem has been resolved by changing the teacher's positioning of the book and/or rearranging the furniture, other problems of student performance can be addressed.

At the schoolwide level, "redline" problems discussed earlier constitute the most fundamental type of problems and should be given the highest priority by a school's leadership as they threaten to undermine the very integrity of the DI implementation. Redline problems include any problems with the fundamental setup steps discussed in chapter 8, such as:

- assessing each student's skills by administering placement tests
- forming instructional groups based on the results of the placement tests
- scheduling sufficient time in the programs for each instructional group

- ordering teacher and student materials that match students' performance levels
- establishing the roles of staff members participating in the DI implementation, which involves teachers incorporating the feedback of expert coaches
- providing initial training in the DI methodology for all teaching staff and ensuring that they "check out" on key teaching techniques
- arranging for practice/in-service sessions twice weekly and more often as needed for all teaching staff.

NIFDI has created a handout on the essential elements of a DI implementation that can be used to identify high-priority schoolwide problems (see Appendix 5).

At the classroom level, the Implementation Priority Pyramid, shown in Figure 10.2, provides a guide for prioritizing problems. In the pyramid, the most fundamental components of a successful DI implementation are placed on the bottom, and the components that depend on the more fundamental components are placed successively higher on top of this most fundamental component.

The most fundamental aspect of a DI implementation is *student engagement*, which can be addressed by the question "are all students engaged in the targeted instructional activity?" In other words, are all students on task? During a DI session, all students should be focused for the full instructional period on the appropriate tasks at every moment during instruction. During group instruction, are students paying attention to the teacher with their finger in the right spot in the textbook or their eyes on the board display? During independent work, are they focusing on the appropriate problems in the correct lesson on the correct page in their workbook? (As mentioned elsewhere, a strong motivational system should be in place to reinforce students for being engaged during all phases of instruction because of the demands on their attention during a DI lesson.)

Note that students should be fully engaged in the targeted activity instead of simply following along without disrupting the class. A student who delays their response and "coat-tails" off the response of the other students is not fully engaged, just as a student who quietly colors at their desk instead of working on the current assignment is not fully engaged. Teachers can use various techniques to increase student engagement and verify that all students are fully engaged, such as calling on students by row or subgroup, providing individual turns during instruction, and monitoring their progress during seat work with periodic announcements to the class about how the students are doing on their work.

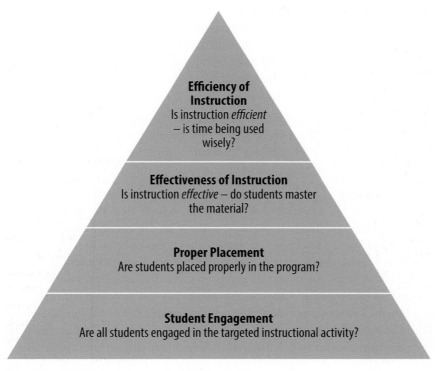

Efficiency of Instruction
Is instruction *efficient* – is time being used wisely?

Effectiveness of Instruction
Is instruction *effective* – do students master the material?

Proper Placement
Are students placed properly in the program?

Student Engagement
Are all students engaged in the targeted instructional activity?

Figure 10.2 The Implementation Priority Pyramid.

Student engagement is the most fundamental aspect of instruction because without it, effective teaching won't occur. Students cannot read a word or story, for instance, if they are not looking at the correct place in the presentation display or their own book. Lack of engagement precludes all other components of the DI model – the careful design of the programs, the allocation of instructional time, the training and coaching teachers have received, the system of data analysis, etc. – from having a positive effect on student performance. So problems of student engagement and their remediation should be given very high priority in a school implementing DI.

A system of positive behavior management should already be in place as part of the initial setup of Direct Instruction (see chapters 7 and 8), and the staff should be trained in how to reinforce students for adhering to rules and for responding correctly the first time during instruction. School leaders should coach teachers on positive behavior management techniques if their students are not fully engaged, as determined through observations. Leaders should help set up reinforcement structures, such as schoolwide recognition for students' accomplishments, which provide additional incentives for students to be fully engaged during instruction.

Note that the requirement of engagement is not exclusive to Direct Instruction. It can also be applied to any learning situation. So many of the techniques used to increase student engagement during DI can be applied to other learning situations throughout the school day.

The second most fundamental aspect of a DI implementation is *proper placement in the instructional programs*, which can be addressed by the question: are students placed properly in the program? Placement is the next most fundamental aspect of DI because if the lessons the students receive don't match their skill level, they won't benefit from the incremental step design of the programs. As discussed previously, each lesson in a DI program contains only about 10–15% new material. The rest of a lesson contains material that has been introduced in previous lessons. For student performance to be maximized, each student's placement in the program should match their skill level *every day* so that the amount of new material each student learns is actually only 10–15% of the lesson. Though challenging to achieve, the closer a school can successfully match all students' skills with their placement, the greater the potential for students' learning to be maximized with DI.

There are several ways to determine whether students are properly placed in the DI programs each day. Placement test results provide a reliable indicator of each student's initial placement, but they only provide an initial snapshot of students' skills. First-time correct responses, discussed in the last chapter, are the single best way to determine in real time whether students are placed correctly in DI. If students are significantly below the first-time correct thresholds of 70% for new material and 90% for material introduced in previous lessons, they may be misplaced in the program. If they consistently achieve 100% first-time correct on all exercises, they may be placed too low in the program and should be moved to more challenging lessons that match their skill repertoire.

Teachers should respond to low first-time correct responses by attempting to bring the students to mastery on the material. They should correct all student performance errors by following the Part-Firming Paradigm, discussed in chapter 5. If the students cannot be brought to mastery after several repetitions on the problem area in the lesson, a next step is to determine where in the program the students are actually at mastery on this particular skill. One strategy is to return to the beginning of the track where the skill was introduced and present exercises to students who had difficulty on the targeted skill. If students answer correctly on these earlier exercises, the teacher should move forward through the lessons until they reach the exercises where the students are not at mastery. This spot in the program may be different for different students on different skills. Once the teacher has determined the layout of students' ideal placement – i.e. the specific exercises in the program that match each student's skills – the teacher and school leaders can develop a plan for addressing each student's skill deficits.

If the deficits are uniform for all students in a group – whether the deficits are small or large – the placement for the group as a whole should be adjusted to match the first-time correct mastery levels of the group on different skills. This can involve proceeding with the lessons as a whole but backtracking to earlier lessons for specific exercises to firm up targeted skills. If the deficits are *not* uniform for all students, but the deficits are small, they can be addressed during a separate intervention period as the group continues to advance through the lessons from their current placement during the regular instructional period. If the deficits are large for individual students who cannot keep up with the rest of the group even with a separate intervention period, the best solution may be to move these students to an instructional group that is placed lower in the program.

The third most fundamental aspect of a DI implementation is the *effectiveness of instruction*, which can be addressed by the question "do students master the material by the end of the lesson?" Are they able to respond correctly after the teacher has corrected all errors? When a teacher implements the Part-Firming Paradigm by giving students the answer after they make a mistake and then repeats the task, do all students perform correctly on every item the last time through an exercise? If the students are not firmly on the skill acquisition step for this lesson, the likelihood that they will be able to retain the skill until the next day will be low. If they are not brought to mastery on every lesson, they will not have a firm foundation for future learning.

An important feature of the Part-Firming Paradigm is the delayed test, which involves the teacher waiting some time while working on other material before returning to the exercises that students had difficulty with the first time through the lesson. These delayed tests can occur throughout the school day to ensure that students retain skills and information for the next day. Teachers and school leaders can ask students the answer to difficult questions before and after recess, before and after lunch, and reinforce students for remembering the correct answers. Delayed tests can be given to the group as a whole or to individual students.

For many DI programs, independent work can serve as an important type of delayed test and an excellent means for determining whether instruction is effective – whether students are at mastery. Some time passes between the time teachers correct errors during group instruction and independent work time. So student performance on independent work is a good test for determining how much students have retained since the teacher corrected the last student performance error. If students demonstrate a high degree of mastery on their independent work (85% or greater), then there is a higher probability that they will remember the material during the next lesson. Independent work is also a convenient source of information for school leaders to access. Workbooks are available at any time, so leaders do not have to schedule a classroom visit to coincide with a specific instructional period. An examination of workbooks reveals what percentage of students answered correctly, whether they fixed-up any errors (using a red pen rather than a pencil), and whether the students' work was checked by the teacher.

The assessments built into the DI programs – checkouts, mastery tests, and cumulative tests – are also important sources of the effectiveness of instruction. Mastery tests and cumulative tests have built-in remedies, which should be implemented with fidelity to ensure that all students master the skills and concepts their group has covered and that they are ready for more advanced material. These assessments are very useful tools for identifying students who are ready for more challenging material as well as those who would benefit from more practice on exercises they've had difficulty mastering. If a student scores 100% on a mastery test or easily passes the rate and accuracy requirements of checkout three times in a row, the student is a candidate for moving to a higher placement. Successively more advanced mastery tests and checkouts can be administered to the student until the student's score indicates a more appropriate placement – 90% correct on the mastery test and within the rate and accuracy requirements of the checkout.

The fourth most fundamental aspect of a DI implementation is the *efficiency of instruction*, which can be addressed by the question "how well is time being used for instruction?" Efficiency has to do with time: are students not only learning essential skills and concepts (mastering them), but are they also learning them at a reasonable rate that will allow them to complete at least a year's worth of material in a year's time? It is important that students master skills and concepts in DI, but their learning will not be accelerated if too much time is required for them to master the material. Acceleration involves mastering skills and concepts faster than expected. So if a group takes three days for students to master a lesson, for example, instruction is effective but not efficient.

When trying to increase efficiency (accelerate learning) teachers and leaders must keep in mind that mastery is a prerequisite for acceleration in the DI programs, hence the more fundamental position of effectiveness in the Implementation Priority Pyramid. Attempting to increase the rate at which students complete lessons only makes sense if students master the lessons as they proceed through the program. Because of the stair-step design of the DI programs, the gap between what students know and what they are supposed to learn each lesson will get larger and larger if students progress through the program without firmly mastering the content of each lesson. If the amount students have to learn exceeds the

10–15% of the lesson that is supposed to be new to the learners, they won't be able to master a lesson in a reasonable amount of time. For students to progress through the program at a high rate, they should not be placed in material that is too difficult for them but instead receive lessons at a spot in the program where they can be successful. If they go through the program too quickly without mastering the content, they will need to repeat the material they didn't master, which will cost precious instructional time.

Many aspects of the DI approach involve the efficient use of time. Choral responses take less time than soliciting a response from each student individually. Scripted lessons allow teachers to present exercises in less time than if they had to construct their own wording and their own examples. Homogeneous grouping allows the teacher to focus instruction at the skill level of the students, which requires less time to bring them to mastery than if they are grouped heterogeneously.

Teachers can augment the built-in efficiency of the DI programs by structuring their classrooms for efficiency. They and the leaders who support them can address the following questions to foster instructional efficiency:

- Are classrooms set up to allow easy flow and access of materials?
- Does instruction start on time and last the full period?
- Are transitions between instructional groups smooth and fluent?
- Are transitions between exercises during a lesson smooth and fluent?
- Is reinforcing students for adhering to rules and performing to expectations done quickly so as not to take too much time away from instruction?

School leaders can help ensure that students practice routines outside classrooms as well as inside classrooms so that instructional time is maximized. In general, leaders can instill a culture of time efficiency as well as student mastery of critical skills and concepts.

Note that the Implementation Priority Pyramid described earlier is student-focused. Each level of the pyramid focuses on a specific aspect of student behavior or performance: are students engaged in the targeted instructional activity? Are they placed properly in the DI program? Do they master all parts of every lesson? Are they learning the material in a timely manner so their performance is accelerated? If leaders can clarify to the staff that the priorities of the DI implementation are all concerned first and foremost with student behavior and performance, this may provide some reassurance to staff members who experience anxiety over observations.

Equally importantly, the pyramid provides a framework for determining the priorities for improving instruction at every level of the school – individual students, instructional groups, classrooms, grades, and the school as a whole. The lower levels of the pyramid must be in place before the upper levels of the pyramid can be effective. If students are not engaged, it's impossible to determine whether they are placed correctly in the programs. If students are not placed properly, they cannot be expected to master the content of the lessons. If they do not master the lessons, they cannot be expected to progress through the programs at a high rate.

However, there are exceptions to the relationship between the levels of the pyramid, which should be seen as a general guide for prioritizing problems rather than a strict sequence of priorities. Upper levels of the pyramid can sometimes influence the lowest level of the pyramid, student engagement. When students are placed properly in the program and master each lesson, they will look forward to the next lesson because they know they will be successful. When the pace of the teacher's presentation is increased, students' attention will often increase as a result (as long as the students still have sufficient think time for each item). The general structure of the pyramid can provide a very useful framework for prioritizing problems in a DI implementation and for reinforcing students' efforts and accomplishments as long as the staff and school leaders keep these exceptions in mind.

CELEBRATING STUDENT ACHIEVEMENT

One of the most enjoyable aspects of teaching and managing schools is celebrating student success. Time in school should be an enjoyable and rewarding experience for both students and staff, which can happen when students receive recognition for their accomplishments in DI.

Reinforcement is key to sustaining student engagement, a key component of an effective implementation of DI, as discussed previously. The potential for reinforcement in classrooms is enormous with DI as there are explicit behavioral and performance expectations for multiple tasks in each exercise with sometimes a dozen or more exercises in a lesson. Celebrations can occur at all levels of instruction and social interaction:

- The instructional group
- The whole class
- A grade level
- The whole school
- Inter-school celebrations.

Chapter 5 outlines the steps teachers can take to celebrate student success at three different time intervals:

- Quick celebrations that take place during a lesson
- Celebrations lasting about 10–15 minutes that occur every few weeks after students reach intermediate goals
- Celebrations lasting up to a whole class period that occur near the end of the school year after students reach their final goals.

School leaders can support the intermediate and final-goal in-class celebrations by visiting the classrooms when celebrations are scheduled to occur. Teachers can provide advance notice to the leadership when the intermediate and final-goal celebrations are going to take place and what the students are celebrating so school leaders can reserve the time to visit the classrooms and help reinforce students for their accomplishments. At the start of the celebration, school leaders can ask students a few questions about what they have learned and then reinforce them for what they know. The presence of the principal as the head of the school with an interest in the specifics of what students learn can act as a powerful reinforcer for students to master the content of the DI programs.

In addition to supporting in-class celebrations, leaders can arrange for schoolwide celebrations of student success, which should also occur at different time intervals. Daily announcements can be used for recognizing such accomplishments as all students in a group passing the most recent mastery test or moving on to a new storybook. The school's newsletter can carry announcements of these accomplishments. Weekly or monthly assemblies can be used for more extensive celebrations. End-of-year celebrations can be used to recognize all groups that completed at least one level of a program at mastery over the course of the school year. These celebrations can involve "challenges" by the principal, who agrees to dance the Macarena, let students paint their face, sit for a dunk tank, or participate in some other way if a whole grade reaches the end-of-year goal. Teachers can increase their students' anticipation of the celebration or recognition, which will increase their motivation to work hard. For instance, a teacher can tell the students: "Remember, if you all pass the mastery test next week, your group's name is going to get mentioned during the morning announcements! You were so close last week. I bet everyone will pass the mastery test this time!"

Before celebrating progress through the DI programs, it is important to verify that students have indeed achieved mastery. It is potentially deflating for students to celebrate moving on to a new storybook or a higher level of the program only to be taken back to an earlier storybook or level if it's discovered later that they didn't actually master the content of previous lessons. For this reason, school leaders might want to conduct in-class spot checks of student performance to verify that students are ready to move on to the next storybook or program level before the move actually takes place. This can take the form of leaders asking students to read passages from the stories and the leader asking comprehension questions, quizzing students on concepts or skills that appear in independent work, or challenging students with scenarios that require them to apply what they've learned in the DI programs. If students answer these questions correctly, the leader can compliment the students on their responses and inform them that she will return in a few days when the students attain the goal.

The opportunity for leaders to verify student performance in advance of their moving on to a new storybook or program level can occur only if leaders are aware of how close groups are to completing the end of a level or reaching some other important milestone in the DI programs. The status of lesson progress and the type of celebrations that are planned should be an integral part of the problem-solving sessions discussed earlier in this chapter.

Inter-school celebrations can augment school-based celebrations of student success. These celebrations can take the form of friendly contests. For several years, Atlanta elementary schools implementing DI each held game-show-style competitions between groups of students on the science and social studies facts taught in the Grade 2 and 3 levels of *Reading Mastery*. The groups received one point for every correct answer and an additional point if they answered in a complete sentence. The winner of each school's competition went on to represent their school in an inter-school contest on science and social studies facts in *Reading Mastery*. Students, teachers, and administrators from each school, as well as district-level administrators, attended the events. The winning team brought home a trophy with the school's name and year engraved on it. The contests acted as strong motivators for the students to learn the facts when teachers and school leaders reminded students of the dates of the contests.

When developing a system of celebrations, teachers and school leaders should ensure that academic recognition of student achievement and improvement takes precedence over other celebrations in the school. If a school places its highest priority on student achievement, celebrations of student achievement should be given the greatest emphasis. At school, there should be celebrations for non-academic purposes, such as birthdays and holidays. However, it is important that these celebrations are secondary in terms of time and attention from adults to celebrations of academic accomplishment and the behaviors that support academic accomplishment, such as perfect student attendance and smooth transitions between classes. If there are too many celebrations outside of DI, the celebrations for student success in DI may lose some of their power to serve as incentives for students to work hard and succeed. Teachers and leaders can monitor the enthusiasm students exhibit for celebrations of academic accomplishment and adjust the frequency of non-academic celebrations accordingly.

To be motivating for students who are working hard but are still not meeting grade-level expectations, the reinforcement system should emphasize improvement in performance. This is especially true for the first year of DI as a new culture of success is being established.

Adults will be reinforced intrinsically by watching their students succeed as any accolades students receive reflect positively on their teacher's efforts. School leaders can augment the reinforcement of staff with explicit recognitions of teachers' accomplishments. For instance, leaders can present staff with a special treat when all teachers complete data forms correctly and submit them on time. Or the building coordinator can post an in-service follow-up form after all teachers demonstrate targeted instructional skills in their classrooms. For the staff, as well as for the students, school leaders should strive to achieve at least a 4:1 positive-to-negative feedback ratio to keep them motivated and enthusiastic about implementing DI.

BUILDING THE CAPACITY OF THE STAFF TO IMPLEMENT DI

For DI to have a long-term positive effect on student performance, it is important that school leaders build the capacity of the staff to implement DI with fidelity. All feedback provided by school-based coaches and external support providers should be designed to increase the capacity of the staff, not just to improve student performance. If directions are given as part of feedback to a teacher, the teacher should also be made aware of the *rationale* for the actions and the *circumstances under which* the actions should be taken. For instance, if a coach asks a teacher to provide individual turns, the teacher should understand that the purpose of individual turns is to check on the mastery of targeted students before proceeding in the program, which assumes that students have mastered the current exercise.

Building the capacity of staff should occur at two levels: within their current roles and in anticipation of future roles they may assume. Chapter 8 described the training regime that should be established for teachers, including initial program (preservice) training, weekly supervised practice sessions, and ongoing in-service training covering classroom setup, behavioral motivation, program delivery and corrections, and data collection and assessment. As described earlier in this chapter, each of those training sessions should be accompanied by follow-up observations or other forms of monitoring to ensure that the instructional staff has fully incorporated the targeted skills into their daily instructional practice.

Building coordinators and other coaches also need to receive training in their roles with targeted follow-up by a DI expert. Building coordinators who do not have a background in DI will need to gain program knowledge by teaching at least one instructional group for a semester as they receive feedback from an external support provider to develop their DI skills.

As indicated in chapter 8, the leadership should identify teachers who demonstrate facility with the DI approach to act as peer coaches who can provide feedback to other teachers on data completion and program delivery. To build up the school's capacity further and ensure the long-run sustainability of the DI implementation, peer coaches can be prepped to serve as the building coordinator should the need arise. So there should be a progression in skills that accompanies the progression in position:

Teacher → Peer Coach → Building Coordinator

NIFDI has developed four levels of coaches' training, which are listed in Table 10.2. The levels represent a logical progression of skills that expands the expertise of the coaches gradually over time. The progression includes a shift from skills that are applied when students are not present (outside of instruction) to skills that are applied during live instruction. In Level A, coaches focus on data completion and data analysis as well as format practice without students present. In Level B, coaches start to monitor and provide support during instruction by conducting some of the fundamental observations discussed in chapter 9 and modeling key instructional formats. At this level, the coach does not give feedback to the teacher during instruction. In Level C, the coach conducts more advanced observations and provides feedback while the teacher is teaching. In Level D, coaches learn to run the weekly problem-solving sessions.

Ideally, coaches can complete all four levels of training in the first two years of implementing DI, but often completing the levels takes longer. New coaches should attend the sequence of trainings from the beginning even if they have been teaching the program for several years as the skills covered during coaches' training can be expected to be unfamiliar even to experienced teachers.

NIFDI also offers more advanced training sessions covering hypothesis formation and testing, which can be covered during the third year of a

DI implementation if coaches complete all levels of peer coaches' training in two years. As with teacher training, coaches' training is designed to introduce new skills and concepts at a rate that allows the participants to master the content of each training fully before being introduced to more advanced content. Coaches' training sessions are followed by structured observations in the classrooms to ensure that the participants can apply the skills and concepts covered during training to the classrooms they support. An expert external support provider should provide the training and then shadow the coaches as they visit classrooms. The visits should be followed by debrief sessions that involve a validity check on the specific problems the coaches observed and the remedies they recommended.

Coaching level	Skills learned	Support provided to teachers
Level A	• Analyze data: LPC, STS, independent work • Participate in problem-solving sessions	• Improve written records • Rehearse with teachers
Level B	• Five-minute observations • Show-off lesson observations	Do all of the above plus: • demonstrate formats or lessons in the classroom • provide in-services
Level C	• Extended observations	Do all of the above plus: • team teach (or otherwise intervene) • provide solutions
Level D	• Participate in data analysis committee meetings • Write effective data analysis reports	Do all of the above plus: • monitor solutions for effectiveness • collaborate with team re: additional solution(s), if necessary

Table 10.2 Levels of coaches' training. Source: the National Institute for Direct Instruction (NIFDI).

As mentioned in chapter 8, in addition to the coaches' training, NIFDI offers the Institute on Becoming an Effective DI Trainer, which prepares experienced DI teachers to become trainers. Once a school has a sufficient number of coaches and a building coordinator who have mastered the content of the coaches' training as well as teachers who have "graduated" from the Institute on Becoming an Effective DI Trainer, the school has all of the expertise it needs to implement DI at a high level of fidelity with little to no support from outside experts. Large-scale implementations of DI can function independently at a high level when district-level personnel have gone through these training sessions, too, and demonstrated that they can apply their knowledge to the schools they support.

ORIENTING NEW STAFF TO THE DIRECT INSTRUCTION IMPLEMENTATION

For the long-run success of DI, new staff should go through the same process that the original teachers went through: learning DI expectations, receiving initial program (preservice) training, participating in semiweekly supervised practice sessions, receiving ongoing training in DI procedures, receiving in-class coaching on delivering DI, and benefiting from expert analysis of student performance data. Teachers who participate in the adoption of DI often have a clearer understanding of the potential effect DI can have on their students because they've witnessed the transformation of student performance at their schools. However, teachers who join the school after DI has been implemented for several years may conclude that an intensive instructional approach is not needed because the students at the school are able to perform at a high level.

For this reason, it's essential that school leaders establish a process for orienting new staff members to the DI implementation. This process should incorporate the essential features of the processes that were used to build consensus in support of the DI implementation for adoption (as described in chapter 7) and establish the roles of staff members at the start of the DI implementation (as described in chapter 8). For new staff hired after the start of the school year, the leadership should ensure that they:

- receive the same background information on DI and its role in the school that the original staff members received
- attend a training on the programs they are expected to teach and pass a checkout of critical delivery and correction skills
- are aware of their responsibilities as instructors in terms of adhering to schedules, teaching to mastery, submitting data, incorporating feedback from coaches, etc.
- demonstrate improvement in implementing the program through coaching observations and participation in the weekly practice sessions.

Ideally, the orientation of new staff should start during interviews of potential candidates to join the staff. These interviews should include questions about the applicant's consent to: teach the instructional groups established by the building coordinator and external support provider; follow the script precisely; adhere to pre-established instructional schedules; incorporate the feedback of anyone who serves as a coach; record critical data on student performance in specific forms daily, etc. Some school leaders bring teacher presentation books into interviews with potential staff members and ask them to teach parts of a lesson in order to convey to them some of the expectations of DI program delivery and to determine whether the candidates would be willing to take feedback on their DI teaching.

Once teachers are hired, they can be assigned an experienced staff member who will act as a mentor. The mentorship provides a personal connection to another staff member who can share their experience with DI and provide encouragement if the new teacher gets discouraged with their progress on mastering DI techniques. The mentor can provide rationale for the components of the DI model and share with the new teacher how each component contributed to the success of the students with DI. Given the high rate at which new teachers leave schools and abandon the teaching profession altogether, it is a small investment for school leaders to provide mentors on DI to new hires as part of a broader orientation of new staff members.

CONDUCTING QUARTERLY REVIEWS OF THE DI IMPLEMENTATION

In addition to the weekly problem-solving sessions described earlier in this chapter, the leadership team should conduct more extensive, quarterly reviews of the school's implementation of DI to determine the extent to which all students are on track to reach end-of-year goals and the steps that can be taken to help students who are not on track to reach the goals. These quarterly reviews should involve 1) projections of the lesson that each instructional group can be expected to reach at the end of the school year if students continue to complete lessons at the same rate of progress (at mastery) to date, and 2) the identification of specific action steps the leadership and/or instructional staff can take to improve student progress at mastery in the short or long run. As discussed in chapter 8, end-of-year projections can be calculated by multiplying the number of days remaining in the school year by the average daily rate of lesson completion to date for each instructional group. The difference between the preset goal for each group and the projected end lesson indicates the additional number of lessons that the students would have to make up to reach the end-of-year goal. If there is no difference between the goal and the projection, the students in the instructional group are on track to reach the end-of-year expectations. If the difference is greater than zero, the group will have to increase their lesson progress to attain the goal. If the difference is less than zero, the students are on track to exceed the goal.

Based on the projections of end-of-year lesson completion at current rates of lesson progress, the school's leadership team can engage teachers in "backwards planning" to determine how many lessons per week each group would need to increase its weekly rate of lesson completion for students to reach the end-of-year goals. A relatively small increase in the weekly rate of lessons, such as an additional lesson per week, may be reasonable for instructional groups who are not on track. To increase lesson completion rates by more than a lesson a week may be an unreasonable expectation. For groups that are very far behind, which may have been caused by contextual factors out of the staff's control, such as school absences due to an illness, maintaining an end-of-year goal that is unreasonable can have a psychologically negative effect on teachers. In these cases, the leadership may add a secondary, more reasonable goal alongside the original end-of-year goal. The revised goal would be based on reasonable lesson progress (at mastery) from the current lesson for the rest of the school year. If an instructional group is 80 lessons off target with only 40 instructional days left in the school year, for instance, the leadership may set a secondary goal of completing 45 lessons for the group. This revised goal would lighten the psychological burden on the teachers and reduce the chance that teachers will "drag" students through the program without completing each lesson at mastery.

Groups that are identified as being "off track" to finish the targeted lesson at mastery should receive more attention than other groups. For the action steps, the leadership should be cautious about issuing a mandate for the teachers of these groups to simply *increase lesson progress* because that may result in teachers going through lessons at the expense of mastery. Instead, the leadership should *identify specific problems* that have been revealed through observations of each group's instruction and analysis of in-program assessments, and they should *formulate remedies for the problems*, which will lead to higher lesson completion at mastery. The remedies may, in fact, include a request to the teacher to pick up the pace of the presentation, which can increase student engagement and allow students to follow the presentation more easily.

For the quarterly review, the leadership team should revisit the essential setup steps described in chapter 8. If any of the setup steps have not been fully implemented, such as scheduling sufficient time in the programs for each instructional group, these items should be given the highest priority. Any problems identified as "redline" or "red-flag" problems through the weekly problem-solving sessions should also be given high priority in the quarterly review. Attendance of the staff at the practice sessions is an ongoing source of data for the leadership to analyze for the quarterly review.

Priorities can also be determined by applying the Implementation Priority Pyramid, described earlier in this chapter. The leadership can address the following questions that result from an application of the pyramid to the implementation of DI at the school:

1. Are students actively engaged in DI during the entire instructional periods?
2. Are students properly placed in the programs on an ongoing basis?
3. Are students mastering the content of the programs?
4. Is time being used efficiently? Are students mastering the content in a reasonable amount of time?

Before the quarterly review, the leadership can take selected data on each of the levels of the pyramid to help answer the questions above. For student engagement, the leadership can conduct a round of two-minute observations. For proper placement, they can conduct a round of first-time correct observations. For each of these items, the leadership should formulate a remedy that details who will take which specific actions to address the problems. The remedies should be prioritized according to the impact they will have on student performance and teachers' capacity to deliver the program effectively.

The main focus of the quarterly reviews should be on improving student outcomes for the remainder of the current school year, but the leadership should also note any adjustments that they will want to make to the DI implementation in future years. For example, if the quarterly review indicates that some teachers are still struggling to implement aspects of the program that should have been in place early in the school year, such as data completion, the leadership may want to pencil in a professional development day early in the next school year to address correct completion of the data forms.

If the school employs an expert external support provider, the provider should be involved in the quarterly review. The external support provider can write a brief report that details the major accomplishments, the major problems, and the specific action steps that will be taken. The report can include a summary of student performance data and observations used to conduct the review. The external support provider can provide their perspective on progress toward building up the capacity of the school to enable it to implement DI independently, which, as discussed previously, is a multi-year endeavor.

The written report based on the quarterly review can take many forms. A simple example is to have two sections:

1. General categories that are implemented well
2. Specific problems along with recommended actions for resolving the problems.

The problems along with their remedies should be listed in the order of priority. If the problems were noted on a previous quarterly report, progress made toward remediating the problem would be noted in the current report. A blank form that NIFDI uses for quarterly reports appears in Appendix 6.

The written reports can facilitate the analysis of the implementation of DI across several schools. If DI is used across a district, student performance data from each of the schools can be compared so district leaders can identify schools that might be able to serve as models for other schools as well as schools that might benefit from extra support. Since the written reports provide a description of the primary obstacles to student success and the specific steps that can be taken to remove these obstacles at each school, the district leadership can use the reports to identify steps that can be taken at the district level to facilitate the implementation of DI, such as providing an in-service on data completion. The district leadership can have its own quarterly review of DI across the district, which would include an assessment of its capacity to support the DI implementation and the steps it can take to increase its own expertise in DI as it works to ensure that all students in the schools are successful with the DI approach.

TOPIC BRIEF 4: HIGHER-ORDER THINKING IN DIRECT INSTRUCTION PROGRAMS

A common misconception among education practitioners is that highly structured lessons involve only rote learning and do not involve higher-order thinking. Supposedly, structured lessons can only involve students repeating and recalling very simple information rather than learning and applying more advanced reasoning skills. According to this misconception, higher-order thinking occurs solely through a process of "discovery," in which students construct their own meaning in an unstructured environment. Supposedly, the more that a lesson or activity is structured, the more that students will be constrained by that structure and the less likely they will be able to learn higher-order concepts.

The reality is that very unstructured activities can sometimes devolve into lower-order learning. Anita Archer, a well-known expert on explicit instruction, describes how she visited an eighth-grade language arts classroom where individual students were supposed to create posters that compared and contrasted the book *Unbroken* with the movie *Unbroken*. However, the students she observed did not focus on comparing the book with the movie as they created their posters. Instead, they focused on various aspects of poster-making: inserting a strong border, selecting fonts for lettering, and using color to make the elements of the poster stand out. In that classroom, the activity of poster-making had taken precedence over higher-order learning involved in comparing and contrasting the book with the movie (Archer, 2018).

In contrast, the Direct Instruction programs ensure that students engage in higher-order learning as they participate in lessons daily. As described in chapter 4, students in the first two levels of the *Reading Mastery* language program master higher-order concepts that lay the basis for more advanced learning. The most fundamental concepts are based on understanding "same," "all," "some," and "none." Skills based on the "sameness" in things in these levels of the program include object classification, analogies, opposites, and synonyms. By the end of the kindergarten level of the language program, children identify differences and sameness between such objects as a bird and an airplane. They note that both an airplane and a bird have wings and can fly, but a bird is an animal with feathers, and an airplane is a vehicle made of metal and has windows.

As students progress through the DI programs, they learn more sophisticated reasoning skills. In Level C of the Comprehension strand of *Corrective Reading*, students learn to use evidence to construct arguments, draw conclusions, and analyze the validity of arguments they encounter. They learn to identify faulty reasoning by applying the following rules about correlations and part-whole fallacies.

Rule	Description	Lesson Introduced
1	Just because two things happen around the same time doesn't mean one thing causes the other thing.	42
2	Just because you know about a part doesn't mean you know about the whole thing.	46
3	Just because you know about a part doesn't mean you know about another part.	61
4	Just because you know about a whole thing doesn't mean you know about every part.	61
5	Just because words are the same doesn't mean they have the same meaning.	67
6	Just because the writer presents some choices doesn't mean there aren't other choices.	78
7	Just because events have happened in the past doesn't mean they'll always happen.	122

Argument rules in *Corrective Reading* Comprehension, Level C. Source: Engelmann, S., Haddox, P. and Hanner, S. (2008b). *Corrective Reading Teacher's Guide: Comprehension C Concept Applications*, p. 43.

As with other concepts and skills taught in the DI programs, the rules are not introduced together wholesale in a single lesson. Rather, they are introduced over the span of 80 lessons to ensure that students have sufficient practice applying the rules to concrete examples before they are introduced to the next rule. The rules themselves are worded simply, but they form a strong basis for students to analyze critically the formal and informal texts (including social media) that they encounter. After students master the rules, the teacher can inform them of the more common term used for the rule. (For instance, the fallacy addressed by Rule 6 is also known as a *false dilemma* or *false dichotomy* argument.)

Whether students learn other labels for the rules or not, they will be prepared to identify faulty arguments, misleading advertisements, and political propaganda, which will serve them well as consumers and citizens after they graduate from high school. As many writers have emphasized, having consumers and citizens who can critically evaluate the media they encounter is a cornerstone of a functioning democracy and a robust market economy. So ensuring that students master the higher-order thinking content in the DI programs benefits not only the students themselves but also the communities where they reside.

TOPIC BRIEF 5: USING DIRECT INSTRUCTION PROGRAMS FOR ONE-ON-ONE INSTRUCTION

As described in chapter 4, two DI reading programs have been designed specifically for one-on-one instruction – *Teach Your Child to Read in 100 Easy Lessons* (TYC) and *Funnix*. Both of these programs were derived from pre-existing DI reading programs (TYC from *DISTAR Reading* and *Funnix* from *Horizons*) and adapted for home use with a single child or as a tutorial program at a school or other setting. Both of these programs can be used for small-group instruction, too, but because the children are expected to touch the book or the screen, the programs are best suited for one-on-one instruction.

In addition to these two instructional programs, any of the other DI programs can be used to tutor children. In order for tutoring to be effective, many of the same setup and delivery requirements for group instruction need to be in place for one-on-one instruction. Each student who receives tutoring in a DI program needs to be placement tested to determine the appropriate level and starting point in the program (described in chapter 8). Students need to receive at least four periods of instruction per week. The teacher or tutor needs to be versed in DI delivery, correction, and motivation techniques. Student performance data should be collected, and data and observations should be analyzed regularly to identify and remediate problems of instruction. Implementing all of these components can be challenging – particularly in schools with strict scheduling constraints and a lack of trained instructional staff. School leaders need to address these challenges before starting a tutoring program to ensure that it is effective.

Another challenge to address when implementing a DI program for one-on-one instruction is to minimize confusing students with two different strategies. The DI programs contain very effective yet often unique strategies for key components of reading, writing, spelling, and mathematics. Examples include: the modified orthography in reading, the "x-box" approach to writing arguments, the morphemic analysis involved in spelling, and the number families approach to performing basic operations in mathematics. (See chapter 3 for more information on the content and task analysis used in the DI programs.) Students may become confused if they are required to apply a new strategy when they've already learned to apply another strategy in the same subject area. Students should not be blamed for confusing different strategies if they receive instruction in more than one program. However, their confusion indicates that the tutor should provide more explanation and practice to ensure that students apply the correct strategy to the appropriate context. The tutor should respond with appreciation to a student's efforts if the student incorrectly applies strategies from one program to another program. At the same time, the tutor should redirect the students to apply the correct strategy in the appropriate context.

If different terms are used for similar procedures, the tutor should explain that the terms mean the same thing. For example, if a child is already familiar with the DI term "take away" to mean subtraction and another program uses the term "subtract," the tutor can pre-teach the new term "subtract" before starting the lesson in which the term is used for the first time. *This requires tutors to screen both the main program and the tutorial program ahead of time for possible areas of confusion.*

Another common challenge that occurs when using a tutoring program is student motivation. Although large instructional groups of students can represent a management challenge, teaching more than one child at a time can actually facilitate instruction. Teachers can use students who are following class rules to manage the group. On-task students provide models of correct answers and appropriate behavior. In a group setting, if a child is not adhering to a behavioral expectation, such as looking at the presentation book during instruction, the teacher can reinforce other students who are on task, which serves as a motivation for the child to look at the book. However, if there is only one child in the group, the teacher cannot use this motivation technique and must rely on other strategies to motivate the child to participate fully in instruction.

Despite these challenges, one-on-one instruction has several advantages in comparison to group instruction. Because only one child is receiving instruction, there is no need for teachers to elicit a choral response. This eliminates the need to repeat material due to "signal jumping" or delayed student responses, known as "coat-tailing" (see chapter 5). There is no need to insert individual turns after group responses, and there is no need to include individual turns during error corrections because every student response is an individual turn. Not only are error corrections simplified, but it is also much easier for a teacher to adjust instruction for a single student than it is for a group of students. If the tutor provides a student with additional practice on a strategy, other students' progress through the program isn't delayed. If the student has demonstrated that they are ready for more challenging content as demonstrated by their performance on mastery tests or other in-program measures, the tutor can move the student to a higher lesson without being constrained by the performance level of other students who may not be ready to skip ahead in the program.

Because the delivery and correction requirements for a teacher or tutor are less in one-on-one instruction than in group instruction, the need for training is reduced. However, tutors should still receive training in program rationale and delivery as well as conducting error corrections and motivating students.

If instructional groups are well managed and students are placed appropriately, students generally prefer to participate in groups rather than receive one-on-one instruction. So if a school is implementing DI as core instruction, students receiving one-on-one instruction should be moved to a group as soon as they catch up with a group that is performing near their skill level. If a school is not implementing DI for core instruction, using DI for tutoring may be a long-term solution for students who are not successful in the core instructional program.

TOPIC BRIEF 6: EXTENDED ACTIVITIES IN THE DIRECT INSTRUCTION PROGRAMS

As described in chapter 2, all DI programs introduce new concepts and skills very carefully with selected examples presented in an instructional sequence that leads to only one interpretation by the learner. This "faultless communication" fosters students' mastery of the new concept or skill as described in *Theory of Instruction* (Engelmann, S. and Carnine, 1991). There is a progression of the content and an evolution of formats in all DI programs as exercises proceed from more structured and teacher-led activities to more independent activities as part of the generalization process. The ultimate goal is for students to integrate skills and concepts fully into their repertoire so they can apply them as needed in any context.

Several DI programs offer extended opportunities for students to apply the skills and concepts they've learned to a variety of contexts. Here are some examples.

READING MASTERY SIGNATURE EDITION (RMSE)

All levels in the reading track of RMSE include a literature anthology and a matching guide for teachers. The anthology in each level contains between nine and 16 readings. The guide specifies when the reading selections can be introduced, as students must master skills that correspond to specified lessons in the main program before they can read the selections independently. The selections are designed to expand upon the skills students master in the regular lessons and provide them with a wider range of literature than they encounter in the stories they read daily for skill development (Engelmann, S., 2008, 5).

The reading track of RMSE also contains detailed guides to research projects for students in Grades 2–5 of the program. There are five research projects per level of the program. These projects are based on the science and social studies content that students learn in the informational reading passages that are part of the daily lessons. The projects reinforce and expand on the content that appears in the lessons, and they provide models to the students for conducting research and consulting with different sources of information. For example, here is the resource list for the third research project in the second-grade program, which deals with the life stages of different insect species:

- Insect identification books
- Magazine articles
- Magazine or book pictures
- Interviews with local experts such as an exterminator, a science teacher, a county extension or agriculture agent, or a university professor
- Zoo
- The internet. (*SRA Research Projects Grade 2*, 2008, 11)

As with the literature anthology selections, the timing of the research projects is keyed to the students mastering designated lessons in the program.

CORRECTIVE READING DECODING LEVEL C

Decoding C, the highest level of the *Corrective Reading* program, includes two bonus information passages every 10 lessons starting at Lesson 58 for a total of 14 extra reading passages. The vocabulary in these passages is tightly controlled to ensure that students can comprehend the passages when they read them independently. However, the sentence structure is more complex, and the word decoding difficulty is greater in the bonus passages. In addition to the bonus passages, the teacher's guide provides directions on how to structure additional outside reading for students. Steps include underlining unfamiliar words, reading and defining unfamiliar words before reading the story aloud, and inserting comprehension questions to check students' understanding of the passages they read.

The *Decoding C Core Resource Connections* supplement contains the full text of 48 leveled passages that are designed to be introduced every five lessons to provide students with additional practice in reading material independently at their skill level. The passages contain a mix of fiction and non-fiction selections. Students are provided with various rubrics to help them analyze the passages. One rubric guides students as they describe the essential elements of a story: the setting, characters, problem, climax, and resolution (*Corrective Reading Decoding C Core Resource Connections*, 2013, C 3). Another rubric prompts students to describe how a passage contains facts vs. opinions (*Corrective Reading Decoding C Core Resource Connections*, 2013, C 10). The supplement also provides a variety of additional writing opportunities.

ESSENTIALS FOR WRITING

Teachers implementing the *Essentials for Writing* program, the most advanced DI writing program, can make use of an optional software program designed to provide additional practice for students on writing mechanics. The software comes in a CD-ROM with 20 separate lessons that cover several skills introduced in the program, such as pronoun use and inserting commas after adverbial clauses or phrases that appear at the beginning of sentences. The software also covers several skills not covered in the program that often appear on many high-stakes tests, such as punctuating sentences that contain direct quotations. In the lessons, students receive practice in common formats that appear in many high-stakes tests (Engelmann, S. and Grossen, 2010, 105).

*

Students will be successful in these extended activities if they've mastered all of the component skills during group instruction, independent work, and in-program assessments. If they haven't mastered these skills, they will have more difficulty performing at a high level in these activities. If, during the activities, students make errors on skills taught previously in the program, the teacher should provide a review of these skills. In this way, students will learn to apply all of the skills and concepts covered in the program more consistently.

The activities can be used for enrichment, and they can be used to help consolidate two smaller groups into one larger group. If two groups are within about 20 lessons of each other, the group that is ahead in the program can perform the extended activities while the other group proceeds through the regular lessons. When the second group catches up with the first group, both groups can be consolidated into a single group because all students will have mastered a similar set of skills.

Teachers and school leaders can save themselves a great deal of time and effort by reviewing all components of the DI programs thoroughly before deciding whether to introduce outside material to supplement the DI programs. If the DI programs address all of the essential standards required, there is no reason to purchase other programs or have teachers spend hours designing their own activities that may or may not build on the DI programs systematically, which the published extended activities are designed to do.

SECTION 3
PITFALLS TO AVOID WHEN IMPLEMENTING DIRECT INSTRUCTION

INTRODUCTION TO THE SECTION

As indicated in previous sections of this book, Direct Instruction is a complex system involving many different components that must be implemented with fidelity to maximize the overall efficacy of the DI approach. If one component is out of place, there can be a disproportionately negative effect on the DI implementation as a whole. So if any of the items discussed in section 2 are not implemented with fidelity, the results can be considerably less impressive than what would occur if all components were implemented fully. Just as a problem with a single component of an automobile can hamper its overall performance – worn-out spark plugs, a cracked radiator, or a warp in one of the brake rotors – a problem with any component of a DI implementation can hamper student performance.

Although a problem with any one component of a DI implementation can serve as an obstacle to full success with DI, some problems are more common and/or more impactful than other problems. This section of the book addresses the most common pitfalls that hamper the success of a DI implementation. The section is divided into two chapters: a chapter on common pitfalls that teachers should avoid, and a chapter on common pitfalls that school leaders should avoid. Each chapter contains the top 10 potential pitfalls for each set of actors (teachers or school leaders). The description of each pitfall addresses, in turn:

- the specifics of the pitfall itself
- the implications of the pitfall – if this implementation component is out of place, what will this mean for student success?
- potential solutions to overcome the pitfall.

There is some overlap between the different pitfalls as they cover concepts that are closely related to each other. The two chapters make extensive reference to previous material in this book to describe the pitfalls, their implications, and potential solutions.

CHAPTER ELEVEN
POTENTIAL PITFALLS FOR TEACHERS TO AVOID

This chapter presents the top 10 most common pitfalls that teachers and other instructional staff may encounter when implementing DI. This list of pitfalls is limited to those problems that are under the control of teachers' ability to change. There are factors other than those listed in this chapter that affect a DI implementation that are out of the control of instructors. Some of these factors are under the control of school leaders and are addressed in chapter 12.

Here are the most common pitfalls, which are explained in detail below:

1. Not learning the scripts before using them
2. Presenting the scripts but not teaching
3. Not teaching everything – and every student – to mastery
4. Letting time get lost needlessly
5. Rushing through lessons with insufficient think time
6. Trying to "enhance" the initial teaching in the DI programs
7. Not applying what students learn in the DI programs to other contexts
8. Not motivating students to learn
9. Not recording data accurately
10. Not realizing that it takes a lot to become skilled in DI.

#1: NOT LEARNING THE SCRIPTS BEFORE USING THEM

POTENTIAL PITFALL

A common misunderstanding about the DI programs is that teachers require little or no preparation before they can present the DI lessons effectively. According to this line of reasoning, all that is required for a teacher to be able to teach DI effectively is for the teacher to be able to read the scripts in the DI programs. As a result, teachers who assume they do not need any preparation before they teach DI may not even glance over the lessons before starting instruction that day. Of course, reading the DI programs is not the same as teaching, which involves an ongoing interaction with students in response to their behavior and performance on the specific tasks depicted in the DI scripts.

IMPLICATIONS

When teachers are not sufficiently familiar with a DI lesson, they become "script bound" with their eyes on the presentation book instead of looking at the students as they present the exercises. The presentation of DI by teachers who have not practiced or reviewed a DI lesson is usually very stilted and halting. They may not emphasize keywords associated with new or complex concepts, and they may make errors in presenting the material. They may not be aware of which scaffolds have been faded in the lesson and which new concepts or conventions are being introduced that build on the content covered in previous lessons. When teachers are unfamiliar with the scripts, the corrections they provide are delayed and sometimes incomplete, especially for new exercises.

As a result, lessons take more time, instruction is less engaging to students, and the potential for students to become disengaged increases substantially. Some students may not respond at all, or they may delay their response and instead "coat-tail" off the responses of other students because the teacher is focused on deciphering the script rather than focused on what the students are doing or not doing. When the teacher doesn't respond to all students' errors by providing a complete and timely error correction for each of them, student mastery and lesson progress are adversely affected.

POSSIBLE SOLUTIONS

To ensure that the instructional staff understands the importance of practicing the scripts before teaching, at an in-service training present the staff with a script they haven't seen before and require them to present it to each other without any practice in a simulated role-play of a classroom in which some teachers play the part of the teacher and other staff members play the part of the students. After teachers have experienced trying to teach a lesson without any preparation in a role-play situation, they can be asked to estimate how much practice they would need to be able to present the script fluently and respond correctly to the errors students might commit. Having the staff as a whole articulate how much time they estimate they will need for practice can help build their support for regular practice sessions. This can be done after they attend a preservice training so they have a better understanding of how much time is required for them to prepare to teach a DI lesson fluently.

To ensure that teachers are sufficiently familiar with the specific DI program that matches their students' skill repertoire, they should attend a preservice (program) training before the start of the school year that focuses at least two thirds of the time on practicing DI delivery skills. The preservice training should include a checkout of each participant's presentation and correction skills, as mentioned in chapter 8. After school starts, teachers should emulate the type of practice that occurred during the preservice training throughout the year. They should engage in small-group practice sessions of essential exercises in new lessons with simulated errors so each teacher in the group can practice and become fluent with the full range of error corrections they might need to implement during the lessons. Practice sessions should have a specific focus and occur at least twice a week for 20 minutes or more per session during the first year of implementation and more often as needed. They should be monitored and supported in person or virtually by an experienced coach (see chapter 8 for more information on practice sessions).

In addition to the supervised practice sessions, teachers should practice or preview each day's lesson on their own so they are familiar with the nuances of the script. Some teachers have even taken the teacher presentation books home with them to practice during the evenings and weekends so they become very familiar with the script. The optimal amount of time for practice and review of the formats is determined empirically; practice should last as long as it takes for teachers to be able to teach the lesson fluently and flawlessly with only a need to glance at the script (to ensure fidelity) so they can direct most of their attention to the students and how they respond to the tasks in the lesson.

#2: PRESENTING THE SCRIPTS BUT NOT TEACHING

POTENTIAL PITFALL

Some teachers focus their attention heavily on the presentation aspects of a DI lesson and much less attention on responding to student performance. Teachers may be familiar with the script, but they may not direct their attention sufficiently to monitoring and reacting to students' responses.

IMPLICATIONS

It is essential for teachers to not only present the lesson as written, but also to be keenly aware of exactly how each student responds to each task. Teachers then need to respond immediately to students' performance. Responses should be in the form of praise and student points for correct answers, and error corrections and extra practice when students either don't respond or respond with an incorrect answer. If teachers do not respond to students' success and errors, students' mastery of the content, their motivation to put forth their best effort, and lesson progress can all suffer.

POSSIBLE SOLUTIONS

For teachers to become more attuned to students who might not be responding consistently during group instruction, practice sessions should include simulations of students who coat-tail or don't respond at all to the teacher's signal. Teachers can also write reminders to themselves in their teacher presentation books to insert more individual turns or to call on subgroups of students (e.g. the back row/front row, or left side/ right side of the classroom), which will help prompt the teacher to pay close attention to the individuals or subgroups that are called upon to answer. An in-service on active monitoring should be scheduled and followed by coaches using the active monitoring follow-up form to ensure that teachers monitor students as they work independently.

#3: NOT TEACHING EVERYTHING – AND EVERY STUDENT – TO MASTERY

POTENTIAL PITFALL

The incremental, step-by-step design of the DI programs is very unusual to teachers when they are first introduced to DI. So they often do not adhere to the maxim that *every task of every exercise of every lesson in a DI program should be taught to mastery*. Mastery is demonstrated when all students answer all items in an exercise correctly the first time they encounter them or in response to a delayed test. Some teachers assume that students will eventually learn the content of the program even if they aren't brought to mastery on every part of their current lesson. For this reason, these teachers may consider the high levels of mastery required to pass the assessments to be too stringent. For them, a much lower level of mastery, such as 75% for mastery tests rather than 90%, would still indicate that students are acquiring a sufficient amount of the content covered in the lessons to proceed in the DI programs. However, 75% correct means that students do not understand 25% of the material covered on the mastery test, which is a very high amount of information for students to learn on top of the 10–15% of the material that will be new to the students each day in future lessons.

IMPLICATIONS

The "double-edged sword" inherent in the incremental-step design of the DI programs ensures that virtually all students placed at their skill level and taught to mastery every day will be able to learn all of the content of the program by the end of the school year. The design also ensures that students who are not taught to mastery every day will experience increasing difficulty with the content as they proceed through the lessons. They will have more to learn in later lessons if they don't master the content in earlier lessons as the DI programs a) build on previously taught content systematically, b) incorporate previously taught material into more advanced exercises, and c) fade the prompts that make learning a concept or skill easier initially. If

417

students do not master a skill when the lesson contains the initial prompts, such as prompts for carrying as part of column addition (discussed in chapter 2), the likelihood is very low that they can master the skill later when the prompts have been faded. Students who do not master all skills as they are taught in the program will need to repeat part or all of the level of the program in which they were placed.

Not only do teachers need to understand the intricacies of the DI program they are teaching, as described in Pitfall #1, but they also need to know how students respond to the specifics of the program – which concepts and formats are easier or more difficult for the students to master. To be successful, teachers must be aware of what each of their students knows, what is new to them, and what they have had difficulty with in previous lessons. If teachers don't have intimate knowledge of each of their students' mastery of previous content before the lesson as well as their mastery of the current lesson, teachers will not know whether today's instruction has been successful. Without that knowledge, it will be difficult for teachers to adjust their implementation of the program to better serve their students.

POSSIBLE SOLUTIONS

Teachers need to teach everything to mastery during every lesson. This involves the teacher noticing all performance errors students make, providing a full correction in response to the error (including delayed tests of the missed items), and repeating parts or all of the lesson later the same day and on subsequent days until all students answer correctly the first time on the delayed tests. Students who are absent, misplaced in the program, or who are not engaged or motivated to work hard require other action steps in addition to implementing the full error correction. For instance, extensive "error correction loops" may indicate that the students need to repeat parts of earlier lessons before they can be successful in the current lesson.

To ensure that students successfully master the content of each lesson, teachers should not omit any part of a lesson, even those that are in the notes. For example, in some lessons, the notes indicate that students should receive individual turns after the group completes part of an exercise. But some teachers may not read the black print in the teacher presentation carefully and only say what's in the blue print, which contains the specific wording they are supposed to say. Omitting individual turns that are indicated in the notes eliminates an important opportunity for teachers to verify that students have mastered the content of the lesson and eliminates an opportunity for the teacher to provide a correction and additional practice as needed for the students to achieve mastery.

It is very helpful for teachers who are new to DI to see an example of students being taught to mastery. The most powerful model for a teacher who is new to DI is to watch an instructional group being taught to mastery at a similar point in the same DI program as the new teacher's students. Once staff members have an image of how teaching to mastery looks – not only an image of the use of error corrections, but also an image of the other instructional components that allow teaching to mastery to take place (attentiveness of the students, clear teacher signals, a brisk pace, an inviting tone and demeanor, familiarity and fluency with the script, close monitoring of each student, use of motivation tools, etc.) – they will be much more likely to fully embrace the vision of teaching to mastery than if they only receive piecemeal feedback on their instruction throughout the school year. Even with a model of teaching to mastery in mind, most teachers will require at least a couple of years of practice and intense coaching before they can implement all of the techniques that allow all of their students to achieve mastery consistently. The use of show-off lessons provides an opportunity for teachers to practice a lesson with feedback until they are able to implement it flawlessly, which reinforces their confidence that they can teach everything to mastery. (See chapter 9 for information on show-off lessons.) For teachers who do not have access to coaching, the video in-services produced by NIFDI can provide guided practice on error corrections and other essential instructional procedures (see www.nifdi.org/videos/video-in-services-2.html).

#4: LETTING TIME GET LOST NEEDLESSLY

POTENTIAL PITFALL

As mentioned in chapter 1, the overriding goal of DI is to accelerate the performance of students, which S. Engelmann defined as "simply teaching more in less time" (Engelmann, S., 2014, 106). The design of the DI programs, DI teaching techniques, and many of the setup steps discussed in chapter 8 support the goal of teaching more in less time. However, in many classrooms where DI is used, time is not used efficiently. Two of the biggest sources of time inefficiency occur when students are not placed properly in the DI programs or not taught to mastery on every exercise in every lesson. In both of these cases, students must repeat lessons until they master the content, which can require spending additional days, weeks, or longer depending on the degree of misplacement and the lack of students' mastery of the material.

A more insidious source of inefficiency is the loss of time in small amounts throughout the instructional day. Instruction may start just a couple of minutes late because the teacher is still gathering materials after the class is supposed to have started. Students may take time to sharpen their pencils or find a specific-colored crayon. There may be a small dispute between two children about where to sit, or the teacher may wait on a couple of students to tie their shoes. Time loss can also occur throughout the lesson. There may be a lack of choral responses so material needs to be repeated. The teacher may go off script to talk with children in too much detail about the academic content. Transitions between exercises may be slow and laborious. There might be some distractions by students who are supposed to be engaged in independent work but are off task. Students may not be at mastery on routines and expectations, which requires the teacher to repeat directions several times.

IMPLICATIONS

Small time losses per day can lead to large losses of instructional time over the course of the school year, which can translate into significant gaps between what students actually achieve by the end of the school year and what they could have achieved with more actual instructional time. As mentioned in chapter 5, losing just six minutes of instruction a day with a student who started DI in kindergarten could mean the difference between performing at grade level and performing significantly below grade level by the time the student finishes Grade 5.

POSSIBLE SOLUTIONS

Specific solutions to the problem of time loss vary depending on the situation, but the general approach should be to:

1. identify potential sources of time loss
2. get ahead of the problem by establishing routines and expectations along with a system of reinforcement when students meet the expectations.

As described in chapter 5 and chapter 8, transitions into the instructional setting and between activities should be practiced to mastery at the beginning of the school year. Practicing these routines should be challenging yet fun for students at the same time if the teacher times the students and then challenges them to see if they can beat their best time right then or again the next day. Students should be reinforced for getting ready for instruction quickly and for transitioning between activities in a quick and orderly manner. Teachers must anticipate these transitions every day. With clear routines in place and an effective system for reinforcing students for following routines and expectations, instruction can get started quickly every day and last the entire period with students' full attention and effort.

#5: RUSHING THROUGH LESSONS WITH INSUFFICIENT THINK TIME

POTENTIAL PITFALL

Some teachers misinterpret the goal of accelerating student performance to mean that they should present lessons as quickly as possible at all times. They may increase their presentation pace past the optimal rate of delivery, which should involve *providing sufficient think time for students to produce the correct answer chorally as a group.* In addition to skimping on think time, rushing may also take the form of omitting parts of the full error correction procedure described in chapter 5. As indicated in Pitfall #3, omitting parts of the error correction will result in problems of student mastery, which should be avoided at all costs.

IMPLICATIONS

When students do not get the think time they require to formulate a response, the first-time correct percentage of the group's performance drops significantly as students make many more errors than they would if they had more time to think before responding to their teacher's signal. With more student errors, the teacher must spend more time providing error corrections and repeating exercises, which delays the group's progress through the program. So trying to go too quickly will actually slow down students' progress through the programs substantially. In addition, behavior problems may develop as a result of too little think time. Students can get discouraged and react in a variety of ways when they don't get enough think time. They may coat-tail their responses off other students, mouth a response but not really respond, turn their attention completely away from the group, or act out behaviorally. Repeating a high number of tasks and exercises can also discourage students as lessons take much longer than they would take if the students had sufficient time to think before they are required to respond.

POSSIBLE SOLUTIONS

The general rule for signaling is that *the teacher should adjust the think time according to the performance of the students, which may vary according to the specific instructional task.* The maximum think time for most material is three seconds, which is actually quite a bit of time for students to formulate a response. Teachers can practice counting "one thousand one, one thousand two, one thousand three" to themselves during practice sessions as they rehearse formats that are new or difficult for students. When teaching DI, the teacher can count in their head before signaling and then praise students when they respond together with the correct answer.

If students answer correctly with three seconds of think time, the teacher can present the exercise again with reduced think time immediately or later in the lesson. The teacher should present the shorter think time as a challenge to the students: "You answered perfectly! Now let's see if you can answer everything correctly when we go a little faster." If the students perform well with a faster pace, the faster pace should be the default for that type of exercise going forward. If individual students still have difficulty, the teacher should provide them with more practice with the slower think time but see if the amount of think time can be reduced in subsequent trials.

#6: TRYING TO "ENHANCE" THE INITIAL TEACHING IN THE DI PROGRAMS

POTENTIAL PITFALL

Many instructional programs are designed to be used as guides rather than as strict instructional sequences to be adhered to closely. As a result, teachers are used to enhancing instructional programs when teaching a skill or concept initially by introducing materials and engaging in activities in addition to those that appear in the instructional programs. In contrast, DI programs are designed to be all-inclusive, with all materials needed to meet the learning objectives successfully unless the scripts indicate that outside materials should be used. As mentioned in previous chapters, the DI programs have been tested and revised based on field tryouts to verify that students who meet the programs' prerequisites and are taught to mastery will learn the content successfully.

Although DI programs are designed to be stand-alone instructional programs with outside materials used very selectively, some teachers regularly make the mistake of providing more explanations and examples of concepts than what's in the DI programs when teaching a skill or concept initially.

IMPLICATIONS

If a teacher adds extra words to those that appear in the DI programs, students can get confused if the wording does not blend with the wording of the scripts, and progress through the program can be delayed. For example, if the word "rainy" appears in the program, a teacher may try to converse with students about how rainy the weather has been lately, which uses up precious instructional time. Or in reading, the teacher may try to teach the short sound /a/ by including the example of "*a* as in alligator." This distracts students from the lesson and may provide an inconsistent example that will confuse students. Teachers may also introduce terms earlier than the program introduces them, which wastes time and has the potential to confuse students because the preskills for understanding the term may not yet be fully taught. In the DI programs, students often learn concepts before they learn specific terms used for the concepts. They first learn concepts using words that are comprehensible to them rather than using terms that are new to the students.

Trying to teach a concept by immediately using a new term increases the chance of confusion. *When a new term and a new concept are introduced at the same time, students may misapprehend the term, the concept, or both.* The success of DI programs is founded on teaching students only one new item at a time and then *building on the knowledge that the teachers know the students know* to teach the next item in a carefully designed instructional sequence. For example, in *DISTAR Arithmetic I,* students learn the prerequisite concepts for subtracting before they learn conventional terms for subtracting. First, students learn to count forward from zero orally. Then, they learn to count forward using a number line, such as the following:

0 1 2 3 4 5 6 7 8

After they can count forward using a number line, they learn to count backward, which is defined in Lesson 67 of the program:

> When you count backward, you count *back* toward zero. (Engelmann, S. and Carnine, 1975, 62)

Students practice counting backward for 15 lessons before they are introduced to the term, *minus:*

> I'm going to **minus** some of the lines… Minuses tell you to count backward. (Engelmann, S. and Carnine, 1975, 64)

Students are able to understand and use the term *minus* successfully because they first learned a prerequisite concept using vocabulary that they understood (counting backward). If teachers immediately start to use the term *minus* on Lesson 67 when students are just learning the concept of counting backward, the potential for confusing students is high. Using other terms, such as *subtract* or *subtraction*, before they are introduced in the DI programs has an equally high potential for confusing children.

POSSIBLE SOLUTIONS

It is important for teachers to follow the DI scripts exactly except 1) when students make an error that indicates that they don't know a term that's used in the program, such as "truck" for students in the United Kingdom, who are familiar with the equivalent term, "lorry", and 2) to provide reinforcement for students beyond the positive statements that appear in the teacher presentation scripts. Teachers should become familiar with the entire scope and sequence of concepts taught (avoiding Pitfall #1) so they understand when and how specific terms will be introduced in the program. If state or national tests require the use of different terms, teachers should teach those terms outside of the DI period and well after students have mastered prerequisite concepts that are taught in the DI programs.

#7: NOT APPLYING WHAT STUDENTS LEARN IN THE DI PROGRAMS TO OTHER CONTEXTS

POTENTIAL PITFALL

The DI programs are designed to provide students with a firm foundation for further learning in a given subject area. Once students have learned a skill or concept and can apply it consistently during group instruction and independent work, the skill or concept should be in the teacher's repertoire to use in other learning activities – from field trips to projects to other (non-DI) curricula. This "generalization" of skills and concepts not only reinforces the skills and concepts students learn in the DI programs, but it also teaches the broader lesson to students that *whatever they learn can be applied to other areas of their lives beyond the instructional setting*, a lesson that can increase their confidence in themselves and their ability to succeed.

Unfortunately, many teachers miss opportunities to solidify and accelerate their students' academic growth by applying what students have learned in the DI programs to contexts outside of the DI instructional periods. They treat the DI programs as something distinct and separate from other learning that takes place at school or at home. They may layer on other teaching that covers the same topics or similar topics to those covered in the DI programs without making explicit connections or demonstrating how the content of the DI programs can be applied to other contexts.

IMPLICATIONS

When the integration of isolated "islands" of learning is left up to the students themselves, some students will be able to make a connection between what is taught in the DI programs and its applications to other contexts, but other students will not. Students who have had greater exposure to the skills and concepts outside of school are more likely to make these connections than those who have not had such opportunities. Thus, not explicitly making connections between what is taught in the DI programs and its applications to other contexts can have implications for equity in learning.

POSSIBLE SOLUTIONS

Teachers should become familiar with the opportunities for students to generalize their skills that already exist within the DI programs. The DI programs contain open-ended questions and extension activities that provide opportunities for students to apply what they've learned in the DI lessons. For open-ended questions during group instruction, teachers should encourage students to share their thoughts (as they monitor the duration and relevancy of students' responses). Teachers should provide feedback and follow-up questions designed to tie students' responses to the focus of the open-ended questions as needed.

Teachers should also keep the content of the DI programs in mind as they plan additional learning activities. For instance, if second-grade students are going to see a video on salamanders, the teacher can give a pop quiz and provide a quick review of what students already learned in the Grade 2 level of *Reading Mastery* about other amphibians (frogs and toads) before they watch the video. The teacher can then ask students to note similarities and differences between salamanders, frogs, and toads as they watch the video. After the video, the class can discuss the similarities and differences they observed, which further solidifies their knowledge of amphibians.

Teachers from the same grade can work together in brainstorming sessions on designing outside activities that make use of the content and skills students have already learned in the DI programs. Each teacher can screen a different outside grade-level book or web-based resource for students and share their analysis with their colleagues regarding the terms and concepts not covered in DI programs that would need to be "pre-taught" to the students before they could be expected to participate successfully in the activity. The teacher's guides for the different levels of the programs and specialized summaries of the content of the programs (*Literature in Reading Mastery Signature Edition* by NIFDI and *Science and Social Studies in Reading Mastery Signature Edition* by Nancy Woolfson) are useful tools to have on hand when planning additional activities. Designing additional activities with explicit connections to the content and skills covered in the DI program can be a very satisfying outlet for teachers' creativity.

In addition to planning activities that make explicit connections to the skills and content in the DI programs, teachers should be on the lookout for spontaneous, unplanned opportunities to make connections between the content students learn and the world around them. Topics in the news, the personal experiences of students, or events at school can provide opportunities to reinforce and expand students' knowledge of the content they learn in the DI programs. If students just learned the term "envelope" and a student walks into the classroom with an oversized mailing envelope for the teacher, this provides an opportunity for a quick demonstration that envelopes can be large and come in different colors, not just be plain and letter-sized. If someone arrives at school on a hoverboard, the teacher can pose the question to students "is a hoverboard a vehicle?" and ask them to apply the rule they learned in the *Reading Mastery* language program: "if it's made to take you places, it's a vehicle."

Teachers should endeavor to make spontaneous, unplanned connections between the DI content and the students' world as brief as possible while still being effective in expanding students' learning. These connections should be made after students have thoroughly learned the concepts introduced in the DI programs. Otherwise, teachers may experience Pitfall #6, confusing students while trying to "enhance" the initial teaching that takes place in the DI programs.

#8: NOT MOTIVATING STUDENTS TO LEARN

POTENTIAL PITFALL

As discussed in chapter 5, managing student behavior is an integral part of DI, as students must be motivated to focus their attention for long periods of time, respond frequently, and repeat material to mastery. Although students experience intrinsic satisfaction in mastering the skills and concepts taught in the DI programs, students may also experience difficulty at times, which requires teachers to have an effective behavior management system for motivating students to keep trying, even when they don't master skills and concepts the first time they go through an exercise. The system should also reinforce students for adhering to rules and procedures the teacher has established, with the goal of maximizing learning time as well as making instruction highly efficient and rewarding for students.

Unfortunately, some teachers establish systems and patterns of interaction that are more punitive than reinforcing by taking on the role of a "taskmaster" in an effort not only to eliminate disruptions to instruction, but also to eliminate any unwanted behavior. "Taskmaster" teachers impose a highly rigid set of expectations that are much more demanding than those needed for effective instruction to occur. In doing so, they interrupt the flow of instruction to focus on such irrelevant and inconsequential "infractions" as students not having both feet flat on the ground, not having their fingers interlocked during group board work, or tapping on the desk softly with their hand. Although students may be trying hard to meet their teacher's expectations, the "taskmaster" consistently provides feedback at a ratio that is far below the 4:1 positive-to-negative ratio that has been demonstrated to reinforce learners for appropriate behavior.

IMPLICATIONS

The taskmaster approach to teaching may result in students who are very attentive to the teacher's requirements, but it does not facilitate maximizing student progress through the DI programs at mastery. Instructional groups in such classroom environments do not move through the program quickly and reliably. The taskmaster teacher's attempt to extinguish all unwanted behavior (not just behavior that interferes with students' learning) slows down instruction rather than maximizing the pace of instruction. Moreover, with a low ratio of positive-to-negative feedback, students may anticipate that they will be criticized for their behavior during the lesson, which interferes with their concentration on instructional tasks. They may make more errors than usual, which results in more error corrections and an even more negative experience for them.

In extreme cases, the taskmaster approach may lead to serious disruptions to instruction as students' frustrations boil over. Negative behaviors can be expected to increase in frequency if there is a lack of attention to "catching kids in the act of being good," a technique described in chapter 5. A preponderance of negative feedback can lead to an adversarial relationship between the teacher and students, with the teacher expecting students to act out and the students expecting the teacher to react negatively to what they do. In these extreme cases, students do not leave school each day thinking that they have worked hard and learned a lot (an important psychological component of any successful DI implementation), and they carry a negative attitude toward school with them when they return to school the next day. Eventually, the result can be a complete breakdown in the flow of instruction as the focus of instructional periods becomes students' lack of compliance to rules and directions as the teacher responds to students' perceived or actual misbehavior.

POSSIBLE SOLUTIONS

Effective behavioral management requires training, support, and practice (in setting up behavioral expectations, reinforcing students for meeting the expectations, ignoring minor behaviors, and reinforcing students for their efforts as well as their accomplishments). Challenging students to "get things right the first time" and reinforcing them heavily for doing so can increase their focus and attention dramatically. Students won't answer correctly the first time every time, but reinforcing them to work hard to do so can help create a very positive classroom climate. The use of behavioral management tools, such as those discussed in chapter 5 (the "Pencils Up/Pencils Down" game, the Teacher/Student game, and the thermometer chart system for independent work) can help teachers motivate students and promote a positive classroom climate. The use of visual representations of students' accomplishments either as points (as in the Teacher/Student game) or as strips (as in the thermometer chart system) can help prompt teachers to pair the awarding of points and strips with positive praise. The visual tools can also signal school leaders that a problem of motivation in a classroom exists (for example, if there are more teacher points than student points or the number of strips on a thermometer chart are low). Recording a session – either an audio or video recording – can help teachers identify when they were being overcritical with students and when they missed opportunities to provide positive reinforcement without interrupting the flow of instruction.

Successful behavior management is facilitated by a goal-oriented relationship between teachers and their students. By explicitly stating a goal for the class, such as getting a set of tasks correct the first time or finishing the grade-level program before the end of the school year, the teacher provides an overarching reason for rules and procedures to exist: the students must abide by the rules and expectations so instruction is efficient and the group can attain the end-of-year goal. If students try their best every day, the teacher will help them reach their goal. Attaining end-of-year goals involves delayed reinforcement that should be supplemented with intermediate goals and celebrations, especially for younger students or students who have experienced academic failure in the past. Without a clearly articulated goal – along with clear evidence of progress toward the goal – instruction has the potential of devolving into a mundane set of procedures and conventions that are followed by staff and students ritualistically for their own sake rather than used as an inspired means of achieving academic success.

Note that placement and teaching to mastery are fundamental prerequisites to making instruction reinforcing to students. Even experienced teachers using a well-implemented positive behavior management system will not be able to make learning fun for students who are seriously misplaced in the program. Ensuring that students are placed properly initially in DI and then taught to mastery daily will lay the foundation for teachers to provide reinforcement to students at a 4:1 positive-to-negative ratio or higher.

#9: NOT RECORDING DATA ACCURATELY

POTENTIAL PITFALL

In-program assessments and independent work provide very useful sources of information to teachers and school leaders on the performance of individual students in the DI programs. Along with in-class observations, these sources of recorded data allow school leaders to monitor instruction effectively and identify potential problems of implementation in a timely manner. However, effective monitoring can take place only when data forms are complete and reliable, as indicated in chapter 9. Unfortunately, some teachers do not fill out the data forms completely and correctly. In these cases, the data do not reflect students' mastery and progress through the programs and cannot be used to identify and remediate problems of instruction effectively.

When recording student performance data, teachers may not understand the critical role that each piece of information plays in managing the implementation of DI across the school. Unless they understand the important role that data play in identifying problems in their own groups and in directing coaching and training resources, they may feel that filling out the data forms is a menial task that is not worth the time and effort.

IMPLICATIONS

If student performance data are unreliable, teachers and leaders are forced to drive the DI automobile with a muddy windshield. School leaders will have to rely on classroom observations or teachers' reports exclusively to determine how well students are performing. Leaders will only be able to identify problems that they observe directly or that teachers report to them, which greatly limits the scope of potential problems that can be identified. This is especially true if teachers are new to DI and can't be expected to identify problems with their implementation of DI when they are just getting used to teaching with DI. If the leadership does not have access to data on the performance of instructional groups across the school, it may not allocate the school's limited coaching and training resources in the most effective way. If leaders do not happen to visit a classroom where students are struggling, they will not know that there is a problem of instruction in the classroom. Thus, in a large-scale implementation, the leadership's ability to catch serious problems of instruction is extremely limited without reliable student performance data as the leadership's time for conducting observations is spread over a greater number of classrooms.

POSSIBLE SOLUTIONS

School leaders should explain how data can be used within each classroom and across the school to make decisions on identifying potential problems of instruction – how accurate and complete data allow teachers to assess student mastery and lesson progress and leaders to then prioritize classrooms for in-class observations, training, and support based on student performance. If the school uses an external support provider (ESP), the ESP can conduct a special training on completing data so teachers have the technical knowledge to fill out the forms correctly. Teachers can be paired with each other as "data buddies" to provide feedback and support to each other on completing data forms correctly before they are collected by the building coordinator. Incentives, such as gift cards, can be given to teachers who complete the forms accurately, completely and consistently. School leaders can also invite teachers to attend a weekly problem-solving session so they can observe how leaders use student performance data to identify problems and direct coaching and training resources.

#10: NOT REALIZING THAT IT TAKES A LOT TO BECOME SKILLED IN DI

POTENTIAL PITFALL

A potential pitfall that underlies several of the pitfalls listed above is *assuming that DI is easy to teach*. While it is true that the scripts eliminate the need for teachers to make many decisions – about the examples used, the order of the concepts introduced, and the specific instructional wording – there is still a great deal more for teachers to learn about teaching the DI programs successfully. As mentioned above, the presentation of each of the instructional tasks and the correction of the full range of possible student errors for each of the tasks require considerable practice. The factors that allow for focused instruction to take place – placement and grouping, classroom setup, positive behavioral management, and data collection and analysis – also require considerable learning and practice. Problem solving, which integrates all of these knowledge areas, requires teachers to develop a hypothesis about a problem of student learning and test a remedy to see if it resolves the problem. Thus, the most successful DI teachers realize that there is much to learn within and without the DI programs that they never learned at university, such as formulating a hypothesis and testing it rather than just implementing a set formula for a given situation.

IMPLICATIONS

If a teacher assumes that there is little to learn about DI because the lessons are scripted, student outcomes can be expected to be mixed. Students who are well placed in the program initially and are naturally attentive and motivated to learn should be successful with DI as long as their teacher follows the script closely. But the outcomes of students who experience difficulty with parts of the program for behavioral issues, absences, lack of attentiveness, or other reasons will probably not achieve their full potential with instruction from a teacher who simply limits themselves to learning the DI basics and apathetically following the scripts. So a teacher's commitment to lifelong professional learning with DI has implications for students' access to a high-quality education and the equitable treatment of all students.

POSSIBLE SOLUTIONS

For students to reach their full potential with DI, it is important for instructional staff to function as a learning community invested in helping each other increase their knowledge of DI and how to apply it most effectively to every student. The specific arrangement and activities of the learning community will depend on the structure of DI at the school – the grades, subject areas, and staff members involved. The broader the implementation of DI, the more the DI community can be synonymous with the school's professional community, and, hence, the easier it is to integrate DI into the schoolwide planning of professional development.

The weekly practice sessions described elsewhere provide one forum for increasing the staff's knowledge of DI. These can be accompanied by other types of professional development. Here are some other examples of ways to build a DI professional learning community:

- A weekly focus across the staff on specific skills (e.g. this week the focus is on *think time* while next week the focus will be on *specific positive praise*)
- Grade-level meetings that focus on the status of DI, specific problems that students and staff encounter, and how to resolve those problems
- Viewing and discussing videos from the NIFDI website (along with the matching study guide)
- Discussing selected readings, such as *Clear Teaching* or *Successful and Confident Students with Direct Instruction* (along with the matching study guide)
- Site visits to a model school
- Attending peer coaches training, described in chapter 10, which provides advanced insights into implementing DI effectively
- Attending other types of advanced training, such as the Coaching Institute or the Institute on Becoming an Effective DI Trainer, which are part of the National Direct Instruction Conference held annually in Eugene, Oregon in late July.

Some of the items listed above can be implemented without the involvement of school leaders, but most of them require the leaders' involvement and support. Indeed, school leaders play an essential role in establishing the conditions for teachers to be able to reflect on their practice and implement DI fully. The pitfalls that school leaders should avoid in implementing DI are the subject of the next chapter.

CHAPTER TWELVE
POTENTIAL PITFALLS FOR SCHOOL LEADERS TO AVOID

This chapter presents the top 10 most common pitfalls that instructional leaders may encounter when implementing Direct Instruction (DI). Several of these pitfalls are directly related to the most common pitfalls for teachers to avoid, discussed in the previous chapter. Most of the pitfalls listed in this chapter are under the control of school leaders exclusively, but some of them, including Pitfall #3 (not scheduling sufficient instructional time) and Pitfall #4 (overlaying multiple instructional programs), are also heavily influenced by district or state requirements that school leaders must satisfy.

Here are the most common pitfalls for school leaders to try to avoid, which are explained in detail later in the chapter:

1. Not providing clear and consistent support for the DI implementation (over-delegating)
2. Failing to set a clear directive to the staff to implement DI with fidelity from the beginning
3. Not allocating sufficient instructional time in the daily schedule
4. Overlaying multiple instructional programs covering the same academic subjects
5. Not placing students at their skill level and ensuring they are taught to mastery every day
6. Assigning the least experienced teachers to the most difficult classrooms

7. Not identifying and using model classrooms
8. Not determining the root cause of student performance problems
9. Not celebrating success in DI sufficiently
10. Not explaining the DI implementation adequately to other stakeholders.

#1: NOT PROVIDING CLEAR AND CONSISTENT SUPPORT FOR THE DI IMPLEMENTATION (OVER-DELEGATING)

POTENTIAL PITFALL

For schoolwide implementations of DI, the involvement of the school principal as the instructional leader is the number one reason for a successful or unsuccessful DI implementation in the long run. The instructional schedule, student grouping, professional development, material acquisition, data collection, and several other aspects of the implementation must be centrally coordinated in order for a schoolwide DI implementation to be successful. Expectations of the staff must be established clearly from the beginning to ensure that all teachers understand what's required to maximize student achievement across the school (see chapter 8). Student performance and teacher delivery of the program must be monitored closely (see chapter 9) and data responded to actively in case there needs to be a "course correction" with the implementation (see chapter 10). These functions must be directed by the instructional leader of the school, i.e. the principal, who must make critical decisions at every phase of the DI implementation for it to be successful.

Unfortunately, many principals are not involved or only marginally involved in the implementation of DI at their schools. They may play an active role in the initial adoption of DI, and perhaps they may also be actively involved in the first year of the implementation, but their involvement diminishes over time as more and more implementation components that require the attention of the school's instructional leader are delegated to others, or essential duties are simply not performed by anyone at the school.

IMPLICATIONS

Without clear and consistent support from the principal, a schoolwide DI implementation is limited in what it can achieve because it requires the cooperation and coordination of the entire staff to be successful. Differing opinions among the staff and different preferences for specific procedures will likely cause the implementation to fray, with negative results for student outcomes. If the principal is not involved, some teachers may choose to abandon the full error correction procedure, for example, while others may choose to place students at their grade level, not their performance level. Some teachers may even reject the feedback of coaches or refuse to record student performance data on the forms provided. The result can be a hodge-podge of instructional practices across the school that do not help students develop essential academic skills consistently and do not provide them with a firm foundation for future learning.

Even if a DI implementation is well implemented for a couple of years at a school, it is very difficult to sustain over time without clear and consistent support from the principal. When new staff members are hired, they need to receive the same training and onsite coaching the original cohort of teachers received so they can be successful with DI and the implementation can maintain a high level of fidelity. In addition to training and coaching, the new staff needs to learn the rationale for DI conventions, and they need to understand the history of DI at the school so they are aware of the before-and-after effects of DI on their student population.

POSSIBLE SOLUTIONS

To ensure a successful schoolwide implementation of DI, the role of each member of the leadership team needs to be clear to the teachers, and the leadership team needs to act consistently in the implementation phases of setup, monitoring, and responding actively. The principal needs to assume a role in all three of these functions, even if another staff member in the building or the district is the primary coordinator of the DI implementation. The principal must be directly involved in the system of monitoring and responding actively, even though other staff members may spend much more time supporting the DI implementation. The principal must be aware of the rationale for the program and the requirements for its success so they can share this information with the staff.

A principal may not be heavily involved in a small-scale implementation of DI, such as a DI implementation in a resource room or a single grade level, but it should be clear to all involved which staff member is primarily in charge of supporting the DI implementation. After a building coordinator or peer coaches have been selected, the principal cannot hand over the management of the implementation to them completely and then not have any further involvement. The principal should still have well-established touchpoints with the building coordinator or peer coaches regardless of the size of the implementation. Also, the principal should still visit classrooms regularly, even for two minutes at a time. Sometimes the principal can accompany the building coordinator or peer coaches, and other times the principal can conduct observations alone. The two-minute observation described in chapter 9 was created so that even the busiest principals would have time to get into classrooms several times a week to observe the level of engagement of students, which is a good initial criterion for determining whether a problem exists in a classroom.

In large, schoolwide implementations of DI, there may be several layers of coaching and management, especially if the district is involved in supporting the implementation directly. For example, the activities of several peer coaches may be coordinated by an assistant principal, who, in turn, receives support from a district-level coordinator. The more complex the management system, the greater the need to define clearly the roles that each person plays in the system. This support plan should be explained to any new staff during their job interview or new-hire orientation. The plan should be revised to accommodate any changes in leadership, with the changes communicated to all staff involved in the implementation during staff meetings.

#2: FAILING TO SET A CLEAR DIRECTIVE TO THE STAFF TO IMPLEMENT DI WITH FIDELITY FROM THE BEGINNING

POTENTIAL PITFALL

In some cases, school leaders may try to ease the staff into the implementation of DI rather than implement all aspects of the DI model fully from the beginning. They may attempt to implement the DI approach piecemeal in the school initially and introduce other aspects of the approach over time. For instance, school leaders may permit teachers to use non-DI programs alongside DI programs to teach the same subject area. Or they may not expect teachers to correct all response errors or require all students to answer in unison during group instruction. The thought behind this approach is that teachers might rebel if they are required to implement DI with fidelity from the beginning because DI involves so many practices that might seem unusual to teachers and too drastic for them to implement fully from the start. According to this approach, teachers might be more willing to implement DI if they are allowed to decide for themselves which aspects of the DI approach they want to adopt initially. After they have experienced success with some aspects of DI, such as choral responses, they may be more receptive to other aspects of the approach.

IMPLICATIONS

Trying to implement DI piecemeal is never successful because it diminishes the effectiveness of the program. When teachers only implement some aspects of DI and not others, lesson progress at mastery is undermined. For example, if a teacher uses a non-DI program alongside a DI program to teach the same topic, students may not have enough time in DI to make adequate progress in the program. Even if there is sufficient time in the daily schedule for DI, students may get confused by the different conventions used in DI versus the non-DI programs. If the teacher does not require all students to answer in unison during group instruction on an exercise, more time will be required to determine whether students have mastered the skills covered in the exercise later in the day. If the teacher does not correct all response errors, students will not master the fundamental skills that are used as building blocks for future learning in the DI programs.

As discussed elsewhere in this book, each of the DI programs introduces fundamental skills and concepts initially that serve as building blocks for more advanced skills and applications. *Seeing students acquire advanced skills and apply their knowledge in new contexts is most convincing to teachers of the efficacy of the DI approach.* Teachers are impressed when they see their students acquire fundamental skills; they are even more impressed (and more supportive of the DI approach) when they observe students acquiring advanced skills through DI. For example, teachers are much more impressed with students reading connected text fluently and comprehending stories than they are with students mastering pre-reading skills (identifying the sounds letters make and blending sounds together to form words). If students are still at the pre-reading stage after several months, teachers may conclude that the program should be used as a supplement and not for core instruction because it covers only basic content.

If DI is not implemented with fidelity from the beginning, it will not have the desired effect, which will undermine the staff's confidence that it will "work" sufficiently well for their students. They may ask themselves why they should follow all of these strange conventions if they are not going to have a markedly positive effect on their students. After several weeks, they may stop implementing the parts of the program that they had earlier implemented with fidelity, which will result in a vicious circle of low changes in student performance and teachers deciding to abandon aspects of the DI approach.

POSSIBLE SOLUTIONS

In order for DI to be highly successful for all children, all components of the DI programs must be implemented with fidelity as described in earlier chapters of this book. A key leadership responsibility is to prepare the staff to implement DI with fidelity from the start of the school year. Regardless of whether the staff has a say in adopting DI at their school, leaders (or an external support provider at the school leaders' request) should explain the rationale for each of the components of DI to the staff. If the staff is allowed to vote, and if the predetermined threshold for adoption has been reached in support of implementing DI (such as 80% in favor), the program should be implemented completely at whatever scale that's been decided upon. All staff members will need to give the program their full support and implement it with fidelity, not just the staff members who voted for it. Staff members who are initially resistant to implementing DI usually become supportive of it after seeing firsthand how well the program works with their students. Therefore, an important leadership objective of the first few months of implementation should be for all teachers to implement the program with fidelity so they can see that all of their students will be successful with DI.

An important distinction needs to be drawn between "easing into" DI and implementing DI in stages. As described in earlier chapters, implementing DI in stages through an initial pilot may be a desirable approach for various reasons, such as financial cost or as a way to demonstrate the efficacy of the approach to hesitant staff members. In many cases, schools adopt the reading and language programs during the first year of a DI implementation and mathematics and spelling during the second year so the staff does not become overwhelmed with too many DI programs at once. For implementations that are less than schoolwide, students should receive the same instruction for the same amount of time that they would receive in a schoolwide, full-immersion implementation. In other words, DI should be implemented with complete fidelity for a pilot of the program and then for each stage of a multi-year schoolwide expansion of DI.

Easing into the implementation should be avoided for positive behavior practices as well as for DI practices. Whatever behavioral rules and expectations that are going to be implemented along with DI should be implemented fully for the grade levels of the students who are identified to receive DI. Positive behavioral practices, such as those described in chapter 5, can be implemented the year before DI is adopted so students understand their teachers' expectations clearly and are reinforced for meeting those expectations, which will allow for a smoother implementation of DI.

To maintain a consensus of staff in support of the DI implementation, the principal may need to reassign staff members to non-DI areas of the school if they decide that DI is not a good fit for them. Sometimes staff members don't realize the day-to-day implications of implementing DI, even if they have been presented with an overview of their responsibilities and shown a video of a DI lesson in action. These staff members may request to be transferred out of the grades that are implementing DI. If they don't request a transfer to another grade, the principal can reiterate the expectations of implementing DI. However, if they still demonstrate an unwillingness to follow the program's requirements consistently, the principal should transfer any staff member who is not willing to implement DI with fidelity out of the grades where DI is being implemented. If the implementation of DI is schoolwide, and there are no positions within the school that do not involve implementing DI, the principal should take steps to replace the staff member. The entire DI implementation may be jeopardized if the staff member is not removed, as described in chapter 8. The process of ensuring full staff support for the model should take place early in the school year to lessen the impact on student performance if replacing a staff member becomes necessary.

#3: NOT ALLOCATING SUFFICIENT INSTRUCTIONAL TIME IN THE DAILY SCHEDULE

POTENTIAL PITFALL

Students not receiving sufficient time in the DI programs daily is one of the most common and serious problems for school leaders to guard against in a DI implementation. As described in chapter 8, time requirements vary greatly depending on the program being implemented. Daily time requirements range from a low of 20 minutes for the Basic Fractions module of *Corrective Mathematics* to 150 minutes for the first two levels of *Reading Mastery* (90 minutes of reading, language, and independent work in the morning and 60 minutes in the afternoon). Often, school leaders adopt the programs without being aware of the time requirements and their implications for the school's overall daily schedule. As a result, leaders may try to fit the instruction of the programs into pre-existing schedules that do not correspond to the time requirements for the DI programs. For example, pre-existing schedules rarely include a second reading period for students who place into the first two levels of *Reading Mastery*, which is essential for accelerating students' acquisition of fundamental reading skills.

Sometimes schools (especially middle or secondary schools) use block schedules with alternating subjects on different days. These schedules may contain the same amount of total time per week that students will receive in DI if time is allocated as recommended in the teacher's guides, but students only receive instruction in DI every other day.

A related problem is the time scheduled for test preparation. A reasonable goal is for students to become familiar with the format of high-stakes tests that they will take as part of state or national requirements. However, many schools spend time on test prep activities all year long, with the amount of time allocated to test prep increasing over the course of the school year until the students take the tests, usually in the spring.

In addition, some school leaders cancel DI to hold assemblies or other events that do not further the academic learning of students. In these schools, instructional time that is lost to assemblies is never made up.

IMPLICATIONS

Not having a regular, daily schedule with sufficient time in the DI programs limits the positive effects of DI on students' acquisition of essential academic skills. If instruction doesn't occur daily, students don't get the distributed practice they may need to master the skills that are introduced in the DI programs. They will have difficulty recalling information and achieving automaticity, which is essential for future skill acquisition. In most school schedules, students already have a break in instruction for two days over the weekend. If instruction doesn't occur daily during the five weekdays, the weekend break may functionally expand to more than two days if DI is not scheduled for a Monday or a Friday. If, for example, DI is scheduled for Monday through Thursday, students will go three days before they receive instruction in DI again. A longer break from DI that includes the weekend increases the challenge for students to master skills as they are being introduced. Moreover, if students are absent for a day or two, the negative effect on their ability to learn and retain information is accentuated with a schedule that does not provide DI daily. This longer gap requires the teacher to spend more time repeating and reviewing material than if students receive DI daily during the work week.

For young and/or struggling learners, the need for distributed practice is even greater, which is why two instructional periods per day by the same instructor are needed for students who place into the lower two levels of *Reading Mastery* or *Corrective Reading Decoding*. Afternoon sessions help students retain and build upon the skills and concepts introduced in the morning. Without the second reading period, students' progress through the program at mastery will be delayed.

If there isn't sufficient time for students to get through a lesson during an instructional period, they may have to repeat parts of the same lesson during the next instructional period. This is because exercises that appear early in a lesson often lay the basis for students to perform well on exercises that appear later in the same lesson. For instance, in the early part of the kindergarten level of *Reading Mastery Signature Edition* (RMSE), a sound identification exercise appears at the beginning of each lesson to ensure that students are firm on the sounds the symbols make before they encounter an exercise that requires them to blend the sounds together to form words. Later in the program, when students read connected text, word attack exercises precede stories in the lessons to ensure that students will be able to read the stories with a high rate of accuracy. If there is not sufficient time in the schedule for students to finish a lesson during an instructional period, the teacher may have to repeat sound identification exercises for students who are in the beginning part of RMSE Grade K and word attack exercises for students who are in higher levels of the program.

Spending time on test preparation beyond familiarizing students with the format of the tests can seriously detract from students' acquisition of essential academic skills. Teaching unfamiliar formats of high-stakes tests to students should only require a few hours per week for up to a month or so prior to the administration of the tests. Students who are already familiar with the testing formats will require a much briefer review of the specific formats that they can be expected to encounter on the tests. If time is taken away from the DI subjects for students to spend more time than is needed to learn the format of the tests, their rate of learning the essential skills and concepts in the DI programs will be delayed needlessly, and, ironically, their performance on the high-stakes tests may suffer as a result.

Excessive test prep in place of DI can also have a negative effect on student morale. For instance, the self-image of middle school students who are in *Decoding B1* and are making strong progress in the program in late autumn may be positive for the first time in their school careers as they experience the joy of "cracking the code" of reading. But if instruction in the program is delayed while students engage in test prep for several weeks, they may not be able to reach the goal of finishing the B1 program and completing the next level of the program, B2, by the end of the school year. Moreover, they will make many more errors on test prep, which is geared toward their grade level, than in the *Corrective Reading* program, which is geared toward their skill level. Thus, prolonged exposure to grade-level test prep has the potential of undermining students' newfound self-confidence with DI as it reinforces their former belief that they are unskilled and cannot be successful at school. The longer they spend in the grade-level material, the greater their morale may be eroded and the positive momentum they experienced with DI will be dampened.

Not having a regular, daily schedule with sufficient time in the DI programs limits the positive effects of DI on *teachers' acquisition of essential teaching skills* as well as the positive effects of DI on *students' acquisition of essential academic skills*. When there is not sufficient time to get through a lesson every day, there is less time for teachers to become familiar with critical instructional formats. They encounter the formats less frequently due to the slow pace of progress through the lessons, which makes it more difficult for teachers to see how the exercises change and incorporate more advanced content over time. The preservice (program) training that teachers receive (described in chapter 8) is usually designed to focus on the first 30 lessons of a DI program, but if the students do not reach Lesson 30 for a few months because of the slow rate of lesson progress, the teachers may not retain the skills they mastered during preservice for delivering the exercises up through Lesson 30. As a result, they will need to relearn the formats of these exercises to deliver them successfully to their students.

POSSIBLE SOLUTIONS

To maximize students' acquisition of skills and concepts with DI, instruction should take place daily for the optimal amount of time indicated in the teacher's guide for each program. Before adopting DI, school leaders should review the time requirements for the different programs as described in the relevant teacher's guides and the *Program Reference Chart* (NIFDI, 2023) and create daily schedules that incorporate these requirements. School leaders may need to be creative to find sufficient time for DI as the daily schedule may also need to meet state or national time requirements for other subjects as well as incorporate such "specials" as music and art. The instructional staff can be brought into the process of creating ideal schedules, which will foster staff buy-in and help ensure that they adhere to the instructional schedules. Optimally, this process should take place long before the start of the school year so the staff is fully aware of daily schedule expectations.

If there is a block schedule of alternating days, leaders should schedule DI for each day. Sometimes elective periods can be repurposed for DI at the middle and secondary school levels. If, for some reason, the full required time for DI cannot be scheduled every day, leaders can insert some additional instructional time during an intervention period. Some schools have incorporated math facts practice for a few minutes for students in *Corrective Mathematics* during their homeroom period, which meets daily.

Sometimes, school leaders may need to prioritize the allocation of time to the neediest students. If only one group can receive a second dose during an intervention period, the period should be provided to the lowest-performing group. The allocation of the extra intervention period can be reassessed after each semester and reassigned to another group as needed. If an assembly regarding safety protocols or some other essential topic can only take place during the time usually reserved for DI, the instructional time should be made up during another part of the day, if possible. Making up for lost time communicates to the staff and students that academic learning is of paramount importance to the school administration and to the entire school community.

Scheduling should also include time for teachers to participate in structured practice sessions, which should occur at least twice a week for the first year of implementation of DI and more often as needed, as mentioned in chapter 8. Grade-level planning times that are in pre-existing schedules can be repurposed for the practice sessions once the DI implementation starts.

As discussed in chapter 8, placement testing should take place in the spring to allow time for ordering materials. Placement testing in the spring also allows adjustments to be made in schedules and personnel assignments before the start of the next school year. As mentioned earlier, two instructional periods per day by the same instructor are needed for students who place into the lower two levels of *Reading Mastery* and the lower two levels of *Corrective Reading Decoding*. If students place into these levels of the programs, the schedules must be adjusted to provide a second reading period. The grouping requirements, as well as the time requirements for the DI programs, differ by level, which can have profound implications for the schedule of specific staff members if students place into the lower levels of programs vs. higher levels of the programs.

Leaders must know and be able to present the rationale for the new schedule to the staff and parents of the students. For instance, leaders should be able to explain to parents that students who place into such basic programs as *Direct Instruction Spoken English* (DISE) and *Corrective Reading Decoding* Levels A and B1 will not be able to participate successfully in content courses until they acquire fundamental skills that are taught in these programs. Consequently, students may not receive instruction in all content courses as they receive an extra period of instruction in the DI programs instead. Once students have mastered the fundamental skills that are taught in these levels of the programs and have advanced to higher levels, the amount of time in DI will be reduced. The students can then attend the content course(s) they missed earlier. Leaders must also be able to articulate to staff the reasons for limiting test prep so as much time as possible is available for instruction. This will accelerate students' progress through the DI programs at mastery as a means of increasing students' acquisition of essential skills and knowledge needed for their long-term academic success.

#4: OVERLAYING MULTIPLE INSTRUCTIONAL PROGRAMS COVERING THE SAME ACADEMIC SUBJECTS

POTENTIAL PITFALL

A common reason for reducing the amount of time with DI is to provide instruction in another curriculum that addresses the same content covered by a DI program. The assumption is that different programs will provide different learning opportunities using different methodologies, which, purportedly, will strengthen student learning because the students will have the benefit of multiple approaches to the same subject matter. This pitfall has much in common with Teacher Pitfall #6, discussed in the previous chapter: trying to "enhance" the initial teaching in the DI programs by introducing materials and engaging in activities in addition to those that appear in the DI program.

IMPLICATIONS

As mentioned in the previous pitfall, if the time scheduled for DI does not meet the program's requirements, students' progress through DI will be negatively impacted. But even if the amount of time allocated to DI is not reduced, using another curriculum that addresses the same content covered by a DI program has the potential to confuse students and thereby impede their acquisition of essential skills and knowledge. This is especially true during the initial teaching of a skill or concept. For adults who have already mastered a given skill or body of knowledge, the use of different methodologies might seem a positive way to "enrich" children's learning. However, the use of different methodologies can have a bewildering effect on learners who are being introduced to a specific skill or concept for the first time, with the potential of frustrating them and reducing their enthusiasm for the subject. For instance, children who receive instruction in the kindergarten level of *Reading Mastery Signature Edition* (RMSE) are not taught the names of letters, as mentioned previously. Instead, they are taught the sounds the letter symbols make. If children are introduced to letter names in another reading program before they master them in the Grade 1 level of the RMSE program, the children may get confused by the differences between sounds and letter names. Another example is teaching students how to carry values during column addition. If students are required to work addition problems involving carrying in a non-DI program at the same time that they are being taught the careful, scaffolded steps for carrying values in *Corrective Mathematics*, as described in chapter 2 of this book, the potential for confusing and frustrating the students is high. *The potential to confuse students applies to any new content that is being introduced to students for the first time.*

POSSIBLE SOLUTIONS

It is vitally important that students are taught one and only one procedure when they are first introduced to a skill. Once students have learned such skills as carrying values during column addition in *Corrective Mathematics*, they can use that skill successfully in a variety of other contexts. With a strong foundation built through step-by-step learning in the DI programs, students can learn other content that presumes mastery of the skills students master in the DI programs. So before being introduced to another program that presupposes specific skills, it is important to ensure that students master all of the skills taught in the DI programs that are necessary for them to be successful in other programs or outside activities. For any activity outside of the DI programs, teachers should ensure that students have the skills to participate successfully. If these skills are taught in the DI programs, school leaders should direct teachers to wait to introduce the non-DI activity until after students reach the point in the program where they have mastered these skills.

If more instructional time is available for a subject, then the entire time should be dedicated to teaching the DI programs. The farther students progress in a DI program, the higher their grade-level performance will be. If more than one curriculum must be used for the same subject area with the same students, then the implementation should be sequential and not simultaneous. School leaders should engage teachers and other staff to conduct a content analysis of the two curricula. An overview of the content of any DI program can be found in the teacher's guides and series guides, which include a "scope and sequence" chart of the content covered in the program. The content analysis should involve identifying the lessons in which specific instructional tracks end in the DI programs and the content of activities in the non-DI programs that assume students have mastered the specific skills taught in the DI programs. In the example of beginning reading, the use of a non-DI program that involves letter names should occur only after students learn letter names in the Grade 1 level of RMSE. In the example of column addition, the use of a non-DI program that involves carrying should occur only after students learn the full series of steps taught for carrying values in the addition module of *Corrective Mathematics*.

When considering the use of a non-DI curriculum, school leaders can ask themselves the following questions:

- *Does the non-DI program cover similar skills to the DI programs?* If the two programs cover similar skills and content, there's no need to use two different programs. Using two different approaches has the potential to confuse students as well as delay their progress through the programs. So instead of accelerating the students' academic growth by using multiple programs, students' growth is stunted in comparison to what students could achieve with a pure DI implementation.

- *Are students able to participate fully in the activities outlined in the non-DI programs?* For the content that is unique to the non-DI program and not covered by the DI program, the leadership should check to see whether the students have the prerequisite skills to participate in these activities. If they do not have the prerequisite skills in their repertoire currently, will they acquire them through the DI program? Students may be able to participate in certain activities later in the school year after they've mastered specific skills taught in the DI programs. The leadership should also analyze the content of grade-level standards to determine which activities required by the state are best to take place later in the school year.

The answers to these questions and any other content analysis can be generated by grade-level teams of teachers, whose work should be shared with any new hires so they understand the relationship between DI and other curricula that the school uses.

Note that the DI curricula contain advanced content and activities that the lessons build toward over the course of a program level. Without a careful analysis of the content of the DI programs, teachers and school leaders might not realize that the DI programs contain activities that are functionally similar to some of the advanced activities in non-DI programs. These activities may be structured differently or use different nomenclature than those in the non-DI program. Once the students master these activities in the DI programs, they can be shown an alternative way of approaching the same topic as it appears in the non-DI programs.

#5: NOT PLACING STUDENTS AT THEIR SKILL LEVEL AND ENSURING THEY ARE TAUGHT TO MASTERY EVERY DAY

POTENTIAL PITFALL

As discussed throughout this book, placing students at their current skill level and ensuring that they are taught to mastery are essential steps for success with DI because of the incremental step design of the DI programs. However, some schools that adopt DI take a cavalier attitude toward the programs' requirements for placement and mastery. Misplacements commonly occur when placement tests are not administered correctly, not scored correctly, or not given to students at all. In some cases, schools use other measures to determine which DI program is appropriate for which students, or they have simply "eyeballed" the programs and decided through a cursory review of the content of the DI programs which program levels should be assigned to which students. Often, leaders assign students by grade level without administering the placement tests, a practice that can result in a huge mismatch between students' skills and the content of the DI programs.

In some schools, students may be placed correctly initially, but a mismatch develops between students' skills and the lessons they are taught over the course of the school year. This can occur when teachers fail to give the in-program assessments as prescribed and live by the results of the assessments, which involves administering the remedies that ensure students master the content of the DI programs as they proceed through the lessons. (See Teacher Pitfall #3 in the previous chapter: not teaching everything – and every student – to mastery.) In some schools, the administration sets a goal for every instructional group to complete grade-level programs by the end of the school year, which can cause teachers to rush through lessons without ensuring that students master the content completely.

IMPLICATIONS

If students are not placed at their current skill level in the DI programs and taught to mastery every day, they will not develop a strong foundation for future learning. If students are placed too high in a DI program, they will not be able to acquire the new skills and learn the new concepts that are introduced in the program because they do not possess the prerequisite skills and knowledge required for success in the lessons where they are placed. If students are placed too low in a DI program, they will be successful in the program, as evidenced by passing the in-program mastery tests and other assessments, but they won't be learning anything new, so their instructional time will be wasted. With a placement that is either too low or too high, students can get frustrated at the mismatch between the content of the exercises in the DI lessons and their skills. *This holds true throughout the school year whenever the content of the lessons and the students' skills don't match.*

POSSIBLE SOLUTIONS

The remedy for the lack of an initial proper placement of students in the DI programs usually involves administering or re-administering the placement tests and starting the DI implementation over if the misplacement is discovered within the first few weeks of school. However, if instruction takes place for more than a couple of months without proper student placement in the programs, a more nuanced approach needs to be taken. When a mismatch has been identified between students' skills and their placement after a couple of months into the school year, school leaders should ask the staff the following questions:

- Can the skill deficits that the student(s) exhibit be addressed at their current lesson placement? In other words, are the skill deficits narrow enough that they can be addressed by reteaching some exercises and providing additional practice while keeping the group intact at their present lesson?

- Or will the student(s) be more successful if they are placed at a different lesson in the program? If so, where is the preferable placement as exhibited through mastery tests or other in-program assessments?

If a student's optimal placement does not correspond to the placement of an existing instructional group, the leadership must make a difficult choice between placing the student in an existing group (preferably at a lower lesson placement) or providing one-on-one instruction to the student.

For schools to be successful with DI schoolwide, it is important that the leadership monitors a) initial placement testing as it occurs at the beginning of the implementation, and b) student performance in the DI programs throughout the school year. As discussed in chapter 9, monitoring instruction can take place directly by school leaders and indirectly through data analysis. A major focus of the weekly data review and problem-solving sessions is to monitor student mastery and ensure proper ongoing placement, as discussed in chapter 10.

When DI is used as an intervention, non-DI measures can be used as initial screeners to determine which students are candidates for participating in the DI implementation. For instance, a school may use DIBELS or another fluency measure to assess which students in Grades 3 and above might benefit from the decoding track of *Corrective Reading*. But once the fluency measure has been used to identify students who are performing below grade level, the outside measure should not be used to determine which level of a DI program is appropriate for the students. The DI placement tests should be used for that purpose (or the in-program checkouts or mastery tests if a student transfers to the school after the start of the school year).

#6: ASSIGNING THE LEAST EXPERIENCED TEACHERS TO THE MOST DIFFICULT CLASSROOMS

POTENTIAL PITFALL

In a schoolwide implementation of DI, there may be a wide range in the degree of difficulty involved in teaching different instructional groups. Overall, groups with students with a history of behavioral problems can be expected to be more difficult to teach than instructional groups with students without a history of behavioral problems. Also, different DI programs require a different set of instructional skills that may be more challenging for teachers to acquire. In many ways, the lower levels of the DI programs are the most difficult to teach as they involve the broadest range of signals and accompanying delivery techniques. As described in chapter 5, the kindergarten level of the reading strand of *Reading Mastery Signature Edition* involves the use of seven major signals, while the Grade 5 level of the program involves the use of a single signal. Students who place into the Decoding A level of *Corrective Reading* may have both low academic skills and a negative image of their own capabilities. For these students to be successful, they require a teacher who is well-versed in DI as well as positive behavior management techniques.

Quite frequently, school leaders are not aware of the potential difficulty of teaching specific instructional groups in a schoolwide implementation of DI when they assign groups to teachers. A common misconception is that lower levels of the program must be easier to teach because the content is more basic than the content of higher levels. But this misconception doesn't take into account the fact that the content is new and difficult for students who place into the programs. These students don't already know the content of the programs, however basic the content may seem to adults, and many of them haven't developed a repertoire of language and thinking skills that are prerequisites for learning new content.

IMPLICATIONS

If a teacher who is just trying to learn DI teaching techniques is assigned the most difficult-to-teach instructional group, the student performance outcomes of the group, as well as the teacher's attitude toward the assignment, may fall short of school leaders' goals. The frustration of new teachers may be exacerbated if teaching assignments are based on seniority and senior staff members choose not to take on difficult assignments. If teachers are new to teaching in general, they will require more coaching and supervision to gain the skills needed to teach the program effectively.

POSSIBLE SOLUTIONS

As a general rule, school leaders should assign the most experienced teachers to the most difficult-to-teach instructional groups. Teachers with strong behavior management skills and a history of successfully working with challenging students should be considered for the most difficult teaching assignments. If all teachers are new to DI, school leaders can examine the results of the preservice checkouts (described in chapter 9) to see which teachers are catching on to the DI approach the quickest and adjust teaching assignments accordingly.

In all cases, teacher assignments should not be based on seniority, and receiving a difficult assignment should not be an initiation for new staff members. The staff should see themselves as a team dedicated to finding the best arrangement for students' learning. Some experienced teachers love the opportunity to have the most difficult-to-teach students in their classrooms, but if an experienced teacher grows weary of having the most challenging groups every year, school leaders should create a plan for building the capacity of the school so other teachers can take on the most difficult assignments successfully.

Leaders must instill in the staff the notion that teaching and classroom management involve skills that can be learned by all staff members and are not dependent strictly on a teacher's personality or inherent talent. Some teachers may require more practice than others before they become fluent in DI and positive behavior management techniques, but these techniques can be mastered by teachers with markedly different personalities. Students adjust quickly to different types of reinforcement, different amplitudes of expression, and other aspects of teachers' personalities.

The building coordinator should teach one of the most difficult instructional groups at least once a week. This sharpens the coordinator's skills while it helps them assess the assignment of the most challenging instructional group and identify what additional steps may need to be taken to improve student performance and the teacher's skills. Having the coordinator teach the most challenging instructional group also sends a signal to the staff that school leaders are willing to do their part to make sure that all students succeed. This can help foster a positive school climate in which all staff members are willing to put forth their very best effort for the sake of the students.

Leaders should ensure that all structural aspects of the DI implementation are in place so all teachers can be successful, including having well-established schoolwide routines and expectations. Positive behavioral practices designed to maximize actual instructional time while reducing behavioral disruptions should be in place for all common areas.

#7: NOT IDENTIFYING AND USING MODEL CLASSROOMS

POTENTIAL PITFALL

As indicated in the last chapter, teaching DI successfully is a complex undertaking that involves learning a host of new delivery, correction, and behavior management skills. Becoming highly proficient in DI can require several years of coaching and practice. (See Teacher Pitfall #10 in the previous chapter: not realizing that it takes a lot to become skilled in DI.) The content of different DI programs usually differs substantially between programs, which requires even experienced teachers to learn new instructional formats if they are preparing to teach a new DI program. And each DI program contains numerous tracks with exercises that change over time as students advance through the program.

It is difficult for teachers to learn a DI program well if they don't have the opportunity to see a model of the program in action. Modeling is an essential step for all learners when they are mastering new skills, which is why DI trainers and coaches demonstrate critical formats and techniques when they are on site at a school. Supervised practice sessions with feedback from a DI expert are essential for teachers' skill acquisition. (See Teacher Pitfall #1 in the previous chapter: not learning the scripts before using them.) The presence of models among the staff in the school provides a great opportunity for teachers who are new or struggling with delivering DI to see how a particular exercise or procedure should look.

Although schools may invest extensively in the professional development of teachers to become effective with DI, many school leaders do not take advantage of the budding expertise of teachers in their own building to help advance the learning of other staff members in the school. If all new staff receive a thorough preservice (program) training as described in chapter 8, they are prepared to teach the initial lessons in a specific DI program. But if they don't have the benefit of a model teacher in their school to show them how to teach lessons that appear later in the program, new teachers must rely exclusively on previewing and practicing the script by themselves or with other novices to try to understand how to deliver new lessons in the DI program.

IMPLICATIONS

If teachers don't have correct models to guide them in their mastery of DI techniques and procedures, they may learn the techniques and procedures incorrectly. As with other learners, once teachers practice a technique or procedure incorrectly, they require more trials to relearn the technique or procedure correctly than if they had the benefit of an accurate model from the start. Even if teachers do not learn techniques and procedures incorrectly, the rate of their skill acquisition can be expected to be slower without having a strong model to guide them. If teachers' skill acquisition is very slow, student performance at mastery can be strongly and negatively impacted. If, as a result, students don't make substantial progress through the DI programs from the start of the school year, both the students' and the teachers' attitudes toward DI can be negatively impacted. As mentioned above, a solid increase in students' skills during the first few months of the school year can help build support among students and staff for the DI implementation. However, this is only possible if teachers learn essential delivery, correction, and behavior management skills correctly from the start.

POSSIBLE SOLUTIONS

School leaders should identify models as part of their regular monitoring of the DI implementation. The presence of models in a school provides a great opportunity for new or struggling teachers to see what a particular technique or procedure is supposed to look like. While they are observing DI in classrooms, school leaders should look for teachers who have mastered the full range of skills needed for successfully implementing DI. They should also be on the lookout for classrooms in which some aspects of DI are models, but not everything in the classroom is perfect.

For instance, a teacher may have excellent materials management but still struggles with providing sufficient think time. In this case, the teacher could be used as a model for materials management only.

Being used as a model can be very encouraging to teachers who are new to DI. For example, if a teacher is struggling with implementing DI in general but is recognized as a model for active monitoring of independent work, the teacher will be reinforced for mastering active monitoring and will be highly motivated to master other aspects of DI. In contrast, if school leaders always use the same staff member as a model of correct instructional practices, other staff members may start to assume that they themselves will never become proficient in DI.

When using teachers as models, visiting teachers should each take a turn presenting the same exercise or transition activity that they observe in the model classroom. This is far more effective than simply observing instruction during the visit. Students should be prepped beforehand that this is going to occur, and they should be challenged to repeat their high level of performance with the visitors. Visiting teachers will have a better chance of replicating the model right after observing it with a class that is already fluent in the skill or routine. They will then have the confidence to implement the same technique successfully in their own classrooms. Although this process requires more time than simply observing the model teacher, the benefits to the visiting teachers of taking a turn here and there far outweigh the extra time it requires.

If school leaders observe staff members who are close to being models in some aspects of their teaching but are not at the model level yet, the leaders can channel more training and coaching resources toward the staff members who are close to becoming models. External support providers can be very helpful in assessing and tracking the skill development of different staff members and determining when a specific teacher is ready to be used as a model for others. During a classroom visit or a practice session, the external support provider can describe to the rest of the staff why the teacher should be considered to be a model in specific aspects of effective instruction. The external support provider can also preview any videos the school leaders make of candidates for model status to confirm that a teacher can, in fact, serve as a positive example for the rest of the staff.

#8: NOT DETERMINING THE ROOT CAUSE OF STUDENT PERFORMANCE PROBLEMS

POTENTIAL PITFALL

As indicated earlier in this book, lesson progress and mastery are the key measures used to indicate how well students are performing in DI programs. If lesson progress and mastery are high for all students, there is a high likelihood that the goal of accelerating their performance through DI will be attained. However, when there is a problem with lesson progress or mastery, some school leaders fall into the trap of simply addressing lesson progress or mastery as the sole problem rather than identifying the root cause(s) of the student performance problem. In other words, some school leaders admonish teachers of groups with low lesson progress to "increase the rate of lesson completion" and teachers of groups with low scores on mastery tests to "increase students' mastery of program content" without providing a solution of how to do so.

IMPLICATIONS

Sometimes, simply communicating to teachers that their students are performing below expectations for lesson progress or mastery can solve a student performance problem. When teachers realize that there is a problem with student performance, they may be able to identify the reason for the underperformance and correct it themselves. But if teachers are doing their best to figure out why their students are not meeting performance expectations but cannot identify the reason for the underperformance, being admonished to "increase the rate of lesson completion" or "increase students' mastery of program content" without being provided with a remedy of how to do so can be very discouraging. It can also be counterproductive if teachers start to take steps that, in turn, discourage their students. For example, if a teacher is told to increase the rate of lesson progress and then, as a result, tries to pick up the pace of a lesson by reducing the amount of think time that students need, students may start to make more performance errors, which leads to an increase in error corrections and an increase in the time it takes students to complete a lesson.

POSSIBLE SOLUTIONS

If there is a student performance problem, it is important for observers to find out why the student performance problem is taking place. It is insufficient just to say that mastery is below acceptable levels or that lesson progress is low. The root cause must be determined so a remedy can be identified that will lead to improved student performance over time.

Sometimes there are multiple layers of cause and effect that need to be addressed sequentially. After one cause of underperformance has been identified and addressed, the next causal factor can be identified and addressed. For instance, if student engagement is low, the initial root causes may be determined to be the teacher's slow pace of delivery and the absence of a motivation tool, such as the Teacher/Student game (a point allocation system described in chapter 5). After these areas of instruction improve, which may take a couple of weeks of coaching and practice, follow-up observations may reveal that the teacher is not implementing the full error correction procedure, and, as a result, the students are not learning all instructional tasks to mastery every day. Since the students are not at mastery, some of the material they are taught in each lesson is too difficult for them, and they become discouraged and disengaged. This second level of cause and effect (lack of complete error corrections) would not have been discovered if school leaders had stopped observing the group after the teacher demonstrated proficiency with the first two areas of improvement (pacing and student motivation).

Because there are often several layers involved in improving student performance and enhancing the skills that teachers need to master to improve student performance, an ongoing record should be kept of each teacher's acquisition of essential DI delivery and correction skills. This record can consist of a compilation of coaching notes for each teacher, the professional development sessions they attend, and follow-up observation forms used to ensure that they acquire the skills covered during schoolwide in-service sessions. (See chapter 9 for a discussion of the use of in-service follow-up forms.)

#9: NOT CELEBRATING SUCCESS IN DI SUFFICIENTLY

POTENTIAL PITFALL

It's common for school leaders to put forth a great deal of effort to develop a positive climate for students at their school. Greeting students individually with a warm welcome at the beginning of the school day, announcing students' birthdays and upcoming events, holding assemblies that are designed to entertain students, and adorning hallways with colorful decorations that change with the seasons are popular strategies used by many leaders to develop a positive school climate. However, many school leaders give far less attention to celebrating the academic success of students than they do to other aspects of school climate. Such academic accomplishments as instructional groups completing a storybook in *Reading Mastery*, finishing a level of a DI program, or passing mastery tests the first time receive scant recognition by many school leaders. In many schools, celebrating students' accomplishments is considered to be an optional activity that can occur in classrooms without the involvement of school leaders. Celebrating the accomplishments of intervention groups in particular is overlooked in schools implementing DI. Students in *Corrective Reading* or other remedial programs often don't receive grades for their work, which can provide a basis for recognizing and celebrating their success in the programs.

IMPLICATIONS

As mentioned in the last chapter, motivating students to learn is an integral part of a successful DI implementation, and a potential pitfall for teachers is to skimp on the amount of motivation they give to students. (See Teacher Pitfall #8 in the previous chapter: not motivating students to learn.) School leaders may not be aware that teachers are skimping on their positive praise to students if the leaders themselves are not involved in celebrating students' accomplishments. Without sufficient motivation for students to learn, the number of behavioral incidents is likely to increase, with a negative impact on school climate, actual instructional time, and students' progress through the DI programs at mastery. This is especially true for intervention groups with students who have not experienced academic success previously.

Where school leaders put their attention sends a message about the priorities of the administration and the school. When leaders are not involved in celebrating students' achievements in DI, it sends a message to students and staff that all of the other areas of the school that leaders help celebrate are more important than the academic work of the school. The message that academic success is not the main purpose of the school is accentuated when DI is canceled for an assembly or other event and instructional time is not made up at some other time during the school day.

POSSIBLE SOLUTIONS

The surest way to develop a positive learning environment is to recognize students' achievements and efforts directly – either individually or as a group. Addressing aspects of the school environment can only marginally help foster a positive learning atmosphere without explicitly addressing students' academic accomplishments and efforts. As mentioned in chapter 10, celebrations can take place at several levels, from the level of instructional groups to the level of inter-school contests and celebrations of students' accomplishments.

School leaders can and should be involved in celebrations at each of these levels, in part to provide positive feedback to the staff. Reinforcing students is a powerful way of reinforcing their teachers, which is especially important to teachers who are new to DI or have been struggling to master fundamental DI teaching techniques. Reinforcing students can help ensure that the overall feedback that leaders provide to teachers is much more positive than it is negative. If teachers only receive corrective feedback on their delivery of the program from school leaders, they can get discouraged. Leaders reinforcing students serves the dual function of motivating students to work hard at mastering the content of the DI lessons and motivating teachers to work hard at mastering the delivery of the DI lessons, as discussed in chapter 10.

The accomplishments of students in the remedial programs should be a particular focus for school leaders as the self-esteem of these students is among the most fragile of any students in their building. Students in *Corrective Reading, Corrective Mathematics*, or other remedial programs should receive written grades for their work, which can provide a basis for recognizing and celebrating their success in the programs. Their scores on checkouts or other in-program assessments can be recorded on a graph, which provides a visual display of their academic progress. In-class celebrations should occur frequently when all students pass their checkouts the first time. These celebrations can help offset the negative feedback students implicitly experience in non-DI classrooms when they are presented with grade-level material that greatly exceeds their skill level.

#10: NOT EXPLAINING THE DI IMPLEMENTATION ADEQUATELY TO OTHER STAKEHOLDERS

POTENTIAL PITFALL

Sometimes principals do not explain the components of a DI implementation to other stakeholders in the district who can influence the long-term success of DI at their schools. Instead of providing the rationale for the DI programs and demonstrating the success of the DI approach to other stakeholders, principals limit their communication about DI to their staff. Upper-level administrators, who wield potential power over the success of the implementation, must rely on reports from others about the nature of DI and its purported effects on student performance if principals do not brief them about DI. Parents of students must also rely on outside information, which may or may not be reliable.

IMPLICATIONS

Even in cases where the decision to implement DI occurs exclusively at the school level, the long-term success of a DI implementation usually depends on others for its success. The support of upper-level administrators is essential for budget allocation (for materials, training, and attendance at the National DI Conference), staffing (paraprofessionals at the lower levels of the programs), and changes in scheduling. The support of parents is also essential as they can lobby administrators and board members to maintain or expand DI because of its positive impact on students. If parents and upper-level administrators are not briefed on the components of DI and the positive effects it has on children's learning and self-confidence, there is a possibility that they will attempt to impede the implementation of DI before there has been enough time for DI's positive effects to become apparent. Staff members who have heard myths about DI and were opposed to the adoption of the DI approach may, consciously or unconsciously, support unfounded fears that parents and upper-level administrators have heard about DI, prompting them to advocate for limiting or eliminating DI from the school district.

POSSIBLE SOLUTIONS

For a schoolwide implementation of DI, the principal should inform parents, upper-level administrators, and other stakeholders about the components of DI, the rationale for the approach, and the positive effects DI has on children's learning and self-confidence when properly implemented. The principal or other school leaders can prepare handouts explaining the need for such components of DI as the following:

- Allocating two reading periods a day to students who place into lower levels of the reading programs so they can acquire essential reading skills quickly, which will allow them to participate successfully in a wide variety of other academic activities

- Placing students at their skill level rather than their grade level to take advantage of the incremental step design of the DI programs, which allows students to build a solid foundation for future learning as they master essential skills every day

- Using signals to elicit choral responses, which provides an equal opportunity for all students in an instructional group to participate and also allows teachers to monitor the performance of all students closely.

Handouts can include excerpts from sources describing myths about DI:

- "Myths and Truths About Direct Instruction" (Tarver, 1998)
- "Myths about Direct Instruction," chapter 3 in *Research on Direct Instruction: 25 Years Beyond DISTAR.* (Adams and Engelmann, S., 1996)

School leaders can arrange for a parents' night early in the school year to explain the use of DI at the school. Demonstrating DI or showing a video of students being taught with DI can be incorporated into the event. If a school is implementing *Reading Mastery Signature Edition* in the primary grades, parents can watch *Why is Reading So Hard?*, available from www.nifdi.org, which explains the fundamentals of the RMSE reading program from the students' viewpoint. The parents' night can be followed by individual meetings with parents, during which the teacher can show the parents their child's placement test protocol and discuss why their child has been placed in a particular program level. The teacher can show the parents the lessons at the end of the program, which the student can be expected to master by the end of the school year.

Demonstrating growth in academic performance and students' self-confidence at the school is key to gaining the support of upper-level administrators. Early in the implementation, the principal should explain to upper-level administrators how DI programs are designed to ensure that students master all of the skills and content covered in the DI programs, which increases their confidence in their abilities in the subject area. As the school year progresses, upper-level administrators should be invited to visit classrooms to see that students are indeed mastering essential academic skills and their self-confidence is increasing. If students are still performing below grade-level expectations during the visits, the principal should communicate realistic projections about when the students can be expected to attain grade-level proficiency. School leaders should be forthright in explaining that several years of DI may be required for upper-grade students who placed into the lower levels of the remedial programs before they can be expected to close the achievement gap. The communication of such expectations will help to mollify any negative reaction from upper-level administrators if there are still performance gaps for some students at the end of the school year.

Parents, upper-level administrators, and other stakeholders should be invited to any intra-school or inter-school contests based on the content in the DI programs. As mentioned in chapter 10, each elementary school implementing DI in Atlanta in the 2000s held game-show-style competitions between groups of students on the science and social studies facts taught in the Grade 2 and 3 levels of *Reading Mastery*. The winner of each school's competition then represented their school in an inter-school contest that was attended by students, school staff, and district-level administrators. In addition to serving as a strong motivator for students to master the content of the programs, the contests allowed upper-level administrators and other stakeholders to see that students' self-confidence was high as they were learning critical content and laying the foundation for their future academic success.

CONCLUSION

As described in the introduction, this book is intended to serve as a guide to teachers, principals, and other educational practitioners as they implement the published Direct Instruction programs. By following the steps described in this book, you will be able to accelerate the learning of your students as they master the skills and content covered in the DI programs. Students will experience an increase in their self-confidence that comes with mastering essential content, which helps lay the groundwork for their future academic success. They will look forward to school and the opportunity to learn more. This will hold true for all students who are placed at their skill level and taught to mastery every day – students who perform at, above, or below grade-level expectations.

THE KEY TO SUCCESS WITH DI LIES BOTH WITH TEACHERS AND SCHOOL LEADERS

Accelerating the performance of all children requires both a master plan for achieving acceleration, as represented by the procedures and requirements described in this book, and the day-in, day-out effort by instructional staff to make the acceleration of student performance a reality. Neither component can achieve this goal without the other. A master plan will not result in the acceleration of student performance without dedicated and well-trained staff who put forth the effort to implement the plan every day. Efforts by the staff to accelerate the performance of *all* students will not be successful unless:

1. the school has been set up to facilitate student learning by scheduling sufficient instructional time, grouping students homogeneously,

purchasing instructional material that matches the students' skill levels, etc.

2. teachers have the tools, training and ongoing support they need to be able to teach all of their students the DI lessons to mastery.

The component that is most commonly absent in schools is the master plan for accelerating student performance. Efforts by teachers and paraprofessionals in the US and abroad to improve student performance are in no short supply. In the US, there are tens of thousands of dedicated teachers who put in an extraordinary amount of effort every day in an attempt to teach all of their students but are unsuccessful in this endeavor because of the absence of the supportive structure and tools that allow them to teach all their students successfully. Without the proper setup and tools, teachers cannot be expected to help all students succeed. Even students with no barriers to learning can fail to reach grade-level standards if their teachers use such approaches as the three-cueing method of reading, which ingrains in children ineffective reading strategies that persist until they are retaught using effective instructional strategies (Hanford, 2022). Students in schools that have bought DI materials will also fail to succeed if the setup of DI is faulty – if students are not placed at their skill level, there is not sufficient time in the program, and other requirements of the DI model are not implemented with fidelity.

For students to succeed with DI, *the form of teachers' efforts must change* once the school has adopted the DI approach. As indicated in this book, teachers implementing DI do not spend time developing traditional lessons. Instead, they must prepare themselves to deliver a script fluently using the correct signals and appropriate pacing, to attend to the responses of each child in the instructional groups, and to respond immediately with corrective feedback when students make an error or praise students when they answer correctly. Teachers must keep track of each of their students' errors so they can return to tasks that were difficult for the students and provide them with enough practice over time to master the tasks. Teachers must monitor students closely when they are engaged in independent work and provide feedback as needed. Teachers must be prepared to adjust instruction in every lesson based on their students' performance on independent work and repeat exercises that were difficult for more than a quarter of the students.

Teachers should prepare themselves mentally for these requirements for teaching students effectively with DI, which will become easier to implement over time. Anayezuka Ahidiana, a longtime DI trainer and coach in Baltimore, gives the following advice, which appears at the end of *Anatomy of a Reading Mastery Classroom*, the third video in the *Reading Mastery Setup and Training Series* (available at www.nifdi.org/videos/reading-mastery-training-series.html):

> You're going to be tired. You're going to be exhausted... But you will come to a place where you own this program... You don't stay up all night practicing. And everybody's going to be smarter. Teachers are going to get to be better. Kids are going to have a future.

The type of effort by school leaders must also change, especially if there is a schoolwide implementation of DI. *For DI to be successful schoolwide, the principal must be the instructional leader* and set up the expectations for the staff, ensure that all of the structural elements of DI (including appropriate scheduling, grouping and placement, material ordering, and staff assignments) are in place, monitor the implementation, and respond to correct any problems that are observed. The principal should have touchpoints with the staff about DI no matter how many responsibilities are delegated to a building coordinator, coach, or teacher on special assignment. *There is always a role for the principal in a DI implementation of any size*, even if it is simply to affirm the effectiveness of the implementation and celebrate students' achievements.

To ensure a successful start to DI, the effort expended by leaders and teachers should be front-loaded as much as possible. This should involve learning about DI, implementing positive behavioral management practices, and taking essential setup tasks *the year prior to implementing DI*. If the staff is fully informed about the program and all of the prerequisite steps have been taken in preparation for implementing the DI approach, the school will have a successful year with DI. If essential preparation tasks are not taken the year before DI is adopted, student performance may improve somewhat in comparison to student performance in previous years, but a dramatic increase cannot be expected to occur unless the setup tasks have been completed before the start of the school year. This also holds true for a mid-year startup of DI, which can occur due to delays in administering placement tests, forming instructional groups, ordering materials that match the students' placements, and completing other setup tasks.

The long-term success of DI depends heavily on the actions of school leaders (and the actions of the district leaders in a multi-school implementation) in several ways. School leaders must perform the following functions after the first year of implementing DI:

- Ordering new levels of the programs as students perform at higher levels than in previous years
- Adjusting teaching assignments to place teachers with the students they can most effectively serve, which may include moving teachers out of the grade levels where DI is used
- Onboarding new staff members – explaining the DI model to them, providing them with the same training and support the original cohort of teachers received, and monitoring their classrooms to ensure that their practices conform to the DI model
- Building the capacity of teachers and coaches to implement DI by providing advanced training from an external support provider.

Because the long-term success of DI depends so much on the school's leadership, a change in leaders can undermine a DI schoolwide implementation quickly. If the principal of a school who oversaw the adoption of DI is replaced by a principal who is not familiar with DI or has negative, preconceived notions about the DI approach, the DI implementation could be in jeopardy. Sometimes, an incoming principal takes steps to dismantle the DI implementation without examining the positive changes in student performance that have occurred at the school since DI was adopted. To prevent this from occurring, the teachers and the outgoing principal can provide background knowledge to new school leaders so they have a better understanding of the DI model and its effect on the school's student population. The new principal can visit classrooms with the building coordinator to see the program in action and observe firsthand the performance of students who have been taught with DI. Similar visits can be arranged for district-level coaches or administrators who are hired after the initial year of the DI implementation. Given the immense power of school and district leaders to alter or change instructional programs, it is essential that new leaders understand fully how the implementation of DI has benefited both students and staff in the schools they oversee.

THE EFFECT OF THE FULL SEQUENCE OF DI PROGRAMS

Research indicates that the longer students receive instruction in DI, the more positive effect it has on their performance level, on average. Table 13.1 shows that the effect of DI on reading performance increases with the length of intervention according to a metanalysis conducted by Stockard et al. (2020) involving over 200 studies. While the mean effect size of a short-term treatment of DI of six months is moderately large, with a confidence interval of the effect size ranging from 0.35 to 0.51, the confidence interval increases with the length of instruction to 0.64–0.84 for a treatment of four years. Similar effects were observed for instruction in mathematics and other academic subjects (Stockard et al., 2020, 128).

Length of Instruction	95% Confidence Interval	Number of Effects
6 months	0.35–0.51	336
1 year	0.42–0.54	761
2 years	0.50–0.62	292
3 years	0.57–0.73	216
4 years	0.64–0.84	227

Table 13.1 Effect sizes of studies on Direct Instruction reading by length of instruction. Source: Stockard et al. (2020, 128).

Not included in the analysis conducted for Table 13.1 were 13 studies that compared the performance of students who received DI for different lengths of time without a non-DI comparison group. The results of these 13 studies affirm the positive, cumulative impact of the long-term use of DI. Stockard et al. (2020) found a consistent trend across these studies – that more instruction in DI resulted in more positive performance effects:

> … when comparisons were made between students in the same setting and with similar characteristics, but with different "dosages" of DI, those who had more exposure to DI had

significantly higher achievement. These results support the findings with our larger sample that students who are taught with DI for longer periods of time have higher levels of achievement and skills than those taught for shorter periods. (Ibid., 129)

In addition, research has demonstrated that instruction with DI has positive staying power. In the 1970s and 1980s, Gersten, Keating, and Becker conducted several follow-up studies to Project Follow Through. (See Topic Brief 8.) The studies involved over a thousand students who received instruction in DI and a similar number of students in the comparison groups. The first two studies, conducted in 1975 and 1976 based on data from students in five sites (Dayton, OH; East St. Louis, IL; Smithville, TN; Tupelo, MS; and Uvalde, TX), involved 1,097 fifth- and sixth-grade "graduates" of the DI model as third graders and 970 fifth- and sixth-graders who did not receive DI. A study conducted in the 1980s involved over a thousand high school students in New York City; Flint, MI; and East St. Louis, IL. The authors found that:

> … the findings tend to consistently favor Follow Through and rarely the local comparison group. In the fifth- and sixth-grade follow-ups, DI Follow Through students did consistently better than comparison groups, especially in reading, spelling, and math problem solving. In the high school studies, better performance in reading and math were found, as well as fewer grade-retentions and more college acceptances. (Gersten, Keating, and Becker, 1988, 326)

Table 13.2 shows data from Uvalde, Texas, a DI Follow Through site, comparing measures on the high school graduation rates between the first two cohorts of students who received instruction in DI as 1st–3rd graders, who started school in 1968 and 1969, with the previous two cohorts of students, who started school in 1966 and 1967. Approximately 85% of the students were eligible for free and reduced lunch, 60–80% of the students were classified as limited English proficient upon entry into the school, and 98% of the students were Hispanic (Gersten et al., 1997, 31).

Cohort	Year began first grade	Number of students	% graduating from high school
Comparison	1966	103	37.9
	1967	97	42.3
Follow Through	1968	87	59.8
	1969	47	53.2

Table 13.2 Percentage of students graduating from high school in Uvalde, TX who received instruction in the Direct Instruction Follow Through model vs. previous instruction. Source: Gersten et al. (1997, 37).

As the table shows, graduation rates jumped considerably for students in Uvalde, Texas who received DI in the primary grades in comparison to the two previous cohorts of students. Less than half of the students before Follow Through went on to graduate from high school. Only 37.9% of the students who started first grade in 1966 graduated from high school, and 42.3% of the students who started first grade in 1967. In contrast, more than half of the students who received DI graduated from high school. Almost 60% of the 1968 cohort received their high school diploma as did 53.2% of the 1969 cohort.

In a more comprehensive analysis of the long-term effect of DI on student performance, Stockard et al. (2020) calculated confidence intervals of effect sizes based on 47 studies for different years to determine how strongly the positive effects of DI are maintained over time. Table 13.3 shows the confidence intervals for effect sizes one and four years after students received instruction in DI.

Length of Maintenance	95% Confidence Interval	Number of Effects
1 Year	0.29–0.59	277
4 Years	0.25–0.58	245
Total	0.28–0.57	522

Table 13.3 Effect sizes of studies on Direct Instruction reading by length of instruction. Source: Stockard et al. (2020, 142).

As the table shows, the confidence interval drops only slightly from 0.29–0.59 one year after DI was implemented to 0.25–0.58 four years after DI was implemented. This result underscores the lasting power of teaching

473

to mastery, demonstrating that once students thoroughly master a skill, they retain that skill over time.

What can be achieved in terms of student mastery and achievement if students receive instruction in the full DI sequence of programs starting from the earliest program levels and extending through the high school level programs (*Essentials for Writing* and *Essentials for Algebra*)? That's still an open question. The full impact of the "cohort effect" with DI from kindergarten to high school is still largely unexplored, in part because of the relatively recent publications of the high school programs. (*Essentials for Algebra* was published in 2008, and *Essentials for Writing* was published in 2010.) Although hundreds of thousands of students have benefited from DI, the full, longitudinal power of the DI approach has been realized with only a handful of students. Project Follow Through, the largest educational experiment in the history of the US (and possibly the world), only involved implementing DI through third grade. Subsequent studies have also focused heavily on the effect of DI in the early grades or of DI implemented as a short-term intervention remedially, in part because analyzing short-term interventions is much easier than longitudinal studies that require following the performance of students for years.

Isolated case studies suggest that a multi-year DI treatment of students with DI would have a very strong, positive effect on student outcomes. As discussed in chapter 1 of this book, the median scores of fifth graders at City Springs Elementary on the Comprehensive Test of Basic Skills (CTBS) went from the 14th percentile in 1998 to the 67th percentile in 2001 (*The Battle of City Springs Epilogue*, https://youtu.be/EjwribR0qbQ). Before graduating from elementary schools, many students in DI implementations in Baltimore, Atlanta, and Nebraska who started DI in kindergarten completed all six levels of *Reading Mastery* and received instruction in *Understanding U.S. History*, a two-volume text intended for middle school students.

The implementation of the full series of DI programs from kindergarten through the high school equivalent programs has been hampered by several factors, including a resistance to accelerating student performance in middle schools. The experience of DI in Gunnison, Utah provides an example of how administrative decisions can slow the acceleration of students' performance after they leave an elementary school where DI is implemented. An exemplary implementation of DI took place at Gunnison Elementary in the late 1990s and early 2000s. With comparatively low rates of student turnover, the implementation of DI resulted in a strong cohort effect by the time students graduated from the elementary school, which extended through sixth grade. The performance of several sixth graders who started DI math in fourth grade was so high that their teacher recommended skipping the seventh-grade math program and placing them into the secondary school's algebra course as seventh graders at the beginning of the next school year. The principal of the secondary school, who opposed DI, rejected the idea of placing incoming seventh-grade students directly into algebra, but he relented after parents of the students protested the decision. After the students were given the end-of-year pre-algebra test twice, seven of the graduates from the elementary school were placed in algebra for seventh grade. Six of the seven students excelled in the course, with four of them scoring in the top five places of all students on the end-of-year algebra test. A later cohort of kids who started DI in first grade included 15 students who skipped seventh-grade math and went straight into algebra as seventh graders (Childs, Hendrickson, and Davis, 2022).

Despite Gunnison's success at accelerating students in math from the primary grades through the secondary grades, DI math was discontinued at Gunnison Elementary after the secondary school principal became superintendent of the district. DI reading and language continued to be implemented at the elementary school, but DI math was removed and replaced by a conventional approach to mathematics.

ACCELERATING STUDENT PERFORMANCE IN ONE OR TWO YEARS

For students who receive DI for only one or two years, the acceleration of student performance can still be dramatic. An example is the progress made by Sebastian Rodriguez, who graduated from the IDEA Quest College Preparatory School in Edinburg, Texas. In a video interview as a twelfth grader in 2013, Sebastian recounted the struggles he experienced as a ninth and tenth grader before he received instruction in *Essentials for Algebra*:

During my ninth-grade year, I struggled through all my math. If I was handed a test, I would just freeze and just even look around ... I see that everyone knows what they're doing except for me. I'll be struggling and start guessing. And that's how I would fail, like, my tests (from www.nifdi.org/about/partner-perspectives.html).

He reported that during his tenth-grade year, he failed almost all of his Texas Assessment state tests, with a devastatingly negative impact on his self-esteem:

I was really... destroyed, like, inside, like, I can't do anything anymore. I can't pass, at all... I would, basically, give up hope, like, I'm not a smart person. I'm not at all.

In the eleventh grade, Sebastian received instruction in *Essentials for Algebra*, and his performance improved remarkably:

Well, that was a big improvement for me. ... As the teacher would give the time to teach me, I would understand the algebra now. I would know the math skills right away. I could easily, like, memorize the problem in my head and know what to do... Besides, I don't need a calculator anymore.

The results of his eleventh-grade score on the Texas Assessment surprised him:

I got commended. I was really excited and happy, and I couldn't believe it. I was thinking in my head, like, "She probably got the wrong person's name, and switched it up." I don't know. I can't believe it at all. I got commended. I never got commended in my life. I would get just a passing grade, but never commended. And I was really happy when I got that, like, I'm going to twelfth grade – I know I'm going to go to college now!

The example of Sebastian's sudden shift in his self-esteem, which reflected the sudden improvement in his math performance, has been replicated time after time in schools implementing DI across the US. This sharp improvement in learners' self-esteem through DI has also been replicated in homes throughout the US and abroad as many children have experienced success early through the use of *Teach Your Child to Read in 100 Easy Lessons.* (See the testimonials by parents and other users of the program at www.startreading.com and Amazon.com.) Sales of the book recently exceeded a million copies, which is a testament to its effectiveness in helping parents provide early literacy instruction for their children.

WHAT MONETARY SAVINGS ARE POSSIBLE WITH DIRECT INSTRUCTION?

It is impossible to put a monetary value on the improvements to Sebastian's self-esteem as a result of careful teaching with *Essentials for Algebra.* Helping students acquire the skills that allow them to succeed and realize that they are smart is priceless. But researchers in Wisconsin have attempted to estimate the savings in the amount spent on remediating students that would occur if DI were used for core instruction for all students starting with the earliest grades rather than as an intervention with students in the intermediate and upper grades who failed to acquire fundamental academic skills when they were in the primary grades. In 2001, the authors of a report published by the Wisconsin Policy Research Institute (aka the Badger Institute) on the use of DI concluded that:

> Direct Instruction holds strong promise for improving the teaching of early reading in Wisconsin. Widespread uses of Direct Instruction would directly benefit children and parents. In addition, improvements gained through competent, widespread use of Direct Instruction would decrease the need for remedial reading programs in the state. Potential cost savings from such a decrease can be estimated by reference to the cost of one important remedial program — special instruction for children classified as learning disabled (LD) — into which many children are now placed when they do not learn to read well in the early grades. A 25 percent reduction in LD placements would yield an annual cost savings of more than $35 million; a 50 percent reduction would yield annual savings of about $71 million; and a 75 percent reduction would yield savings of $107 million. (Schug, Tarver, and Western, 2001, 1).

These estimated cost savings were calculated using 2001 dollars. The present-day valuation of the savings would be at least one and a half times as much. Moreover, this estimate represents the projected cost savings in one state with less than 2% of the total US population. The cost savings on a national scale in the US would be in the billions of dollars annually. This large-scale monetary cost savings would be accompanied by a marked increase in students' self-esteem and a corresponding decrease in the incidence of many self-destructive behaviors.

The Wisconsin Policy Research Institute study examined possible savings from implementing DI to reduce expenditures on special education. The Education Consumers Foundation (ECF) offers a free calculator for determining the lifetime cost of public taxes for students who do not learn to read proficiently by the third grade. According to the ECF, the average lifetime state and federal taxes that taxpayers will pay for the welfare, health care, public safety, and training in support of a student who does not read proficiently by the third grade is approximately $90,000 for an individual who drops out of high school and $30,000 for an individual who graduates from high school but is unprepared for college or the workplace (see https://education-consumers.org/efc-cost-calculator/). If the cost of the DI programs, training, and support seems high, the cost of not implementing DI with fidelity as core instruction from the earliest grades is much higher in the long run.

PILOTING DI WITH YOUR STUDENTS

If accounts of students' success with DI seem too good to be true, if you are skeptical about the effects of DI, you are not alone. The romantic version of teaching and learning is the predominant paradigm in the educational system in the US and in many other countries around the world. The institutions of higher education that offer courses on upper-case DI are very few and far between. For that reason, the DI approach may seem unusual and even "inappropriate" to you. It is understandable – even laudable – to be skeptical about an approach that is accompanied by great claims of student success. Many of the strongest supporters of DI started out as skeptics of the approach.

If you are skeptical, you can visit a school that has experienced success with DI to observe it in action and talk with the staff to hear about their experiences with DI. Visits can also take place virtually, although in-person visits allow observers to get a better all-round feel of the school, its climate, and the relationships between the staff and students. There are also many resources that can help you understand what's involved in implementing DI, which you may want to access before you visit a school (see chapter 7).

One way to determine whether DI will increase the academic success of your students is to pilot it with them. A pilot should take place only if all of the requirements of the DI programs can be met. If the requirements are not met, the implementation may not lead to great improvements in students' performance and self-esteem. If all of the requirements are met and the programs are implemented with fidelity, you will see a noticeable improvement within the first few months of implementation. Over time, you will see the remarkable results that occur when students are taught at their skill level every day to mastery, which leaves them ready and craving to learn more. As longtime teacher and coach Anayezuka Ahidiana says about teaching children with DI:

> It's the most incredible experience on the planet to see kids make a chance for themselves.

A word of caution to those who pilot DI with fidelity: once you see how much more students can achieve when they are all taught at their skill level every day to mastery in a way that provides a firm foundation for future learning, you may insist on using DI. Scores of teachers who have implemented DI have decided that they only want to work in a school where they can teach all of their students to be successful. They are not willing to go back to watching a large percentage of their students struggle when they could be soaring, developing harmful habits and attitudes when they could be learning with confidence, and missing out on essential skills rather than mastering skills. Many of these teachers either attempt to persuade school leaders to adopt DI schoolwide and set up the school structurally to accommodate the grouping, scheduling, and other requirements necessary for DI to be successful, or they decide to move to a school with a more supportive environment for implementing DI.

If you implement DI successfully, you too may have difficulty in the future watching students fail to receive effective instruction, just as you would have difficulty watching children fail to receive proper nourishment when there is an abundant supply of food that could be made available to them.

PARENTS CAN TEACH THEIR CHILDREN TO READ

You may consider this comparison of providing food with providing effective instruction to be inappropriate since it is much easier for modern societies to provide food than it is for them to provide instruction that meets the needs of every student. Indeed, DI is not easy to implement. As this book indicates, DI requires considerable training, practice, coaching, and effort from teachers for them to deliver it effectively, and it requires the adoption by school and district leaders of specific practices for setting up, monitoring, and troubleshooting the DI implementation for it to be successful with every student. But if parents can teach their children to read successfully, shouldn't the educational system be able to do so, and not just be able to teach all students to read, but also to acquire other skills students will need to succeed in college, career... and life? The numerous testimonials by users of *Teach Your Child to Read in 100 Easy Lessons* referred to earlier underscore how parents using the program for as little as 20 minutes a day with no training can successfully teach their children to read, even children who have been labeled dyslexic or learning disabled. If parents, as unpaid, untrained novices to teaching can use a program successfully with their own children, shouldn't schools be able to do the same for all students? After all, schools and districts have resources that greatly exceed those available to parents, and districts are staffed with professionals who have spent years attending teacher training colleges and other institutes of higher education.

Because schools are responsible for providing students with the skills they need to succeed in college and career, the schools – and the colleges and universities that graduate and certify teachers and school leaders – should be reformed until they can ensure that all students succeed. The tools, procedures, and programs that lead to student success through the comprehensive DI model have been available for decades. All that's needed for students to succeed with DI is the will, organization, and sustained focus to implement the model with fidelity.

TOPIC BRIEF 7: META-ANALYSES OF THE DIRECT INSTRUCTION RESEARCH BASE

A meta-analysis is an analysis of studies conducted on a particular topic or program. Typically, the author of a meta-analysis gathers all known studies on a topic or program, examines each study to determine the effect that the program or intervention demonstrated in each study, and then aggregates the effects into an overall effect size. Often, a study has more than one effect size because the authors of the study used more than one measure to analyze the program or intervention. The overall effect size of the meta-analysis is positive if the program or intervention demonstrates a net positive effect across the studies (i.e. students who received the program or intervention performed better than comparison students who did not receive the program or intervention), or the effect size is negative if the program or intervention demonstrates a net negative effect across the studies (i.e. comparison students who did not receive the program or intervention performed better than students who received the program or intervention). In this way, meta-analyses provide a more comprehensive assessment of the effectiveness of a program or intervention than any individual study.

At least six meta-analyses have been conducted on DI over the years, all of which indicated that DI has highly positive effects on student achievement. The most recent meta-analysis on DI was conducted by Jean Stockard and colleagues and published in 2020. In *All Students Can Succeed: A Half Century of Research on the Effectiveness of Direct Instruction*, Stockard and colleagues examined over 500 studies encompassing nearly 4,000 effect sizes, which makes it *the largest meta-analysis ever published on a single instructional method!*

The authors found that DI's effectiveness was consistently strong and positive across different school environments, which held true for student self-confidence as well as academic achievement. The authors concluded that DI's positive influence on student outcomes increases as the duration of the implementation of DI increases, and that DI could be used to overcome the gap between performance of students from low-income households and national norms on the National Assessment of Educational Progress (NAEP), the "nation's report card." According to the authors, the results of the meta-analysis indicated that:

... the longer students were taught with DI and the more that their schools and teachers followed the implementation guidelines, the greater the effect. The data show that DI's effectiveness is significantly greater than alternative programs, even when used for short periods of time and under less than optimal conditions. But, when students were exposed over a period of years and with careful attention to implementing the program as designed, outcomes were extraordinarily strong. Most important, the effects with this optimal exposure surpassed the effect associated with the difference in NAEP scores of students from low-income households and other students. (Stockard et al., 2020, 147)

In addition to confirming DI's overall high level of effectiveness, Stockard and colleagues dispelled various myths that have developed around DI over the years:

In chapter 1, we outlined a range of criticisms of DI. For instance, critics have suggested DI may be effective in teaching basic skills but not those that require some type of higher-order understanding; or that it will be effective for low-performing students but not high performers. They have also suggested that it will destroy students' love of learning, harm self-esteem, or promote behavior problems; and that teachers and students simply don't like the programs. The data, however, did not support these claims. While there were some minor differences in estimates of effects regarding different skills, all of the estimates were large or very large and far greater than those found in studies of other interventions. There was no indication that effectiveness was restricted to students with certain characteristics or in certain settings. Nor was there any indication that it can somehow harm students or that students and teachers do not like the program when they have used it. (Ibid., 2020, 147–48)

A synthesis of meta-analyses published a decade earlier confirmed the positive effect of the DI approach on student achievement. Instead of examining individual studies, John Hattie examined over 800 meta-analyses on a wide variety of curricula and instructional approaches, including DI. He concluded that the evidence base for DI's effectiveness was "high" in comparison to other educational methodologies:

> Every year I present lectures to teacher education students and find that they are already indoctrinated with the mantra "constructivism good, direct instruction bad". When I show them the results of these meta-analyses, they are stunned, and they often become angry at having been given an agreed set of truths and commandments against direct instruction. Too often, what the critics mean by direct instruction is didactic teacher-led talking from the front; this should not be confused with the very successful "Direct Instruction" method as first outlined by Adams and Engelmann (1996). Direct Instruction has a bad name for the wrong reasons, especially when it is confused with didactic teaching, as the underlying principles of Direct Instruction place it among the most successful outcomes. (Hattie, 2009, 204–205)

TOPIC BRIEF 8: PROJECT FOLLOW THROUGH

Project Follow Through (1968–1977) was the largest educational experiment in the history of the US and, by many accounts, the largest in the world. (For example, see Stockard et al., 2020, 49). At its peak, it involved 75,000 students annually in 180 communities located across the country with a wide variety of demographic characteristics (Becker, 1977). The purpose of Follow Through was to analyze the effect of different approaches to classroom instruction on the performance of at-risk students at schools receiving Title 1 support. The "models" representing the approaches participating in the study covered the full spectrum of educational philosophies – from discovery-oriented approaches, such as the Cognitively Oriented Curriculum and Responsive Education, to teacher-directed approaches, such as Behavior Analysis and DI (Watkins and Slocum, 2004, 59). Parents from participating communities selected the model that they wanted implemented in the schools their children were attending. Matching schools with similar demographic characteristics were selected as comparisons to the "experimental" schools implementing the Follow Through models.

Student performance in Follow Through was measured in two broad categories:

- Content-area performance (reading, math, spelling, language)
- Performance on different skill sets (basic skills, cognitive skills, and affective measures).

The models were classified according to the type of approach they were perceived to employ. The three categories were: Basic Skills, Cognitive-Conceptual, and Affective-Cognitive models. DI was classified as a "basic skills" approach.

In 1977, the performance of third-grade students who started Follow Through in first grade or kindergarten was measured. Nine out of the 22 original models met the requirements for a minimum number of sites needed to participate in the final evaluation. The results demonstrated that *students who received instruction in the DI model performed higher on all measures, including cognitive skills and affective measures, than students who received instruction in the other models.* Abt Associates, the company hired by the US Office of Education as the official evaluator of Project Follow Through, concluded that:

> The Direct Instruction Model of the University of Oregon, a basic skills model, had substantially higher average effects than did any other model. (Stebbins et al., 1977, xxv)

And that:

> ... most Follow Through intervention produced more negative than positive effects on basic skills test scores. The only notable exception to this trend was the Direct Instruction Model. (Ibid., xxvi)

The following chart displays the net number of outcomes favoring each model's sites in comparison to the local sites that served as controls. A zero score indicates that there was an equal number of outcomes favoring a model's sites in relation to the comparison sites. A positive score indicates that there were more outcomes favoring the model's sites. A negative score indicates that there were more outcomes favoring the comparison sites. The first three bars in the chart indicate that there were nearly 300 outcomes favoring the DI sites in basic skills, about 350 outcomes favoring DI sites in cognitive skills, and over 250 outcomes favoring DI sites in affective skills relative to comparison sites.

Number of Significant Outcomes for Basic Skills (B), Cognitive Skills (C), and Affective Measures (A)

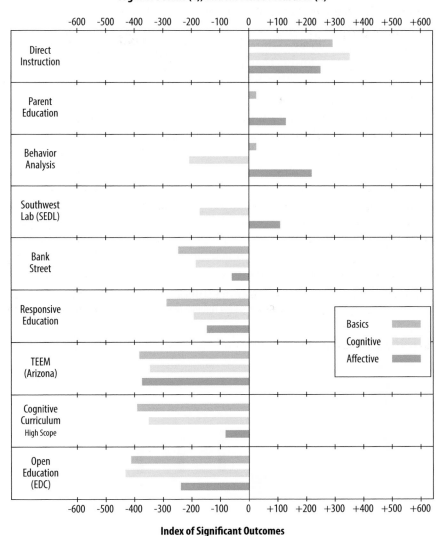

Index of Significant Outcomes

Source: Engelmann and Carnine (1991, 356).

As the chart shows, *the DI model had the highest number of positive outcomes in all three skill categories – cognitive outcomes, basic skills, and affective outcomes.* Students in only three other Follow Through models performed higher than the comparison schools in any category (with net positive outcome scores). Students in most of the other Follow Through models performed lower than the comparison schools in all three categories (with net negative outcome scores).

In terms of content-area performance, students in the DI model scored first in reading, mathematics, spelling, and language with percentile scores above 40% in all of these subject areas. As the chart below shows, third-grade students in the DI model achieved close to or slightly above the national average on the Metropolitan Achievement Test (MAT) in math, spelling, and language. Students in only one other model, Behavior Analysis, scored above the 40th percentile in any of the content areas (spelling). The Behavior Analysis model did not specify a particular curriculum, and several of the sites operated by this model used DI programs. The content-area percentile scores for all other models were much closer to the Title 1 average (20th percentile), and students in several models scored below that mark.

PERCENTILE SCORES
Across nine Follow Through models

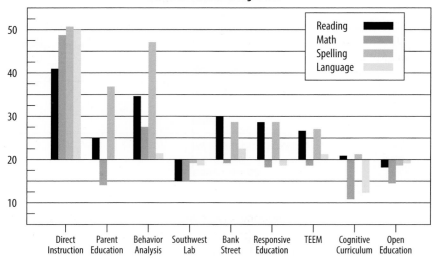

Source: Adams (1996, 51).

Students in the DI model achieved these results despite the inclusion of the Grand Rapids, Michigan site in the final evaluation. The developers of the DI model stopped supporting the site several years before the evaluation due to a deliberate lack of implementation fidelity by the local administration (Engelmann, S., 2007, 138–40). The performance of students at the site was noticeably lower than the performance of students at any of the other DI sites. The evaluators noted in an interim report on students in the second cohort of Follow Through:

> When Grand Rapids, which appears to be an outlier, is dropped from the total, the average performance of the other sites is at or above grade level in each subject. (Stebbins et al., 1976, 169)

Although the results surprised many observers at the time, the evaluators explained why DI was effective in the Cognitive-Conceptual domain:

> Although the instruction is programmed, the emphasis is placed on the children's learning intelligent behavior rather than specific pieces of information by rote memorization. (Bock, Stebbins and Proper, 1977, 65)

And why DI was effective in the Affective domain:

> To some observers the performance of FT children in Direct Instruction sponsored sites on the affective measures is an unexpected result. The Direct Instruction Model does not explicitly emphasize affective outcomes of instruction but the sponsor has asserted that they will be the consequence of effective teaching. Critics of the model have predicted that the emphasis of the model on tightly controlled instruction might discourage children from freely expressing themselves and thus inhibit the development of self-esteem and other affective skills. In fact, this is not the case. (Ibid., 73)

The Follow Through results demonstrated that students' self-esteem increases when they experience academic achievement daily and are recognized for their accomplishments – two important components of the DI model.

The federal government was fully aware of the comparative effectiveness of the "Basic Skills" models in general and the DI model specifically. When the district of San Diego wanted to switch models in 1974, three years before the final evaluation of Follow Through, the US Office of Education forced the district to choose between DI or the Behavioral Analysis model sponsored by the University of Kansas (Grossen, 1996, 6).

Despite being fully aware of the effectiveness of the DI model and despite a legislative mandate to disseminate the results of Project Follow Through, the US Office of Education contributed to the systematic repression of the final evaluation's findings. Contrary to the legislation that enabled and funded Follow Through, information about individual *sites* instead of the educational *models* was disseminated. In a letter to US Senator Bob Packwood, Ernest Boyer, the US Commissioner of Education, explained his department's reasoning for not disseminating information about the performance of students in the different Follow Through models:

> Since the beginning of Follow Through in 1968, the central emphasis has been on models. A principal purpose of the program has been to identify and develop alternative models or approaches to compensatory education and assess the relative effectiveness through a major evaluation study which compared the performance of Follow Through children with comparable children in non-Follow Through projects over a period of several years... The evaluation found that only one of the 22 models which were assessed in the evaluation consistently produced positive outcomes. The central finding of the evaluation was that there was substantial variation in effectiveness among the sites in almost all of the models. Accordingly ... we are funding 21 of the successful sites as demonstration sites this year so that other schools and educators will learn about, understand, and hopefully adopt the successful activities and procedures taking place in these effective sites. In summary, while the initial emphasis of the program was on designing and implementing models, the evaluation results forced us to shift attention more to successful individual projects. If the evaluation findings had indicated that the various models tested were either generally effective or generally ineffective, then the

subsequent demonstration and dissemination activities could have proceeded along model rather than individual project lines. However, with the exception of the Becker–Engelmann Direct Instruction model, this was not the case. (Engelmann, S., 2007, 248) (The full text of Commissioner Boyer's letter is available for download at www.nifdi.org/what-is-di/project-follow-through.html.)

Boyer also addressed Senator Packwood's query about the federal government expanding the implementation of models that were shown to be effective in Project Follow Through:

> With respect to your question about funding selected models on an expanded scale, with the exception of the Direct Instruction model this could not responsibly be done since, as I noted above, positive evaluation evidence for the other models is lacking. The same problem applies to your question about funding sponsors to disseminate information on Follow Through programs on the college and in-service levels. Since only one of the models, and therefore only one of the sponsors, was found to produce positive results more consistently than any of the others, it would be inappropriate and irresponsible to disseminate information on all the models which carried the implication that such models could be expected to produce generally positive outcomes. (Engelmann, S., 2007, 249)

Boyer's logic runs counter to all sound scientific practices. When results of a study in any field of science are disseminated, it doesn't matter whether only one approach or several approaches are found to be effective. If a study comparing the effectiveness of different vaccines, for instance, concludes that only one type of vaccine is more effective than other vaccines, the results are disseminated just as readily as the results of a study indicating that several vaccines are effective.

The federal government's suppression of the Follow Through results has contributed to the paucity of knowledge about DI among education practitioners – despite an ever-expanding evidence base demonstrating the effectiveness of DI. Without the dissemination of the results of Follow Through, and with very few institutes of higher education offering courses on Direct Instruction, very few teachers or administrators are aware of DI's effectiveness, especially in the cognitive and affective domains. Not only are they unaware of the results of Project Follow Through, but they are also unaware of the longitudinal, follow-up studies of students who participated in Project Follow Through, which demonstrated that the positive effects of the DI treatment were sustained into ninth grade and beyond. (See the conclusion of this book as well as Adams, 1996, 51–56.)

With coursework that paints DI as a "basic skills" approach effective only in helping students learn rote facts, many teachers shy away from using DI programs or explicit instructional methods. As Cathy Watkins observed, "the instructional methods a teacher uses are most likely to be those taught during his or her own training" (Watkins, 1996, 64). Instead of using effective teaching methods, teachers often employ ineffective and sometimes deleterious practices, such as the three-cueing system, which prompts students to guess when reading words, as described in *Sold a Story* (see Hanford, 2022). Until and unless institutes of higher education incorporate DI and explicit instruction into their course offerings, the instructional methods teachers employ can be expected to perpetuate student achievement gaps and prevent all students from attaining their full potential.

TOPIC BRIEF 9: BEHAVIOR SPECIALISTS ON DIRECT INSTRUCTION

In September 2021, two academic journals published by the Association for Behavior Analysis International – *Behavior Analysis in Practice* and *Perspectives on Behavior Science* – devoted special issues to Direct Instruction. While behavior specialists are the chief intended audience of the special issues, several articles in the issues will appeal to a broader audience. Topics addressed in the special issue of *Behavior Analysis in Practice* include applying the DI approach to teaching social skills, developing instructional materials for teaching any concept, training parents to implement explicit instruction with their children, and implementing DI at a public charter school serving students with autism spectrum disorders (ASDs). Topics in the special issue of *Perspectives on Behavior Science* include "faultless communication" and other DI design features, the use of a specific observation tool for assessing teacher–student interactions during explicit instruction, and Siegfried Engelmann's philosophical, theoretical, and technical contributions to the field of education. The introduction to each special issue can be downloaded for free at:

- https://link.springer.com/article/10.1007/s40617-021-00639-8 (*Behavior Analysis in Practice*)
- https://link.springer.com/article/10.1007/s40614-021-00314-x (*Perspectives on Behavior Science*).

The special issues provide a variety of additional reading and useful references for anyone who is interested in learning more about the history, philosophy, theory, and practical effect of explicit instruction or Direct Instruction.

APPENDIX 1
ACTIVE MONITORING

Through proper **active monitoring** a teacher can keep students on task and, just as importantly, keep them accurate in their responses.

Circulate. When students are working independently on written assignments, the teachers should move around the classroom looking closely at students' work. The teacher should not be seated at a desk. It is not possible to scan student work from one position. The teacher must get close enough to read what students have written. Desks and chairs should be arranged so the teacher has easy access to each student.

Reinforce correct answers. The teacher should show that they *care* whether or not students are getting the material right. Active monitoring is most effective when the teacher appears to be excited about students getting correct answers. Giving recognition to students with correct answers motivates students to care about their work.

Check student work while walking. The teacher can complete a lot of checking while walking around the room. The teacher can put a star next to every correct item they have looked at on a student's paper. Those items won't have to be reviewed later. The teacher should spend no more than 30 seconds with each student.

Point out errors. An equally important component of active monitoring is to indicate when items are wrong. The teacher should make a mark on the student's paper next to the incorrect item and tell the child something like, "Oops. That one is wrong. Look carefully and try it again."

Do not reteach individuals. The teacher can be sympathetic but should NOT stop to teach a student who has made an error. If the teacher teaches students individually, students will learn that they don't have to pay attention in class during instruction because the teacher will help them individually.

Reteach the whole class. If three or more students have the same error, the teacher should immediately stop the class and provide a whole-group correction. The correction should be worded exactly as in the original instruction.

Reinforce good behavior frequently. It is critical for the teacher to have a system in place where they can frequently reinforce students for following classroom expectations. Here's the rule: **The teacher should reward good behavior at least four times as frequently as they correct inappropriate behavior.**

Correct off-task behavior. The teacher needs to provide consequences for students who are not on task. The teacher can take a point as part of the Teacher/Student game. The teacher can say something like, "Gee, I'm sorry you're not working, I get a point. When I see you working, you can get a point."

Reprinted with permission from the National Institute for Direct Instruction.

APPENDIX 2
COORDINATOR DIRECT INSTRUCTION SUPPORT FORM

School _____   Date _____

Name of Coordinator _____

Name of Reviewers _____

Score _____ *of 100 TOTAL SCORE*

Score _____ *of 40*   **Daily classroom observations**

1. _____   Award 1/2 point for each extended observation made with notes on form—on average per week, for example, 30 classroom visits per week = 15 points, 15 visits per week = 7 1/2 points. *(Collect at least 3 weeks' worth of forms to find the average.)* Maximum—15 points.

2. _____   Observes teachers and groups targeted in data review meeting within the week.

0	1 pt.	2 pts.	3 pts.	4 pts.	5 pts.
never	sometimes	frequently	mostly	almost always	always

3. _____   Completes monthly summary form on classroom observations/interventions.

0	1 pt.	2 pts.	3 pts.	4 pts.	5 pts.
never	sometimes	frequently	mostly	almost always	always

4. _____   Spends 100% of time working directly with teachers and students in classrooms during instructional periods and 75% of time supporting the program outside of instructional periods.

never (0 pts.)	rarely (1 pt.)	sometimes (2 pts.)	usually (3 pts.)

5. _____   Uses conference call summaries to provide feedback to teachers that is clear, effective and based on student performance.

never (0 pts.)	rarely (1 pt.)	sometimes (2 pts.)	usually (3 pts.)

6. _____   Provides data to document the results of his/her interventions with classroom teachers based on conference call summaries.

never (0 pts.)	rarely (1 pt.)	sometimes (2 pts.)	usually (3 pts.)

7. _____ Demonstrates model lessons or models lesson parts when appropriate in programs where comfortable.

  never (0 pts.)   rarely (1 pt.)   sometimes (2 pts.)   usually (3 pts.)

8. _____ Documents implementation of thermometer charts or 90% club on 5-min observations.

  never (0 pts.)   rarely (1 pt.)   sometimes (2 pts.)   usually (3 pts.)

5 pt BONUS

_____ Independently discovers problems, determines solutions and/or prioritizes problems.

Comments:_____

_____

_____

Score _____ *of 17*   **Weekly data review meetings and conference calls**

1. _____ Oversees weekly collection of LPCs, STSs and independent work summaries.

  never (0 pts.)   some of the time (1 pt.)   usually (2 pts.)

2. _____ Sends data to NIFDI personnel in a timely manner.

  never (0 pts.)   some of the time (1 pt.)   usually (2 pts.)

3. _____ Examines classroom data (LPC & STS forms) before data meeting or call.

  never (0 pts.)   some of the time (1 pt.)   usually (2 pts.)

4. _____ Specifies problems in sufficient detail for solutions to be evident before meeting or call.

  never (0 pts.)   some of the time (1 pt.)   usually (2 pts.)

5. _____ Works with NIFDI and coaches specifying solutions.

  never (0 pts.)   some of the time (1 pt.)   usually (2 pts.)

6. _____ Prioritizes red flags if any as appropriate and works to solve red flag problems until completed.

  never (0 pts.)   some of the time (1 pt.)   usually (2 pts.)

7. _____ Follows up and determines whether or not solutions worked within a week.

0	1 pt.	2 pts.	3 pts.	4 pts.	5 pts.
never	sometimes	frequently	mostly	almost always	always

2 pt BONUS

_____ Provides confirming data that demonstrates effectiveness of solutions.

Score _____ *of 21*   **Instructional details**

1. _____ Conducts assessments and identifies student grouping possibilities, and with NIFDI input regroups students based on tests and performance.

  never (0 pts.)   rarely (1 pt.)   sometimes (2 pts.)   usually (3 pts.)

2. _____ Oversees placement of new and continuing students, and insures groups are appropriate size.

    never (0 pts.)   rarely (1 pt.)   sometimes (2 pts.)   usually (3 pts.)

3. _____ Assists in establishing the schedule for DI instruction and monitors classrooms to see that the schedule is implemented.

    never (0 pts.)   rarely (1 pt.)   sometimes (4 pts.)   usually (6 pts.)

4. _____ Identifies students who need additional instructional time and assists in arranging for it.

    never (0 pts.)   rarely (1 pt.)   sometimes (2 pts.)   usually (3 pts.)

5. _____ Anticipates and updates list of needed instructional materials for principal.

    never (0 pts.)   rarely (1 pt.)   sometimes (2 pts.)   usually (3 pts.)

6. _____ Communicates accomplishments of students to principal and arranges for schoolwide recognition.

    never (0 pts.)   rarely (1 pt.)   sometimes (2 pts.)   usually (3 pts.)

*Comments:*_____

_____

_____

Score _____ *of 8*   **NIFDI Visits**

1. _____ Accompanies NIFDI personnel on classroom visits.

    never (0 pts.)   some of the time (1 pt.)   usually (2 pts.)

2. _____ Takes notes during NIFDI observations.

    never (0 pts.)   some of the time (1 pt.)   usually (2 pts.)

3. _____ Ensures that staff and self are prepared for NIFDI visit.

    never (0 pts.)   some of the time (1 pt.)   usually (2 pts.)

4. _____ Meets daily with NIFDI personnel during visit—to review and prioritize problems.

    never (0 pts.)   some of the time (1 pt.)   usually (2 pts.)

Score _____ *of 14*   **Training**

1. _____ Conducts program training and in-class follow-up coaching for new staff within their first week.

    never (0 pts.)   some of the time (1 pt.)   usually (2 pts.)

2. _____ Conducts in-service practice/training sessions.

    never (0 pts.)   some of the time (1 pt.)   usually (2 pts.)

3. _____ Creates an agenda for in-service practice/training sessions and documents teacher participation through attendance sheets.

    never (0 pts.)   some of the time (1 pt.)   usually (2 pts.)

4._____ Organizes, supports, and monitors attendance at program format practice sessions.

        never (0 pts.)   some of the time (1 pt.)   usually (2 pts.)

5._____ Designs and delivers in-service sessions in response to specific common problems.

        never (0 pts.)   some of the time (1 pt.)   usually (2 pts.)

6._____ Arranges and participates in peer coaches' training sessions.

        never (0 pts.)   some of the time (1 pt.)   usually (2 pts.)

7._____ Works with peer coaches on training and observation techniques.

        never (0 pts.)   some of the time (1 pt.)   usually (2 pts.)

Comments:_____

_____

_____

Reprinted with permission from the National Institute for Direct Instruction.

APPENDIX 3
PRINCIPAL DIRECT INSTRUCTION SUPPORT FORM

School _____   Date _____

Name of Principal _____

Name of Reviewers _____

Total Score _____ ***of 100 FOR DIRECT INSTRUCTION SUPPORT***

Score _____ ***of 20***   **Classroom observations**

1. _____   Accompanies Implementation Manager and makes observations (5 minute or extended) with notes on form each visit. (1 point each)

2. _____   Follows up on recommendations from Data Review meeting with the delegated person or directly with the teacher.

0	1 pt.	2 pts.	3 pts.	4 pts.	5 pts.
never	sometimes	frequently	mostly	almost always	always

5 pt BONUS

_____ Discovers problems, determines solutions and/or prioritizes problems.

Score _____ ***of 18***   **Weekly data review meetings or conference calls**

1. _____   Has carried out tasks assigned in previous data meetings or conference calls.

0	1 pt.	2 pts.	3 pts.	4 pts.	5 pts.
never	sometimes	frequently	mostly	almost always	always

2. _____   Contributes and participates in data meetings and conference calls.

0	1 pt.	2 pts.	3 pts.	4 pts.	5 pts.
never	sometimes	frequently	mostly	almost always	always

3. _____   Takes immediate action on Red Flag items.

0	1 pt.	2 pts.	3 pts.	4 pts.	5 pts.
never	sometimes	frequently	mostly	almost always	always

*Comments:*_____

_____

_____

Score _____ *of 12*   **NIFDI Visits**

1. _____   Ensures that staff are aware of and prepared for NIFDI visit.

        never (0 pts.)   some of the time (1 pt.)   usually (2 pts.)

2. _____   Accompanies NIFDI Project Director on classroom visits.

        never (0 pts.)   some of the time (1 pt.)   usually (3 pts.)

3. _____   Completes observation form or takes notes when observing in classrooms.

        never (0 pts.)   some of the time (1 pt.)   usually (2 pts.)

4. _____   Meets with NIFDI personnel regarding visit—either in data meeting or other time.

        never (0 pts.)   some of the time (1 pt.)   usually (2 pts.)

5. _____   Ensures that actions are taken on identified problems.

        never (0 pts.)   some of the time (1 pt.)   usually (3 pts.)

Score _____ *of 20*   **Coordinator oversight**

1. _____   Actively supports coordinator's efforts to implement NIFDI recommendations through written and verbal communication to the school's staff.

        never (0 pts.)   some of the time (1 pt.)   usually (4 pts.)

2. _____   Meets weekly with coordinator to review implementation, establish priorities and plan observation schedule for coordinator.

        never (0 pts.)   some of the time (1 pt.)   usually (2 pts.)

Monitors to ensure that the coordinator

3. _____   conducts and documents daily classroom observations and provides support to the DI implementation amounting to 100% of the time during instructional periods and 75% of time outside of instructional periods.

        never (0 pts.)   some of the time (1 pt.)   usually (2 pts.)

4. _____   follows up on specific problem remedies with specific teachers within one week and documents the outcome.

        never (0 pts.)   some of the time (1 pt.)   usually (2 pts.)

5. _____ assists teachers with student performance issues and documents.

      never (0 pts.)   some of the time (1 pt.)   usually (2 pts.)

6. _____ conducts program training and in-class follow up coaching for new staff within their first week.

      never (0 pts.)   some of the time (1 pt.)   usually (2 pts.)

7. _____ creates agenda and conducts in-service practice/training sessions and documents teacher participation through attendance sheets.

      never (0 pts.)   some of the time (1 pt.)   usually (2 pts.)

8. _____ conducts assessments and regroups students based on tests and performance.

      never (0 pts.)   some of the time (1 pt.)   usually (2 pts.)

9. _____ keeps track of decisions made in weekly data review meetings/conference calls.

      never (0 pts.)   some of the time (1 pt.)   usually (2 pts.)

Comments:_____

_____

_____

Score _____ **of 20**   **Policy implementation**

1. _____ Schedule sets up additional time (2nd reading) for low-performing students and all students in K–2 grades.

      policy *not* established (0 pts.)   policy *is* established (4 pts.)

2. _____ Schedule allows appropriate minutes for each subject.

      policy *not* established (0 pts.)   policy *is* established (2 pts.)

3. _____ Schedule allows cross-class and cross-grade grouping.

      policy *not* established (0 pts.)   policy *is* established (2 pts.)

4. _____ DI time is protected from competing activities.

      policy *not* established (0 pts.)   policy *is* established (2 pts.)

5. _____ Purchase of needed DI materials before and throughout the year is enabled.

      policy *not* established (0 pts.)   policy *is* established (2 pts.)

6. _____ All staff are trained in programs they will teach.

      policy *not* established (0 pts.)   policy *is* established (2 pts.)

7. _____ Coordinator's schedule is free to observe in classrooms during time when DI is taught and given a group to teach if DI experience is needed.

      policy *not* established (0 pts.)   policy *is* established (2 pts.)

8. _____ Peer coaching training is arranged and peer coaches are released for it.

                    policy *not* established (0 pts.)   policy *is* established (2 pts.)

9. _____ Coordinator is freed up to train all new staff within their first week.

                    policy *not* established (0 pts.)   policy *is* established (1 pt.)

10. _____ Professional development time for DI is protected with no competing initiatives.

                    policy *not* established (0 pts.)   policy *is* established (1 pt.)

2 pt BONUS

_____ Schedule arranges to free up peer coaches to get into classrooms.

Score _____ **of 10**   **Follow up** (*1 point each for the following*) Follows up to ensure that

1. _____ DI schedule is followed in classrooms.

2. _____ DI instruction begins on time.

3. _____ DI groups are appropriate size.

4. _____ groups or students are not moved without consultation.

5. _____ teachers complete and turn in all data forms weekly.

6. _____ student data is sent to NIFDI on time each week.

7. _____ conference calls begin on time with everyone present.

8. _____ problem solutions are followed.

9. _____ thermometer charts are posted and being used.

10. _____ academic achievements are celebrated in the school.

Comments:_____

_____

_____

Reprinted with permission from the National Institute for Direct Instruction.

APPENDIX 4
PROBLEM-SOLVING SESSION SUMMARY TEMPLATE

School:	
Date:	
From:	NIFDI Implementation Manager
To:	Principal, assistant principal, Building Coordinator (BC), Coach #1, Coach #2
Cc:	Project director, district person
	(P) = Participated in the call

Follow-up to last week's actions		
	YES	**NO**
1. Timely follow-up has been completed as per BC's response received mm/dd/year.		
2. Number practice sessions occurred. This met expectations.		
3. Number targeted training sessions occurred. This met expectations.		
4. Daily Mastery Tests (DMTs) were completed in a timely manner if needed.		

This week's review of student performance data and observations				
Teacher	**Problem Description**	**Remedy**	**Follow-up by whom?**	**Follow-up by when?**
Coach #1: Teacher #1				

Coach #1: **Teacher #2**			
Coach #1: **Teacher #3**			
Coach #2: **Teacher #4**			
Coach #2: **Teacher #5**			
Coach #2: **Teacher #6**			
Coach #2: **Teacher #7**			
Accolades			
Accolade #1:			
Accolade #2:			
Accolade #3:			
Red Flags/Red Lines			

Problem Description (Red Flag = unresolved issues on three previous summaries/Red Line = issue with an essential implementation element)	*Remedy*	*Follow-up by whom?*	*Follow-up by when?*
Problem #1:			
Problem #2:			

Push Backs			**Accelerations/Jumps/Test ups**		
Group	**Current program/ lesson**	**New program/ lesson**	**Group**	**Current program/ lesson**	**New program/ lesson**

General comments:

APPENDIX 5
ESSENTIAL ELEMENTS FOR IMPLEMENTING THE FULL IMMERSION MODEL OF DIRECT INSTRUCTION

NIFDI's mission is to produce schools that replicate the high levels of student achievement that have occurred when the comprehensive Direct Instruction (DI) model is fully implemented and to promote lasting systemic change that allows schools to continue to function at a high level independently after a three-to-five-year initial implementation period. We have observed that the following elements need to be in place in each school in order to accomplish these goals:

ENSURING FIDELITY OF IMPLEMENTATION

☐ Only DI programs in use in the school(s) for agreed-upon grade levels and subject areas. The model generally focuses on reading and language together in the first year of implementation, expanding to include mathematics and spelling in the second year.

- ☐ An academic kindergarten with reading and language instruction.
- ☐ Two literacy periods a day (90 and 60 minutes) for a) all students in kindergarten and first grade and b) below grade-level learners in grades two and above. Sufficient time scheduled for other DI programs, according to program requirements.
- ☐ A commitment to begin DI instruction the first week of school and teach instructional groups until the end of the school year. Suspension of DI groups for test preparation and administration will be kept to a minimum.

REACTING TO STUDENT NEEDS

- ☐ Student placement for instruction by skill level and a commitment to regrouping students based on student performance as indicated by NIFDI consultants.
- ☐ A commitment to supply NIFDI with student progress and student mastery data in a timely manner and to follow the advice of NIFDI consultants.
- ☐ An understanding that any factor interfering with student performance or progress, such as a lack of cooperation or performance on the part of an instructor, will be treated with urgency and followed up until resolved.

PARTICIPATION OF PERSONNEL

- ☐ Full participation of the entire staff in support of the model. This includes following schedules, using DI techniques and curricula, incorporating advice of NIFDI consultants, and submitting required data in a timely manner (weekly).
- ☐ Instructional aides in grades K–2, at least, to ensure necessary student–teacher ratios.
- ☐ A full-time, onsite (building) coordinator in each school employed by the district to facilitate the implementation. The coordinator functions as the lead coach with teaching responsibilities for at least the first half-year of implementation. The coordinator accompanies NIFDI consultants when they are on site and takes notes about key action steps.

☐ Principal and district leadership as demonstrated through participation in meetings and weekly problem-solving calls, accompanying NIFDI consultants when they visit classrooms of concern, conducting in-class observations when NIFDI consultants are not on site, and setting priorities that support the implementation of the model.

☐ Lesson practice sessions scheduled twice weekly and more often as needed for all teaching staff. Sessions are monitored by the coordinator and NIFDI personnel to provide targeted practice and feedback on skill development.

☐ Development of peer coaches to assist the coordinator and support instructional staff.

INITIAL AND ON-GOING PROFESSIONAL DEVELOPMENT

☐ Participation by a testing team in a full-day training on administering initial program assessments (placement tests) to each student. This includes sending the protocols for the completed placement tests to NIFDI to help form initial instructional groups based on student performance, not grade level or age.

☐ Full participation of the entire staff (teachers, aides, and leaders) in:

- initial preservice program training. This includes completion of the lesson checkout process by all instructors and the building coordinator before beginning instruction with students or providing coaching to staff

- *Routines and Expectations Road to Success: Keys to Developing a Positive Learning Environment*

- a one-day training on data collection and analysis. Instructional staff and leaders attend other in-service sessions as indicated by NIFDI consultants.

☐ Attendance by the building coordinator at the Coaching Academies over multiple years of implementation or the Coaching Institute at the National Direct Instruction Conference.

☐ Attendance by the school and district leadership at the Administrator Institute at the National Direct Instruction Conference prior to the implementation of the Direct Instruction model.

BUDGET

☐ A budget that supports:

- release time for DI training and other elements of the model, including training staff members who missed the initial preservice program training
- funding of all instructional materials needed for teaching students at their instructional levels across the school year.

APPENDIX 6
QUARTERLY REPORT FORM

School:		Date:
From:		

General categories that are implemented well:

Major problems (be specific) and recommended actions (in order of priority):

APPENDIX 6
QUARTERLY REPORT FORM

BIBLIOGRAPHY

Adams, G. (1996). "Project Follow Through: In-depth and beyond." *Effective School Practices*, 15(1), 43–56.

Adams, G. L. and Engelmann, S. (1996). *Research on Direct Instruction: 25 Years Beyond DISTAR*. Seattle: Educational Achievement Systems.

Archer, A. L. (2018). *The Time is ALWAYS: Quality Instruction for All.* 44th National Direct Instruction Conference Keynote. Available at: www.nifdi.org/videos/national-direct-instruction-conference-keynotes.html

Archer, A. L., Gleason, M. M. and Vachon, V. (2005). *REWARDS (Reading Excellence: Word Attack & Rate Development Strategies) Teacher's Guide.* Boston: Sopris West.

Archer, A. L. and Hughes, C. A. (2011). *Explicit Instruction: Effective and Efficient Teaching.* New York: Guilford Press.

Barbash, S. (2012). *Clear Teaching: With Direct Instruction, Siegfried Engelmann Discovered a Better Way of Teaching.* Arlington, VA: Education Consumers Foundation.

Barker, S. (2019). "How Direct Instruction can improve affective factors." In Boxer, A. (ed.) *The researchED Guide to Explicit and Direct Instruction: An Evidenced-Informed Guide to Teachers.* Melton, England: John Catt Educational, Ltd, pp. 109–16.

Becker, W. C. (1977). "Teaching reading and language to the disadvantaged: What we have learned from field research." *Harvard Educational Review*, 47(4), 518–43.

Becker, W. C. and Engelmann, S. (1996). "Sponsor findings from Project Follow Through." *Effective School Practices*, 15(1), 33–42.

Becker, W. C., Engelmann, S. and Thomas, D. R. (1975). *Teaching 1: Classroom Management*. Chicago: Science Research Associates.

Bereiter, C. and Engelmann, S. (1966). *Teaching Disadvantaged Children in the Preschool*. Engelwood Cliffs, NJ: Prentice-Hall, Inc.

Berkeley, M. (2002). "The importance and difficulty of disciplined adherence to the educational reform model." *Journal of Education for Students Placed at Risk*, 7(2), 221–239.

Bock, G., Stebbins, L. B. and Proper, E. C. (1977). *Education as experimentation: A planned variation model, volume IV-B effects of Follow Through models*. Cambridge, MA.: Abt Associates. (ERIC Document Reproduction Service No. ED 148491).

Bowler, M. (2001). "Teaching method makes the grade." May 27, *The Baltimore Sun*. Available at: www.baltimoresun.com/bal-rd.edbeat27may27-column.html

Bowler, M. (2003). "An urban oasis of flowing hope." June 15, *The Baltimore Sun*.

Boxer, A. (ed.) (2019). *The researchED Guide to Explicit and Direct Instruction: An Evidenced-Informed Guide for Teachers*. Melton, England: John Catt Educational, Ltd.

Carnine, D. W. (1980). "Two letter discrimination sequences: High-confusion-alternatives first versus low-confusion-alternatives first." *Journal of Reading Behavior*, 12(1), 41–47.

Carnine, D. and Kame'enui, E. J. (eds.) (1992). *Higher Order Thinking: Designing Curriculum for Mainstreamed Students*. Austin, Texas: Pro-Ed.

Carnine, D. W., Silbert, J., Kame'enui, E. J., Slocum, T. A. and Travers, P. A. (2017). *Direct Instruction Reading*, 6th edn. Boston: Pearson.

Chenoweth, K. (2003). "Direct Instruction gets direct results." December 4, *The Washington Post*. Available at: www.washingtonpost.com/archive/local/2003/12/04/direct-instruction-gets-direct-results/f86326fa-d33e-4d8f-aa6c-fd4a1effcd88/

Childs, K., Hendrickson, R. and Davis, G. (2022, November 28). Personal communication [Personal interview].

Clark, R. E., Kirschner, P. A. and Sweller, J. (2012). "Putting students on the path to learning: The case for fully guided instruction." *American Educator*, 36(1), 6–11.

Corrective Reading Decoding C Core Resource Connections. (2013). Columbus, Ohio: McGraw Hill Education.

Crawford, D., Engelmann, K. E. and Engelmann, S. E. (2008). "Direct Instruction." In Anderman, E. M. and Anderman, L. H. (eds.) *Psychology of Classroom Learning: An Encyclopedia.* USA: Macmillan Reference Library.

Dixon, R. and Engelmann, S. (1999). *Spelling Mastery Series Guide.* Columbus, Ohio: McGraw Hill Education.

Dixon, R. and Engelmann, S. (2007a). *Spelling Mastery Series Guide.* Columbus, Ohio: McGraw Hill Education.

Dixon, R. and Engelmann, S. (2007b). *Spelling Through Morphographs Series Guide.* Columbus, Ohio: McGraw Hill Education.

Education Consumers Foundation. (2023). *Cost of Reading Failure: Any US School.* Available at: https://education-consumers.org/efc-cost-calculator/

Engelmann, K. E. (2020, February). "The application of design of instruction to implementation." *Special education as specially designed instruction: In recognition and honor of Zig Engelmann* [Paper presentation]. Council for Exceptional Children (CEC) Annual Meeting, Portland, OR.

Engelmann, K. E. (2003). "City Springs set the standard… again." *Direct Instruction News*, 3(2).

Engelmann, K. E. (2014). "Creating effective schools with Direct Instruction." In Stockard, J. (ed.) *The Science and Success of Engelmann's Direct Instruction.* Eugene, OR: NIFDI Press, pp. 99–122.

Engelmann, K. E. and Stockard, J. (2008). *Academic Kindergarten and Later Academic Success: The Impact of Direct Instruction.* Technical Report 2008-07. Eugene, Oregon: National Institute for Direct Instruction.

Engelmann, S. (1967). "Teaching formal operations to preschool advantaged and disadvantaged children." *Ontario Journal of Educational Research*, 9(3), 193–207.

Engelmann, S. (1969a). *Preventing Failure in the Primary Grades.* Chicago: Science Research Associates.

Engelmann, S. (1969b). *Conceptual Learning.* San Rafael, CA: Dimensions Publishing Company.

Engelmann, S. (2000). "About reading – a comparison of *Reading Mastery* and *Horizons.*" *Effective School Practices*, 18(3), 15–26.

Engelmann, S. (2007). *Teaching Needy Kids in our Backward System: 42 Years of Trying*. Eugene, Oregon: ADI Press.

Engelmann, S. (2008). *Reading Mastery Signature Edition Grade K Literature Guide*. Columbus, Ohio: McGraw Hill Education.

Engelmann, S. (2012). *Critique of Lowercased d i (direct instruction)*. Available at: https://zigsite.com/Critique_of_Lowercased_di(direct_instruction.html

Engelmann, S. (2014). *Successful and Confident Students with Direct Instruction*. Eugene, Oregon: The National Institute for Direct Instruction.

Engelmann, S. (2018). *Strategies for Teaching Students with Severe and Low-Incidence Disabilities*. Khoury, C. R. and Stockard, J. (eds.) Eugene, Oregon: NIFDI Press.

Engelmann, S. et al. (2008a). *Corrective Reading Decoding, Level B2 Teacher's Guide*. Columbus, Ohio: SRA/McGraw Hill.

Engelmann, S. et al. (2008b). *Reading Mastery Signature Edition Series Guide for the Reading Strand*. Columbus, Ohio: McGraw Hill Education.

Engelmann, S. et al. (2008c). *Reading Mastery Signature Edition Grade 4 Textbook B*. Columbus, Ohio: McGraw Hill Education.

Engelmann, S. et al. (2008d). *Reading Mastery Signature Edition Teacher's Guide Grade 5*. Columbus, Ohio: McGraw Hill Education.

Engelmann, S. et al. (2008e). *Reading Mastery Signature Edition Literature Guide Grade 4*. Columbus, Ohio: McGraw Hill Education.

Engelmann, S. et al. (2008f). *Corrective Reading Decoding, Level B1 Teacher's Guide*. Columbus, Ohio: SRA/McGraw Hill.

Engelmann, S. et al. (2008g). *Corrective Reading: Decoding B1* (Teacher's Presentation Book, Student Material, and Teacher's Guide). Columbus, OH: SRA/McGraw Hill.

Engelmann, S. et al. (2014). *Connecting Math Concepts Comprehensive Edition Series Guide*. Columbus, Ohio: SRA/McGraw Hill.

Engelmann, S., Becker, W. C., Carnine, D. and Gersten, R. (1988). "The Direct Instruction follow through model: Design and outcomes." *Education and Treatment of Children*, 11(4), 303–317.

Engelmann, S. and Bruner, E. C. (2008a). *Reading Mastery Signature Edition Teacher's Guide Grade 1*. Columbus, Ohio: SRA/McGraw Hill.

Engelmann, S. and Bruner, E. C. (2008b). *Reading Mastery Signature Edition Teacher's Guide Grade K.* Columbus, Ohio: SRA/McGraw Hill.

Engelmann, S. and Bruner, E. C. (2008c). *Reading Mastery Signature Edition Grade K Teacher Presentation Book A.* Columbus, Ohio: SRA/McGraw Hill.

Engelmann, S. and Carnine, D. (1975). *DISTAR Arithmetic I Teacher's Guide,* 2nd edn. Columbus: Science Research Associates (SRA).

Engelmann, S. and Carnine, D. (1991). *Theory of Instruction: Principles and Applications (rev. ed.).* Eugene, OR: ADI Press. (Originally published in 1982, New York: Irvington Publishing, Inc.)

Engelmann, S., Carnine, D. and Steely, D. (2005). *Corrective Mathematics Series Guide.* Columbus, Ohio: SRA/McGraw Hill.

Engelmann, S. and Colvin, G. (2006). *Rubric for Identifying Authentic Direct Instruction Programs.* Eugene, Oregon: Engelmann Foundation.

Engelmann, S. E. and Engelmann, K. E. (2004) "Impediments to scaling up effective comprehensive school reform models." In Glennan, Jr., T. K., Bodilly, S. J., Galegher, J. R. and Kerr, K. A. (eds.) *Expanding the Reach of Education Reforms: Perspectives from Leaders in the Scale-Up of Educational Interventions.* MG-248-FF, Santa Monica, CA: The RAND Corporation.

Engelmann, S. and Engelmann, O. (2012a). *Connecting Math Concepts Level A Teacher Presentation Book 1.* Columbus, Ohio: SRA/McGraw Hill.

Engelmann, S. and Engelmann, O. (2012b). *Funnix Reading Programs Teacher's Guide.* Eugene, Oregon: Royal Limited Partnership.

Engelmann, S., Engelmann, O. and Carnine, D. (2012). *Connecting Math Concepts Comprehensive Edition Level B Teacher's Guide.* Columbus, Ohio: McGraw Hill Education.

Engelmann, S. and Grossen, B. (2010). *Essentials for Writing Teacher's Guide.* Columbus, Ohio: SRA/McGraw Hill.

Engelmann, S., Grossen, B. and Osborn, S. (2008). *Reading Mastery Signature Edition Language Arts Teacher's Guide Grade 5.* Columbus, Ohio: SRA/McGraw Hill.

Engelmann, S., Haddox, P. and Hanner, S. (2008a). *Corrective Reading Teacher's Guide: Comprehension A Thinking Basics.* Columbus, Ohio: SRA/McGraw Hill.

Engelmann, S., Haddox, P. and Hanner, S. (2008b). *Corrective Reading Teacher's Guide: Comprehension C Concept Applications.* Columbus, Ohio: SRA/McGraw Hill.

Engelmann, S. and Hanner, S. (2008). *Reading Mastery Signature Edition Teacher's Presentation Book B Grade 2.* Columbus, Ohio: SRA/McGraw Hill.

Engelmann, S., Hanner, S. and Johnson, G. (2008). *Corrective Reading: Series Guide.* Columbus, Ohio: SRA/McGraw Hill.

Engelmann, S., Johnston, D., Engelmann, O. and Silbert, J. (2011). *Direct Instruction Spoken English Level 1 Teacher's Guide.* Longmont, Colorado: Cambium Learning/Sopris.

Engelmann, S. and Osborn, J. (2008). *Reading Mastery Signature Edition Language Arts Teacher's Guide Grade K.* Columbus, Ohio: SRA/McGraw Hill.

Engelmann, S., Osborn, J. and Davis, K. L. S. (2008). *Reading Mastery Signature Edition Language Arts Teacher's Guide Grade 1.* Columbus, Ohio: SRA/McGraw Hill.

Engelmann, S. and Silbert, J. (2005). *Expressive Writing 1 & 2 Teacher's Guide.* Columbus, Ohio: SRA/McGraw Hill.

Engelmann, S., Silbert, J., Engelmann, O. and Carnine, D. (2013). *Connecting Math Concepts Comprehensive Edition Level D Presentation Book 1.* Columbus, Ohio: McGraw Hill Education.

Engelmann, S., Silbert, J. and Hanner, S. (2008a). *Reading Mastery Signature Edition Language Arts Teacher's Guide Grade 3.* Columbus, Ohio: SRA/McGraw Hill.

Engelmann, S., Silbert, J. and Hanner, S. (2008b). *Reading Mastery Signature Edition Language Arts Presentation Book A Grade 3.* Columbus, Ohio: SRA/McGraw Hill.

Engelmann, S., Silbert, J. and Hanner, S. (2008c). *Reading Mastery Signature Edition Language Arts Presentation Book B Grade 3.* Columbus, Ohio: SRA/McGraw Hill.

Gersten, R., Keating, T. and Becker, W. C. (1988). "The continued impact of the Direct Instruction model: Longitudinal studies of Follow Through students." *Education and Treatment of Children*, 11(4), 318–327.

Gersten, R., Taylor, R., Woodward, J. and White, W. A. T. (1997). "Structured immersion for Hispanic students in the US: Findings from the fourteen-year evaluation of the Uvalde, Texas program." *Effective School Practices*, 16(3), 30–38.

Grossen, B. (1996). "The story behind Project Follow Through." *Effective School Practices*, 15(1), 4–12.

Hanford, E. (2022). *Sold a Story: How Teaching Kids to Read Went So Wrong*. Available at: https://features.apmreports.org/sold-a-story/

Hart, B. and Risley, T. R. (1995). *Meaningful Differences in the Everyday Experience of Young American Children*. Baltimore: Paul H. Brookes Publishing.

Hattie, J. (2009). *Visible Learning: A Synthesis of Over 800 Meta-analyses Relating to Achievement*. London and New York: Routledge.

Herman, R. et al. (1999). *An Educators' Guide to Schoolwide Reform*. Arlington, VA: Educational Research Service.

Hirsch, E. D. (2006). "The case for bringing content into the language arts block and for a knowledge-rich curriculum core for all children." *American Educator*, Spring. Available at: www.aft.org/periodical/american-educator/spring-2006/building-knowledge

Hollingsworth, J. R. and Ybarra, S. E. (2018). *Explicit Direct Instruction (EDI): The Power of the Well-Crafted, Well-Taught Lesson*, 2nd edn. Thousand Oaks, California: Corwin, A SAGE Company.

Hughes, C. A., Morris, J. R., Therrien, W. J. and Benson, S. K. (2017). "Explicit instruction: Historical and contemporary contexts." *Learning Disabilities Research & Practice*, 32(3), 140–148.

Jones, G. (2019). "Electrolysing Engelmann." In Boxer, A. (ed.) *The researchED Guide to Explicit and Direct Instruction: An Evidenced-Informed Guide for Teachers*. Melton, England: John Catt Educational, Ltd, pp. 55–73.

Kame'enui, E. J., Carnine, D. W., Dixon, R. C., Simmons, D. C., and Coyne, M. D. (2001). *Effective Teaching Strategies that Accommodate Diverse Learners*, 2nd edn. Upper Saddle River, New Jersey: Merrill Prentice Hall.

Korbey, H. (2020). "Is it time to drop 'finding the main idea' and teach reading in a new way?" July 28, *Edutopia*. Available at: www.edutopia.org/article/it-time-drop-finding-main-idea-and-teach-reading-new-way

Marchand-Martella, N. E., Blakely, M. and Schaefer, E. (2004). "Aspects of Schoolwide Implemenations." In Marchand-Martella, N. E., Slocum, T. A. and Martella, R. C. (eds.) *Introduction to Direct Instruction*. Boston: Allyn & Bacon, pp. 304–34.

McCourt, M. (2019). *Teaching for Mastery*. Melton, England: John Catt Educational, Ltd.

Mitchell, B. A. (2020). "Why Johnny still can't read." October 10, *National Review*. Available at: www.nationalreview.com/2020/10/public-schools-passing-students-who-cant-read/

NIFDI. (n. d.). *Closing the Performance Gap: Student Performance Results on the Nebraska Statewide Writing Assessment: Before and After NIFDI Support*. Available at: www.nifdi.org/docman/presentations/218-gering-data/file.html

NIFDI. (n. d.). *DI and the Common Core State Standards*. Available at: www.nifdi.org/programs/about-the-programs/di-and-ccss

NIFDI. (n. d.). *Helping Kids Soar: Children Reaching Their Full Potential with Direct Instruction*. Available at: www.nifdi.org/how-to-be-successful/success-stories/431-helping-kids-soar.html

NIFDI. (2013). *Literature in Reading Mastery Signature Edition*. Eugene, Oregon: NIFDI Press. Available at: www.nifdi.org/programs/reading/reading-mastery.html

NIFDI. (2023). *Program Reference Chart*. Eugene, Oregon: NIFDI Press. Available at: www.nifdi.org/resources/free-downloads/programs/program-reference-chart.html

Palfreman, J. (2002). *Why is Reading So Hard?* Available at: www.nifdi.org/videos.html

Ramaswamy, S. and Davies Lackey, A. (2023). "Instructivism in literacy as a means for social justice: An effective path forward with Direct Instruction reading." *Behavior and Social Issues*, 1–31.

Recht, D. R. and Leslie, L. (1988). "Effect of prior knowledge on good and poor readers' memory of text." *Journal of Educational Psychology*, 80(1), 16–20. Available at: https://doi.org/10.1037/0022-0663.80.1.16

Rosenshine, B. (2008). *Five Meanings of Direct Instruction*. Lincoln, Illinois: Center on Innovation & Improvement.

Rosenshine, B. (2012). "Principles of instruction: research-based strategies that all teachers should know." *American Educator*, Spring, pp. 12–19.

Rosenshine, B. and Stevens, R. (1986). "Teaching functions." In Wittrock, M. C. (ed.) *Handbook of Research on Teaching*, 3rd edn. New York: Macmillan, pp. 326–91.

Schug, M., Tarver, S. and Western, R. (2001). "Direct Instruction and the teaching of early reading." *Wisconsin Policy Research Institute Report*, 14(2), 1–29.

Scott, T. M. (2017). *Teaching Behavior: Managing Classrooms Through Effective Instruction*. Thousand Oaks, California: Corwin.

SRA/McGraw Hill. (2008). *The REACH Higher System: System Guide*. Columbus, Ohio: McGraw Hill Education.

SRA Core Resource Connections Decoding B1. (2013). Columbus, Ohio: McGraw Hill Education.

SRA Research Projects Grade 2. (2008). Columbus, Ohio: McGraw Hill Education.

Stebbins, L. B., St. Pierre, R. G., Proper, E. C., Anderson, R. B. and Cerva, T. R. (1976). *Education as Experimentation: A Planned Variation Model* (Vol IIIA). Cambridge, MA: Abt Associates. (ERIC Document Reproduction Service No. ED 148489).

Stebbins, L. B., St. Pierre, R. G., Proper, E. C., Anderson, R. B. and Cerva, T. R. (1977). *Education as Experimentation: A Planned Variation Model* (Vol IV-A). Cambridge, MA: Abt Associates.

Stein, M., Kinder, D., Rolf, K., Silbert, J. and Carnine, D. W. (2018). *Direct Instruction Mathematics*, 5th edn. Boston: Pearson.

Stockard, J. (2014). *The Relationship between Lesson Progress in Direct Instruction Programs and Student Test Performance* (NIFDI Technical Report 2014-1). Eugene, OR: National Institute for Direct Instruction.

Stockard, J. et al. (2020). *All Students Can Succeed: A Half Century of Research on the Effectiveness of Direct Instruction*. Lexington Books: Lanham, Maryland.

Stockard, J. and Engelmann, K. (2010). "The development of early academic success: The impact of Direct Instruction's *Reading Mastery*." *Journal of Behavioral Assessment and Intervention for Children*, 1(1), 2–24.

Stoten, H. (2019). "Is this right for my school?" In Boxer, A. (ed.) *The researchED Guide to Explicit and Direct Instruction: An Evidenced-Informed Guide for Teachers*. Melton, England: John Catt Educational, Ltd, pp. 117–30.

Tarver, S. (1998). "Myths and Truths About Direct Instruction." *Effective School Practices*, 17(1), 18–22.

Teach.com. (2020). *Teaching Methods*. Available at: https://teach.com/what/teachers-know/teaching-methods/ (Accessed: 12 July 2020).

Thales Academy. (2016). *Direct Instruction: A Thales Academy Short Film.* Available at: https://youtu.be/GIrldg89g54

Watkins, C. L. (1996). "Follow Through: Why Didn't We?" *Effective School Practices*, 15(1), 57–66.

Watkins, C. L. (1997). *Project Follow Through: A Case Study of Contingencies Influencing Instructional Practices of the Educational Establishment.* Cambridge, MA: Cambridge Center for Behavioral Studies.

Watkins, C. A. and Slocum, T. A. (2004). "The components of Direct Instruction." In Marchand-Martella, N. E., Slocum, T. A. and Martella, R. C. (eds.) *Introduction to Direct Instruction*. Boston: Allyn & Bacon, pp. 28–65.

Weitzel, K. (Transcriber.) (2012). *Closing the Performance Gap: The Gering Story.* Available at: www.nifdi.org/docman/video-supplements/transcripts/223-transcript-closing-the-performance-gap/file.html

Woolfson, N. (2014). *Science and Social Studies in Reading Mastery Signature Edition*. Eugene, Oregon: The National Institute for Direct Instruction.

Zimmer, B. (2010). "Ghoti." *The New York Times Magazine*, June 25. Available at: www.nytimes.com/2010/06/27/magazine/27FOB-onlanguage-t.html